Jody,
Enjoy the Ride!

A BICYCLE BUILT FOR
TWO BILLION

A Bicycle Built for Two Billion
ISBN: 978-0-9961372-0-1 Paperback
          978-0-9961372-1-8 eBook

Copyediting by Mark Burnstein
Cover design by Neal Prentice and *the*BookDesigners
Interior page design by *the*BookDesigners www.bookdesigners.com

Printed in the United States of America

Published by:
LUDELA PRESS
2029 Oliver Avenue,
San Diego, CA 92109
831.465.4787

www.abicyclebuiltfortwobillion.com

Second Edition, July 2015

About the Second Edition: The first edition of this book was, like far too many projects in my life, rushed into fruition. I did not get a chance to truly "heart-check" the book and I let my editor have far too much creative freedom in "being me" and sharing my thoughts, feelings and even dialouge. This edition has been Jamie-ized and is from the heart and totally true to the best of my recollection.

A BICYCLE BUILT FOR
TWO BILLION

A MEMOIR

JAMIE BIANCHINI

FOR

_____

RICHARD BIANCHINI
For all your hard work and sacrifices.
For sticking with me every pedal stroke of the journey

GARRYCK HAMPTON
For looking past my ego and into my heart. For your forgiveness. For
your friendship.

MAMACITA
For dropping everything, every time, all my life, to support my
passions

GUAPA
For your love, tolerance, patience and support

ACKNOWLEDGEMENTS

I HAD NO intention whatsoever to ever write a book when I embarked on this odyssey. If it were not for the support and inspiration of a heck of a lot of amazing people you would not be ready to join me in the following pages.

Topaz Adizes, thanks for sharing your wisdom and pushing me to dive into this form of storytelling. And my amazing editor and writing coach Franz Wisner for believing in my story and forcing me to pen the entire book myself. Even through my darkest hours of self-doubt you believed in me, this story and the impact it can make in the world. He also came up with the title and went such the extra miles I am forever grateful. We did it!

Kristoph Lodge, you are the man. This book would not be here without your support. Big thanks to Coley Brady, Mike Creech, Steve Lidy and Chris Hermaon at Heartland RV for believing in my vision of the *Family Book Tour*. And to Mike Gast and Pat "PK" Kelsey at KOA for hosting our gypsy family with so much graciousness and generosity. God is good indeed!

When this dream was just on paper certain people came on board as early adopters of our dream. This helped us gain momentum and manifest an expedition that exceeded our expectations 100 fold. Merideth Tennant, Ken Pollard and Neal Prentice thanks for the logos, websites and creative love over the years. James Bleakly at Black Sheep Bikes, thanks for the killer steeds. Erwin and the Assos team in Switzerland thanks for the quality gear and for giving us so much more to keep the wheels turning. Jeff Scully & the Ortlieb crew—man those goodie boxes were a blessing. Terry Shorrock, thanks for pushing us through the maze of Panasonic and believing in us. Eric Shutt & Michael Zellman at SRAM you made sure we were always rolling and then some. Andy Genewick at Sierra Designs you were the master of the hookup. The Race Face crew in Canada—took the same crank set all the way. Wade at Spokesman Bikes in Santa Cruz and the wrenching skills of Casey always got my tattered tandem back in order.

Out on the road and back at home some folks really went the extra mile to help make this vision a reality—believing in me, the project and assisting me to grown personally and spiritually. Big Rich Nason you always pumped me up. My brothers Gino and Nick, my sister Tally and all my nieces and nephews thanks for the prayers and open arms when I came back to crash on your couches or park my VW in your driveway. Shannita thanks for the multiple visits and always being there, wherever "there" was.

Mr. Yamafuji you opened my heart. Ursa and Bojana thanks for saying yes and opening the doors of compassion for me. Brandon and Kimberly Barrett for the love and hospitality over the years. My precious Godchild Kaya you inspired me to come home safely. Sean and Tessa for making me feel at home every time I came home. Les Stroud for believing in me and being such an epic mentor and friend. Andrew and Ben my Kiwi brothers—I'll never forget you guys. Dean and my Tassie Crew—wow.

Vanessa Lurie for Living and Giving Big in South Africa. Special thanks to East Africa crew Maruti, Shaul, Natalie, Mohammed, Tony, Polly, Jeanne, Costa, Bernard, Hugh, Toffy, Spencer, Clayton, Pardon, Claire, Moonga, Kingsley, Michael and Elijah, Cactus Agony, Wayne & Lucy at Houseboat Company in Zambia, Gift, Joseph, Richard, Warren, Innocent & Family, Pascal, Johann and Anna Saggioro the Principessa.

In West Africa Hugo Van Tilborg was my savior—thanks brother! Also Mathieu Thouemen, Koudede, Sambo, Booba, Kwame and Gina, Isaac, Bridget, Dave at Footsteps in Gambia, Emma, Ousainou Njie, Nadia, Mohammed

In Europe I rode with 100's of people and every one of them was priceless. But I have to give extra thanks to Antonio, Anna & the Saggioro family, Helene, Ursa and Luka, Svamir, my Butterfly Goga, Nevena, Milan, Mirela, Michel & Gabo for helping me find my lost family in Slovakia, Zaya & the Fabian family, Irena, Tim & Sybille, Mette, Vibe, Paula—I still have the flag! Carina—thanks for caring year after year. Mark my brother from another mother, Monica, my most lucky Irish brother Sean, Janina in Wales, Jo & Paul in England, my Dutch Princesses in Holland, Phillip in Belgium, Drew Grahm at Cobblestay in Paris (wow, that was awesome!), Melanie, Jean Michel, Sophie, Aviva la Loca, Ricardo, Maricio and the Surf Castle crew in Baleal, Portugal. Somehow I managed to spend under $500 on accommodation on a 26-country tour of Europe.

On my Latin adventures I give special thanks to Gil, Natalia, Lucas, Oliver, Roberto Corona, Juan Angel, Jose Rubio, Eduardo, Julia, Jorge, Roberto Leon in Cali, Carlos and Irma in San Jose, Dave Corridor—thank you, Pedro in Nica, Esfrain and Mauricio in El Salvador, Ori and Gula in Guatemala.

To my family in Spain, Os Quiero! Jose y Nieves—gracias por hacerme sentir parte de la familia desde principio. Nieves y Pepe—gracias.

And the final stretch home and to now the crew in Canada Vanessa, Kellie, Natalie, Dave Marino, Eilish and the Murhpy family. Kris and Stacie Moore thanks for the welcome back to USA and Kris—the words of wisdom to stop a spiral. Tad—always with me in spirit, Willie—thanks for canceling the cougar hunt.

I'm sure I forgot hundreds of mentions but these are what came to me at 11.26 pm and I've been doing so many late nights I forget what normal sleep feels like so please know I'm grateful for everyone who put any ounce of love and support into making this dream a reality.

To Garryck, you are my guru of just about everything. Thanks for co-creating the amazing dream with me and being by my side when I deserved to be abandoned. To Mamacita, it's beyond words and you know it. Just feel it—endless gratitude and awe coming your way. And to my most amazing wife and children—thanks for putting up with my late nights and writing retreats. It's time to celebrate and see the USA together!

A BICYCLE BUILT FOR TWO BILLION WORLD ROUTE

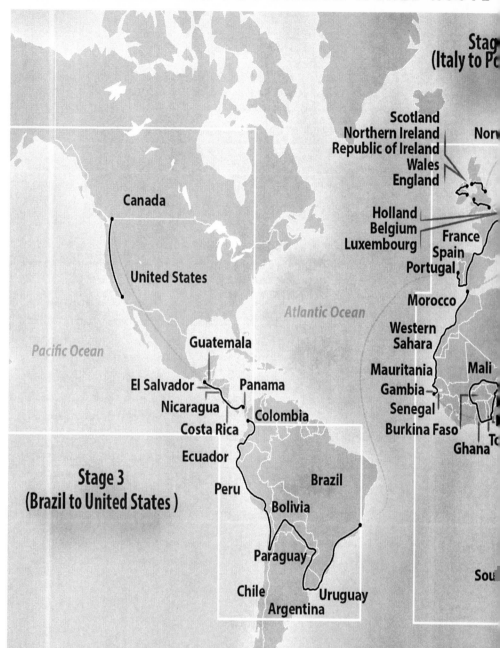

Scotland
Northern Ireland
Republic of Ireland
Wales
England

Nor

Holland
Belgium
Luxembourg

France
Spain
Portugal

Canada

United States

Morocco

Atlantic Ocean

Western
Sahara

Pacific Ocean

Guatemala

Mauritania

Mali

El Salvador

Panama

Gambia

Nicaragua

Colombia

Senegal

Costa Rica

Burkina Faso

To

Ecuador

Ghana

Stage 3
(Brazil to United States)

Peru

Brazil

Bolivia

Sou

Paraguay

Chile

Uruguay

Argentina

(South

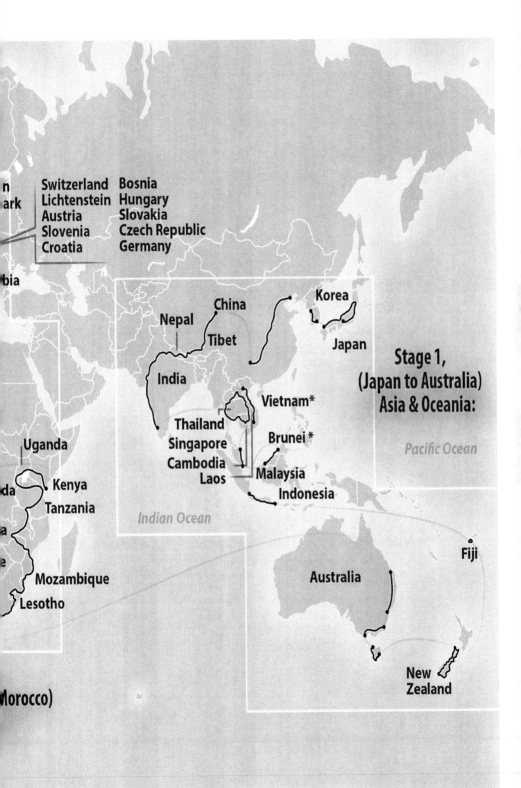

Switzerland Bosnia
Lichtenstein Hungary
Austria Slovakia
Slovenia Czech Republic
Croatia Germany

Korea

China

Nepal

Tibet

Japan

India

Vietnam*

Stage 1,
(Japan to Australia)
Asia & Oceania:

Thailand
Singapore
Cambodia
Laos

Brunei *

Pacific Ocean

Uganda

Malaysia

Indonesia

Kenya

Tanzania

Indian Ocean

Fiji

Australia

Mozambique

Lesotho

New
Zealand

Morocco)

TABLE OF CONTENTS

PROLOGUE.
BURLINGAME, CALIFORNIA. USA.

---►

ON THE LOUDEST day of my childhood, what I remember most is the silence. Big, billowy silence that muffled the morning cacophony still resonating from the living room. Silence you could touch.

I felt it as soon as I saw my bike. There she was, reclining against the garage wall like a high school buddy leaning against his car after class, just waiting to scoop you up and conquer the open roads.

Some kids still swore by the old Schwinn Stingrays with their banana seats. But c'mon, who designs a kid's bike with three-speed stick on the crossbar? You needed a cup to ride it. Other boys made the shift to fancy 10-speeds. Or 12-speeds! But what about the jumps and the puddles and curbs? Was a 10-year-old boy just supposed to give those up?

No, for my money, or, make that my parents' money, only one bike would do—the Mongoose BMX. And not just any Mongoose BMX, a royal blue *Supergoose*. With a tough neck stem, KKT lightweight pedals, and an NOS pad set covering all bike parts most likely to inflict pain during one of my regular, and spectacular, crashes.

I seized her handlebars and felt the cool metal on my palms, the grips having been worn to tatters. Nobody inside would miss me. They probably wouldn't even notice I'd gone. After the fighting stopped, my brothers and stepbrothers would go back to their comic books and heavy metal music. My getaway would be a clean one.

I opened the garage door and sped out into the Northern California fog that would burn off by noon, past neighborhood kids on their front lawns sporting their new Hang Ten shirts and OP shorts and tube socks pulled up to the knee, tossing new footballs and staking out croquet wickets for a family competition before lunch. "Merry Christmas," said a friendly neighbor as I raced past his house. If he only knew.

In the silent whir of the ride, I thought about the bomb that had just gone off inside our house.

Whenever I met a new kid at school, I'd explain my family was "just like the Brady Bunch." That would buy me at least couple weeks until he'd find out my home life was far from prime-time. Mike Brady would never unstrap his belt for someone telling a white lie. No, about the only thing our family shared with the Brady Bunch was its size. If you count Alice, that is. And you have to count Alice. Nine in all, including my brothers Nick and Gino, my mother, my stepdad Jim, stepbrothers Paul and Tim, and stepsister Jenny. Plus Pete, who was Mom and Jim's baby. Oh, and me.

To this day, I wonder what would have happened to all of us had my Uncle Jack lived longer. My mom's older and ever-doting brother Jack filled his life to the brim. He had 11 kids and he fawned over each one, with leftover time and TLC going to my mom. A stroke shrunk his world to an intensive care unit. His two sons, aged 15 and 13, were staying at my house when the final call came from the hospital that he'd passed away. He was 39.

Numb from the loss of her hero and chief champion, my mom helped organize a black tie memorial service with Jack's boss, Bob. Bob loved Jack, and soon he took Jack's place in my mom's life, giving her the time and attention she craved. Scotch-and-water finished the job.

My dad, Dick, was also spending his days with a new love. He had sold a couple of his liquor stores to open Bianchini's, his dream Italian restaurant. Everything about it was big—the menus, the portions, the glowing sign out front…the time he spent at the bar…the amount of inventory and profits stolen by his employees.

When the restaurant failed, he came home to find that his marriage had failed too. My mom broke the news to me. When the moving van arrived, she asked me to ride my bike down the "big hill" to a new address.

Dad went from the large house in Hillsborough to a small apartment in Daly City. My brothers griped about the neighborhood, but I thought the inside was nice, with brown shag carpets throughout. We shared a room. I liked that he didn't oversell the place. Instead he let us do whatever we wanted—illegal fireworks off the balcony, anything-goes wrestling matches and TV dinners devoured during R-rated movie sessions. I learned a lot of words from Clint Eastwood. Every other weekend we'd pile in to his old silver Porsche 924, with the sour smell of wet carpet and seats that weren't really seats. We'd fight over the window position and babble about the anarchic fun ahead.

I thought I was handling everything in stride. That's what I told the counselor. My mom arranged for me to go, saying something over the phone about me "slipping." I didn't feel like I was slipping. The weeks slid into years and when all else failed, there was always my Supergoose.

I wasn't thinking of a bike ride earlier that morning. Like most 10-year-olds on Christmas day, I was consumed with molded plastic possibility. *Maybe it's Simon! Or, better, Nerf Rockets!* As I scurried through the boxes in search of any with my name, Jenny modeled her new Guess jeans and Tim cranked up "You've Got Another Thing Coming" from his bedroom. I didn't find a package with Simon, or Nerf Rockets. Just a couple shirts and some board game I didn't recognize. I didn't complain. There was always the envelope from Uncle Howie. His five-dollar cash gifts helped bridge the gap between redemption and disappointment.

"Hey, Mom," I said. "Can we open the cards?"

"Clean up this mess first."

Mom scurried around in the kitchen, trying to finish yet another large meal without having it consume an entire morning. I could smell the bacon and eggs on the cast iron skillet. I grabbed a plastic garbage bag and started to cram it with ribbons and torn wrapping paper. After a few handfuls, I could see the floor again. Jenny and my brothers chipped in, chatting about the planned purchases ahead. Only Tim, two years my senior, avoided the chore, preferring to test the limits of his stereo and his eardrums with the wailings of Judas Priest.

Peeking around the corner into the living room, my mother shot us a smile. All go.

The orderly assembly quickly dissolved into a free-for-all as we scoured the tree for a card with our name on it. One by one, everyone found and tore open their envelopes. Good ole Uncle Howie. I grinned and nodded along. Oh the wonders a five-dollar bill could buy!

But…is it back here? Or on the floor?

My mind on hyper-speed, I noticed Tim's card wasn't there either. *He'll buy drugs with it.* I ran into the kitchen.

"Mom! Tim stole my Christmas card and money!"

"Are you sure honey?"

"He must have! It's gone. And so is his. He's locked himself in the bedroom."

I knew my mom would take my side. She almost always did. And the more our family spun out of control, the more she sided with my brothers and me, even when she knew we were in the wrong. This wasn't a home any more. It was a courtroom. Admit nothing. Accuse, accuse, accuse. She slammed the door with her palm, forgetting about the eggs as she paced down the hall.

"Tim, you open this door up right now and turn off that godforsaken music!"

Silence.

"Get out here," she said. "Now!"

After what seemed like the world's longest guitar solo, he finally opened the door. This only deepened my conviction. *Pot. Definitely pot.*

"What do you want?" he said, one hand on the door.

"You stole my Christmas card from Uncle Howie. You loser!"

"I didn't steal anything, you little brat!"

"Yeah? Then why is yours missing *and* mine is missing too? You stole it!"

"I took mine this morning. I didn't take yours."

"You stole it to buy drugs you…devil worshipper!"

Tim lunged toward me, swinging a fist at my temple. I ducked behind my mom and his arm struck air.

"Tim, for Christ's sake. It's Christmas day. Give Jamie back his card from Uncle Howie now!"

The other kids neared the commotion

"How do you know he stole it?" said Paul.

"You guys steal everything," said Gino.

"Ah, piss off!" yelled Tim. "All of you, piss off!"

My brothers and I paused for a beat before acting in unison. This moment was long overdue. We stepped around my mom and sprang toward Tim and Paul, swinging fists and grasping for hair and arms. They shot back with a few punches, months and years of built-up tension now being unleashed in the hallway brawl. I cried and swung at anybody with a "step" in his name.

"You jerk!"

"Go to Hell!"

"Stop!!!" came the scream from below. My mom had dropped to the floor on her knees. I could see the tears pouring down her face like a leaky garden hose. A drop of blood dripped from her cheek. "It's Christmas

Day!" We paused to look at her. "Please, please stop this."

We looked at our torn clothing and scraped knuckles, then each other. At that moment we all realized we had disintegrated into a collective mess far beyond the limits of the definition of the word "family." Brady Bunch? We needed a Brady Bill to stop any further violence. Brawling on Christmas morning was about as low as a family could get. We all knew it.

Go.

I headed toward the garage. Gino grabbed me before I could leave. One minute, he motioned. He picked up the phone, dialed a number, and handed it to me.

"Merry Christmas, son!"

"Dad. We need to get out of here."

"What's going on? Did he hit you guys again?" he asked, his voice rising in concern.

"Dad...we, we...we can't do it anymore."

I could hear him pace, trying to piece it all together.

"Give me a few weeks, and I'll work something out. Let me talk to your mother."

I dropped the handset, letting it dangle from the wall. Gino picked it up and filled my dad in on the details of the morning. I was already gone. Off and into the solace that came with every curb jump and oversized mud puddle. There. That one. Faster, harder. Silence.

Go!

My bike became my best friend and companion soon after the divorce

1

XI'AN, CHINA

--->

"TELL JAMIE NOT to come home."

I'd logged off the computer long before, but those words remained frozen. My mother, a few continents away, had undergone emergency open-heart surgery the day before. Gino sent me an email, giving me a handful of disconnected details, but assuring me that her prognosis from the doctors was optimistic. "Tell him not to worry," she told Gino as the attendants rolled her in to the operating room. "I'll be fine."

Everyone says he or she will be fine. I'll bet it's the most popular last word in the history of the world. But fine is one of those words that should come with a DEFCON rating. Are you *fine* fine or *not-fine* fine? That's why I paced around all day until I could talk to her by phone. I wanted to hear the emotions that came with her "fine."

I was anything but fine. I clinched a cheap Chinese cigarette in one hand and slugged a local Hans beer in the other. Xi'an had its faults, but beer wasn't one of them. *Must be water from the nearby mountains and the German brewing techniques adopted by Tsingtao,* I thought as I drained the last of the lager.

There are few things as helpless as being a half-world away from an ailing mother, unable to give anything to the woman who had given me everything. My mind whirred in reverse over the last several months. Were there any signs I missed? A time when I should have called off this whole crazy mission?

I tried to stay positive, telling myself that she was strong and would make it. But I felt like I was slipping into a bottomless pit of sad and lonely. *That's not what she needs. Buck up.*

Up until the news from home, my two months on the road were

bunny-hops of bliss. In South Korea, I scored free tickets to World Cup Soccer, was showered with meals and camaraderie from locals and expats, and logged thousands of vertical feet of single-track mountain biking. The hills of Seoul are a mountain biker's utopia—dramatic and demanding, with sweeping views of the metropolis and beyond. The descents are tight and challenging, even for experienced riders. An even bigger challenge is getting back up the hills. They'll zap every ounce of strength and leave riders on fumes for the rowdy downhills, increasing the odds of a crash.

A handful of expat riders came up with a solution they called Bongo surfing. At the base of a hill, they'd grab onto the hatch of a Kia Bongo, the popular, low-powered Korean pickup truck. They'd nod "okay" to the driver, then hang on with all their strength as the truck powered its way up. Other motorists tended to give ample space, not wanting to be the one to flatten a gringo that day. I was hooked. My left arm burned within minutes, but the pain was more than worth it, affording me ample strength to rocket down trails with names like Middle Finger and Hell's Gate.

Pedaling on to China, I joined the bicycling masses in Beijing, with its wide streets teaming with commerce and curiosity. Chinese attitudes toward bicycling had shifted in recent years, as the growing middle class set aside their spokes in favor of exhaust-spewing cars, a black smoke signal to countrymen they had made it in the new China. *Maybe they'll see this bald American rider with his bright yellow Assos jersey and ever-present smile and realize that bicycles are still cooler than cars. Anyone?*

I carried on, undeterred. I might not have convinced many Chinese citizens to abandon their motoring dreams, but I did get them to stare. During my time in China, I saw no other tandems, and certainly none that carried a crazy Yankee who'd ask any able-bodied local if they wanted to join him for a ride. No, I'm sure that was a first.

China was the third country on my quest to pilot a tandem bike around the world while inviting strangers to join the journey as my guest riders. By now, I had learned that sign language and smiles were the best way to communicate. Keep it simple. Don't try to explain the entire trip or my reasons for taking it. Just smile, point to seat, and nod yes.

I was discovering that road walkers were the best bet to accept a ride. They walked because they couldn't afford any other means of transportation. Locals at the bus stop seemed to be a good second bet, especially if the buses were crowded or the service spotty. School kids were likely candidates. Then came the lollygagging groups of men. You could usually count on the men to goad someone from the group to get off his butt and get on the seat. Most of them would panic once they realized they had zero control (brakes, steering, speed), a rare occurrence in male-dominated Asia.

None of this mattered at the moment—the guest riders, the countries visited, and the many to come, the reason for the quest in the first place. Every ounce of my brain focused on my mom as I waited in a dimly lit phone cabin for the right time to call. Midnight. Eight in the morning, California time.

"Mamacita! Oh my God, how are you?"

"Darling. I'm fine," she said. Her voice was crackly and weak. I put my hand over the receiver to muffle an oncoming sob.

"Mom, are you okay? I wish I could be there."

"Don't you cry, Jamie. I'm going to be just fine. I'm just weak and need a little time to get my strength back."

I froze, not knowing what to say, feeling guilty for not being by her side.

"Well, get it back soon. I want to get you back out on the road with me."

My mom had joined me for the kickoff leg of the global tour, spending a couple weeks with me in Japan. I knew she was a long way from climbing on a bike again, but I wanted to give her something to shoot for in her recovery. As soon as the words left my mouth, I worried they came across as insensitive. She'd talked about joining up again in Nepal, my "dream destination." She had waxed poetic about the mountains and mystery atop the "Roof of the World." I also knew she wanted to share some quality time in a place that was important to me.

"It all depends on what the doctor says. But don't think about that now. Just get back on your bike."

"I didn't mean to..."

"Stop worrying about me," she said sternly, clearing her throat to make her point.

I snapped out of my funk. Once again, here was my mom restoring order, even from the other side of the earth. I had my marching orders. I promised to call her in a few days.

Her strength fueled my ride back to the hotel, and I decided to pedal through the Muslim Quarter, the ancient starting-off point for the Silk Road and home to Xi'an's Muslim population. Fitting, I thought. Her words were like a green flag allowing me to restart this insane journey I'd concocted with my best friend, Garryck, years before.

I smiled to myself as I cycled past aging mosques and a handful of remaining street vendors packing up their stalls for the day. Tomorrow morning they'd be out anew, selling mutton "burgers" and hand-cut noodles, quail eggs, and songbirds in cages. Power lines hung across the street like jumbled jungle vines. An elderly man threw a tarp over souvenir dolls carved to resemble the nearby Terracotta Army. I envisioned the warriors laying siege at night, a trinket takeover to an area traditionally dedicated to food. Was there any way to stop it? Was there any way to stop tourism's onslaught anywhere?

Well, I'm not a tourist, I told myself as I pedaled through the still streets. This trip was about a deeper, more honest connection. That's why Garryck and I had somehow managed to get two tandems and several bags of gear and spare parts into the heart of China. Our whole way of travel not only embraced connection with locals, it depended on it.

Garryck would be thrilled to hear my mom had come out of the surgery in good spirits. We might just get her back on the road yet. The rest of Asia was probably out of the question, but maybe she'd join us in New Zealand or Australia.

I looked forward to Garryck's and my evening routine of discussing the roads ahead. He was in charge of the gear and supplies, everything from chains to rope, extra tires to gears, rice to clean water. I focused on the route options, an arduous task made even more difficult thanks to our outdated maps with only Mandarin characters. The rough plan: down to Chengdu, then up into the Himalayas to Tibet and Nepal.

The greater plan: become the first people in history to take tandem bicycles around the world, powered by strangers who would hopefully become friends. Optimistic? To a fault. Naïve? Sure. Dangerous? Yes. It didn't matter. Nothing could dissuade us from doing something to build a little camaraderie on this planet of ours, one rider at a time.

The journey was the culmination of a dream hatched years before, delayed countless times, scrubbed and rebooted, cursed and forgotten, now in full bloom in central China. I widened my smile as I walked into our hotel lobby. *We're doing it. We're finally doing it.*

The next afternoon in the hotel lobby, while finalizing our route to Tibet, a soft tap on my shoulder interrupted my daydream. A young, timid

hotel worker informed me I had a phone call. *How could I have a phone call?*
Nobody knows I'm here.

I walked with him to the front desk, grabbed the phone, and heard
the deep breathing before any words. Garryck.

"Bro, the bike is gone!" he said. "It's gone, man!"

"What are you talking about?"

"Someone stole my bike from in front of a busy supermarket. It's gone!"

No, no, NO!

"Um, okay. Relax. We'll find the bike. Trust me."

"God, no. There's no way. There's gotta be a billion bikes out there."

"But no titanium tandems, right?"

"The parts. This thing is probably already scrapped and sold."

"No. We'll find it."

We have no choice.

He paused.

"I gotta go," he said. "The police are here."

"Hang in there! We'll find the bike!" I yelled. But he had hung up.

I raced through the possible fixes. Have another bike shipped over?
Ask friends for money? Go with the remaining tandem and give up on
the goal to share rides with the world? Worse of all, would Garryck quit?
None of the scenarios seemed possible or desirable.

Garryck with our first Chinese friend and Guest rider Wai Li in Beijing

Proud best buddies ready for the Himalayas, just a few days before the bike theft

2

SOUTH CENTRAL LOS ANGELES, CALIFORNIA. USA

---▶

THE FIRST THING I ever noticed about Garryck was his faded blue JanSport backpack, fraying at the strap ends. I saw it a few steps ahead of me early one evening as I made my way down a crowded sidewalk toward the moral turpitude that is Pre-Rush Week at the University of Southern California. I noticed the pack was bulging and slightly wet at the bottom. Closer up, I heard the dull, aqueous clanging and echoes. I hustled to get beside him, matching his athletic gait stride for stride.

"Whatcha packin'?" I inquired.

He looked over at me, confused, as if I'd asked a trick question. Then he smiled.

"Coors Light," he said. "Of course."

He raised the can in my direction. Cheers.

"Finally! Someone else who gets it. Pack your own."

I turned as we walked to show him my fully stocked backpack as well. He nodded in approval.

"I don't get the people down here," I said. "They would rather stand around empty handed in a long keg line when they could just have a beer whenever they wanted."

There was something about Garryck that put me at ease and made me feel like I'd found a kindred soul. Perhaps the way he strode—laid back yet erect and with confidence, like he knew exactly where he was going. It made him seem bigger than his 5'10" frame. His smile was genuine and his easy-going nature matched mine. He tossed around California slang, though he said he was from Washington. When I talked to him, he didn't look over my shoulder to see if anyone else was around. He consumed conversations like they were a Sunday feast.

I needed a friend like Garryck. After a few weeks on campus, I was beginning to feel I might have a huge mistake enrolling at USC. I shared with Garryck the differences I observed between me and the rest of the student body. Pressed Reyn Spooner aloha shirts vs. my faded t-shirts. BMWs vs. his my tattered Toyota pickup. I noticed a few people tossing repulsed stares at our wet, worn backpacks. When I offered a beer to someone in the keg line I got a few takers, but just as often received confused denials of disgust. But it didn't matter with Garryck. With Garryck I felt like at least someone understood me.

I chose USC after a conversation with my friend Ron Sciandri, a straight-A student who could do things like list every president backwards and forwards. Ron had been accepted to Duke University. And while most of my friends chided USC as the University of Spoiled Children, Ron had a different take. "It's the University of Superior Connections," he told me after a rugby game. I interrupted one of my dad's daily CNN marathons to break the news.

"So, I'm thinking about going to USC," I said.

He turned away from Wolf Blitzer and let my words sink in.

"Well, you picked the most expensive one," he said.

I glanced up at the screen to see the crisis du jour.

"I can go somewhere else if we can't afford it. But that's where I want to go if I had my choice."

"No, no. Your grandparents left you boys money to go wherever you want to go. We can make it work. Trojans it is! Rose Bowl champions. Junior Seau's going to be a great pro."

I didn't care about football, but if Junior Seau and his Trojan teammates made my dad happy, great. We talked about the business school and the social network I could build. I knew he was proud. I pictured all the times he'd give updates to his customers at the liquor store. He had a TV in the shop. It would now be tuned to USC games.

That first night with Garryck began a regular routine of trips to the infamous Fraternity Row. By the time rush week formally started we knew we wanted to continue the party, and we both concluded that the best parties seemed to take place at Sigma Chi. "If we're going to pledge, let's pledge at the top," we told ourselves. The fraternity reveled in fame of alumni like John Wayne and Tom Selleck, and promised limitless business connections ahead. Sold. We toasted our last warm Coors Lights at the end of another long evening. "To Sigma Chi." Together, we'd do it. "Laser dedication," we promised each other. And if we failed, we would try again in the spring. It was the best, or nothing.

To our shock, not only did the house accept us, they elected us to leadership positions in the years to come. *We did it*, we told ourselves. We were now leading one of the most storied fraternities in the country. Let the celebrations begin.

But after about the fiftieth sorority party with the DG's, the Kappas, and the Pi Phi's, I started to grow restless. If I heard "Play that Funky Music" one more time, I was going to dismember someone.

One night I looked up into the sky and saw yet another LAPD helicopter circling over gang-infested South Central. Was this really the American Dream? The next week, Garryck and I passed on the party and escaped to the San Gabriel Mountains for the first of many hiking and camping trips. Away from the disco lights and floodlights, I felt energized.

Garryck was the one who added mountain biking to the mix. He'd recently upgraded to a Cannondale with front suspension, and gave me his old Nishiki Alien rigid bike. In typical fashion we dove right in, tackling steep and rocky trails. If the hikes and camping gave me vigor, the mountain biking made every sense feel heightened and alive. We took turns leading the tight, cactus-lined, single-track terrain around Strawberry Peak in Angeles Forest, screaming in delight. One wrong movement and we'd fly into the trees or off a cliff. I became addicted to the sounds of off-road biking, our chains slapping the frame *clack, clack, clack,* the grinding crunch of a sharp turn, all combined with our hoots and hollers. Grasping the handlebar as tightly as I could, I felt I finally had my life in my hands.

It wasn't long before our college spring break vacations migrated away from pure beer drinking binges to include mountain biking and camping trips to Utah and Colorado. We'd lay in our sleeping bags under the countless stars philosophizing until dawn while promising ourselves that we would never pursue careers just for the money, that we would always follow passion and, hopefully, purpose. Forget career tracks. Let's create our own tracks.

After graduation, Garryck accepted a job as a bike technician at REI while I scrubbed toilets as an entry-level worker at the Balmer's Herberge youth hostel in Interlaken, Switzerland. "You went to USC for that?" our parents asked us. They didn't get it. We were learning about fields we loved and planning for the roads ahead.

But our plans were like photos left in the sun, vivid and real at first, then fading every day until their images are beyond recognition.

3

PALO ALTO, CALIFORNIA, USA

--➤

NO COLLEGE COURSE prepared me for this moment.

Half a decade removed from college, I sunk deep in the living room couch, gazing at the TV. Outside, a handful of trees dropped their leaves, a quiet reminder that real seasons existed beyond Palo Alto. On the nearby table sat a file folder stacked with papers for my upcoming bankruptcy court appearance. I took a deep breath and slumped deeper into the couch. No job, no prospects, no more loans or balance transfer offers. Even the minimum payments on my credit cards had grown impossible to meet. I numbed myself with daytime television. I hated television.

What am I doing here?

After a lengthy channel surf, I paused on the movie *City of Angels*. Meg Ryan, Lake Tahoe, an idyllic bike ride. Meg closes her eyes and spreads her arms wide. She's free and trusting to the planet, alive for the first time in her life. Then, wham! A truck kills her. Nicholas Cage, her angel-turned-boyfriend, appears by her side. Cage had just given up eternal life to be with her. Now she was gone. Forever.

Suddenly, a tsunami of sadness consumed me. The pit of my stomach tightened into a crippling mass, dropping me to my knees on the pet-stained carpet. Quickly they came, the waves of loss and regret. Failed jobs and loves, shuttered plans and college dreams. I felt the tightness creep up into my neck, choking my breath and forcing me to crane my head for air as loud, voilent cries erupted from the depth of my being.

The beginning seemed so good. My humble, soulful plan after college was to pursue a simple life and career in travel, starting with a job at the hip Balmer's Herberge youth hostel in Switzerland. Looking back, I realized the plan started to veer when I won the coveted Best Business

Plan from USC's Entrepreneur Program. Instead of saving money and learning the hospitality trade, I decided to pour every penny I had into a Harley Davidson import business. This despite the fact I knew nothing about Harleys or importing or the laws of Switzerland. Within the year, I came back to California, broke, a bit bruised, but still determined to start my own business.

While in Switzerland, I escaped one afternoon to bounce on a trampoline with a sun-dappled American woman named Ali. With the Alps in the background, we leapt around and wrestled and laughed about life. Ali had an older brother; she not only chuckled at my fart jokes but could cup a stinky ripper and inject it into both my nostrils with expert skill. Family was important to her. I got that right away. So was optimism. We saw each other frequently before she flew back to North Carolina. We kept in touch, and soon she was living with me in California. Ali asked for little. Yet for some reason I decided money, lots of money, was the key to our relationship.

Easy, I concluded. We were living in the San Francisco Bay Area during the dotcom boom. People were making millions just by purchasing clever URLs. Craft a business plan that had anything to do with e-commerce (or pets!) and write your own check. Forget about follow-up or actual results. This was the economy of ideas, something I had in long supply.

A few months later a friend called me from Utah. I had worked for Filippo while in college, selling Cutco Knives to earn a bit of spare cash. When he pitched me on his new venture—a multilevel marketing ("MLM") company called NuSkin—I was hesitant, but I respected Filippo and was curious about his excitement. When he invited me to Provo to visit the company headquarters and do a little skiing, I accepted.

Filippo picked me up from the airport and drove me to a sparkly mansion owned by a NuSkin founding member. We met the bigwig at the door and went straight back to his heavily leathered home office. He showed me several six-figure income checks as casually as pointing to family photos. *Monthly checks.* This guy made more than a million dollars a year. He had money *and* an incredible lifestyle since his "downline" did all the selling and consuming while he traveled and enjoyed time wtih his famly. It didn't get any better. But he was a "Blue Diamond" and Filippo was a "Lapis." If I wanted the view mansions and that freedom lifestyleks I'd have to start at the bottom of the pyramid and work my way up.

Their sell job worked. I used nine credit cards to buy thousands of dollars' worth of anti-aging creams, wrinkle reducers, and recruitment videos to send to friends and family. I convinced Ali to join me. This was now *our* dream. We'd achieve it *together*.

I called every friend, relative, classmate, and stranger I could track down. "Could you use a little extra spending money?" "Are you done trading time for money?" "How about a revolutionary and all-natural product to remove those wrinkles?" My intentions were pure. I wanted to experience both time and finacial freedom alongside my closest friends and family. But the mountain of skin care boxes refused to shrink and I quickly began to question my career choice.

To save money and help reach the NuSkin millions, Ali and I moved in to my dad's house. By this time, Ali and I had had racked up more than $30,000 in debt and sold approximately three jars of hand cream. Undeterred, I organized dinner parties where I plied my friends with Merlot and Camembert before pouncing on them with my true intentions. When they rebuffed my offers, I flew to the Philippines and Thailand to start "down lines." "That's where the real money is," I promised Ali.

But she'd had enough of the painful sales pitches and friendship-killing rejections. She shed NuSkin and landed a job as an executive assistant at an advertising company. Her small salary allowed us to buy groceries and little more. She worked days, coming home exhausted while I came alive at night, pitching the MLM dream on the phone or darting off to recruitment events held in hotel meeting rooms. Come back to us, she whispered. Come back to bed. We met on a trampoline. We'll bounce back.

Soon, I promised. As soon as we make our first million. But soon destroys relationships. She moved out of the house and left me alone with the boxes.

I drifted and dabbled. Desperate for a way out of my situation and a way back to Ali, I accepted an invitation from a cheery young man to join his Bible study class. I figured my life could use a little spiritual grounding. So I went to one Bible study, which led to another, then another. I stopped proselytizing about aloe moisturizers and started spreading the word of a New Age Christian church. I put a "Got Jesus?" sticker on my dilapidated Subaru. If I had any friends left from my multi-level marketing escapades, I'm sure I pushed them aside with my newfound moralizing. My calls went unreturned. And when I failed to bring guests with me to church, the parish gave me the evil eye as well.

So I re-invented. Literally. I came up with two "brilliant" inventions that would allow me to win Ali back, save face with friends, and propel me anew on the path toward entrepreneurial success. I started traveling the country looking for licensing deals for a pocketknife-carabineer I had designed. The deals never materialized. Debt soared.

I shifted again, building prototypes in my bedroom for an eyewear retainer–carrying case combo that would be my redemption. Both designs had merit and simply needed capital, capital as distant as those college bike rides with Garryck. I knew I should set aside my pride and seek investors and partners. But that's not how I wanted the story recounted at the USC Entrepreneur Program. My debt climbed to nearly $90,000 and Ali stopped returning my calls and emails. I was stuck with Nicholas Cage.

A dangerous hand of cards to play for a recent graduate with a massive ego

4

PALO ALTO, CALIFORNIA. USA

- ▶

SLOWLY I ROSE from the floor, groggy and stunned like a heavyweight fighter felled in the later rounds. I crawled over to the couch and took inventory of my hands, my feet, my surroundings. All there. In a strange way, I saw a new person. I took a deep breath and was filled with a peaceful feeling. Everything was going to be just fine. Divine, even. In fact, I felt my life was finally ready to begin.

When I finally caught my breath after the power cry of the century I felt lighter and clearer than I had in years. Though still weak and queasy, I felt like a successful exorcism had just been performed on me. The demons had left my body (though the demon's debt remained). The crippling dread that shrouded me began to lift like a winter coat being packed away in spring. Sure I was humiliated. And broken. I was also liberated.

First, I let go of my all-consuming desire to win back Ali. She was gone, and if I cared one iota about her I wouldn't disrupt her new path. The "check-ins" and ema weren't helping her. Or me. Not every relationship is meant to last a lifetime. I finally saw that this one was through.

Behind Ali lurked dozens of bruised relationships and abandoned promises. "I'll get the money back soon." "This will work. Trust me. I researched it." Well, they could see me in all my pathetic splendor now. Broke, failed, alone.

And it felt, well, okay. I didn't have to pretend any longer. I was a loser. And proud! I could start having real conversations again. Goodbye to the lies. I smiled at the thought there was no longer anything forcing me to stay in any one place. I could roam anew. Free. I still needed to sort out my affairs with the bankruptcy court, but...

I launched myself off the couch and ran into bedroom. I logged into Yahoo Messenger. *I have no idea what time it is in Korea, but maybe he's there. Be there. Please be there!*

I typed a quick note. Nothing. Hello? Still nothing. Just as I stood up, I saw the words pop up on the monitor.

"Ya, Mon! What's up? Rahhhspect!"

Garryck had moved to South Korea to teach English. While I'd abandoned passion in favor of riches, Garryck had stayed true to his heart. To him, Korea was the mother lode. He could work half the day, then mountain bike the rest. He kept his life simple and built his savings and friendships.

"Outrageous idea," I typed. "Let's go around the planet...by bicycle! Let's live our dream, bro! I'm ready to make a commitment. Today."

The screen sat idle for what seemed like hours. *Did he even remember the travel plans we had hatched a few years ago? Was his life too good to disrupt?* Garryck understood me better than anyone. He knew firsthand my ability to disrupt lives with my crazy schemes. Hurricane Jamie.

"Okay. Let's do it! I just paid off the last of my student loans."

"Perfect! I don't have a red cent saved. So I'll need a little time. How about two years?"

"Deal. We leave in two years no matter how much money we've saved, okay?"

I hesitated to bring up another issue.

"We both need to commit 100%. No marriages, serious girlfriends, or jobs that would make us ditch the trip."

"Ha! I don't know if you're joking or what, but okay."

I exhaled. Looking at his words, I knew we were on.

"Hey, I may be able to find you a job teaching English out here," he said. "The money is good and cost of living low, so it's easy to save more than $1,000 a month here."

"Yeah, I'm interested. See what you can do for next semester. I'm going to find some work now and start saving. Get a real job. It's about time!"

A few days later, I hauled myself into a nondescript government building with its prerequisite florescent lighting and stench of decay and delay. A bored receptionist pointed me to a room down the hall. All the while I scanned the premises for representatives of the thirteen creditors to whom I owed more than $80,000. Inhaling deeply, I entered the room

expecting a crowd. There was only one person at the table. Not one cred-
itor showed up. I set down my papers and motioned to the man that I'd
like to get started. *Now. Before anyone shows up.* And in less than an hour
I was 100% debt free. I walked out of the office, did a double victory
fist pump, hopped in my car, and headed to a temporary employement
agency. Time to find a job.

My mood changed as soon as I pulled into the parking lot. That
feeling of freedom and possibility ground down into the reality that my
entrepreneur days were temporarily on hold. I didn't owe the money
anymore, but I would always carry the debt of failure. While my USC
classmates negotiated bonuses and cashed out stock options, I lowered
my head and begged the temp agency to give me something. Anything.
They put me through a vigorous Microsoft PowerPoint, Excel, and Word
proficiency test, gauging my skills and typing speed.

Two days later, I reported to a temporary assignment at a dotcom
startup called InPurchase. Being a chronic entrepreneur, I had no problems with the chaotic atmosphere. I dove right in, doing everything
from PowerPoint proposals for the marketing department to Visio dia-
grams for product development. I envisioned myself a Swiss Army knife,
a worker who could do it all. The founder and CEO was a handsome
Harvard MBA named Sundeep. He had raised $7 million dollars simply
by showing a handful of slides to a few local VC firms. He needed a jack-
of-all-trades type to work for the company full time.

Just as I was starting to excel at InPurchase, Garryck sent me a note
saying he had a teaching job waiting for me in Seoul if I wanted it.
Perfect, I thought. I can ask Sundeep for a fulltime post with a good salary. If he balks, Korea here I come.

Sundeep did better than offer me a fulltime job. He tossed in stock
options, generous benefits, and a salary that would allow me to accumu-
late more money than I would have saved in Seoul. Sold.

But I didn't want the trip dream to drift away as it had in the past. To
keep the preparations on track, Garryck and I created roles for ourselves.
I became the official "Administrative Expedition Leader" and Garryck
adopted the post of "Technical Expedition Leader." Now all we needed
was an expedition name and identity to begin soliciting sponsors to help
offset the hefty equiment expenses.

I was reading any self-help book I could get my hands on at the time, seeking answers and inspiration on my new path. This led me to a quote attributed to Gandhi: *"Be the change you want to see in the world."* I put the book down. I'd heard this quote dozens of times before, but never had the words resonated like they did now. The failure compellation returned—Harleys in Switzerland, network-marketing nightmares, losing Ali, destroying my reputation and going bankrupt. This time, my reaction was different. Rather than feel resentment, I was filled with a new resolve to learn from the failures and use them as stepping stones to grow and evolve. I had to take responsibility for where I was in my life, and be honest with my weaknesses.

Looking back, I realized the common denominator to all my failures had been my sole focus on *me*. It was about *my* big award from USC. *My* big trip I wanted to do for *me*. *My* million-dollar bank account for *me* and *my* future family. *Me, Me, Me*. Wasn't there more to life than just doing and acquiring for my own sake? I tried to trace the roots of my selfishness. Upbringing? Alcoholic parents? Divorced family? I couldn't be sure. All I knew was that my approach and values clearly failed to deliver the rewarding life I knew was out there for me.

Suddenly the ride took on a new purpose. I needed to be open to new views and values. I resolved to start doing things differently in my life, to take time to listen, connect, and lear. The ride was the ultimate opportunity to do so. I caught Garryck online later that night.

"Hey, bro," I said. "I've been thinking. I'd really like this ride to mean something more than just a pure pleasure trip for ourselves."

"Totally agree. I was thinking the same thing. Maybe riding for a charity?"

"How about partnering with LiveStrong and riding for cancer research?"

"I don't know. I'm sure we'd get a lot of followers, but I don't have any connection to cancer. It wouldn't feel authentic."

We tossed around a couple other charity suggestions, but settled on nothing.

I lay awake that night, thinking more about the Gandhi quote, asking what change I wanted to see. *Be the change you want to see. But what is change and what is me? Be the change you.....* It hit me. I'd ping Garryck in the morning.

"Dude, I found our team identity and name. Peace Pedalers! The domain www.peacepedalers.com is open too! What do you think?" I typed.

There was a long delay in responding. *Not a good sign.*

"Um. It's all right, I guess. What about Planet Pedalers?"

"Bro, there's no soul in that. No purpose. Check this out! We can have a logo with a bike that has a WORLD in one wheel and a PEACE SIGN in the other. Super cool, eh?"

"Hmm. I like the logo idea. But I'm not about to do a ride around the world preaching against war. I'm just not an anti-war guy. It wouldn't be authentic."

"I'm not saying that we're anti-war. Being 'anti' anything is just feeding what you are 'anti' against. I'm talking about *being* peaceful people and riding into each town in peace. That's just who we are naturally— peaceful and loving guys. Get it?"

"That makes a bit more sense since you put it that way, I guess. I still don't totally love it."

We chatted back and forth, and I shared with him the Gandhi quote and how *peace* is what came to me first. I asked him to trust me in my role as the Administrative Team Leader and stressed the importance of having a catchy, unique team identity, something that represented who we were and how we rolled.

I tried to keep my arguments on a practical level, leaving my hip-pie-at-heart sentiments out of the equation for the time being. I deeply wanted to see more peace, love, and understanding in our world, and had the audacity to believe that a couple well-meaning bicyclists could affect such a change. I had experienced and witnessed enough unnecessary fear, negativity, and prejudice in my lifetime.

When I told friends and family about the trip, many said I'd get killed, robbed, kidnapped, die from malaria or food poisoning, get taken as a white slave, or go native and never come back. My father led the chorus of worriers. I chalked it up to the television news that consumed his waking hours. From the breakfast table to his days at the liquor store to his evening entertainment, there was always a TV nearby, blaring Fox or CNN. I could see fear taking him over, leaving behind a wake of distortions and prejudices about foreign cultures, religions, skin. This trip would be about conquering those biases and fears. I'd send him postcards and short videos from my stops to show him what was really going on in the world.

Above all, I wanted to help create just a little more peace in our world. So, according to Gandhi, I had to "be" peace. Hmmm. How the hell do you "be" peace?

"If you really like the name and think it will help us get sponsors, then let's do it," said Garryck. "I agree we come in peace, and it would be nice if we had an identity that would help us meet new people and convince folks to come hammer their favorite mountain bike trails with us. I'm in."

"Super! Thanks, man. I promise we're doing the right thing."

I doodled the logo of a bike with a peace sign and a globe as wheels, then gave it to Merideth, a friend and graphics expert at work. She loved the concept so much she offered to help get a website up and running, as well as create a logo for free. I sent every piece of progress to Garryck. *See! Cool? This thing is for real now.* We now had a web presence and an official expedition identity, "Peace Pedalers: A Global Mountain Bike Expedition." On the website, we shared our simple expedition mission: "To use bikes as a vehicle to create intercultural friendships across all religious, racial, and language barriers."

We had no idea exactly *how* we would use bikes to create friendships, but we both were aligned with our cause. It was us, the change. In our minds, we were off on the road. Now we just needed to figure out a way to pay for everything.

Our official expedition logo and intention for peace

5

MOUNTAIN VIEW, CALIFORNIA. USA

--▶

THE REJECTIONS STREAMED in so fast I thought the potential sponsors must have had some kind of anti-Jamie autoreply on their computers. The excuses were all the same. "We get hundreds of proposals just like yours every year. There is a limited amount of funds and equipment we can donate. We're going to pass on Peace Pedalers. Try us again after you're on the road a year or two."

I now dreaded the calls and chat sessions with Garryck. I'd promised him the Peace Pedalers approach would help us land sponsors and support. But after dozens of requests, we'd only received a couple Oury handlebar grips and a ThudBuster suspension seatpost for my bike courtesy of Cane Creek. I tried to sound optimistic. "It's not a 98-percent fail rate, it's a two-percent success rate! We just need to ask a couple hundred other companies for help."

We told each other we were going to do the ride with or without sponsors, but having their support would allow us to use our expedition funds on living expenses instead of costly gear. We could go farther, and do more. I sent out more requests and followed up with the marketing managers. The responses remained the same. Pass. Thanks, but no thanks. Good luck.

I rose early one morning to jog with my dog, craving that stillness between dawn and full light. Lawn sprinklers sprouted to life. Paperboys zigzagged empty streets. In that hour, everything was possible. Still soaked in sweat after the run, I fired up my computer and saw the message from Garryck.

"Crazy idea to start your day," it read.

"Share it," I replied.

"I just re-read *Fear and Loathing in Las Vegas*. There is this great scene in the book where they are driving to Las Vegas and they decided to stop and pick up a hitchhiker to make the trip more interesting."

"Yeah, yeah. Hunter and his buddy. His attorney. What's his name?"

"I was thinking," he continued. "How sweet would it be to bring a *tandem* bike around the world instead of a single bike."

A tandem? For the two of us? Or maybe he…

"So you mean piloting a tandem by yourself with the rear seat open and picking up hitchhikers?" I asked

"Yeah! Whadda ya think?"

"Well…it would be sweet.….but wouldn't it be a lot heavier?" I asked. I still wasn't sure where he was headed with all this.

"Yeah, but then we'll just get stronger," he said.

That was Garryck's answer to adding any nonessential weight to our bikes as we began to compile equipment lists. He could handle it. Garryck crushed even the most challenging rides. I wasn't as confident.

"But with a tandem you would miss out on all the epic mountain bike trails. That would be a bummer."

"Yeah, I was thinking about that too. What if we could build a bike that could be *both* a single *and* a tandem?"

"What? That's not possible."

"I've seen it done before with a road bike. And I think there's a way to design one that can allow us to mountain bike hard-core trails and still be able to change it to a tandem to pick up strangers and invite them to join us."

"I don't know."

"I'm going to try to design it."

Well, he was the Technical Expedition Leader of the ride. He deferred to me on the expedition name. I needed to do the same in return. Who knew? Maybe he could pull off the impossible and we could embark on something that had never been done before.

Forty-eight hours later he sent me a Microsoft Paint document detailing his design of a bike he called the "Tangle" (a **tan**dem-sin**gle**). It was ingenious, a design that would allow us to do the bulk of our riding on a tandem bike, picking up strangers at every step of the way, then quickly transform the frame into a mountain bike by removing the middle section via frame couplers.

Garryck believed we could find someone to execute the design. So did I. The more I studied his drawing, the more I wanted to hit the road. Immediately. The Tangle was the ideal way to achieve our goals and have a little fun. And one Tangle wouldn't do. We decided to launch the tour with two.

We also agreed on a few ground rules. The bicycles would be open to anyone who wanted to join us for a ride. No language, age, or gender discrimination. Guests could ride as long as they wished. They just had to pedal. In exchange, we'd offer to pay for their food, lodging, and a bus ticket back to where they started the ride. They would become our "Guest Riders." This would be our small contribution to the world of peace and connection, one bike ride at a time.

With the Tangle approach, we now created a new identity: Peace Pedalers: The Worldwide Invitation to Ride. We also modified our mission: "To use bikes as vehicles to create more peace in the world by inviting total strangers to join the journey to build friendship that cros language, cultural, political, or religious barriers." I was sure Gandhi would have hopped on for a ride. We would naturally *be* peaceful on a day-to-day basis by traveling with this spirit of openness, trust, vulnerability, and acceptance. Here was an expedition in alignment with our passion, aligned with our souls. We were both more than ready to ride.

Invigorated, I re-crafted and re-sent all the previously denied sponsorship proposals. In them I shared our new concept and approach to the journey. We now had something unique and newsworthy, something packed with heart and soul. I was convinced we could now capture their attention and cut through all the other sponsorship proposals on their desks. I skipped the part about the bike only being a concept. It was still just a dream and these marketing managers had seen a lot of dreamers come and go, walking away with their valuable marketing product and never delivering on their end of the promise. I didn't want to give them another excuse to say "no."

But I needed to do more. I determined I had to get face-to-face with the potential sponsors, starting with a company that could build the frame. "No"s are much harder in person. I knew there was one event each year where they'd all gather: Interbike, in Las Vegas, the largest bicycle expo in the country. Legally, I was banned from attending. I was not a vendor, retailer, distributor, or even in the bike business. The convention is open to trade only. I didn't care. The success of Peace Pedalers depended on me finding a way through the door. I booked a flight.

After a series of pleas and small talk, I convinced an exhibitor to slip me an extra badge. Beaming, I walked through the doors at the Las Vegas Convention Center promptly at 9 a.m....then received my first rejection promptly at 9:15 a.m.....then 9:40...10....10:25...11 a.m.... Every major frame builder said they'd be happy to make a prototype of the Tangle. "For about $12,000." "$15,000." "$20,000." Design, labor, materials, parts. "Thanks, but I have a budget of about zero thousand dollars," I replied.

All it takes is one believer, I kept telling myself. There's gotta be a "yes" out there in the multitudes. I did the calculations in my head. If the email rejection ratio held true, I'd need to talk to, well, um, only 45 more builders that day. *Yeesh.* Then right around lunchtime, I met an unassuming yet talented bike builder named James Bleakley. A contract welder for multiple manufacturers, James had overheard my pitch earlier in the day and was intrigued by the ideals and vision of Peace Pedalers.

"Sharing the cycling experience with strangers around the world is a noble cause," he said.

"So can you design and build them for us?" I asked.

"Listen, I'm just launching my own company called Black Sheep Bikes. I would love to build these bikes for you, but I can't afford to cover the cost for all the materials. If you can find a way to get me the materials, in whatever flavor you want—aluminum, titanium, steel—I will design and build them for you."

It took me a few seconds to register what he said. Then, *Wow.* I held out my hand. Deal. Even though I had no idea where I'd find the materials he would need, I knew for the first time that the Tangle would become a reality. And soon. As far as I was concerned, Black Sheep Bikes was our sponsor and the Tangle frames were officially "in production."

Armed with the good news, I redoubled my pace and ran around the trade show floor like a coked-up broker on a bull market day. I had only five more hours to secure all the gear for the trip. I shoved a few energy bar samples into my mouth and scrambled to find all the marketing managers who'd received my earlier requests and blown me off. The Tangle news changed everything. Forget about the old trip. This one was bigger, better, and well on its way. If a sponsor still hesitated, I'd return to their booth hit them up again. With a smile, of course. I wanted them to understand how deeply I felt about Peace Pedalers, and that I'd do anything to make it a success. I was going away, but I was *not* going away.

By the end of that year, we had roped in the support of a several dozen sponsors who donated tens of thousands of dollars in products, including:

- Black Sheep Bikes: two custom titanium Tangle frames
- SRAM: shifters, chains and new XO derailleurs
- AVID: mechanical disc brakes
- Race Face: cranks, rings, posts, bars, and stems
- Chris King: hubs and headsets
- Manitou: suspension forks
- Assos: cycling clothing
- Old Man Mountain: racks
- Vaude: panniers and packs
- Sierra Designs: tents, sleeping bags and clothing
- Cane Creek: suspension seat posts for stokers (guest riders)
- Camelbak: hydration
- Ancotech: titanium tubing
- Paragon Machine Works: titanium parts
- Geax: 2.25" Sedona mountain bike tires plus road tires
- Sun Ringle: rims
- Benchmade: knives
- Leatherman: tools
- Martin Guitar: Garryck's travel guitar

The successful sponsorship mission allowed us to keep more cash in our bank accounts, but we knew we needed to do more. I set my personal goal to save $50,000 to pay for the trip, but we were committed to go regardless how much money we had saved. So in addition to working a couple of side businesses—Garryck imported high-end bikes to Korea, while I spent my spare time selling phone and Internet services to small businesses—we launched "Operation Frugality."

This entailed daily analysis of every expense, equating each to a line-item on the trip. For example, one beer at a bar in Palo Alto cost the same as a one-night stay in Asia. Ouch. One meal out with friends equaled six meals in Africa. Out went Starbucks frappuccinos and endless sushi fests. In came microwave noodles and "pre-partying" at home. I thought

Operation Frugality would toss a wet blanket over my lifestyle. Truth is, I hardly noticed the difference.

It even became fun, a game. I saw it as a military operation. The enemy was a creeping capitalism always looking to infiltrate the slightest crack in my defenses. Tip jars that sprouted in places like ice cream shops and hardware stores. *Maybe I should carry one around myself?* Parking meters a block away from streets with free parking. All those mystery expenses on credit card bills, charges for "processing" and "administration." The enemy lurked everywhere.

The operation proved so successful, I opened an offensive on another front. I called it my "Opportunity Radar." This mission required a heightening sense of awareness and a no-holds-barred approach to seizing any opportunity to make a buck. If I heard a friend or associate say, "Yeah, we're installing a bunch of new Unix servers next quarter," my Opportunity Radar would sound off. "I know the perfect guy for Unix installs," I'd say. "Do you mind if I have him give you a call?" I'd then network around with friends and associates to find a Unix expert and give them the hot lead with the proviso I receive a finder's fee if the deal went through. Everyone walked away happy.

A few years later Garryck and I were cashed up and ready for the ride. For the first time since college graduation, I had my arms wrapped tightly around something I knew would be a success.

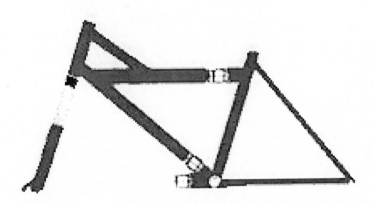

Single Mode

The titanium Tangle's single mountain bike mode

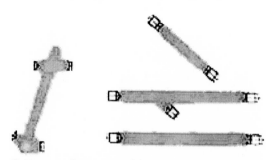

Custom frame tubing and couplings

Just add titanium S and S couplers and tubing

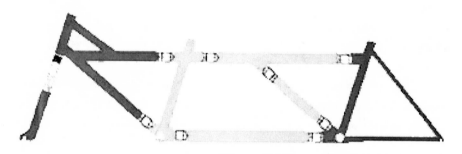

Tandem Mode

Voilà. A tandem ready to pick up strangers and make friends

6

DANA POINT, CALIFORNIA. USA

--➤

"DAMN, HE'S CHEAP," I thought as I looked at his clothes. I laughed to myself. My dad had worn socks until at least three toes protruded out of them. Three! His shoes had to have no soles left before he would even consider any replacement. Even then, it wasn't a sure thing. And God forbid if my brothers or I had attempted to purchase any clothing items for him. "You're just wasting money!" I could hear him say.

No, he had insisted on putting his money into something with greater returns. Hopefully us. My brothers and me. Education, cars, and, yes, clothes. Every one of my crazy entrepreneurial efforts or MLM ventures. "No, he's not cheap," I corrected myself. "He's the most generous man I know."

I looked around before touching his hand. "Goodbye, Dad."

Propped up in his coffin and surrounded by velvet, he looked like something you'd see in a jewelry store display, a Rolex watch in an open box. Had I not known the occasion, I wouldn't have known it was him. His jowls drooped in every direction, forming a fleshy collar, while his skin was pumped with chemicals, giving him an amber hue. The only thing recognizable was his worn brown suit, likely purchased a decade prior for a major event. Maybe for Gino's high school graduation. Maybe for mine. He was 67.

When I first heard news of his death, I was devastated but not surprised. Dick Bianchini survived polio as a teenager, which left him hunched and twisted. He lived each day of life in enormous physical pain and refused to take the doctor's prescriptions. He medicated himself, with cigarettes and bourbon and comfort food. *His death means an end to his daily suffering*, I told myself.

Staring at his corpse, I felt…nothing. This wasn't dad. Not the one I knew. Why do we do these rituals at death, changing loved ones into cold statues? I chuckled again at the suit. Of course they could only find an old suit to put on him. Every other dime in his life went to my brothers and me. Time, encouragement, love—he gave us everything he had.

I kept staring at him and holding his cold hand. I had yet to shed a tear and was wondering when they would come. *Are people looking at me like I'm an uncaring automaton? I love this man more than anyone.* My mind shifted from the present to the future. And that's when it hit me, like a battering ram to the castle gate. There would be no future with him. My father would never see me succeed as a man. He wouldn't dance with my future wife or hold my kids for hours. I felt the tears slip over my cheekbones and on to the floor. I knew there'd be no stopping them now, and I didn't attempt to try. Dick went to his grave having only witnessed me struggle and fail and embarrass myself. He watched me dial friends and pitch them my wild MLM visions in front of a Duraflame fire in his living room. He supported my late night prototype-building missions with the inventions. He loved Ali dearly and had been excited for us to get married. He cooed about being a *Nonno*, grandfather.

On one of my last visits to his modest condo in Dana Point, I talked with him about my growth and realizations after the bankruptcy. We both agreed that the wealth and materialism that surrounded me at USC and in the Silicon Valley changed who I was, and reshaped the values of simplicity and modesty he had tried to instill in us. I told him that I needed change, far-reaching change, and that the Peace Pedalers mission would hopefully spur that transformation. He smiled and told me "a man's gotta do…" I knew he had reservations about the trip, thinking it was a waste of my education. That made his support even more treasured, and his death even tougher. I'd show him the value of the journey. I'd prove to him that I could finally see something through to completion.

I love you, Dad. You've given me everything I ever needed.

As the funeral service came to a close, I stopped crying and felt a wave of peace and joy wash over me. I had an unexplainable yet clear knowingness that he left his pain-ridden, broken-down body by choice. He knew I was departing soon on my world tour, and he didn't want to miss it. I smiled at the thought he was wise enough to know that leaving his body would allow him the freedom to become my guest rider on the tandem. Anytime, anywhere. When he wasn't with me, he could ski with Nick or play a round of golf with Gino.

I returned back to his corpse one last time. I held his hand firmly. "We're going totrrrss finish, Dad. This one's different."

Richard Bianchini with his son, Jamie

7

SAN MATEO, CALIFORNIA. USA

I QUIT MY job in March after two and a half years of working and saving. I walked out with box of junk under one arm, slapping high-fives with the other. I had been telling co-workers daily about ho I was going to quit and take a tandem around the world. They said nice things, but didn't believe me. They reacted to me the way a parent talks to a child when he says he's going to build a roller coaster on the moon.

On the way out, Sundeep, the CEO, handed me a $15,000 bonus check. He had turned a blind eye to my use of the office phones and printers for Peace Pedalers activities. He also signed on as a corporate sponsor by converting the office's phone and data service contracts into my name. I'd receive a small stipend every time his employees made a call or sent an email. We didn't talk much about the trip, but I knew he embraced the mission.

On the other side of the Pacific, Garryck taught his last English class and shut down his bicycle import business. We were both now officially unemployed. Garryck moved out to California to live on my floor as we started "Operation Sell Off." Through eBay, garage sales and word-of-mouth we sold everything we could, from clothes to furniture to cars.

What we couldn't sell, we gave away. In the end, everything we needed for the trip fit into the panniers of our bikes. The more we shed, the more empowered we felt. The process became addictive. Garryck and I felt sick to our stomachs thinking about all the money wasted on storage units that housed items we'd long forgotten and never planned to use. Most of Garryck's belongings from his storage unit were moved about 100 feet to a nearby trash bin.

The night before we kicked off, I thought about all the questions I wanted to ask the world. What is love to you? What is beauty? How do you stay hopeful in dire situations? Coke or Pepsi? Do you floss?

I wrestled with expectations deep into the night. We slept, or attempted to sleep, at Garryck's sister Gwyn's apartment in the Marina district in San Francisco. Without an alarm, I woke at dawn and took a look at the sky. Spotless and crisp. Surely a good omen. I looked over at Gwyn's living room floor, packed with bodies and sleeping bags and gear. Garryck rose without a word and just smiled. This was it. Day one.

We decided the first leg of our journey would also be a little test run, a relatively easy jaunt from San Francisco to Los Angeles. We'd then board a flight to Japan. I convinced my friend and former colleague JJ to come along as my first guest rider. Garryck roped in our mutual best buddy Big Rich. JJ and I had done a couple rides together on the Peninsula. She was only 5-feet tall, but she packed a strong power-to-weight radio. I knew she could handle an unhurried 400-mile ride to L.A.

Rich received the "Big" tag not because of his size, but because of his outsized personality. He always found the lighter side of life and fueled his friends with hilarious wisecracks and endless optimism. I could think of no better person to join our kickoff tour. However, from a cycling perspective, Big Rich was not packing his normal physical prowess. He was a two-time marathon runner but had fallen into a rut and let himself go in the months prior to our ride. To make matters worse, Rich and Garryck did not have any time to strategize their gear or do any training rides together like JJ and I did. Without any coaching on what to pack for a bike tour Rich packed like he was going to Vegas, with heaps of heavy jeans, jackets, and shoes. His bag felt like he'd included golf clubs, and Garryck soon nicknamed it The Pig.

But we all laughed it off, and we all felt upbeat as we quickly packed our gear and belongings into bags and strapped them onto the tandem bikes. I gave my bike seat a quick adjustment, doused on a little sunscreen, slipped my camera into my pocket, and 3-2-1. GO! Or, more like 'go'. The "GO!" would have to wait until we reached our official kick-off point, the Golden Gate Bridge.

Free of the traditional morning fog, the bridge pierced the skyline and pulled us to her like a vamp. The tourists were out early, taking photos of the orange icon and treading across her deck. I wondered how many of them knew this was also one of the most popular suicide spots on the planet. Stay long enough and you're sure to see someone hurl himself over the railing. Stunningly gorgeous, with unmatched views and a whiff of danger, the bridge seemed the perfect place—and a perfect metaphor—to begin the expedition.

I considered all of this as we stood on the Marin County end and looked across the bridge and the Bay to the Transamerica Tower and the high-rises of the financial district. The next time I'd stand in this spot I'd be returning from a six-continent world tour. We were actually doing it. I looked aloft in hopes to see my dad.

And, GO! We pushed off and headed south over the bridge. JJ grinned ear-to-ear, and Big Rich screamed in ecstasy as we navigated the narrow bike lane.

From the beginning couple of pedals, Garryck and I paid special attention to our tandems. They were first-of-a-kind prototypes that had never been tested. The trip to L.A. would allow us to uncover any design flaws and get them fixed in the United States before heading to Asia.

JJ and I hit a groove from the beginning. Her light pack and strong cycling legs were the magical ingredients to keep us merrily motoring over countless hills as we headed down the coast, out of San Francisco, through Pacifica, and then down to Half Moon Bay. At our pace, we'd be in Los Angeles a day ahead of schedule.

Behind us, Garryck and Rich struggled on Highway One's steep and dangerous climbs. Rich's virgin biking legs, poor conditioning, and massive pack made a tough trek ruthless for Garryck. Just few minutes into the ride he had already discovered the first mechanical failure, a collar that did not want to hold the seat post in place. Garryck was frustrated but resourceful. He fashioned a homemade shim out of a discarded tin can until he could figure out a permanent solution.

The broken collar was just the beginning. The largest chain ring on Garryck's bike was hitting the frame, forcing him to ride without using it. He thought we could still make it to Los Angeles, but the rapid cadence on the flats and downhill sections of the ride was doing a number on Richard's injured knee. It became clear by the end of day one that doing a world tour without a full set of gears would be foolish.

Even facing an uncertain future of our tour to Los Angeles our crew remained in a surprisingly ecstatic state. After our first day of tough touring we landed a free campsite steps from a pristine beach. Mamacita brought us food and gave back rubs to our tattered team. The fresh air, ocean views, camaraderie, and feelings of childlike freedom had us all grinning ear to ear by the time we remounted our steeds for day two of the ride.

JJ and I cruised in to Santa Cruz on the end of the second day. We hugged and babbled about tackling Big Sur the next morning. But our plans came to a crashing halt when we took inventory of our reality. The bike frame had to be sent back to Black Sheep Bikes in Colorado and our flight left in a few weeks to Japan. On top of that, the two-day mission without a big chain ring had transformed poor Big Rich's knee into a puffy, almost unidentifiable member of his body. There was no way he'd be able to climb the challenging Big Sur peaks. Garryck and I looked at each other and knew what we had to do. We'd have to shut it down. We'd decamp at my mom's house nearby and regroup.

Two days and we'd already lost a bike, and that was in America, where we could summon a UPS driver and have our problems solved in a few days. I knew there would be many more challenges ahead. I had no idea how we'd disentangle them.

Day 1 with JJ on my bike, Rich on Garryck's. And our gracious host Christina

8

SADO ISLAND, JAPAN

--▶

THE SKIES DIDN'T help. Garryck and I could see the dark clouds tracking toward us like an oncoming train, big and black and powerful. We'd already spent the night in a torrential downpour at a public park on Lake Kamo and were now scrambling to pack up all our gear before the next deluge.

The scenery and area's history didn't do much to brighten my mood either. Sado Island, off the west coast of Japan, is a land of ghostly forests and silent wooden fishing villages, of ancient exiled monks and slave laborers brought from the mainland to operate the gold mines centuries prior, of hardscrabble livelihoods carved out of mountain and sea. It's eerily beautiful, but I didn't need the "eerily" part that late afternoon.

In the words of a five-year-old, I needed my mom.

She and Jim had decided to join us in Japan for a few weeks as we kicked off the big trip. I still couldn't figure out why she'd stuck with him for all these years. Low self-esteem, probably. Convenience. The strain of change.

"Why does he rattle you so much?" asked Garryck.

"He's a clown," I said.

"So he's a little goofy. A lot of people are goofy."

"No, you don't understand. He puts on a make-up, a red nose, and fake boobs and goes out with clown friends or just does his act on the street. He's a *clown* clown."

"Nah, you're full of it. Does he have a clown name?"

"Busty."

I fantasized they'd split after a big clown fight, a knockdown over a joy buzzer or a squirting flower. I pictured him trying to make a serious point with a rainbow wig on. Apparently, he'd been putting on the red nose and doing his clown bit in the past couple cities they'd visited here in Japan. I gave him credit for coming, though. He did like to travel, especially on her airline discounts.

After my parents divorced, my mom took a job as an American Airlines flight attendant. The pay was awful and the passenger requests beyond inane. "Do you have any dog food for my pet Shih Tzu?" "May I open a window? It's a little stuffy in here." But the work gave her—and her family!—free tickets to the world. Literally. She'd since retired, but we could all still fly anywhere on the planet for next-to-nothing. That career decision helped make the whole trip possible.

Beyond the tickets, her energy fueled me during the first couple weeks of the journey, helping me overcome the myriad sentiments surging through my body. Relief, apprehension, elation, panic, pride—name an emotion and I was feeling it, usually in ten-second bursts that quickly changed to the next emotion in the spin cycle.

She's a toucher, a hugger. Leave a limb near her and she'd caress it, always with an all-consuming smile people sometimes mistook as disingenuousness. I knew she was extra elated to be doing her two favorite things—exploring new places and spending time with one of her sons. For the past three decades, she'd refocused her life for moments like this.

She and Jim had just left us to return home. I wouldn't see her for many months, while it would be several years before I moved back to California.

Garryck and I went about packing our bikes in silence. I turned my back from him so he couldn't see me fighting tears. I felt like a homesick boy at camp who spends extra time in the bathroom. I finished packing and looked up to air-dry my eyes. I turned around and saw Garryck standing next to me. He put his arm around me and nodded, it's okay.

When my tears had finally disappeared, Garryck put both hands on my shoulders and stared into my eyes. "I'm your family now," he said.

I nodded and attempted a smile. He was right. If we were going to survive this trip, we'd need to be family for each other.

We saddled up our steeds and cycled in silence, past rocky coves, wooden temples and persimmon orchards. The rains caught up with us as expected, but after an hour the sun took over. I began to feel lighter, freer, stronger, and more grateful than ever. I was pedaling my way south on Sado Island with my best friend. Suddenly the landscape didn't seem as bleak.

Massive raindrops peppered my jacket, creating a symphony of cold, wet beats. *Pip, pap, pip, pab, blang.* This opus dragged on like Wagner's *Ring Cycle.* That and the weight of the tandem and gear made these climbs painful and slow. I looked ahead to Garryck, waiting for me at a summit. He lived for this kind of riding. The steeper the climb, the more challenging the elements, the better. I prayed he didn't want to do this all day. Finally I caught up with him.

"Look, bro," he said. "A winery."

"No way!"

"What do you say we get out of this rain and drink some wine?"

Reason No. 14 why Garryck is a great friend—his thoughtfulness and consideration of others. Reason 745—his knowledge of my love of wine. I knew he would have preferred to keep riding that afternoon. Small gestures have amplified results on the road. So does petty bickering.

As we pedaled our bikes over to the wooden structure, a man walked out to meet us. Based on his graying hair and crow's feet, I guessed he was in his sixties, but his sinewy and athletic build had me reconsidering.

"Wow! Wow! Wow!" he said. "What are you guys doing out in this weather? Are you crazy?"

Garryck and I paused. Was the winery closed for the season?

"Come inside. Right away. Put your bikes under the cover over there and come get warm," he said, motioning to a tarp over a couple vines.

"Thanks a…" I said.

"My name is Mr. Yamafuji."

His home was simple and uncluttered, with warm wood floors that made me feel comfortable.

"Come try some of our wine," said Mr. Yamafuji, pouring a couple glasses for us. "It's not French, but we like to think it's some of the best wine in Japan."

"Kanpai!" I said with a grin, offering a cheers. *This certainly beats pedaling in the rain.*

For the next few hours, Mr. Yamafuji queried us about our experiences in Japan thus far. We marveled over the country's numerous free shelters, often complete with kitchens, changing rooms, flat benches, and sturdy roofs. He cocked his head as if to say, "Doesn't every country provide free refuge to those in need?" Yes, the country was expensive, he said. But then he clapped his hands in agreement when we told him we had saved a few yen by camping in Buddhist temples and feasting on bento boxes sold in gas stations and food carts.

"Do you have to ride off today?" he asked. "Because if you are flexible with your plans, I would like to invite you to an *onsen.*"

I looked over at Garryck, knowing he would want to get back on the road as soon as the rains cleared.

"We'd love to join you," said Garryck.

"Excellent!" he said. "My daughter and grandson are coming over tonight for dinner, and I would like you to join us. Perhaps you can spend the night as well. Tomorrow the rain may lighten up a bit."

We got out of our wet clothes, hung them out to dry on our bikes, and hopped in Mr. Yamafuji's car to head to a nearby onsen mineral bath. Once there, Mr. Yamafuji instructed us on the proper procedures—to clean your body before entering, avoid splashing or loud talk, and wear your towel on your head as you soak, if you wish. As I reclined in the waters, I could feel the stolen glances from fellow bathers, all local men. I closed my eyes and sank deeper into the warmth.

We returned to Mr. Yamafuji's house to find his daughter, Tomoko, and her cherubic two-year-old son, Ryosuke. We all sat on the porch, sipping wine and giggling away, with little Ryosuke on my lap. Next came an authentic Japanese feast of expertly cut sushi and sashimi, juicy tempura veggies, and a steamy soba noodle soup, all accompanied by several bottles of Mr. Yamafuji's delicious red table wine. Soon his wife, son, and mother-in-law joined the festivities for an evening of storytelling, music, and belly laughs. Little Ryosuke ripped up the harmonica, while Mr. Yamafuji played his flute and Garryck and I hacked away at the guitar and drums.

To cap the evening, we were invited to tea with Mr. Yamafuji's mom. She did not speak a word of English, but informed her son she wanted to meet us. We managed to communicate, through sign language and smiles, how much we enjoyed her company and her excellent tea, and she was able to let us know she was having a tooth pulled the next day. The wordless conversation gave me hope for the roads ahead.

At bedtime, we retired to surprisingly comfortable futons on top of tatami mats. We were both exhausted and amped up at the same time.

"How cool was that?" said Garryck. "Dinner, drinks, and music with four generations of Yamafujis."

"I'm still in awe that he is trusting us with his entire family," I said. "Especially how we arrived, unannounced, all wet and stinky, on a couple weird-looking bikes. Would you be that accepting? I don't know if I would."

"Maybe it's *because* we pulled up that way that he trusted us."

"Yeah, maybe the bikes allow people to put their guard down a bit."

We woke to a traditional breakfast spread of rice, miso soup, zesty *takuan* radishes, and sweet *umeboshi* plums. Mr. Yamafuji waited patiently as we devoured every morsel.

"I'd like to take you up on your offer for a bike ride," he said, putting on his jacket

"Let's do it!" I said.

What better person to host as my first international guest rider? He hopped aboard, and we pedaled around the winery then through the neighborhood, giggling like Ryosuke for most of the ride. He patted me on the shoulder as we coasted down a large hill and back to his house.

"Jamie, it's been nice having you stay with our family," he said, reaching out to put his hand on my shoulder. "We don't get many solo travelers up here. Usually just the tour buses."

"Thank you for the hospitality and...well...for trusting us with your family, Mr. Yamafuji. This has been very special for us."

"You are most welcome."

As he patted me on the shoulder, I caught a glimpse of how intimate the rides with guests could be. A ripple of sadness passed through me. I didn't want to leave.

"My cousin Ryoko lives in a town called Tsuruga, which is on your route to Kyoto. I called her this morning and told her you will be coming. She welcomes you to her home and will cook you a big meal. Even better than mine!" he said, laughing at himself.

Mr. Yamafuji asked us if we wanted to stay longer, to take a helicopter ride and spend more time with his family. I brightened at the suggestion, but knew Garryck was eager to get back on the ride. Before we left, Mr. Yamafuji handed Garryck a small bottle of dessert wine.

"We'll drink it on the ferry to Korea," said Garryck.

The long rides between towns gave me the opportunity to do something I'd avoided during the past decade—think. Not like some Buddhist monk who'd practiced meditation for decades, but actually spending a bit of quiet time, away from the cell phones and emails, to cogitate on the options and possibilities in life. I was shocked how many big decisions I'd made with little to no thought, choices about careers, relationships, faith, and, well, life. Without realizing it, I'd ceded control to bosses and bill collectors and conventional wisdom.

Out here on the road, my mind had nothing behind which to hide. And that scared the heck out of me. It felt like we didn't know each other, two brothers who once shared a home only to part ways and move to opposite ends of the country. In a foreign country we were becoming reacquainted, though I had no idea where the discussion would lead.

Sometimes my brain focused for hours on the tedious or inane—a saddle sore, lunch options, or which gear delivered the best efficiency on the flats. Ever the entrepreneur, I also set some sort of a record trying to think up the next Rubik's Cube. But since the stay with Mr. Yamafuji, the contemplations had drifted into deeper waters. Like, what the hell were we doing here?

I'd been reading and researching more, which scared me as well. On this day, my long lost noggin focused on the Law of Karma. According to this law, every event that occurs in life will be followed by another event whose existence was caused by the first, and this second event will be pleasant or unpleasant depending on if the first event was skillful or unskillful. Skillful events are free of cravings, delusions, or selfishness. Unskillful events have self-centered agendas. My brain grabbed on to that notion, then mixed in some "sow what you reap" sermons from Catholic school and a little "If you do good, you do good for yourselves; and if you do evil, you do it to yourselves" language from the *Qur'an* I'd stumbled across.

I know Garryck and I are not out trying to save the world or start some big charity that's going to lift a country out of poverty. But was this purely joyride or could riding a tandem with an empty seat and inviting strangers to be friends and share our passion of cycling be considered a "skillful" event worthy of such amazing Karmic beneifts like the homestays with Mr. Yamafuji and Ryoko? Or landing 40 corporate sponsors to launch our dream?

I thought about Mr. Yamafuji and the gifts he gave us, including trust, hospitality, and openness. He seemed like he enjoyed the time together as much as we did. Maybe more so. *Could we do the same?*

After checking into a cheap hostel in Kyoto I took a late afternoon ride along the Kamo River. Students lazed on the grassy banks while a few riverside restaurants stretched out for business. I ignored the green signs—the ones with an icon of a bicycle and a line slicing through it— and pedaled on. That's when the internal argument began.

Why are you passing up all these potential riders?

You know ten Japanese words, and when you say them you sound like Pikachu.

Just smile and motion to the bike.

They're either going to laugh or run away from the imminent kidnapping.

Can't help you on the abduction front, but if they laugh, who cares?

I do. It feels terrible to be rejected.

You should act more like a kindergartener.

Huh?

Kindergartener gets rejected, what does he do? Mope or turn to the next kid and ask him to play?

Ask him to...

Exactly. Go for it!.

I slowed my bike, took a deep breath, and began to look for able-bodied strangers. Several times an athletic looking man or woman would approach, smiling and glancing at the bike. Each time I smiled back... then rode on by.

After a few more timid attempts, I thought back to the smiling face of Mr. Yamafuji, his daughter Tomoko and her son Ryosuke, and all the people whom we had met so far. To a person, they were excited to connect with a new friend from a faraway land. *Why would these people be any different? Man up, Jamie. This is what Peace Pedalers is all about. It's time to get over this funky fear once and for all.*

I approached two young women from behind, slowing my bike so I was riding at their walking pace. We caught eyes. I smiled. They both smiled back.

"Hi. My name Jamie. Do you speak any English?" *Um, maybe lose the baby talk.*

"Ahhhh. Leeeetle," said one of the women.

They looked at the bike and let out a muffled, staccato giggle. That got me giggling. Then we were all giggling.

"What's your name?" I asked

"My. Name. Is Nanami."

"Nice to meet you, Nanami. You want come for small bike ride? Maybe drink some tea?"

Instead of answering me, she continued to giggle and chat with her friend. I thought they were trying to ignore me, but I didn't give up. I kept coasting alongside them. Nothing happened. They went quiet, so I decided to go quiet. It's an old sales trick. First one to speak usually loses after you go in for the close.

"I go," said Nanami, nervously.

"Uh. Great. Hold on," I said, just as nervous. I pulled my bike over to the side of the path and they walked over slowly.

"I hold the bike. I have it. Okay?" I assured her, looking her in the eyes and grasping the bike extra firmly. "You. Put your feet here."

Nanami got on the bike as I held it tightly. I saddled up and looked back at her.

"Ready?" I asked her.

"Uh. Yes. Ready."

"One-two-threeeeee," I yelled as I made the first pedal stroke.

"Whoooooooooooooo," Nanami screamed with delight, followed by more contagious giggles that continued for several minutes as locals and her friends stared at our crazy tandem machine meandering our way along the river. Then, as if the novelty wore off and the mission kicked in, the giggles evaporated, and we rode in a comfortable, euphoric state of silence for ten minutes. *Yes! If you can get a shy young Japanese woman on a bicycle, you can get anyone on a bicycle.*

"Where's your favorite place to have tea?" I asked after several more minutes of pedaling.

Nanami guided me into a small restaurant, and we both got off the bike. Small sweat beads fell from her forehead, and her pale cheeks were now rosy pink. We were both ecstatic.

Over tea in a small teahouse, we hacked our way through a conversation using my miniscule Japanese lexicon, her limited English, drawings on napkins, sign language, and a tiny dictionary she carried in her purse. I didn't remember a word, only that I loved every moment.

Kanpai! Sure beats the rain

Ryosuke had better skills that Garryck and I. Seriously

My first international guest rider Mr. Yamafuji

I was happy I faced my fears that day. So was Nanami

The mesmerizing scenery out touring Japan

9

XI'AN, CHINA

THE XI'AN CHIEF of police dropped Garryck off at the hotel well after midnight. He looked much younger than any police chief I'd met in America, a small-framed man with bright red lips. Garryck had spent countless hours giving statements, meeting with interpreters and waiting around. His eyes looked puffy and worn. I gave him a big hug. We didn't say a word. I left some food for him up in the room, but his stomach was too wound up for him to eat. I said a few half-hearted words of encouragement, then went to sleep to the muffled sound of him weeping into his pillow.

When I woke, I brightened at the thought that last night was only a bad dream. That evaporated as soon as I looked over to Garryck. His bike was gone, and possibly the trip as well. I didn't talk to him as he dressed to go do Tai Chi. Garryck had found a free class in a nearby park. He was always much more relaxed after his sessions and I hoped today's class would help lift his spirits. I sensed his mood had changed when he walked back into the room.

"How you doing, bro?" I asked him, giving him another hug.

"Better than last night, but still..." he said, shaking his head in disbelief.

"We have to find the bike"

"How?"

"We offer a huge reward. Get everyone in town on the lookout. It's a titanium tandem, for God's sake. It can't hide for long."

"I guess..."

"Garryck, it's not an option *not* to find your bike. Just like it was not an option not to do this ride, remember?"

We shared our plan with Kane, the owner of the hotel restaurant, Kane's Kafe. Handsome and outgoing, Kane was part of a new breed of Chinese businessmen who opened hotels and restaurants that catered to the increasing number of Western tourists. Cold beer. Hollywood movies. He was always eager to lend a hand with travel advice, including translating our maps. When we told him about the theft, he was very sympathetic to our situation.

After breakfast, Kane suggested we arrange to have a reporter from the most widely read newspaper in Xi'an come by to do an interview and take some pictures. He made a call, and later that day we shared our story with an earnest young woman who spoke excellent English. We told her we were offering a 3000-yuan reward for the person who found and returned the bike. This amounted to about $500, more than most locals earned in a year.

"Tomorrow is Sunday," said the reporter. "This is the day that more people read the paper than any other day. I'm going to try to get this article into the Sunday edition. I can't promise you but I'm going to try my very best."

I then suggested we hang flyers near the scene of the crime and pepper the reward all over town so we could build a team of supporters. Kane helped us translate a paragraph detailing the Peace Pedalers project and how we needed the bicycle to carry on the mission. We took the translated paragraph to a local Internet café, where the friendly staff typed it up and arranged it on a page complete with a digital picture of my bike. They did it all free of charge. We made 300 copies of the flyer and were ready to begin the operation.

As in any country, there are the well-meaning, the nefarious, and those in between. In the past 24 hours, we'd experienced China's full range. It made me realize how pointless it is to ascribe a characterization to a country. Every country has every personality. The question is only which voices are the loudest.

We plastered the flyers near the supermarket and handed them to anyone who had paused out of curiosity. I know it was hard for Garryck to return to the scene, an all too vivid reminder that his one-of-a-kind creation was now gone.

The following morning, we made the front page. "Two Foreigners Offer 3000 Yuan to Find Their Beloved Bicycle" read the headline. A large article detailed the theft and included a photo of Garryck and me looking pissed off.

"You should be happy with this article," said Kane. "It will inspire the residents of Xi'an to keep an eye out for your bike."

"And the reward is going to get people to start talking about it too," added a restaurant customer.

But it didn't. We waited around the hotel hoping for a phone call that never came. I went to bed disheartened, wondering how, and if, we'd continue. I woke up the next day feeling lower. It was July 1st, my dad's birthday. I stayed back at the hotel and let Garryck continue handing out flyers.

As I lay in bed, I had a crazy notion. *Yes, sure, why not? Dad, happy birthday. I hope you're celebrating. I know you're a selfless man who always put his kids first. So I'm checking in to see if you can work some magic with the angels and saints and apostles and Jesus and Mohamed and Allah and whoever else you're hanging with up there. Please help us find the bike and get us back on our dream journey.*

By the time Garryck returned to the hotel, we had a small group of locals and expats and locals actively looking for the bike. The article, and, more important, the 3,000-yuan reward, had created a small herd of bounty hunters. He was exhausted but seemed more hopeful and determined than he was the days before.

That evening, we received a surprise visit from the chief of police. He was dressed in street clothes, and came with his wife and son. He invited us to dinner to an upscale restaurant, where the staff genuflected as soon as we entered. The waiters filled the table with dishes before I could unroll my napkin. The chief waited before speaking. I put down my chopsticks.

"Garryck, I am sorry for the loss of your bicycle," he said.

"Thank you."

"Listen closely. We are going to find your bike. We know where they sell stolen bikes and have already begun looking for it."

"But you have not found it yet, right?"

"No, we have not. But we will. We will find your bike. But I need to ask you a very important favor. Please do not talk to the newspaper again. When this article came out yesterday our station began to receive many, many phone calls from the citizens of Xi'an. There have been so many people calling that we can't make or receive any phone calls. Our citizens are furious about this theft and are demanding that the police do not let you leave China without your bike. Nobody wants you to leave with a bad feeling about our country."

I was floored by the news. And heartened. Our predicament, and our mission, had prompted countless strangers to take time out of their day to aid our cause. Would I have done the same had I read an article in the *San Francisco Chronicle*? I'd like to think so, but I wasn't sure.

We heeded the chief's request and focused on handing out more flyers in the coming days.

Kane was waiting for us on our return on evening. "Good news, Garryck," he said.

Thanks, Dad!

Garryck and I went to the main police station only to learn that we were going to have to wait awhile until he could take possession of the bike. Something about "legislative paperwork." Garryck had to first produce a legal document showing the price of the bike. He was told the cost of the bike would help determine the severity of punishment. The custom-built Tangle had an estimated value of more than $10,000. A theft that pricy could mean a long prison sentence or even death for the thief. China doesn't take lightly to criminals who steal from foreigners. We learned the man was trying to sell the bike on the black market for $45 when the police captured him.

Finally, we were summoned to the station to retrieve the bike. We followed a young, serious police officer up a dimly lit stairway to an office to sign the case papers. On the way, the officer stopped to stare into a dingy, unlit room. In there sat a man handcuffed to a chair. His soiled shirt was half unbuttoned. He hung his head to avoid our gazes. The officer looked at him with disgust before leading us to another room. The chief arrived and we signed the paperwork.

"Sir, is there any way we can influence the sentence for the thief?" I said. "We don't want him put to death or beaten."

"Sorry. You have no say in what happens to him. He will receive the punishment he deserves."

"But we...I mean, can't we drop the charges or anything?" I asked.

The chief shook our hands and motioned for his subordinate to escort us out.

We rolled out of the station, ecstatic to have our bike, but I was numbed by the thought of what might happen to the thief. *He knew the consequences when he did it. But maybe he has a family, and no other way to support them. There was nothing else we could do. Right?*

The endless canvassing, the search parties, the stress and fear—the whole ordeal had taken its toll. We were both more than ready to leave town and ride away. We also felt grateful to all the people who had helped us, and we wanted to say thanks.

We were more than prepared to part with 3,000-yuan reward if someone had located our bike. But since the police found it, we did not have to pay. However, it was not just the police who found the bike. It was anyone who took a flyer, called the police, or spread the word.

"I think we owe that money to everyone," I said to Garryck as we made our way back to the hotel.

"Was thinking the same thing," he said.

Instead of giving the money to the group of supporters, we decided to spend it on a large party with free food and drinks for the hotel crew, Internet café staff, newspaper reporters, police, and anyone who lent a hand.

Nobody had done more than Kane. So we invited everyone who helped to join us for a night of celebration at Kane's Kafe. After we'd made the arrangements, I realized the party would take place on July Fourth. Perfect, I thought. We'd make it an independence party. A freeing of our bike...our journey...and any misperceptions we had about China.

On the night of the party, I surveyed the empty plates and drained beer glasses. A couple hotel friends from Ireland provided the evening's impromptu entertainment, playing a few drinking songs on their guitars. Above it all I saw the compassion and altruism in the faces of the dozens of people who'd donated time and energy to help a couple strangers realize their crazy Peace Pedalers dream. The stolen bicycle didn't dampen our quest; it fuelled it, bringing together an international cast to solve a common problem. That's what the journey was all about, right? I felt the anxiety leave my body, and in its place a warmth.

I looked around the room again. Garryck and I had hosted dozens of guest riders, but had yet to invite anyone to come on an extended overnight expedition with us. Maybe I wasn't ready or confident enough. Now I was. I scoured the crowd for someone to ride with me south towards Chengdu. I stopped on Phillip, a backpacker staying at the hotel. A Belgian man in his mid-thirties, he sported a dark goatee that matched his large, furry eyebrows. He was touring China by bus and train, and when I broached the bicycle option, he admitted he was eager to see more backcountry.

"Phillip, my Belgian waffle," I said, properly inebriated and putting my arm around him. "Your belly is getting a little big, yeah? All those train rides."

"Oh, yes, too big," he said, chuckling and rubbing his stomach. "You must be very happy to be finally riding tomorrow. Congratulations."

"I am, Phillip. But do you know what would make me even happier?"

"Tell me."

"I would be ecstatic if you accompanied me and became the first long-distance international guest rider. I want you to ride out of Xi'an with us tomorrow and pedal down to Hanzhong and see the real China. Away from the tour buses. That would really make me happy, Waffle."

He stood there in silence for a moment, processing the invitation. Then his smile grew larger, and I knew he was in.

I found it hard to sleep that night. It had taken two months to convince someone to join us on a multi-day trip. I reflected back how Mr. Yamafuji's benevolence had given me the confidence to invite my first roadside guest rider, Nanami, on the bicycle. Now here in China, an entire community of people, strangers all, showered us with kindness and compassion as well. Perhaps that's what inspired me to reach out and invite Phillip to dive deep into the heart of China's back roads with me. I lay there facinated about how this journey was unfolding and drifted to sleep filled with gratitude.

寻找特别的自行车
赏金: *3000*元

　　2002年6月28日在西门附近的人人乐超市，发生了一起令人震惊的失窃事件，小偷偷走了我们独一无二的自行车。我们来自美国（名字是汉普顿和杰米）准备骑这自行车环游世界，这是一个十分特别的双座脚踏车，我们已经骑着它到过了日本和韩国，中国是100个国家中的第三个国家。

　　但28日下午，有人偷了它，同时也偷走了我们的希望和梦想。我们的计划在中国旅行两个月，我们要去学校、孤儿院、福利院帮助那些有身体缺陷的老人和小孩实现骑车的梦想，但是那些小偷不仅偷走了自行车，而且也偷走了老人和孩子的欢乐，如果你有关于这辆自行车的消息或想将它物归原主，请与我们的朋友Kane联系。

手机：13571882937
地址：丰禾路11号

The flyer translated by Kane and produced by the Internet café staff

Our front-page article in the main Xi'an paper

Celebrating with our hero Kane

10

XI'AN, CHINA

WE STOPPED AT our favorite breakfast joint for a final taste of their Muslim-influenced pita bread filled with egg, lamb, bamboo shoots, peppers, and mystery fillings. Xi'an had become a little home away from home over the last several weeks, and I began to feel sad about leaving. We owed a lot to this community.

Before we left, Kane handed me a piece of paper. "Forget the city maps," he said in a paternal fashion. "You'll need this."

I unfolded a handcrafted map with notes and routes penned by Kane. It proved to be a godsend during the chaotic Xi'an morning rush hour, and a final gift from the city. After an hour of twists and turns, we escaped the beeping horns and found ourselves in the quiet countryside.

Then it hit me. We had entered into "Real China," I told myself, defining "real" as areas with minimal Western influences. No longer could we escape to a modern hotel or restaurant with menus in English. We were all in, and with our first long-term guest rider. In some ways, it felt like the trip had finally begun. I looked at Phillip on the back of my bike. Neither of us cared where we were heading that day. We wanted only to see Chinese life behind the tourist curtains.

Kane's map led us onto a tree-lined street with minimal traffic. The road eventually took a detour onto muddy, rocky terrain and through farmland, peasant villages and backcountry roads. I felt like a spectator at a fireworks show, with bursts of color that exploded in the region's pale haze—bright, buttery sunflower fields, orange roofs, rich green rice fields.

"Real China" also gave us another real adventure—flat tires. We averaged at least three a day, each one attracting local fellow cyclists eager to cop a closer look at the tandem machines and their pale-skinned riders.

The men would approach slowly though steadily, often ending up just a few inches away. They'd stare as we wrestled off the tire, sandpapered the tube, applied glue, then added another bright orange patch. Personal boundaries didn't seem to exist with Chinese men. If locals wanted to touch something, they'd touch it. Or bend it, or pull it. The episodes were disconcerting at first, though by the third or fourth one I grew accustomed to the gatherings. On the rare occasion when bystanders didn't approach, I wondered if I had done something wrong.

The humid heat turned our team into a sweaty, stinky mess by the end of each day, and nothing cools better than a clean mountain river. So whether it was 20 kilometers into our ride or 100, when we found a decent local inn near a river we'd call it quits for the day. We'd park the bikes, pay a couple dollars for the room, devour any food they had on hand, grab a couple cold 25-cent beers, put on our board shorts and head down to the water.

"Say, Waffle, how does bike touring compare to backpacking?" I asked Phillip one day as we were drying our bodies on a riverbank.

"Come on," he said, shaking his head in disbelief. "Theez. Theez, izz like living a dream. I tell you. Jeezz."

At dinner, local men approached our table, eager to try broken English learned from TV, school or the Internet. The local women, on the other hand, had courteous, distinct boundaries. They hung together like a tribe, often three generations strong, as they cleaned, cooked, served and handled the bulk of the work. They wore simple cotton pastel-colored pants, shirts and sundresses, and sported short-cropped hair with pigtails and braids that matched their outfits.

Before retiring for the night, we'd give rides to dozens of tittering kids while their parents and families cheered nearby. We'd make loop after loop until everyone in the village who wanted a ride received one. I couldn't help but feel like a kid as well, one who had wandered over into another neighborhood, not far from home. I didn't know my playmates, but the games and experiences were the same.

On the umpteenth day of this pleasant routine we met an English-speaking boy who escorted us to another perfect local hotel on the banks of a river. Soon we were sitting on the porch, laughing with dozens of kids and an 88-year-old man with a long white beard and a perma-grin. Phillip had a special talent for making everyone around him laugh, even if they didn't understand a word of his jokes. He used exaggerated facial expressions and sound effects to win people over.

This time, the merriment screeched to halt when two stern-looking men greeted us just before dinner. Police, explained the boy, as they asked for our passports. This was not an official, tourist-authorized hotel. We would have to leave. Garryck, Phillip and I decided to eat dinner and hope the police would go away. We were tired and hungry. The last thing we wanted was to pack up our bikes again and ride in the dark.

Unfortunately, the men returned with a no-refusal offer to drive us 30 kilometers to a government-sanctioned hotel in Foping. The hotel rate would be nearly ten times what we were paying at the inn. Garryck and I looked at each other. Heck no. We'd rather camp somewhere than give in to the corruption and bureaucracy of the local Chinese government.

To the surprise of everyone, that's what we did. At 10 p.m., we packed up our bikes, put on our headlamps, said goodbye to the disappointed townspeople who did not want us to leave, and started pedaling under a clear, starlit night. One challenging aspect about biking and camping in China is that nearly every piece of fertile, flat land is actively farmed. After a being chased from a few impromptu campsites by bombastic dogs, we found a vacant piece of land on a lumpy, dried-up rice field.

I went to bed dirty and sticky. Next came the mosquitos that displayed zero cultural bias, attacking us with abandon. A wild dog roused us out of our sleeping bags and into our panniers in search of knives and pepper spray. Still, we'd shown up the police and their silly regulations. Hadn't we?

I felt better in the morning as the fog parted to reveal a mountain ridge skyline dappled in green and white. Then the reality of the climb set in, as did the realization we had no food. We had forgotten to stock up at the last stop.

"There should be a town up ahead," said Garryck.

"Uh, not according to the map," I replied.

Garryck did not do well without food. His body composition was almost pure muscle, unlike Phillip and me, who had plenty of reserves of good old lard. After climbing for several hours, we pulled over to devour our remaining crackers and drink honey from a bottle filled by a local beekeeper. We convinced ourselves that an upcoming speck on our map would be the Chinese equivalent of a McDonalds drive-in. When we finally arrived, the village was deserted. Our stomachs screamed anew.

An hour later I asked a cement worker if we could buy some food from him. He pointed me down the hill where we just came from. Phillip and I made it to the top of the pass first. We began drinking our honey in order to generate as much energy as we could. But I was worried about Garryck. He was riding without extra leg power and lingered far behind. To our surprise, Garryck caught up to us. He was grinning ear to ear.

"I found a bread tree!" he said.

"What eez a bread tree?" asked Phillip, not sure if he had heard him right.

"Some guy pulled alongside to give me a thumbs-up sign. I used my hands to ask how far to food. He motioned a long way and tossed me bread and peppers! I didn't have to say a word."

We sat in a tunnel at the summit and devoured the entire bag of hardened bread along with the rest of our honey. My fears gave way to a comfort that that we'd be okay, that citizens of this common planet of ours would help whenever they were able to. We'd survived the challenge, and went back to our routine of riverside hotels and joy rides for locals. Phillip relished the moments, using pantomime to ask villagers about the minute details of their lives, like how they washed their clothes or which kid was the fastest runner. We couldn't have picked a better multi-day guest rider.

"It was an unforgettable journey. Thank you for including me," said Phillip as we soaked in our last moments together.

"How is your belly? Did you lose any weight?" I joked.

"I need more than five days for this belly of mine. It took me five months to grow it!"

"I'll miss ya, Waffle. It won't be the same riding China without you."

"We'll ride again one day. When you come to Belgium, okay?" he said.

"You promise?"

"I promise," he said, reaching out for a hug.

We had a long hug. Then, just like that, my seat was empty. And I was left wondering who might be next.

One of our many flat tire stops with the curious locals

Phillip working his magic

Phillip and Jamie refueling on honey and bread tree fruit

11

KANDING, CHINA
(FORMER GATEWAY TO THE TIBETAN WORLD)

WE COULD SEE the road winding up the massive mountain in front of us, steeper and longer than any we'd encountered before. We had begun our climb into the mythic Himalayas. Garryck and I took a break on the side of the road to stretch and, more important, mentally prepare ourselves. Without warning, he let out a loud *Owwwwwwwooooohh!*, and I joined in.

As we dropped into our granny gears, I looked at Garryck and decided something felt different about him. About us. Big challenges usually brought out the best in him. A college final, a grueling climb, a stolen bicycle. I also sensed that we'd shed a few barriers between us. These days he was more approachable, less guarded. I hoped I was as well. The guest riders came more easily for us after these months on the road. And something was shifting in both of us. I was eager to see how it all resettled.

The temperatures dropped with each foot of altitude. 10,000 feet, 11, 12. We now cycled in freezing conditions. My foul-weather cycling duds, which had kept me warm and sweaty for hundreds of miles, now fought a losing battle against the elements. I started to shiver, and grew concerned. The sun was going down, and there wasn't an inn or lodge for at least ten kilometers.

I looked at our current guest riders—Ursa and Bojana, two adventurous, blonde Slovenians—and felt a crushing weight of responsibility. Neither of them had extreme weather sleeping bags or mats. Camping in the wildflower-filled meadow was not an option. We needed to find shelter, and fast.

We stopped the bikes in front of the only structure for miles. The dark and weathered wooden house had smoke coming out of a small chimney. A barking dog sprinted toward us at full speed until a chain stopped her pursuit mid-attack. We waved and smiled innocently at a woman in the window, motioning for her to come down. Please.

She approached cautiously, keeping her distance from the fence, yet close enough for me to see her leathery skin and deep wrinkles. I mustered some phrasebook Chinese for "sleep." No response. She spoke Tibetan and I knew none.

Ursa and I switched quickly to an award-worthy mime show. We acted out how we would first unpack our long-wheeled machines, then roll out our sleeping bags and sleep like babies on the floor of her house. Marcel Marceau would have been proud. Success! She understood! Then she nodded her head, no, and walked back into the house.

What do you mean no? After that performance?

We stared at each other, stunned. We'd freeze unless we found shelter. There could be no "no"s. That's when I started to laugh. I looked at the others and laughed harder. To amuse ourselves earlier in the day, we had plastered temporary tattoos on our foreheads from chewing gum packages. Bojana had a green dragon, Garryck a purple whale, Ursa sported one of a little yellow girl, and I had a blue bird propped between my eyes.

Garryck and I had descended into Luding a few days earlier, feeling strong, skilled and confident having navigated the wild, muddy, rutted roads to the base of the Tibetan highlands. That's where we met Ursa and Bojana, both experienced riders. We quickly became a powerful team tackling days of relentless climbing into the mountains. Our planned one-day ride stretched into ten-day adventure up towards the town of Litang, near the Tibetan border.

We had been able to find lodging in Kanding and were hoping to make our way to the next town, which had several options for lodging. But our pace was slowed by regular stops to take photos of elaborately decorated horses and to meet numerous colorful characters on the road.

"We rrreally must deeescover some way to sleep here, Jamie," said Ursa.

"I know, I know. We'll think of something."

Garryck joined me as we opened the gate and made our way towards the building, setting off the dog anew. *I hope that chain holds.* A short Tibetan man in a soiled business suit emerged from the front door.

"Try your Chinese," said Garryck.

Yes. Good call. I was the official Mandarin translator and had been listening to tapes and studying the language since we entered China. The woman had sent him out because he could speak Mandarin. Of course.

But before I had a chance to say a word, he took one look at us and turned around and went back inside. The dog continued to wail, but we weren't going anywhere. The man peeked out the window, and we waved for him to please come out. "Puppy dog eyes, puppy dog eyes," counseled Garryck. We walked up to the door and knocked gently. Nothing. We knocked again. Finally he opened the door. He had bloodshot eyes, stained teeth, and cheeks so red I thought they were painted on.

"*Ni-hao-ma,*" I said, opening my Mandarin phrase book and pointing to the characters for "Can we sleep here?" He shook his head, no. I pulled out some money and offered to pay him. No. My heart sank. I felt a surge filling my body as the gravity of the situation settled in. No amount of money or puppy dog eyes was going to change his mind.

We looked behind him and saw a rotund woman chatting with another woman who looked like her sister. As a last ditch effort, we motioned to them. Tents. Cold. Ignore the silly tattoos. Then something clicked. The aliens are not looking for a hotel, they seemed to indicate. They have their own gear. They will not abduct us.

The man's facial expression morphed from confused and cautious to welcoming and compassionate. We were in. I looked back at Ursa and Bojana and gave two thumbs-up signs. Our host introduced himself as Yeshe, and showed us to our sleeping area, a one-room shack attached to the main building with a wood floor stained with mud, spit and spilled food. He then vanished only to reappear a minute later with a wicker basket of boiled peanuts. He then left again as quickly as he came in.

"They must be in the next room saying, 'We'll give the aliens some peanuts and see if they eat them,'" said Ursa, giggling in her sleeping bag as she tried to raise her body temperature back to normal.

Yeshe returned again with bowls of warm noodles. We had planned to eat our own food, but knew it was considered rude to refuse hospitality in Asia. We slurped down the noodles, then gave Yeshe a Tootsie Pop as a thank-you present. He smiled. Wide. His family had little, yet he treated his guests and accommodations like a concierge in a four-star resort. *He's proud*, I thought. And that made the noodles taste even better.

Garryck made strategic calculations on how to maneuver our two sleeping mats so all four of us had core body protection from the hard and cold floor that night. Bojana, my guest rider, would be sleeping right next to me. Although she had a boyfriend and I promised to honor a hands-off rule, I struggled not to reach over and spoon her. I craved the companionship.

But once Garryck blew out the single candle lighting the room, we began to drift into a deep slumber. Crazy to think we could sleep so well on a stranger's floor fouled by spilled food and dirty shoes. I didn't care a lick. Those four beautiful walls kept us from hypothermia. A simple shack had never looked as regal to me.

Yeshe's hospitality fueled our giant climb to more than 14,000 feet the next day, our first summit. "We did it!" yelled Ursa at the apex. We joined in, screaming at the top of our lungs, a mixture of ecstasy, adrenaline, and oxygen deprivation. We snapped our victory photo and quickly began our high-speed descent soon after to avoid losing body heat. The descent afforded long views of rich green pastures dotted with yaks and herder tents.

We were now in the Tibetan plateau, undulating between 4,000- and 5,000-meter summits. We stopped often to gawk at mountain peaks so sharp they looked like they cut the sky, give rides to cackling locals, eat *tsampa* with villagers, and chat with humble Tibetan families in front of their elaborately painted wood and stone homes. The pristine air and high altitude made the blue sky seem neon, with clouds so white and vivid and close you wanted to grab them like handfuls of popcorn.

The climbs consumed every ounce of energy we could muster. Equally taxing was the mental aspect of the cycling. One missed pothole when you're descending at 50 miles per hour can cost a bike, a limb, a life. So Garryck and I kept our eyes glued on the road and worried even more. Having passengers aboard more than doubled the focus.

Late one afternoon, we'd had enough. Our legs smoldered and our stomachs howled from a full day of granny-gear climbing. There was no way we'd make it to the next town. We needed to secure accommodation again with a local family.

After a few failed attempts, Ursa and I spotted an elderly man sitting cross-legged next to the road. His name was Toshi, he declared. Ursa and I launched into our mime routine again. Act 1: "Riding in the hot sun all day." Act 2: "So darn tired and hungry we're ready to faint." Act 3: "May we sleep at your house?" Toshi nodded yes and opened up his front gate.

We wheeled the bikes inside the fence, being very careful not to step on any steamy, multilayered landmines left by Fred, a giant pig roaming the yard. We climbed up steep stairs to enter a large single-room dwelling painted every color of the rainbow on the inside. Toshi's wife, Yara, had a covered pot cooking on the open fire inside the house. She motioned that we were invited to eat with the family.

After cleaning up down at the river we returned to the main room, eager to wolf down some dinner. Two leathery-faced Tibetan men entered after us, carrying a mysterious item wrapped in a filthy tarp and tied with worn rope. They tossed the package on the wooden floor. *Thump!* The floor shook, and a man in a grubby orange shirt untied the rope and began unwrapping the contents.

The first thing I noticed was an eye the size of a billiard ball, glossy and still, staring up at us. *Cult. Humans next. Run!* Then I saw the deep folds and wet black nose, curled horns, and a shaggy, bloody mane. A yak head. A thousand-pound, deader-than-dead yak head.

Before I could ask Yara what was going on, I felt a *swoosh* and heard a *crack!* One of the men began to wage war on the skull with an ax, spraying chunks of bone, hair, and blood in every direction. *Smash!* We dove for cover near Yara as the other men detached the horns, hair, and skin with the skill and efficiency of an ER team. Bones, hair, and skin went in one pile; everything else in another. My stomach waged a war itself. Half wanted to retch with every whack of the axe, but the other portion cried out for food, *fooooood!*

My internal battle continued for the next two painful hours as Yara boiled yak head parts in a musty, earthy broth. And when the soup was ready, we all slurped down a bowl and asked for more. And another, please. The Himalayan pile of yak skin and bones didn't slow my feast for an instant. Neither did the one-year-old baby who wailed in terror, though apparently not from the yak butchery. He was scared of the ghost faces in the room, Toshi told us, and laughed.

As in many Tibetan homes, there were no separate bedrooms in the structure. Everyone slept in the large open room with several wooden columns painted in brilliant crimsons and aquamarines. I mimed to our hosts our desire to go to sleep. Yara pointed to the butcher's corner, where ample evidence of the mutilation remained. I flicked away a few of the larger bloody remnants and slept for ten hours.

Garryck and Ursa crossing the 10,000 foot elevation

Our tattooed Slovenian guest riders Ursa & Bojana warm, dry and fed in Yeshe's simple house

Our proud USA-Slovenia team crossing a 14,000 foot pass

Beautiful yet demanding high altitude touring

Yara was enjoying the experience as much as we were!

12

LITANG, CHINA.

---▶

LHAMU REACHED FOR my hand with her soft little fingers. Pema, her younger sister, pulled my other hand with all her vigor, tilting her body to a 90-degree angle. They led me through a mountain field speckled in purple, yellow, orange, and white wildflowers. The fading sun lit up the field with a sepia glow. I wished the scene would last forever.

Lhamu was eight and Pema was five. They were the daughters of our host for the evening, Nima. Fearless Lhamu showed me a few wildflowers in hand, and I stared at the vibrant petals and delicate stems. Small cups of beauty in an unforgiving clime. I couldn't remember the last time I stared at a flower. Switzerland, perhaps? Childhood? To stop and smell the roses you first need to see the roses. I pointed to my handlebar bag and motioned that I'd love to have a bouquet for the next day's ride. Lhamu's eyes lit up. She led me to a field rife with flowers just a few hundred feet from their front yard.

The sun escaped behind the local peak, chilling the air like an opened refrigerator door. I could smell wafts of soup streaming from Nima's kitchen. Like children everywhere, the girls ignored dinner and darkness in favor of adventure. *Yong, yong!* Come! They led me farther away. We picked a handful of purple and orange flowers, then *yank*, they pulled me off to the next field. Then another.

Although I was enjoying the quest, I kept trying to pull the girls back closer to their house so that we'd be in view of Nima. Every so often I'd ditch the girls and jog back to the house to make sure Nima was not worried. And every time I'd see the same thing—Nima inside cooking, perfectly content to let her daughters roam around fields with an adult stranger. Lhamu and Pema sprinted to fetch me. They grabbed my hands and pulled me back to the fields to continue our mission.

As they raced to pick blossoms, my mind whirred back to Northern California and the early bike riding lessons, the yells and encouragement from my father, and the wiped tears after the inevitable falls. To kindergarten, when a classmate approached me and asked simply, "Do you want to be my friend?" To the panicked searches when my new friend Paul and I would break curfew, again, conquering dirt trails on our BMX bikes in the dark.

Paul's father and my mom got married. Paul and I stopped being friends as soon as they did.

Maybe that's when the fear set in. It does for most children at some point. Fear is ultimately going to set in, but a good friend can postpone it. He can shield you from worst-case scenarios and point you toward the possible. *Would Lhamu and Pema ever have that type of fear*, I wondered. Probably not in the foreseeable future.

I looked back to the house, to Nima, and thought about the countless times I'd been warned against talking to strangers, let alone frolicking in a wildflower field with them. She'd given her daughters a gift, one they were now sharing with me.

I sat down and both girls came over to present their creations. Lhamu had assembled wildflower crowns for the both of us, the king and queen of all that can be seen. Pema handed me a wilting bouquet that still looked prettier than anything I'd ever seen in an FTD window. She reached for my hand, and I acted like she was a superhero wrenching me up from the ground. She laughed, and then she laughed some more.

"*What the hell* is that horrible noise?" I asked Garryck after hearing a grinding screech from my bike that seemed to worsen with each pedal.

"'I'm not sure exactly."

"Sounds pretty serious, bro."

"I'll take a look when we get to our campsite," he said, keeping his head fixed on the road ahead while spinning the pedals at a blistering pace.

The 20-tooth granny gear was our best friend and savior on the Himalayan climbs, but today it seemed to question the relationship. A few hours after I noticed the grinding, Garryck's bike began to make a similar noise. By the time we found a flat camping spot for the night, both bikes sounded like they'd been possessed by demons.

"Bro, you have to look at this and get it dialed in," I said. I rolled my bike over in front of his tent and set it down by his side.

When Garryck and I had concocted the Peace Pedalers expedition, we each chose roles based on our skill sets and passions. I was proud of the work I'd done, securing dozens of sponsors and overseeing the administrative side of the project. I expected him, as Technical Team Leader, to do everything possible to make sure the bikes worked properly. After examining the tandems, he called me over.

"Our bottom brackets are toast," he said with the look of a mad scientist.

"Uh, what do you mean they're toast?"

"Look at it!" he said, holding a disintegrated mess of ball bearings and bushings. "The only way to keep riding is to use the front bottom bracket and put our bikes in single mode."

"What about spare bottom brackets?"

"No, I didn't think we'd go through them so fast."

"I don't understand. You are a trained master bike mechanic. You packed every spare part and tool known to man, but somehow you forgot to pack critical drivetrain parts that only weigh a few measly ounces?"

He tilted his head, and set the pieces down on the ground.

"I'm sorry. That's all I can say. It's just this one part. Everything else is fine."

"And what about our tires? You had two years to research the best tires. All four of our touring tires have had blowouts. We could have been hurt or even killed. Now we're touring heavy tandems on lightweight mountain bike tires, for God's sake. Super slow and dangerous, bro."

Whoa, whoa. Who was the "Administrative Team Leader" who insisted on the inferior tires in the first place as a way to save money? Uh, me. And when a sponsor sent us the wrong bottom brackets who was it who said "they'll be fine" instead of buying the very best like Garryck suggested? Yep, me again.

"We'll get parts sent up to Kunming. Better tires and more bottom brackets to keep in our spare parts stock." Garryck said.

For the past four days we had crossed numerous 5,000-meter sum-mits together, hosted Tibetan monks at our campsites and locals on our bikes, accepted invitations to sip butter tea with yak herders and soaked in endless mountain vistas. We tackled the challenging, athletic rides Garryck adored and the human interactions I craved. This was the embodiment of the expedition. And now it was over. No more tandems.

Although deep in my heart I knew I had no right to, I blamed Garryck for the breakdown. *He should have insisted on the right gear. That's his job* I told myself. I was not only angry, I was also a burnt out. We had been living in close quarters from morning to night for over six months and I was feeling a strong need for some solitude to recharge. So after a few words of explanation, I shifted my bike into single mode using the one functioning bottom bracket and pedaled away from our campsite for a multi-day mission on the rugged roads to Zhongdian.

From the moment I left, the rhythm and energy of the expedition changed. I stopped when I wanted to stop. I picked flowers until my han-dlebar bag looked like a float at the Rose Parade. I mingled with the locals on the side of the road, even if I had just stopped five minutes before to tickle a cute baby. I took a nap in a field and a butterfly landed on my face. I ambled along, just fast enough to keep the bike moving, allowing me to soak in every detail of the area's mountains, trees, rivers, villages, and peo-ple. The slow, sporadic pace would have driven Garryck crazy.

With each day alone I could also feel a growing confidence to con-nect on a deeper level with locals. In the past I'd hesitate whenever I sensed Garryck wanted to keep the bikes in motion. I didn't want to upset him, so I'd keep pedaling and ignore my desire to slow down. *But that's not what the trip was all about*, I told myself. I missed that sense of connection. Here on my own I could write my own daily touring plan. Stop riding early in the day to find the perfect homestay for the night. Sit with the locals and hack through dictionaries and sign language. Listen and learn. I was free.

By the time I approached Zhongdian, I began to realize that my vision for the trip was different from Garryck's.

Yet this wasn't just my dream. It was equally his. Plus I missed him—his support, his enthusiasm, his friendship. I couldn't imagine going it alone.

Lhamu's crown of flowers

Pema's bouquet in my handlebar bags

My first solo campsite where I slept in listening to birds

Connecting with the locals was easier as a solo cyclist

My bike after a tough day solo cycling

13

EVEREST REGION, FORMER TIBET

THE EXCITEMENT OF arriving at a Mt. Everest basecamp postponed any deep discussions about the future of the ride. Garryck and I would wake early, zip open our tent, and watch the sun flicker on, gaining strength and brilliance as it painted the world's tallest mountains in ever-changing shades of gold and gray and white. My legs ached like they did every morning, but after a few minutes of stretching they felt like they wanted to return to the bike. A carpenter reaching for a hammer, a singer reaching for a mic.

I looked out the tent to see a young Tibetan boy in an oversized blue sport coat slowly inching his way towards me. Behind him came a small entourage of friends. Six or seven years old, I guessed. I motioned their leader to come closer and take a look at the bike that had drawn them to the tent. His face lit up as he touched the tires, grips and seat.

His buddies slowly gathered around, five curious kids looking for a morning adventure. I pointed to the front and the rear seat and motioned that I wanted to give them all a ride. They bounced and poked each other. I grabbed the smallest of the bunch and put him on my front handlebars. Two other boys piled on the stoker seat and my seat. I checked back to make sure they were stable and counted *1...2...3!* And off we went, screaming into the void that filled the still village nearby. *Aweeeeeoooohhhh!*

The yelps of joy attracted more kids, who came running down from surrounding houses to collect their rightful turn on the tandem bike. *Ahhhhhhhheeeeee!* I spent the next hour giving rides to anyone who asked. Seconds. Thirds! I started to worry I wouldn't have enough strength for the rest of the day's ride. They begged for the experience to continue. One boy indicated that the morning was a gift. He was right. But what he didn't know was that the gift was more mine. By the time we pedaled out of town and towards Nepal, my mood was as high as the surrounding tors. The crew of giddy Tibetan boys kept giving until the end, running full speed alongside us until they could run no more.

Their unadulterated joy stuck with me. Those smiles found a home deep in my heart. I rode solo for the rest of the day, preferring to think about the pure bliss of those boys. Life is perfect at that age. Decisions are made without fear or bias. We simply pursue passion. We want to connect with anybody who shares that passion. At some age we are told that passion is frivolous and connections can be dangerous. We become ashamed of screaming at the top of our lungs or dancing around the house in our underwear. Only decades later, when we're looking back over our lives, do we talk about the importance of passion. Often it's too late.

Before my senior year in college, my mother gave me some unpleasant news. Once I graduated, I would no longer be eligible for the cheap plane tickets she could secure through her job at American Airlines. "You're not going to be a dependent anymore," she explained, encouraging me to take advantage of the deep discounts while I could. I grabbed a flight book and started making reservations for Boston, Barbados, Chicago, anywhere with a friend's couch or cheap accommodation. I yearned to see more of the world, but I also had something else I wanted to uncover.

Idling at LAX while awaiting a standby flight to New Orleans for Mardi Gras, I approached a businessman next to me. I'd done so dozens of times that year of power traveling. After some small talk, I asked him the question that lingered inside me.

"Did you go to college?" I asked.

"I did," he said.

"Ok. Then I'll ask you this. If you could go back in time to when you were just graduating college and do one thing differently, what would it be?"

"Now, that's a good question."

"I've asked more than a hundred people the same question."

"Really? And what have they said."

"I'll tell ya after you give me your answer."

"Smart aleck. Hmmmmm. Lemme think."

I could tell the question resonated with him, and that he didn't want to dole out some pat response. I took the issue seriously as well. I saw the questions as a personal senior research project. The answers were slowly changing the way I looked at the world and influencing my thoughts for life post-graduation.

"I guess if I were to go back to 1983 and do something different I would have....Hmmm. Honestly, I would have just delayed getting so darn serious so soon."

He looked down at his feet, then picked up his head to look back at me. He seemed ashamed.

"Can you elaborate on *serious?*"

"Yeah. I would have delayed getting tied down to a mortgage, two car payments, and children. Don't get me wrong. I love my wife and kids. But if I could do it all over I would have strapped on a backpack like you have right there and gone out and enjoyed my freedom for a while to see the world before tying myself down to so many commitments."

"That sounds..."

"Truth is, nobody really took me very seriously in my twenties anyway in the business world. I could have explored my interests of music and the arts for several years and come back to start my career later and been just fine."

"That sounds all too familiar," I said.

"So what other answers have you received?"

"Honestly, just about everyone has shared their unique version of the exact same answer you just gave me. In the end, everyone seems to be telling me to enjoy freedom and youth instead of waiting until some elusive retirement or financial milestone."

"Well, we can't all be wrong, can we?"

"Nope. I've interviewed too many people to dismiss it as coincidence."

"You're a wise man asking all this advice."

"Thanks."

"You'd be even wiser to heed it."

Here on the road from Tibet to Nepal, I thought about that business-man and his advice. I thought about all the answers I heard that year. Was this trip one last grasp at the joy and carelessness of being young? *No*, I said to myself, beaming. If by giving someone a ride or even passing them on the street, you can make a local's life a little lighter, the expedi-tion is a success. I saw that the "peace" in Peace Pedalers applied not only to goodwill between cultures, but an internal harmony as well. This gave me a high. And an idea.

I thought about it for the rest of the day as I soaked in the last of the lunar-brown scenery and bright white snowcapped mountains off in the distance. That night I found an Internet connection and sent an email to my mom.

Dear Mom,

I was just thinking about you on this evening's ride here in Tibet. I was thinking about how you and I were planning on riding together in Nepal. I was sad that you are not going to be able to join me. But then I came up with the next best way for your spirit to flourish in Nepal.

Do you still have access to those little teddy bears that you sent in the last care package? Can you send over a huge box of teddy bears, stickers, lollipops, and any other little small gifts that are light, easy to send, and easy to carry on the bike? I've been giving rides to the little kids here in Tibet, and got inspired to bring more smiles and joy to some of the kids in need down in Nepal.

I am not going to be able to access the Internet for a while, so if you could get this package together as soon as possible ready to send to our hostel in Kathmandu that would be ideal. I'll email or call you as soon as I get to the next town with phone or Internet.

Jamie

Loading up the local kids for a spin

My morning riding crew as ecstatic as I was

14

KATHMANDU, NEPAL

- ▶

"**WHAT DOES DOUBLE D** stand for?" I asked the cheerful young Nepali man after meeting him on the streets in Kathmandu.

"Desires Delight," he said.

"Wow, that's awesome! Sounds like dessert topping or a porn....What do you do for a living, Double D?"

"I fix refrigerators. I'm good at it, and it makes people happy."

Double D did happy well. His shaved head and omnipresent perfect-teeth grin gave him a friendly, mini-Buddha vibe. *How do so many people in developing-world countries have perfect teeth? Maybe because they eat real food instead of foodstuffs that have been packed with fructose and manipulated beyond recognition.*

In many countries, "friends" hung around foreigners in hopes of becoming paid guides or, at least, scurrying you to a shop or restaurant that would in turn give them a tip. Double D wasn't a tour guide and didn't want any money. He loved showing people around Kathmandu and quickly realized the tandem was an ideal new way to do so.

He led Garryck and me on panoramic rides and hikes in the hills, ferried us around the tangled backstreets and rickshaw-clogged roads, brought us to hidden Sadhu temples, and made sure we enjoyed a side of Katmandu often ignored by tourists and trekkers. Before long, Double D and I began tackling the city alone because Garryck was off implementing Road Rule Number 9: If you make a love connection and wish to break away for a few days, go forth and prosper. He went off to trek the Annapurna region of the Himalayas on a travel honeymoon.

Double D showed me sacred pujas and daily rituals, haggling at the markets, and secluded spots to escape Kathmandu's grip of chaos and noise. One afternoon, I noticed a severed goat head next to a few scattered flowers. Then another. Then two on the next block.

"Hey, Double D. Are you trying to get my goat?" I asked.

"You have a goat?"

"It's an expression. Means to anger someone."

"Are you angry?"

"No, no, no. What's up with all the goat heads?"

"*Dashain.* They are sacrificed to please the goddess Durga."

"I see the heads, but where are the goat bodies?"

"Feasts all day!"

Seeing the mutilated heads spread across town did little to prime my appetite. But the more Double D explained the rituals, the less repulsed I became. We did the same thing in the U.S., after all. Worse. We did our slaughter in mega meat-processing centers. Rarely did we give thanks to the animals we killed or incorporate them into our spiritual ceremonies. *At least these animals had a party before they died.*

"You know something," I said as we shared a ride on our last afternoon in Kathmandu. "The only overnight riders to join us so far on the tandem have been other Western backpackers."

"Really? Why?"

"I don't know. Tough for many locals to break away."

"Yes, it's expensive. People have to work."

In the much of the developing world, vacations are as real as tooth fairies and politicians' promises. The thought of getting away for a few days is a chimera for movies or wealthy Westerners.

"What if I invited you as my guest of honor to do a three-day ride to Pokhara beginning tomorrow?" I said. "I'll take care of meals and lodging. And when you're ready to come home, I'll buy you a bus ticket back."

"I, I have never been to Pokhara. I have never left Kathmandu."

"Would your parents let you go?"

Like most unmarried young men in this part of the world, Double D lived at home.

"I don't care. I would not miss this for anything."

"Tomorrow we ride."

"Hey, would you like to come see my village and sleep at my home tonight? I would like to pay you back."

"Deal. Let's go to the hotel and get my stuff."

Though the next morning offered textbook conditions for riding—clear skies with a slight breeze at our backs—we both knew the road between Katmandu and Pokhara was the most dangerous in all Nepal, jammed with trucks and aggressive motorists and with little space for bikes. We set our expectations low, predicting we'd spend most of the day dodging busses and gulping diesel exhaust. To our surprise, the road was practically deserted. Maoist terrorist challenges in the country scared away tourists and locals.

Double D did double duty that day, giving it his all on the pedals and looking for opportunities to impart his wisdom about his home country. "We don't greet people with a handshake here. You put two hands together and bow, saying '*Namaste.*' It means 'I salute the God within you.'" He taught me several Nepali words and phrases, all the while mixing in more of his unique philosophies on life, service and love. "Being of service to others is being service to yourself. You can't give and not receive."

Our conversation continued as we passed simple thatch houses where Nepalese families bounced, waved and cheered us on. During breaks I played with the local kids while Double D went to work lining up the best available food in the area. He presented each meal with passion and earnestness, making sure I understood the ingredients, could say the name properly, and ate more than my fair share. There was the daily staple of *dal-bhat-tarkari* and silver *thali* plates of rice, spicy lentil soup, vegetable curry, spicy chutneys and pickled veggies.

After our tough day in the saddle we found a riverside hotel and received permission to set up our tent on the beach. We then had a long swim and a huge *dal bhat* feast with a dozen sweet-and-sour side dishes before drifting off into a deep sleep against the backdrop sound of the gurgling river. *Maybe Double D could travel with me beyond Pokhara?*

"Jamie. Jamie. Wake up," he urged at first light. "Please wake up."

"What's wrong, Double D?" I asked, sitting up in my sleeping bag.

"Please, get out of the tent and look at my face."

I crawled out of the tent and peered into his eyes. They had a burning yellow tint. He then showed me the palms of his hands, now the color of a pale banana.

"I don't know what to do. I am very, very tired. I feel very badly."

"Yeah, Double D, you don't look good. You need to get off the bike and go see a doctor."

"I really want to keep going. But I'm afraid I am just too ill. I'm so sorry," he said, his buttery eyes now beginning to tear up.

"Listen, let's head up to the main road and we'll find a bus back to Katmandu. You're going to be fine. Okay?"

I pushed the bike and gear up the hill while Double D struggled to carry himself and his small daypack. I was worried. I had read about the yellowing of the skin and eyes being a symptom of hepatitis, malaria, or jaundice. He needed medical care as soon as possible.

"I'm very sorry this happened," he said with tears now falling from in his eyes.

"I will come with you to the doctor. You'll be fine"

"No, no. Jamie, you ride on. I can go to the doctor on my own. You find a strong rider to join you to Pokhara. Please."

"Listen, Double D. These last couple days have been the highlight of my entire trip. You, my friend, are why I am chasing this insane dream. You."

"Come back and visit one day. Please. We can continue our ride to Pokhara then."

He reached his arm around me.

"One day," I said, though we both knew the odds were against it happening anytime soon.

A bus came soon after we arrived at the main road. I gave him plenty of money for the doctor and made him promise he would not spend it on anything but medical care. Given his generous nature I knew he would think about helping others. He promised to take care of himself. He boarded and we slapped a high-five from the window as the bus rolled away.

As the bus vanished over a horizon, I was filled with a wild mixture of emotions. I was depressed to lose Double D after only one full day of touring, and concerned about his health. Did I put him at risk? Should I have insisted on joining him to the doctor?

But those feeling gave way to an enormous dose of joy. *Desires Delight! How can you not love a person named Desires Delight?* I peered down the hill to our camping spot. *He did it. We did it. Who cares if we didn't make it to Pokhara. Double D showed me the way.* If I wanted a deeper connection with the world, I'd convince more locals to join me on overnight rides. I lifted my hand to give him another high-five.

Birsha clutched her soft white teddy bear as I reached down to pick her up. She shook her head no and turned away. I loved her look—bright green flip-flops and dangling earrings, a tomboy face and long brown hair.

"I'm not going to take your bear," I said. "I'm just trying to get you up on the bike for a ride."

"You have to forgive her, Jamie," said Raju. "She's never had a toy."

Raju was one of the volunteers at the Children Welfare Home, an orphanage Garryck and I decided to visit to distribute some of the teddy bears, animal purses and clown noses my mom had sent from California. Raju, with his ruby red *tilak* (a *bindi* on women) and calm demeanor, assured Birsha her bear was safe and that she could mount the bike without worry.

"The children do not get many visitors," he explained after a dozen tandem rides with the hooting kids. "Your visit means more than you think."

"It's my birthday," said Garryck. "And I can't think of a better place to celebrate."

"Please tell Birsha that as a present for Garryck's birthday we want her to take a bike ride around the yard with us," I told Raju.

As he explained everything to the shy little girl she looked at her bear, then the bike. And with the poise of a Broadway actress ready to go on stage she slowly handed the bear to Raju and climbed aboard. Within minutes her screams were as loud as any we'd heard all morning. "Again, please, sir," she said. Raju clapped for her with the fuzzy arms of the bear.

I lived for those moments, and began to crave them more and more. Over breakfast later that morning I talked to Garryck about my days with Double D and the deeper payoff of overnight local riders. I was hooked, I explained.

"I'm itching to find a Nepali rider myself," he said. "Let's make it happen."

"Why don't you head over the bike shop and ask around. I'll stop by some of the outfitters and see if we can't rustle up someone for an adventure."

Within a day of hunting around Pokhara we managed to find two willing and able Nepalese guest riders. Garryck struck up a conversation with Santos and Ramchandra, two teenagers curious about the tandems and looking for a little excitement. They agreed to meet us at a bike shop the next day at 8 a.m. and pedal south towards India via Bardia National Park. They both seemed earnest and eager to ride.

In the morning we rode to the shop and heard the bad news. Santos had become ill and couldn't join the group. I suggested Ramchandra ride with Garryck, hoping they would forge a partnership as rewarding as mine with Double D. I wanted him to share my growing addiction for deeper connections with locals. Since it looked as if I would ride solo, I would have to redouble my efforts to keep up with them on the 480-km journey.

Ramchandra was seventeen, a high school junior, and all of about 100 pounds. He showed up wearing jeans, a button down shirt and flip-flops, with a comb in his hands at all times to sculpt his glorious black hair, parted on the side and clipped to the ears like a banker's haircut. I worried his frame wasn't big enough to help motor the bike, but Ramchandra, an experienced cyclist, had strong legs and just a small pack.

"Plus this guy does the most amazing goat imitations," Garryck said during a break. "He mimics their sounds and the goats reply!"

As we climbed up out of Pokhara, I picked up several guest riders, young and old, most walking on the shoulder of the road. Some carried their weight; others were dead weight. Garryck and Ramchandra stopped to let me catch up. Just as I was about to reach them, a motorcycle with two riders pulled up alongside us.

"Hey, Jamie, remember me?" said the rider on the back of the motor-cycle. "It's Madan! You gave me a short ride yesterday."

"Hey, Madan. What are you doing up here?" I asked.

"The guys at the bike shop told me about Santos getting sick. So I got permission from my parents. Can I ride with you guys?"

"Hell, yes!"

My legs felt better before he even mounted the bike. Madan, a 23-year old college student on break, sported a red bandana and Liverpool FC t-shirt with large block lettering that proclaimed "You Will Never Walk Alone." Though not as proficient a rider as Ramchandra, Madan had a personality that fit well on the tandem. He was mostly laid back and soft spoken, though he'd burst into commentary from time to time with the confidence of a drunken poet. On breaks he'd break out a joint and quote reggae musicians while pointing out his favorite flowers or butterflies.

"Love the life you live; live the life you love."

The gentle climbs and easy descents, landscapes bejeweled with evergreens and sparkling wildflowers, quaint villages with kids yelling "bye, bye," and two affable and industrious (and sometimes stoned) locals giving their all to the pedals helped make this the most gratifying ride of the trip so far. Mesmerizing, even. After a few miles my body settled in to a comfortable lull and my mind shifted into low gear. *You're peace pedaling, brother.*

We arrived in a small village with only one lodge, and landed a room with four beds—perfect to continue the engaging conversations with our new friends. After another delicious and inexpensive meal of *dhal bhat,* Nepal's rice and bean staple, we chatted like summer campers, bonded over a couple games of cards and a few puffs of Madan's ganja, and drifted to sleep the minute our bodies reminded us of the 80 kilometers clocked earlier that day.

Garryck woke me shortly after dawn.

"Dude, I went downstairs to the toilet and just about pooped my pants!" he said.

Still in a dream state, I didn't know whether to be scared or amused.

"Did you eat something bad?"

"There's at least five guys in street clothes packing FAL assault rifles! Maoist terrorists are eating breakfast at our hotel!"

Maoist terrorism and the daily drumbeat of stories detailing their atrocities had had a chilling impact on tourism. The insurgents were demanding an end to feudalism, a new constitution, and the establishment of a Nepali republic. They swore they would stop at no end to reach their objectives, bombing and killing in their path. Garryck and I made a vow to avoid conversations about politics whenever possible. Did those discussions ever solve a problem or change a mind? No, our expedition was about the opposite of politics. It was about exploring commonalities.

In Nepal, we couldn't avoid the politics. Locals on the bike and off gave us their opinions and warnings. Most made it clear the terrorists did not wish to harm tourists. However, they warned, if you happened to find yourself in the wrong place at the wrong time, the consequences could be deadly.

Knowing all this, we gathered our belongings and crept downstairs, trying to act as natural as possible. *Breakfast? No, no. Just a bunch of cyclists. Need to be on our way.* Madan nearly tripped over an assault rifle leaning against the wall. I held my breath and hoped the crew of grizzled men didn't notice. They seemed to be far more concerned with their porridge. *Desk manager? Where the heck is the desk manager when we need to pay?* A young man finally appeared from behind a door and took our money. We were nearly home free.

I heard a car approach and park outside. *Oh, no! Cops! We're going to be trapped in the middle of a shootout.* The car turned out to be a hotel worker's. We exhaled and loaded the bikes at record speed, fastening packs and gear so haphazardly I was sure we'd lose half of it.

And even after we'd boarded the bikes and pulled away we still worried, choosing to ride in silence rather than tempt fate. Our collective mood started to ease only after the three-hour climb to Tansen. We were all relieved and looking forward to the long decline to Butwal. The smooth, glorious downhill section had racetrack turns and a grade that allowed us to coast the whole way. The bikes seemed more than appreciative, effortlessly gliding through each turn with minimal action required. *Ahh, breathe.* There was very little traffic on the road, allowing us to focus on the scenery and finally open up about the morning. "Garryck, you're right about pooping yourself," I yelled. "Those pants look a little brown."

Garryck and Ramchandra had fallen about 100 yards behind us when a large bus settled in between. I turned to give Garryck more grief. "Might want to jump in a river or...." And that's when I saw the rocks. There, around the turn. Jagged and strewn across the smooth pavement, the size of jawbreakers. I went from poop jokes to a high-speed, high-stakes slalom course. "Hold on!" One, then another. *Where the hell did these come from?* To another, and we're almost through. Until, *no! Smack!* We hit one straight on at 40-miles an hour. Boom! The front tire gave way immediately.

At the time, Ramchandra and Garryck were howling at the sight of a guy who had his head stuck out the window and was expelling the contents of his lunch down the side of the bus. When Garryck looked ahead to make sure I saw the Technicolor display, he caught our slow-motion crash in full view. The bike slammed us to the ground then slid on the right-side panniers. Madan and I bounced a few times and grasped at the ground in a frantic attempt to halt the skid. The bus would reach us in a few seconds. I looked to Madan, who wasn't wearing a helmet. *No, no, please no.* I'd heard about similar crashes on mountain roads, usually involving motorists who traveled at far too high speeds. *No!*

For whatever reason, the bus slowed as it made the turn. The driver pummeled the brakes and brought the transport to a halt just a few feet before flattening us. Maybe the curves made the driver slow his speed. Maybe the barfing passenger. *That's the most beautiful vomit I've ever seen.*

This was our first crash in more than seven months on the road. We took a quick inventory of ourselves and the bike. We both had impressive scrapes and strawberries on our bodies, and Madan had a large bump and cut on his head. We threw some iodine on the abrasions, patched up a half dozen holes in two tubes, and gathered the shrapnel of bags and gear to reload them on the bike.

Off we rolled, this time much more slowly to make sure it did not happen again as the road continued to deteriorate. Before I had time to worry about Madan, he slapped me on the shoulder and chuckled. "Ha! It's like what Bob Marley says: 'Though the road's been rocky, it's sure feels good to me!' Ya know! Ya know, Jamie!"

I felt a wave of relief, and a small dose of guilt, when we pulled into Butwal, our final destination for the day. I could have killed us both out there. Guest riders put their lives into my hands. Literally. I had to ride more safely, more responsibly, when anyone joined me. I looked to Madan. "I'm sorry, my friend."

One of the many benefits of biking with two Nepalese guest riders was the ability to send them into a hotel reception area while we hid outside. As was the case in most countries, the locals were able to get local rates, usually a 50-75% discount from the tourist rates. After scoring the group a few cheap rooms for the night, Madan and Ramchandra would then take us to a favored local restaurant, where we were served delicacies not found on the menu. I tried to blend in, though I tended to out myself as a tourist the moment I used my left hand to eat. "We use that hand to wipe," laughed Ramchandra.

After a few more days of stress-free touring we finally made it to Bardia National Park, a 100-square-kilometer wildlife reserve that is normally chock-full of tourists. But due to the current terrorist activities, we saw only one other visitor. The hotel manager was so desperate to fill his facility he rented us private bungalows for a few dollars each. The same rooms normally fetched more than $50 a day.

Garryck and I were thankful for all the insights and experiences we shared with Madan and Ramchandra, though neither of us could get used to the Nepali custom of tilting your head to the side to say yes. We kept thinking they were rebuffing our offers. We wanted to give them something to say thank you, even though they explained they'd been enriched by the ride just as much as we had.

On our last day together I treated them to a guided jungle walk in search of rhinos, tigers, and elephants. It was the end of the season, so the likelihood of seeing the big game was slim. None of us cared. Instead we saw fresh tiger paws, rhino prints and elephant dung, and laughed about what would happen if we did encounter the animals.

As the pleasurable day was winding to a close we spied a man riding an elephant. *Yes, that's it. Send these guys off in style.* After a quick explanation of the Peace Pedalers expedition, the man allowed us to hop on top of the gentle elephant for an unforgettable ride across the river.

"You know," said Ramchandra. "Before this week, my best vacation was to make a small picnic in my village. This trip has been the best thing to happen in my life. Thank you."

"No, thank you guys!" I replied "It's been the best travel experience of our lives as well."

"You will come back one day and visit us again, right?"

"I don't know when," said Garryck. "But we'll be back."

"Remember what Nepal stands for," said Madan. "*Never Ending Peace And Love.* Don't you forget it!"

He had told us this many times on our journey. Now we knew why

The colorful and slightly disturbing Dashain sacrifices

Leaving Double D's home town of Patan

Sharing my home with my first overnight native guest rider

Another load of giggling, grateful orphan in Pokhara

The children were overjoyed by our visit

Ramchandra the pedal master

The road rash from our high-speed fall

An unforgettable final adventure

15
RAJASTHAN, INDIA

"OKAY, BUDDY. LET'S figure out the plan of attack to Goa," I said.

"Oooooh K," said Garryck, staring at the menu.

"I was thinking we could ride to Surat first so we can at least hit the ocean, and then down to Mumbai. It's about, oh, 1,200 kilometers."

"Fair deal of that will be pretty uninspiring touring."

"We're just spoiled after Tibet and Nepal. Plus it's still another 600-plus kilometers to Goa from Mumbai."

"2,000 kilometers. There's no way we'll do that in two weeks."

"Yeah, by lingering in Japan, China, Tibet and Nepal we just don't have as much time as we thought we'd have."

We sat there for a few beats in silence, noshing on chapati bread and spicy chutney. Neither of us wanted to be the first to admit the unspoken truth on the table in front of us. I cracked first.

"Bro, I have to be honest. I'm fried. My enthusiasm level has dropped for Peace Pedaling right now. All I've been thinking about lately is a quiet beach in Goa where I can swim, listen to music, and try to rustle up some female companionship."

"As much as I hate to admit it, I'm with you. We need some down time."

"Yeah, eight months on the road, and two-and-a-half years of planning. No wonder we're feeling burnt."

Now. Talk to him.

"So let's go from Mumbai to Goa," I said. "A 600-kilometer spin is no Sunday stroll. Gives us a long ride in India and will still land us in Goa with plenty of time to beat the holiday crowds."

Coward.

"Deal," he said. "As much as I hate trains, I prefer riding down south where it will be more lush and green. Enough of this gray, dusty touring."

We caught the overnight train from Jaipur to Mumbai, and just as quickly settled into our unique rhythm on the roads of southern India. We'd ride each day before dawn, clicking off 30 kilometers by breakfast. Garryck and I viewed each sunrise like the unfolding of the Sunday paper. Each day brought unique sights and experiences right up to our noses—women in vibrant saris carrying water on their heads while their male counterparts lingered on doorsteps; children in British school uniforms asking for rides, which we gladly provided; cows, cows, and more sacred cows.

For lunch, we'd stop in a town and search out the favored samosas. In general, Garryck and I tended to avoid fried foods during the day. They'd fill a belly, but leave you feeling sluggish and slow. Indian samosas proved to be the exception. The deep-fried pastries filled with potatoes, lentils, peas, onions and possibly lamb, and savored with delicious mint and curry sauces, would entice us during the late morning hours and power us through the afternoons.

But my favorite part of the day came later, after we'd found a room for the night and headed to a patch of open space to join one of the omnipresent cricket matches. Grass, dirt, or pavement—the pitch didn't matter. Children and men staged matches on any free space they could find.

Cricket in India is a daily Super Bowl and a Sunday revival, a presidential campaign and a sandlot free-for-all. Combined. Everyone is invited, everyone is excited, and everyone has an opinion. I tried to learn the rules quickly. *It's kind of like baseball. Squished into two bases, with two pitchers and a ball that looked and felt like a round brick. Don't get hit by the brick.* Within minutes after stumbling upon a match, a local would toss me the ball and invite me to bowl...then proceed to blast shot after shot over parked cars and idle cows. "Hey, I've just clocked 100 kilometers!"

But cricket was more than cricket. Cricket was India. Massive, complex, both tolerant and fanatical. Dominated by men, with legions of girls increasingly eager and able to give it a try. Like baseball, cricket offers ample time to chat about anything other than the game. And the locals were more than willing to share their thoughts on the growing economic power of India, the advantages of an arranged marriage, the latest must-see Bollywood movies. The more time I spent on the cricket pitches, the more I realized how much I needed these deep intercultural experiences to carry on. When we got back on the bikes, I often resented having to leave so soon.

And the balance began to shift. Picking up the occasional local for a quickie-giggly ride was losing its allure. I was starting to feel that the only reason we were hosting guest riders was to snap a photo of them on the bike for our website. These surface connections were the only kind we'd make unless we slowed down and lingered in the villages like we did in Pokhara to find Ramchandra and Madan.

But I knew this was the last thing Garryck wanted. He was a cyclist, first and foremost. He wanted to ride. He needed to ride. I could see him start to pace and bounce around whenever we were delayed. I was hoping a nice long respite on the beach would help resolve the conflicting desires, though deep down I feared it would not.

Four days later we rolled into Anjuna, Goa, the ideal place to celebrate Christmas and New Year's. No crowded malls or inescapable renditions of "Santa Claus Is Coming to Town." Just sand, serenity, and a few of the area's famous house music parties at night. Santa Claus was welcome to come to town. He just better bring some SPF-50 and enough beers to share.

But when we arrived, the town seemed to move to a different beat. Instead of upbeat house music we envisioned, the clubs and bars blared dark and heavy trance. The mechanical, mind-numbingly repetitive beats attracted a zombie-like crowd of partiers and young former Israeli soldiers looking to forget their mandatory three years of service. Anjuna was perfect…if you were in search of strong and cheap drugs of dubious origin, ranging from ecstasy to ketamine to horse tranquilizers.

This zoned-out, stoned-out reality did not match the idealistic vision we had painted for ourselves during the punishing and frigid riding in the Himalayas or the long dusty days touring India. Instead of paradise, we found beaches crowded with hash-smoking expats. The only lodging we could muster was a run-down old house with multiple dogs that barked at every car, housefly, gust of wind, or anything else that moved. "This was worth it, right?" we told ourselves with ever decreasing conviction.

"You know," I said. "A year ago, I could have carved out a good time here. Ten years ago, I would have talked about staying for good."

"I wanted to chat with you about that," said Garryck.

"Cool. Maybe we head to new town. I hear south of Goa…"

"I'm just not feeling it here, bro."

I paused. I could see he was nervous. He had something to share.

"I got an offer to teach English for the rest of the winter back in Korea," he said.

"Oh…okay."

"I told you about this before, bro. I need the money."

"I don't remember you saying anything. Dude, we just got here. Really?"

"It's nothing personal."

"Nah, of course not."

I don't remember the rest of the conversation, only that he'd leave. Soon. I was crushed. Maybe he did tell me about it some time in the past but I just didn't think he'd do it. As he continued to explain his reasons, I kept thinking that I'd done something to cause the split. "Just for a couple months." "Just to get some cash." *Maybe he was expecting a massive cycling trip when you envisioned a massive connection trip.* "We'll reconnect in Thailand in a couple months." *Maybe.*

Maybe not.

One of rural India's countless village Cricket matches

Connections like this was why I was out Peace Pedaling

16
KOH KONG, CAMBODIA

CROSSING THE BORDER from Thailand into Cambodia I felt like I had just exited a time machine. Pavement gave way to dust. Horse-drawn carriages outnumbered cars. The sun's rays practically dripped with power-zapping humidity. No A/C or indoor toilets or any sort of relief for miles. And I loved every minute. This was the Southeast Asia Garryck and I dreamed of touring. Most important, we'd ride it together.

We'd planned to reconnect in Thailand, but since Garryck had already toured most of the country, he opted to train for a 24-hour mountain bike race while I meandered around the nation by myself. He not only finished, he won, besting the other riders by more than a couple hours. When I saw him he looked exhausted but overjoyed, a thoroughbred after being allowed to race. We'd meet in Koh Kong, we told each other via email.

As I pedaled toward the town, a young kid on a scooter pulled alongside. "There's a man with a bike like yours up ahead," he said. I redoubled my pace on the sooty, 20-km ride and quickly spotted Garryck's tan skin and yellow cycling jersey at a ramshackle fruit stand.

"Ya, Mon!!" I yelled.

"Bra! Guess what? We're in Cambodia!" he yelled back.

We gave each other a huge hug. And then another. I missed him, and could tell he had missed me as well. We spent the evening swapping adventure stories about our solo escapades in India, Korea, and Thailand. Peace. Pedalers. *The time apart has strengthened us,* I told myself. *It's made me appreciate him more, a champion rider and an even better friend. We can make this work.*

Garryck and I rode side by side on nearly empty roads as we made our way towards Phnom Penh. *"Susadai, Sudadsai!"* Hello, hello, yelled villagers from "hammock huts" and shaded areas under houses on stilts.

If there was a child under ten with clothing, I didn't see him. The country's newest generation roamed naked and free.

The Cambodian back roads also introduced us to a new phenomenon—the "Two-Pump-Chump." That's the name we gave to the men who jumped out of their hammocks or came sprinting toward us from their homes, curious and excited to accept our invitation to ride. They'd nod repeatedly as we gave them a pantomime overview of the dos and don'ts of tandems. "Yeah, yeah, yeah," they would say. "Go, go, go!" They'd hop up on the bike, laugh hysterically, give one or two pumps to the pedals, then jump off the bike and run back to their families and friends.

Here in the land of the monstrous Khmer Rouge, ground forever scarred with the blood of millions of innocent Cambodians slaughtered in one of history's worst genocides, the most prominent sound we heard was laughter. And not just laughter aimed at us and our crazy tandems, but belly laughter shared with everyone during all the day's events. Laughter so infectious and overshadowing it forced me to sit and listen. *Whatever they're taking, I want some.*

Over the coming days we attempted to give longer rides to locals, but succeeded only in signing up a couple European backpackers and an Aussie named Nic, who carried only a bike messenger bag.

"Just what I need," said Nic. "My flute, my notebook, my toothbrush, a spare shirt and shorts, and a rain jacket."

"That's it?" I asked.

"The less I bring the more happy and peaceful I am."

Nic's lighthearted joy lifted my journey for the next several days as we cycled on to Siem Reap and the Angkor Wat temples. But as each day passed, I began to feel the longing once again for more local connection and contribution with the local Cambodians. So before leaving town I recruited Garryck and Nic to pedal down to a local orphanage to deliver some free rides and positive energy to the children. I experienced more joy in one hour with those kids than I did in in three days gawking at the ancient Angkor temples. Each snapshot of a stone-carved face made me yearn for a real one.

Garryck started to open up about his desires as well. He was itching for some hardcore mountain biking as much as I craved a deeper dive into Cambodian culture. We agreed to make our way to Banlung in the northeast corner of the country. There we'd log some single-track riding around a 700,000-year-old crater lake, and hopefully find some residents to share the adventure with us.

Lazing that afternoon in a hammock, I wrestled with our two urges. I loved mountain biking as much as Garryck. But a little voice inside me kept nagging, *this is not what you came here to do.* The solution thwacked me like a two-by-four between the eyes. *I came here to ride with locals. What if I could show them some mountain biking, too! Would they be as jazzed to do it? Would the experience increase the thrill for me?*

I had to find out. Without telling Garryck, I rode down into town and began my search. The easiest pickings, we had learned, were at budget hotels. I spotted Lek, a genial young man I'd met days prior, cleaning some tables.

"Hey, Lek! How's your day going?" I asked.

"Very good, sir," he replied.

"If you call me sir again, I'm going to punch you," I said.

"Sorry, sir. Jamie."

"What time do you work tomorrow?"

"I work in the morning until 3 o'clock."

"How about a bike ride? A mountain ride on the long bike I showed you yesterday. Maybe you can show me where you live and we can go exploring."

"I would like that very much, sir."

I raised my fist like I was going to slug him.

"I'll pick you up tomorrow at three."

When we rolled up to the hotel the next day, Lek ran down to greet us, flashing a bucktooth grin. He tucked his black slacks into his socks to prevent them from getting caught in the chain. After a quick trip to his house to swap his work clothes for shorts and to promise his family we'd bring him back in one piece, we biked to our favorite loop. After climbing for about 15 minutes, I was impressed with the power in his legs.

"So what do you think so far?" I asked. "You're not scared, are you?"

"No, not scared. Should I be scared?"

"Just trust me when we start going down. We've been doing this trail for a few days."

"Okay, Jamie," then "Whooooooooaaa. Whooooooooooooaaaaa!"

"Stay in the center and relax!" I yelled back to him.

"Ooohhhhhhhhhhh. Wooooooooooooooooo. Ahhhhhhhhhhhh"

Yes! Lek was getting his first taste of a snake section that Garryck and I loved. He couldn't see what was coming next, so all he felt was a whipping sensation and the accompanying stomach churn. *Yes, YES!*

He settled in more and more with each turn, following my lead to pedal during the flat sections. *Faster, faster! Okay, that's fast enough. You promised to bring him home alive.* After a few more loops we retired to the crater lake for a brisk swim.

"I can't wait to tell my friends about this," he said.

"Maybe we can ride more tomorrow. Hey, perhaps down to the Laotian border!"

"I am free tomorrow. But I want to take you to meet my parents and see the house my father and I built."

"Maybe we can all eat together. I would love to eat a typical meal from this region."

"Oh yes, we can cook! It would be our pleasure, sir."

I raised my fist in jest again.

I felt a repeated tapping on my back as we approached his house the next day. I'd never seen anything like it, an expertly crafted abode on stilts with a roof that stretched almost to the ground. His mom came out to greet us, scurrying dozens of chickens in the yard. I looked at one and wondered if we would eat his brother for lunch. Inside, Lek's mother had laid out an oversized bowl of *kuy teav* soup with noodles and broth, hardboiled eggs, vegetables from their garden, cashews from their trees, and other mystery goodies. After gorging ourselves, Lek took us to tour the rubber plantations and to a secret waterfall he was dying to share with us. We felt special. *The best trips are the ones with the least amount of planning.*

The entire experience was idyllic and ideal, a traveler's "greatest hits" moment...until exactly eight hours later, when Garryck and I jockeyed for space around the single toilet in our hotel. Lek's chickens had their revenge. Cambodia-belly. I could tell that Garryck had it worse than me. I was able to function and walk around. He was a blob of flesh, and in need of constant care. I hobbled out to fetch him bread, bananas, and bottled water. We'd be delayed for a few days.

Thanks to an inane standoff with corrupt border police and Garryck's slow pace due to his illness, we didn't enter the Mekong Valley in Laos until midday, just as the sun staged its most potent attack. The roads were vacant. Anyone with an ounce of experience or common sense knew better than to do anything other than sleep after lunch. Garryck swore he could handle an afternoon ride, but we both regretted the decision as soon as the border guard started talking about mysterious fees and unofficial forms that "should have been completed."

By the time we reached the guesthouse, Garryck's olive skin glowed an alarming tinge of crimson, and our brains felt like they would soon start bubbling out of our ears. No matter how much water we drank, we could not seem to get our temperatures to go down. We swore off any more afternoon rides in open sun and hoped a long night's sleep would allow us to rise early and tackle our tour of Laos.

I woke up feeling human, but not great. Garryck, not so much.

"I'm pretty sure I've got giardia," he said. "I'm worked."

Giardia is a nasty intestinal infection caused by a parasites found in areas with poor sanitation and unsafe water.

"How about knocking it out with the Cipro antibiotics once and for all?" I suggested.

"I don't know, bro. I really don't like taking that toxic stuff. Try to save it for emergencies."

"Five days with Cambodia-belly?" I said. "That's almost 911 territory. Take the pills. You'll be good tomorrow."

Staring at the bikes outside, I was now I was in a pickle. I was expecting Garryck to be ready to join me on of a magical ride along the west side of the Mekong River I'd been dreaming of for weeks. A Swiss cyclist urged me not to miss the section for its rich cultural diversity and picture-perfect touring. One part of me wanted to explore and connect, but the other felt I should stay with Garryck and make sure he was okay. *He'll take the Cipro. He'll be fine. Works in 24 hours.*

"Hey, Garryck," I said. "Would you be okay if I go it alone up the river? I was thinking we could meet in Pakse in a few days."

He did a slow-motion double take.

"Um, well, I'm pretty messed up," he said.

"Yeah, of course."

"But do whatcha gotta do, bro. I know you really want to ride this section of the Mekong."

After the many months together, we could both decipher the language behind the words. I could tell he was not pleased, and I knew he would not have left me if I were in the same condition. But he also knew

I was itching to ride. We both froze for a minute.

"I'll stay if you're really worried," I said. "But I think you're going to be fine. Just chill, drink water, and eat that Cipro."

"I know. I'll be fine. Do whatcha gotta do."

"Thanks, bro! I promise you'll be fine. I'll, I'll take plenty of pictures."

I excitedly loaded up my bike, though the weight of Garryck's condition made everything feel twice as heavy. *You should never leave your best friend when he's sick.* I hesitated and looked back to the room. *He's an adult. It's just a tummy ache. He'll be fine.*

I hopped a boat to a small town on the west side of the Mekong, doing my best to leave my guilt on the other side of the river. The Swiss cyclist was correct. The area was a rider's Eden, with a small dirt path that ran along the river through picturesque villages with smiling kids, freer-than-free-range chickens, wallowing pigs, curious dogs and welcoming residents waving and greeting me with sincere *"Susadai!"* calls. I took a break to swim in the river and met a Laotian schoolteacher named Kasem. Better, he taught English. Better still, he agreed to ride with me for the rest of the day.

We stuck to the shady, flat, charming and car-free dirt roads. I had a new friend to explain the cultural landscape, like how weddings are arranged between families and how bodies are cremated after death. "Family is everything," said Kasem. "We say: 'Don't take a straight path or a crooked path. Take your parents' path.'" *Yes, this is Peace Pedalers to perfection.* I answered numerous questions he had about the U.S., and we embraced the commonalities of our two homelands. *Perfection...except for Garryck.*

At the end of the day, just as we were boarding a small, rickety boat piloted by a couple of ten-year-old boys, I reached for my camera, only to come up empty. Hurriedly I searched the other bags. It was gone. Kasem and a team of boys helped me backtrack my path for the next hour in hopes that we'd find it. We did not. *Ironic. One of the most picturesque days of the entire trip and you lose your camera. Or maybe not ironic. Maybe more like karmic.*

The next day I shook off the loss of the camera and managed to convince a Belgian backpacker named Clara to ride with me for 20 kilometers to Paske. We both had detailed maps showing a small trail that went along the west side of the river, hopefully similar to the blissful roads I took on the day before. Instead we ended up on a muddy, steep, nasty walking trail. It was nearly impossible to push the bike, let alone ride it. We spent five hours mud-wading and bushwhacking in the scorching heat. All the while, the guilt of leaving Garryck behind made me feel I deserved it or even attracted it. Luckily, Clara was a good sport and thanked me for the "adventure."

When I arrived at the hotel, I found Garryck playing his guitar in the shade, eating juicy guavas and grinning from ear to ear. He had taken the Cipro and improved in about a day. If he was mad, he didn't seem it.

"Lemme see some pictures," he said.

I was angry. Angry at the previous day's trip-from-hell. Angry at myself for deciding to do it.

"Up for a long ride tomorrow?" said Garryck.

I was also angry at us, and at me for not talking to Garryck about us. Since rejoining in Cambodia, we'd both compromised on our wishes. Garryck lingered longer in the villages and I gave in to his extended, challenging rides, usually without local passengers. But the common ground turned out to be as muddy as my ride on the Mekong. Neither of us seemed happy or inspired and we both had our fair share of resentment.

The ten-country journey to date had inspired and awoken in me a far different vision for Peace Pedalers, one that involved using the tandems more as vehicles of connection and service than bikes for hardcore athletic journeys. I wanted to slow down, stay longer in the villages, keep my rear seat full of new local friends, and be open to finding ways to make a difference in the communities we visited.

Since the first days of our friendship, Garryck and I were both passionate about our goals and hard workers in order to achieve them. Put another way, we were some stubborn SOBs. This epic journey was a definitive dream for both of us. It had become clear to me now that our differnet dreams were going to continue to cause friction and resentments unless something changed. We both knew this. But neither of us had a clue what changes were necessary to relieve the pressure.

A good friend had emailed me with news that he soon planned to be married. "If you come home, you can be one of my groomsmen," he said. I politely declined the invitation at first, but now decided to accept it.

"He's a close friend. I should go," I told Garryck, unconvincingly. "You go on to Malaysia. I'll join you in Indonesia in a few months. We'll work it out."

A rare guest rider who resisted the two-pump-chump temptation

Cambodia may have a low GDP but they sure laugh a lot

17

SAN FRANCISCO, CALIFORNIA. USA

--►

I COULD FEEL the imbalance as soon as I soon as I picked up my bike and gear at SFO. I was toned, tanned, and healthier than ever due to four months of vegetarian-based diets, alcohol-free living, and regular yoga and meditation practices. I was looking forward to spending the summer in the San Francisco Bay Area visiting family and friends before rejoining Garryck in Indonesia in September. The mutual resentments we both harbored had grown unbearable and I hoped this trip back home for a few weddings would hopefully recharge our enthusiasm for the partnership.

After Garryck left in India I checked into a yoga ashram where I was inspired to give my body a break from alcohol and meat for an entire year. I was proud of myself for lasting four months and felt great. But at the first wedding I grabbed a glass of champagne off a tray. It's a wedding. We're supposed to celebrate. The bubbly didn't kill me, so I grabbed several more. Steaks with dinner? Sure. Late night cocktails? While we're at it.

I woke up the next day feeling horrible. So horrible I grabbed a can of chewing tobacco and started up my most abhorred habit of over 15 years that I was so thankful I had finally kicked out on the road. And before I knew what hit me I was back to my old routines—fine wine, red meat, cold beers, fat lips full of tobacco. What's happening to me?

Reality set in a few days after the wedding. My friends feigned interest in my travel stories, but had a hard time relating. I felt like we spoke different languages. And I realized how little time they had for topics like international bike rides. So I repacked my stories and did what everybody else was doing—try to earn money. I had a summer to kill before the next wedding so I rented a bedroom from a lesbian couple in San

Francisco, bought a used car and dialed for dollars, trying to convince more companies to use telecommunications services that would give me a percentage of sales.

In my bedroom I crammed my bicycle panniers and anything that had to do with Peace Pedalers in the closet and out of sight. I decided I needed a proper break from Peace Pedalers and the busy days working and late nights partying would do the trick. But soon the dinner drinks became beer o'clock and "it's gotta be happy hour somewhere." Before I knew it I was back to my old pre-ride self. Worse.

I started dating local woman at night, tending to my telecom business during the day, and reconnecting with friends and family during the times in between. I was having fun, plenty of it. But it was surface fun. The kind you'd curse in the morning, promise you'd never do again, then accept an offer to meet a friend for drinks and start the carousel all over again.

As in Asia, I had that nagging "you're out of alignment" voice echoing in my head. My salvation was the fact I had the opportunity to hit the reset button, get back on the road again and realign myself. I had Garryck. He could often straighten me out with a look and a curt "dude..." I wondered how the road was treating him and had started taking a few spins on the tandem to get back in shape. One mildly hung over morning I sat on the porch in foggy San Francisco, sipping a coffee and catching up on email. Garryck copied me on a group email from Kuala Lumpur, Malaysia.

Everything went wrong on the 27th of September. Matt and I were having a fantastic day out riding. The trails were in perfect condition, and we took some good photos of some drops. I was feeling great, and my riding was fluid. I guess it was too fluid. As I stopped to lower my seat as we were coming onto a fast section of the trail, the last section, Matt rolled past.

I had been jamming on that section of the trail all week, and it wasn't long before I started inching up on Matt's tail. I took my eyes off the trail for a second to judge the distance between us. It was then that I hit a small mound in the trail right before a slight bend. At the speed I was going, my bike lifted off and carried me over the trail. I tried to get the bike pointed back in the right direction with some body English, but the bike abruptly stuck in the soft shoulder as it touched down. From there it was a fast blurring of momentum and motion. I can only assume that the sharp, nearly instant stopping of my bike caused me to be flung to the side at a high rate of speed. There was a quick flash of the large hard-wood tree, enough to cause my reflexes to get my right arm up to deflect the impact. That is about all I remember from the crash itself.

The next memory is the extreme pain that was shooting throughout the right side of my body and the sound of my own scream of terror and agony that seemed to enclose me. The surrounding jungle was just a blur. The force of the impact was so violent that it spun me completely around to the other side of the tree. My whole chest seemed caved in, and my breathing was coming in gasps, and leaving in guttural outcries of pain. It was too intense to cause tears. I yelled out once for Matt. Only the monkeys heard it. As soon as I could begin to breathe somewhat nor-mally, and then fully comprehend what had just occurred, I knew that my arm was broken.

My first thought was to check and see if the bone was protruding through the skin. I slid my left hand down the length of my arm and then checked my palm to see if there was any blood. If I was able to feel relief at that point, I must have felt a little. It took everything I had to suppress the pain enough to get my arm secured under the sternum strap of my CamelBak. In my first attempt to stand up I nearly collapsed straight over. Instead, I dropped to my knees and focused on keeping from passing out. Time passed, and the world leveled out. I stood up again and walked over to my bike. As crazy as it sounds, I think I actually looked over my bike for damages. I picked it up by the stem and started to walk out. I only made it about ten steps before the pain forced me to stop, buckle over and rest my head on my stem. I had to hold on. It continued on that way: ten or so steps, stop, get it together, another ten more, and on.

The results of my x-rays were not good. I had fractured my right forearm and the fourth rib on my right side, shattered my right elbow and punctured my right lung. The puncture wasn't a major one. Had it been, my lung would have likely collapsed back in the jungle, but it was enough to create a trapped pocket of air in my chest.

Under different circumstances the news would have been more devas-tating, but I was just relieved that the pain had ceased. The reality that I would be off my bike for three months wouldn't sink in until much later.

They put me on the operating table the next day, put an injection into the catheter in my top of my hand, put the oxygen over my mouth, and that's the last thing I remember. The next thing I know, I hear my name and open my eyes to see the nurse standing over me. My first question was if I had a chest tube. The doctor had said that there was a possibility that I would need one. I was relieved when she told me I didn't.

After three-and-a-half days in the hospital, I was elated when the doctor came in and said that I could be released. It wasn't too long after that my world came crashing in. I got a call from Jamie's and my insurance company to inform me that my policy had expired. I was devastated....

I stopped reading. No! No no no!!! I felt a wave of heat and wanted to vomit. No, this can't be happening. Our travel insurance sponsorship lasted for one year of coverage. It had expired the month I came home, the month I put Peace Pedalers in the closet. The phone rang a few days later.

"Bro, you were in charge of sponsorships. What happened?" said Garryck.

"I'm so sorry, man. I didn't renew any sponsorships this summer, including our travel insurance sponsor."

"Did you get an insurance policy for yourself this summer?"

Guilt, shame and disbelief hit me so hard I grew dizzy and sick to my stomach.

"Yes," I said.

"Dude, you got yourself a policy but didn't bother telling me? Do you realize how messed up that is?"

"I'm so sorry. I just came home and put everything having to do with Peace Pedalers on the back burner to have a break. I had no idea something this crazy would happen."

"I'm going to have to get a bunch of surgery done and rehab as well... it's going to be super expensive."

"I'm so sorry this happened, bro."

"Not good."

"When do you think you can come back on the road?"

"The road? I don't even know when I'm going to get out of bloody Malaysia!"

"I'm sorry."

The line went silent and I checked to see if the call had dropped.

"You go on ahead," he finally said. "Like we agreed, if someone gets hurt the other keeps riding. Maybe I'll meet you in Australia or something."

When I got off the phone I sat there, stunned. I started to get up, then felt so dizzy I had to sat back down. I stared blankly at my bike... then started to break down. *What is this pattern you seem to follow of success-failure-success-failure? And why can't your bloody mistakes and binges only impact you?*

I felt paralyzed. Garryck was out for at least three months, and I worried our friendship would never recover. My short-term lease was up in a few days. Was I really going to go to Indonesia by myself? I searched through old emails with the insurance company and found the policy. Maybe there's a loophole? The fine print confirmed the worst.

I needed help; I needed answers. More than anything, I needed a savior. I needed my mom. I packed up my bike and all my things and drove eight hours down I-5 to her house in San Diego.

Speeding through the flat fertile farmland, I started the ride with a few rounds of mental self-immolation. Try as I did, there was no escaping the sin. I pummeled my thighs with my fists and slammed the steering wheel. Then around Harris Ranch, a giant cattle farm that greets riders with a malodorous wallop from miles away, I tried to shift my thoughts. I used meditation techniques gleaned in India to still my mind and allow myself to simply witness my thoughts. I focused on my heart and my breathing. After a few minutes of this, I became at peace with the present moment. I asked God for help in healing and growing from this experience.

I arrived late at night, unloaded all my gear onto her garage floor and made my way inside. I walked into her living room and found her sitting on the couch with a candle burning, warm tea steaming, and an unmarked box in the middle of the table. I put my head on her lap.

"Jamie, you have to remember that this event is not who you are as a man," she said, rubbing my head. "It's an event, not you."

"I just keep replaying it in my mind like a broken record. And a crummy one at that. Backstreet Boys or Hootie or something."

"Listen, each experience we have in life builds on the next; it makes us who we are now, right now. And right now you not the man you were last week. You will grow and learn from this."

"I can't believe I'm going alone, without Garryck."

"You have the opportunity to take this experience and have it mold you closer to the man you really are. Peace Pedalers is your calling, and it's a higher calling. This event is part of the calling revealing itself in some way. You have to just trust this."

We had a long, silent hug by the candlelight.

"Jamie, listen. Here's a piece of paper. Write what you want God to handle for you and put it in my God Box."

"I dunno, Mom. I know you love this…"

"Sweetie. Listen. I've seen this God Box do miracles more times than I can count. Ask and trust."

I sat there for a moment with the pen in my hand. I didn't even know what to ask for. For Garryck to get better soon? For his forgiveness?

God,

Please assist Garryck and me. Help in finding forgiveness for my past mistakes and the very best steps for our future. And please help us both be at peace knowing that we are on the best path to take us where we need to go from here.

More than anything, I sought mercy, peace and clarity. I wasn't sure if I should continue the ride or dream anew. Anything was possible. I felt lost and vulnerable.

The next morning I woke up, rolled over on my side, and gazed over at my dusty tandem and filthy panniers. They needed a good cleaning. I grabbed a couple rags and started in, coaxing dirt from neglected nooks. Each scratch and ding had a story, many that came back to me in a powerful swell. The wrecks and near-misses. The curious old men and two-pump chumps. And the children. Those inspiring children with their infectious grins.

I prayed for a minute, then sunk into my favorite yoga position, Child's Pose, collapsing on my knees for several minutes in a relaxed ball. When I opened my eyes, I knew the answer. The ride must go on. I'd learn from this mistake and allow it to shape my own character and future decisions. It was time to shift the values and intentions of the expedition to include a deeper sense of contribution, meaning, and purpose.

That same giddy feeling of eagerness and anticipation Garryck and I shared on our first pedal strokes in Japan started to return once again.

Inside me churned fears of the unknown mixed with adrenaline, curiosity, and a strengthened resolve to fulfill the Peace Pedalers' mission. I wasn't giving up. I couldn't give up. You listening, Dad?

I tossed on a semi-clean t-shirt and strolled into the kitchen, which smelled like fresh coffee and fried pork. The morning San Diego sun filtered through the window, clashing with the smoke of the cooked bacon.

"So, how did you sleep, honey?"

"Well. I'm feeling better."

"You look better. I told you. The God Box works wonders."

I grabbed a piece of bacon, then set it down.

"I'm going to be riding solo for the next few months, starting in Indonesia."

"Maybe that's part of God's plan, too. For you to ride into a Muslim country by yourself and share some peace and love. To dispel the myth that Muslims are dangerous"

"I hope. Or maybe my bad karma will come catch me."

"Well let's get that good karma back. If your intentions are pure it doesn't take much."

Mom was right. All great things start with good intentions. I packed a several dozen extra teddy bears and hoped Garryck would heal enough to join me soon.

Garryck ripping up the trails of Kuala Lumpur, Malaysia

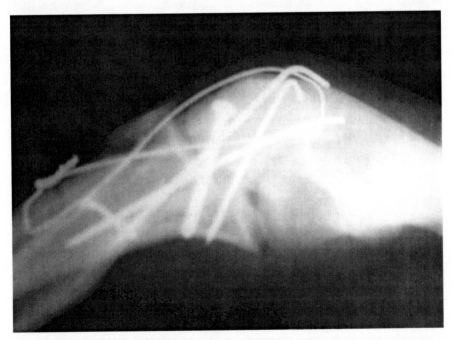

Garryck's elbow after the surgery

18
SIGATOKA, FIJI

---➤

I HAD NO idea what to expect when I turned off to look for surf at Sigatoka, a sugarcane hub and sand dune haven on the southern edge of Viti Levu, Fiji's main island. I hit the only lodge around, and was told by the owner I could use any of the surfboards lying around.

Surfing had become a passion since my ride in Indonesia. Though I'd lived most of my life in California, I never understood the surfing fanaticism. It seemed time-consuming, cold, and frustrating. Sitting on a board, peeing in your wetsuit to keep warm, all to catch a wave that lasted at most a couple seconds? Give me the bike any time.

But Bali had a way a lulling visitors into a change of mind. As I watched riders from all over the world catch wave after perfect wave, a tall, tan surfer approached me. I'd met Jonas the night before.

"Looks pretty fun, eh?" he asked. "You going to surf?"

"I'm not sure. I don't have a board."

"Man you have to get out there. It's perfect"

"Yeah, I just…"

"I have an extra board, why don't you use it?"

"Really?"

"Of course. You share your seat on your bike, so I share my board! Go have fun! Go on."

The afternoon waves were perfectly suited for my beginner abilities, and the left-hand breaks were a godsend for my goofy-foot stance. I'm not sure what kind of wax or juju Jonas, a Swede, put in that board, but I managed to catch three addicting waves - long, fast, steep ones that ended with me flying off the top and landing in bathtub warm water while looking up at coconut trees and Q-tip clouds. By the third dose

I was hooked. Glancing out toward the next set, I suddenly understood why surfers travel the world in search of the perfect wave.

Though planted on my bicycle, I kept a keen lookout toward any inviting waves throughout Indonesia and now here in Fiji. Fellow travelers raved about Sigatoka, but with my limited experience and knowledge of the break, I was unwilling to jump in solo. There'd be more waves ahead, I convinced myself as I mounted the bike and started to pedal away.

"*Bula!*" yelled a man about a hundred yards away.

"*Bula!*" I replied.

"You are not leaving already, are you?" said his taller friend. "You haven't seen anything yet."

I pedaled over to introduce myself.

"Nice to meet you, Jamie. I'm William," said the man with a hat like Gilligan's. "He's Simon."

"Can we help you with anything?" said Simon slowly.

"This is going to sound crazy, but I'm doing an around-the-world cycling adventure with this bike here, inviting strangers to join me and create friendships. I also love to surf so my plan was to grab some waves and then head up into the Nausori Highlands with someone. You guys up for a ride?"

They were stunned at first. They stared at the bike, then each other.

"Today was our last day of work," explained Simon. "We are closing for Christmas so we could accompany you to Nausori. How about I find my own bike and William can go on your bike?"

"Great! May I buy you guys a beer? We can check out some maps."

"Let's go to my village of Kula Kula," said Simon. "We'll play some pool."

He hopped on my bike and, just like that, I had my guest riders. Simon was the more serious of the two, a "cool guy" with frosted tips on his short afro, Oakley sunglasses, and a wife-beater tank top. William had deep crow's feet from all his laughing. Both were rail thin but blue-collar strong. Over a few games of eight-ball and a couple beers, we hashed out a plan to surf at 8 a.m. the next day and then depart in the afternoon for the highlands. "Tomorrow," we toasted.

Tomorrow. 8 a.m. Nobody showed up at the hotel. Forget 9, 10, and 11 a.m. as well. *What the hell!* Simon and William strolled in with their boards and surf trunks at noon.

"Okay, Jamie, let's go get some waves!" said Simon.

"I thought we said 8:00, guys. We were supposed to be riding out of Sigatoka by now."

"Relax, Jamie. Fiji time," said William.

"It's going to be too late."

"Have a surf, Jamie," said Simon. "Chill out. Tonight you can stay with my family; meet my baby girl and my wife. We'll leave early tomorrow morning."

I looked at him, askance.

"I promise," he said.

After a relaxing surf session, William and I took a ride to his house, where I fell in love with his three children. I piled them all on the bike, then added three more neighborhood kids to set the record for most riders on the tandem! We rode together through the village of Kula Kula, laughing and screaming together as the neighbors came out of their homes to cheer us on.

There was no "Fiji Time" the next morning. Simon and William gently rocked me at 5 a.m. sharp. I could see by their arched eyebrows they were excited for our journey into the highlands, a first for all of us. One thing we did know was that it was going to be tough. We fueled up on Milo (a chocolate malt beverage) and bread, a combo they assured me would give us maximum power.

William had the strongest legs of any guest rider to date. We motored at a fast pace up a deserted gravel road along the Sigatoka River. The scenery of flowers, exotic native bush and lush rock formations provided constant sensual bombardment, while the broken clouds kept the air relatively cool.

Halfway up to a 3,000-foot summit a man stuck his head out of a passing bus and yelled something I couldn't understand. "That's my friend, Joe," said William. "He lives up here somewhere." I didn't think anything of it until later that afternoon, when three kids popped out of the wilderness while we were taking a short break.

"Are any of you William?" one of them asked.

"I'm William."

"Joe is expecting you at the junction."

"Okay. Thank you," said William.

And when we hit the junction, there was Joe was on horseback, wearing a red polo shirt and an Outrigger Resort sarong. He led us to his village, then to his home, next to a rugby field. He introduced us to his family and the village chief, a thirtyish man with a short gray beard. I knew what would come next: kava.

"If you are going to go traveling in the highlands, you must bring kava," an affable, 250-pound Fijian rider told me earlier. "And all kava is not the same. Bring the best possible kind so you are welcomed."

Simon helped me prepare my kava offering to present to the chief, who was shocked I had brought kava, let alone the good stuff. William, Simon, and I took turns pounding the kava root with a heavy pole in a thick iron bowl. After a several turns of sweaty smashing, the kava morphed into a powder, ready to be placed on a fine cheesecloth, soaked in cool water, then strained to the make a drink.

Slowly we walked toward Joe's house, at a pace so leisurely it felt like an Old West showdown. "It is time for your welcoming ceremony," said Joe. "Once the ceremony is finished, you are a part of this village and are welcome to stay anytime, as long as you desire." We entered the house, a simple cinderblock structure, and were joined by the chief and several other villagers.

The ceremony involved first accepting a half-coconut cup full of kava; a *bilo*, Joe said. As instructed I drank my full cup in one gulp and followed that with a hand clap and a robust *"Bula!"* *"Bula,"* echoed the others. After William and Simon followed suit, we were asked to sit with the gang around the huge wooden bowl, a *tanoa*.

Simon explained that kava, a natural sedative, has been used for centuries as part of a sacramental ritual to strengthen relationships and keep interactions between Fijians mellow. *Brilliant. Maybe the United Nations should do the same.* After several cups of kava, Joe saw me wobble while trying to sit cross-legged on the thatch floor.

"Jamie, it's okay to lie down if you are tired," he said.

"No, but I want to be in the kava circle and part of the ceremony," I said, determined yet exhausted.

"You can still be in the circle lying down. We'll tap you when it's your turn."

Again, brilliant. And another tip for the U.N.

Over and over they did it. I would drink a large bowl of kava, then shut my eyes and recline, soaking in the good energy and conversation until another villager would tap me again. We did this for hours, until

William and I finally passed out. Simon, on the other hand, stayed up until about 4 a.m. drinking kava and bolstering friendships.

The next morning I was up early, hoping to get on the bikes before the heat and rain. I was worried about a kava hangover, but my mind felt fully operational and clear.

"Hey, Simon," I whispered, tapping him gently. "We should start packing up."

Nothing. "Simon." No luck. We were back on Fiji time. We had a late meal and didn't saddle up until about 11:30 a.m. According to the map, we needed to cover roughly the same distance to loop back to Nadi as we had the day before. It was also clear the terrain would be challenging. I did my best to relax and trust my Fijian friends, but I knew we were in for a tough day.

Right off, we faced a brutally steep 2,000-foot climb in the strength-stealing midday heat. When we hit the first false summit we all got excited on the descent, only to find yet another precipitous hill.

"You doing okay, Jamie?" asked William, noticing my silence.

"I'm okay. I just really wish we tackled these hills in the morning like we planned. We have a lot of terrain to cover, and we're not making good time with the hills and heat."

"Yes, I agree. This morning was not the morning for Fiji time."

As we made our way deeper into the thick jungles of the highlands, the clouds began to thicken and transfigure from white to gray to black to fire-hose. The rain continued its onslaught until we pulled in to a small village to fuel up on tinned fish and crackers.

"Looks like we have a good 15 kilometers to go to the next town, Simon," I said. "We should hit the road."

"We have plenty of time. Let's have a game of pool," he said.

"I have plans tomorrow to go to the Yasawa Islands to meet a friend for Christmas celebrations. He's expecting me. Can we starting riding, please?" I begged.

"Relax. Fiji Time. One game of pool, then we'll go," said William.

"I don't have a good feeling about this, guys," I said, grabbing a pool cue. "And I'm going to whop your butt in this game. Fast and then we go."

I lost, and we stayed. And stayed. And stayed until the rain slowed and we hustled back on the road. After a few minutes, the clouds opened up again, dampening my mood and my ability to soak in the waterfalls, rolling green hills, tuneful birds and glistening flowers. The sun gave up for the day, and the road turned into a mud pit. The chain on my bike became extra sticky, and we had several cases of "chain suck," where the chain gets swallowed into the rings.

At 9 p.m. we were jolted with a loud *CRACK*. The pedals froze.

"What was that, Jamie?" asked William.

"I don't know, but I know it's bad," I said, turning my headlamp on high to get a closer look.

"That was very loud," said Simon.

"Of course it was loud! We just destroyed my derailleur. Ahhhhhhhhhhhh!"

"It's okay, Jamie, we are almost to Nausori Village," said William, as he put his hand on my shoulder.

"You have been saying that for the last two hours, guys! We would be in Nadi now sipping a cold beer together if it was not for your silly Fiji Time."

"Chill out," said William. "Simon and I will push the tandem. Just take Simon's small bike. You need a break."

I exhaled.

"It will all be okay, Jamie," said Simon. "Part of Fiji time is to trust. You have to trust it will all be okay. It will be okay."

You know he's right. Why can't you convince the rest of your body and mind?

Trust, this trip is all about trust, I told myself as we pushed our bikes into the blackness. I apologized to the guys for snapping. Shortly before midnight, we arrived in Nasori with no idea where we'd eat or sleep. We were all covered in mud from numerous falls, smelly enough to scare away most living creatures, and so hungry our stomachs panged in harmony. Simon and William walked up to the first house with a light still on.

"We are very lucky," said William, returning. "This is the village head's house. His name is Tuk, and he has offered us a place to stay. His wife is preparing food now."

"Thank God," I said, almost in tears of relief.

Tuk, a gray-haired elder with a pink Aloha shirt, led us to the back of his house where we stripped naked and took cold bucket showers. By the time we were done, the food was ready. I inhaled every morsel, while Tuk and the boys chatted away. After dinner, Tuk took us to a thatched roof hut in the backyard. "A *bure*," explained Simon. "A traditional Fijian house." Tuk had arranged mats, blankets, and pillows on the hardwood floor. I wanted to kiss him. *Trust.*

The next morning we woke to sunny skies and clear views of the surrounding mountains. With any luck we'd make it to Nadi in time for me to meet Willy, a friend I'd met a few weeks prior. I had gotten to know Willy, a cheery and stout commercial fisherman, while killing time near the harbor waiting for my lost luggage to arrive from Indonesia. He had invited me to enjoy a traditional Christmas with him and his family on the Yasawa Islands, and I eagerly accepted and looked forward to the experience with great anticipation. We were supposed to meet that morning and catch a boat shortly thereafter. I called him from Nasori, but was but was informed he had left already. My Yasawa Christmas was not going to happen.

"I missed Willie," I informed the guys. "The boat's gone."

"Sorry, man," said William.

Do you still trust?

"Listen, Jamie, join our families back in Kulu Kulu village for Christmas," said William.

"Much better than Yasawa Islands," said Simon.

I looked up at them.

"Well...that's...that sounds great, guys. Thanks."

"And I know how much you love surfing, so I promise we will surf a lot," said Simon, putting his arm around me and giving me a squeeze. "There are no waves in Yasawa, so you see, it was meant to be."

We had no choice but to hitch a ride to Nadi in the back of a truck. Giving up a downhill ride after a grueling ascent is like skipping the makeup sex after a knock-down, drag-out fight. It's just not done. But the bike was toast, and we were all eager to get in a little last-minute shopping on Christmas Eve. In addition to my luggage not arriving, my wallet also had disappeared on arrival to Fiji. I only had a handful of dollars in my pocket, just enough to purchase some more kava and a few gifts for my hosts.

On Christmas morning, I woke to no flashing tree, no mountain range of gifts, no early wake-up by the kids. Simon helped me into a *sulu*, a sarong for men used on special occasions. He then gave me one of his *bula* shirts with a soft flower print to complete my Fijian ensemble.

We walked the long way to William's house, through the villages and past churches teeming with worshipers. Islanders nodded and wished me "Merry Christmas," and I felt as connected to a community as I ever had on a Christmas morning. The de-emphasis on gifts and consumerism eliminated the traditional Christmas stress that came with the gifts. And instead of everyone focusing on their latest electronic gadget or game, we spent the morning talking, reminiscing, and sharing stories about family and the commonalities between our cultures.

After a quick surf in warm rolling waves, we headed to William's house for a large *lovo* dinner, where the food is wrapped in banana leaves then cooked underground in hot rocks for hours. Out in the waves I laughed out loud to nobody in particular. *This sure beats multi-volume assembly instructions or those endless basketball games the NBA now crams in on Christmas Day. If Jesus were alive today, I'm sure he would prefer we be out here in natural creations, enjoying something that doesn't need AAA batteries.*

When I entered William's house, the kids dragged me to the center of the room and began dancing to traditional Fijian songs. William turned up the music, and within a minute the entire household joined the festivities. We twisted and hopped around, a giant sweaty mass mix of age-old customs and dance moves gleaned from *American Bandstand*. And it worked. Every shimmy and headshake. *Merry Christmas.*

When the music ended, we sashayed to the porch for a holiday kava ceremony. In between cups, I served as the new toy for the village kids. They climbed on my lap and cuddled up with their heads on my chest. One little girl fell asleep on me. "Uncle Jamie," William announced. Each of his children received just one gift for Christmas, modest ones at that. A homemade dress. A used action figure. Crayons and paper. I looked at them and wondered if I was ever that happy on Christmas Day.

After a lengthy *lovo* dinner—I counted 16 different dishes pulled from the ground, including fish, pork, chicken, and root vegetables from the family farm—we loosened our *sulus* and walked with the children to the sand dunes to catch the sunset. A brief shower amplified the smell of the beachside flowers and coated the scenery in a reflective sheen of orange and red. *Merry Christmas, indeed.*

The only thing missing was Garryck. But he'd be back soon, and we'd be able to share these moments together again.

Fiji Time led me to William's house for some record-breaking village spins

Pounding my kava gift with the village chief

The next morning I surveyed the damage in light. Our Fiji expedition was over

Taking a break from the punishing, muddy climbing

Tuk was a gracious host and treated us like family

Ready for Christmas. Fiji style.

Removing food from the lovo underground oven. Amazing!

William's mother prepping the massive feast

The best Christmas dinner I've eaten. Ever.

19
CHRISTCHURCH, NEW ZEALAND

WITH GARRYCK STILL on the mend I looked for people to take his place—kindred souls, hardcore riders, true believers in the Peace Pedalers' mission. In New Zealand, Andrew fit the bill. I felt a connection with him within minutes of meeting, a bond beyond just our matching bald noggins. We loved surfing and mountain biking, adored feel-good music and nature, and nodded our heads in agreement when we talked about spirituality. My "soul brother from Down Under," I called him.

Andrew and I spent many days together after meeting in the seaside town of Kaikoura on the South Island. We ate crayfish dinners and washed it down with Marlborough white wines. Like nearly every Kiwi I met, Andrew not only embraced the concept of a multi-year walkabout, he envied it. "You're living my dream," he said enthusiastically and with a hint of sadness.

I'd spent several months in the country, adventuring around the entire South Island, spending a grand total of zero dollars on accommodations and enjoying priceless rides through verdant wine regions, along windswept coastlines, by ancient glaciers, and around a mountain range aptly named The Remarkables. Although I had a constant stream of soulful Kiwi riders, my favorite times occurred with Andrew and his friends, camping, surfing, and solving the world's problems. I felt depressed having to leave him and his crew just days before I left for Australia.

"Jamie, I love you like family," he said as we hoisted a final beer together at Christchurch Airport.

"Yeah, I love you too, man. Feel blessed to have a Kiwi brother like you." *Cheers!*

"Brothers. Yeah, brothers. So as your brother, I need to tell you something."

"Shoot."

"The boys and I were talking at the festival, and we all love your gift of being able to get people together, to have a good time. Your energy is contagious and you inspire people to stop what they are doing, take a day off work, and join in the fun and adventure. It's a gift."

"Um, thanks. Appreciate it."

"But there is one part of your personality that will not go over well with the Aussies. I know because I used to live there."

"Really?"

I could tell he was nervous and had rehearsed the delivery.

"You need to learn to participate and contribute more at the events you organize. See, you disappear when the actual work starts. Like setting up camps, shopping, preparing food, cooking, doing dishes. You know, the dirty work."

The words caught me off-guard. I scrambled to respond.

"Really? Oh, man, I'm sorry. I had no idea. I mean, I guess, I don't recall the setups and cleaning, and, darn. Now that I think about it, I'm, sorry. I appreciate…"

"Kiwis let that stuff slide. We're laid back. Aussies will shove it in your face. I'd give a little more effort if I were you."

"I will. Thanks for having the courage to tell me. It shows you care. I promise to take it to heart. I'm doing my best to grow on this journey, to become a better man. Thank you."

We had a long hug, and I boarded the plane to Australia with a full bag of emotions, ranging from that excitement for new adventures to despondency for leaving behind my Kiwi crew, to shame and embarrassment.

"Last Gas for 184 Kilometers" read the sign. I felt inspired to stop and take a photo to document the moment, proof to friends and family the journey hadn't turned into a complete joy ride. My mother was planning to arrive in less than a week. I had lost my peak fitness in New

Zealand. I needed a rapid fitness rejuvenation to build up enough pedal power for the both of us. This solo run would take me through some of the most beautiful, remote, and physically demanding terrain in all of Australia—Tasmania's remote West Coast. I rode through the endless eucalyptus forests, canopies of red, green, orange and brown, suffusing the air with sinus-clearing mint. I camped on isolated beaches, sang with exotic birds, and didn't see another person for several days.

This pristine area of western Tasmania tested my physical limits, with daily rollercoaster rides of 80 kilometers and up to 7,000 feet of climbing. The snakes, kangaroos, wallabies, and possums didn't seem too sympathetic. Slowly, *too damn slowly*, I worked my sluggish body into shape. By day three, just as I was beginning to feel the progress, I felt something far more disconcerting. The granny gear on the bike went out. I had just put a new chain on and hoped it would mesh with my worn gear until Mamacita came down. Now I was stuck with just a medium and a large front chain ring. I was in the middle of nowhere trying to take a fully loaded tandem bike up numerous 14-percent grades without a granny gear. My knees screamed *noooo!* My pace slowed and I became exhausted within the hour, with heavy cramping and insufficient levels of food and water needed to recover.

Now I really, *really* missed Garryck. His mechanical skills bordered on magic. No parts or time to wait? No problem. Voila! We'd be up riding before the next motorist passed us by. But since I'd gone solo, I noticed the condition of my bike had gone south—blown headset in Indonesia, dead rear derailleur in Fiji, missing frame coupler tool in New Zealand. And now a blown rear cassette and issues with my granny gear! *That mad climber would probably love this. C'mon, amigo. Get your butt back out here.*

After a few grueling days of quad-busting climbs and long pushes, I finally made it back to Somerset, spent but excited to meet with my mom again. It had been more than a year since she had joined me on the road. Would she be as active as before her heart surgery? Would I be able to pedal hard enough for the both of us if she wasn't? I checked email to see if her flight information was still the same. But the headline above the email from American Airlines is what grabbed my attention first. "My Future with Peace Pedalers." *Yes! You've finally answered my emails! When and where are we going to meet?*

I smacked the return key to pry open the note and read it with giddy anticipation.

Garryck explained the crash turned out to be much more serious—and expensive—than either of us imagined. The first reconstructive surgery on his shattered elbow drained his travel bank account. It would take him a year to recover financially. Now, he was in the process of selling his beloved tandem to pay for yet another surgery and the rest of the rehab work. *No, man. Money's not an issue. We can raise the money. I'll get more sponsors.*

We wouldn't meet in Australia like we'd planned. We wouldn't meet anywhere. Garryck was quitting the ride.

The reason was more than financial, he went on to explain. We wanted drastically different things from the journey. The ride did not meet his expectations, he wrote. I did not meet his expectations. *I did not meet his expectations.*

The words now blurred. Stubbornness. Selfishness. The same ones Andrew used. I did not meet his expectations.

I sunk my head into my hands for a long, long time. *No. No. Give me a chance. I can change. This is OUR vision. Inspired in the halls of USC, nurtured in the years after graduation, then realized! We did it!* Until we didn't. There'd be no more we.

Not wanting to sink deeper into depression, I opened an email from my mom. "Thanks for inviting me to come join you. You not only accept me, but you invite me to be part of your life. This is the best gift you can give a mother. I'll see you in Australia soon." My cousin Shannon, a walking dose of feel-good energy, and her friend, Heather, planned to join the festivities as well. The timing couldn't have been better.

I waited at the airport with an odd mixture of anticipation and curiosity, washed over with a cloud of gloom and disappointment. My mom had been Peace Pedalers' biggest booster from day one. Now it was her turn to experience being a long-term guest rider. I told myself I'd withhold the news about Garryck until later. But seeing her freed my vow like a bird from cage.

"Honey, is everything okay? You don't look like your normal Jamie self," she said over dinner, reaching across the table to hold my hand.

"I have some really bad news, Mom. Garryck quit the ride. I'm alone now."

"Sweetie, I'm sorry. I know this must feel terrible. But who said you have to be alone?"

"Mom, he *quit* the ride. No more Garryck. I may have some visitors like you and a few riders here and there, but it's not the same. I don't know if I want to do the rest of it alone."

"Everything is in divine order, Jamie. For whatever reason, God has chosen for you and Garryck to go your own ways. You can do it. I know you can."

"Yeah, I guess ever since I've been riding without him, I've been traveling and staying with new local friends, having the experiences I craved."

"And your mission is to share the message that *anyone* can head out into the world, connect with new friends, and be embraced by strangers, right?"

"Yeah," I said, beginning to feel better. "I just miss Garryck. A lot. And feel horrible about this entire experience."

"Listen, Jamie. This is your calling. You have a higher purpose, and you have to trust that all these events are part of the evolution of you and this mission you are on."

"The thought of riding in Africa, alone, scares the life out of me, Mom."

"Great."

"Come again?"

"When you are alone you are vulnerable. And it's that vulnerability that breeds trust, trust that will allow you to connect with people who will help you navigate Africa safely."

"Thanks for coming, Mamacita. Every time I've needed a lift on this wild journey, you've been there."

Shannon and Heather arrived the next day. Shannon lit the room, as much by her beaming personality as her voluminous and kinky red hair. Heather, I soon discovered, was equally upbeat and curious about the new surrounds. I hugged them all, hard and probably a bit too long. Shannon dropped her smile for a second before I waved her on. "C'mon. Let's explore Tasmania."

All three brought a boatload of can-do energy I desperately needed. Unfortunately, they brought a boatload of possessions as well, especially my mother. I immediately surveyed their belongings in an effort to lighten their bags. Mom's luggage won the prize for biggest loser, with an electric toothbrush, lethal amounts of cosmetics, glass containers, and a library of hardback books. I loaded all the excess items into a large duffel bag and made arrangements to stash it in town.

Unburdened and uplifted, we boarded a boat to Port Arthur, where a steward promptly handed us ginger tablets to stave off seasickness on the rough waters. Everyone chugged them down in a sign of unity. "Team Harmony," we dubbed ourselves. My mom pulled out bright yellow smiley-face balloons, which we inflated and stuck to our panniers. Heather and I found stuffed animals and zip-tied them on our helmets. Ichibubu the Echidna sat atop my dome, a Platypus crowned hers. We debarked and rode from the port through rolling farmlands, lakes, and bays to the town of Marion Bay, with its crescent-moon beach.

The day was a success no matter how you measured it. The ginger tablets worked their magic. Heather and Shannon were hooked, chatting about the adventures ahead. My newly repaired tandem rode as smooth as a bowling ball down a well-oiled lane. And Mamacita cried only once, tearing up during a steep climb. Any day she cried only once was a success. *Definitely inherited that gene.*

"To Team Harmony!" we toasted after sitting down for a seafood feast and a divine red, purple and orange sunset. We had the entire beach to ourselves, inspiring an after-dinner fire after a brisk swim in the ocean. That night I shared my new tent with my mom. Even her otherworldly snoring couldn't put a dent in the day. I stared at her in the moonlight and admired her courage for being here.

Team Harmony made its way up the east coast of Tasmania through charming villages, camping on unspoiled beaches, tackling steep climbs, screaming down the descents, enjoying great meals, and sharing our passion for family, adventure and nature together. Their presence was like adding wood to a fire that had started to burn out. When I broached the idea of quitting now that Garryck was no longer involved, they shot me down quick.

After several days of long rides and lengthy conversations, Shannon and Heather left Team Harmony to return to the U.S. while Mom and I shared one last adventure before she departed, a trip on the legendary Great Ocean Road. "We're doing it, we're actually doing it," we told each other as we soaked in soaring cliffs, towering rock stacks, relentless surf and peaceful bays, lush forests and quirky, colorful towns. We camped every night and only lingered in towns long enough to get supplies. Most tourists lingered on the coast, but we gave equal billing to the fern grottos and mossy rock rivers inland.

"I hugely appreciate you coming down here, Mom."

"Of course," she said, waving me off like she'd just walked across the street to meet me instead of trekking halfway around the world.

"You give me so much."

"With your children, it's not giving. It's just parenting. You'll see that one day."

I gave her a hug and decided not to roust her when the nightly snoring fest cranked up again in our tent.

As the trip with my mom wound down, thoughts of Garryck popped in to my head. I worried I'd done irreparable harm to our friendship. *Strange how Mom enters the picture during times of strain. Or maybe not strange at all.* I thought back to that little boy on the BMX, escaping the house on Christmas morning. I thought about her standing up for me that day and every day since. She was a good mom. Perhaps the time with her was exactly what I needed to allow Peace Pedalers to continue.

My bro Andrew at the Roots Festival in Kaikoura

20

BYRON BAY, AUSTRALIA

FUELED BY MY time with Mamacita—as well as shamed from the one-two punch from Andrew and Garryck—I made a vow to focus as much energy as I could possibly muster on being selfless and helpful to anyone I encountered. It worked immediately. The new attitude led to a constant stream of colorful Aussie guest riders and rich homestays where I pummeled the hosts with offers to cook and clean. The positive experiences compounded, leading to more open doors, more referrals, more guest riders, and more overall satisfaction all the way up the east coast of Australia.

During one stay, I was invited to a "full moon" party being held at a stunning Craftsman home deep in the bush of Mullumbimby, a small hippie town outside Byron Bay. Most of the guests were devotees of Sai Baba, an Indian spiritual guru with followers around the world. The energy created by so many loving souls, chanting away to the full moon, created a palpable buzz. Their faces literally glowed.

Looking across the living room, past numerous hugging couples, I noticed a woman listening intently to a companion. She'd smile with her eyes, and I could see she was processing every word. *Wow. Listening is so sexy.* She had a naturally erect posture, which made her seem confident and hale. Her movements were slow and deliberate. I couldn't take my eyes off her.

She must have sensed my stare, because she immediately turned to face me after her conversation ended. She gave me a warm, welcoming smile. Slowly I walked over.

"Hi, I'm Jamie."

"Hello. I'm Sophie," she said, reaching out for a hug.

Oh, that hug. It seemed to last forever and each millisecond felt like another layer of uncovered intimacy. I felt her heart beating. Her tall, slender body melted into mine. She smelled like natural oils and soaps.

"Do you own this house?" I asked.

"Oh, no. I wish! This is a friend's house."

"I don't know why I thought you did. You just looked so…at home," I said, feeling a bit embarrassed.

"It's a beautiful house. And grounds. I was just going to go outside by the fire. Would you care to join?"

"I'd love to."

She extended her soft, svelte hand and grasped my calloused, bruised paw. Despite the differences, our hands fit perfectly, like they belonged to each other. We found a seat next to the fire, and she began to chant along with the others.

"I like it, but I have no idea what any of these chants mean," I said. "So I'll just listen."

"That's perfect. Just feel the energy."

As the chanting grew faster, Sophie inched closer. We began to melt into each other without exchanging any words. When the chanting stopped she turned to face me. I was scared our moment was over. A large mango tree loaded with fruit and cackling kids caught my attention.

"Want to go climb that tree with the kids?" I asked.

Really?

"I'd love to."

We followed the children up and down branches, listening to their instructions, peering over at each other amidst the chaos. Her smile was so genuine and all-encompassing, and her eyes nearly closed every time she grinned. There was something special about Sophie, something I had to explore.

The next day we met at a park. I'd been looking forward to her embrace all night. Our connection still simmered, even without the fire, full moon, or the hypnotic chanting. I took her on a long ride on the tandem and detailed everything about the Peace Pedalers project, including the loss of Garryck.

"It's a beautiful endeavor, Jamie," she said in her soft, sweet Aussie accent. "You should be proud of yourself for making it this far."

"I am. It's, well, it's just a lot easier to do a trip this intense with a partner."

"Really, what kind of partner are you looking for?"

"Somebody to share the adventure with, to explore the beauty of our world. Someone who shares the same passion to connect with others."

"I'm sure it won't be hard to find a new partner. I would love to do something like that, and I'm sure others would too."

Did she just…

"Really? You would be open to riding bikes around the world?"

"For sure."

Those words floated in my head after we hugged goodbye.

"For sure."

"For sure!"

Later, I met her at the beach, and we walked under the moon, hand in hand. We stopped at a park bench to stare at the ocean and its moonlit ripples. I felt her turn to me, and I returned the gesture. Beat, beat, beat. Then we kissed. A long soft, warm, wet kiss. I'd heard Brazilians could tell if a romance would last based solely on a first kiss. I knew. I was falling for Sophie. Hard.

I suppose it was no accident she entered my life at that time. I attributed the attraction to my openness to be in love. Just a few weeks prior, I had grabbed my journal while camping by myself on a secluded beach outside Sydney.

Love. A life partner. I had originally envisioned waiting until Garryck and I finished our ride. But since he left, there is no reason not to have full-time partner to ride alongside me and share the magical connections of Peace Pedalers. Hoping to put the message out into the universe, I listed a bunch of adjectives to describe such a partner. *"Passionate about travel." "Courageous." "Independent." "Athletic." "Spiritual." "Fun." "Sexy."*

At the time, the journal writing was no more than daydreaming. People who looked for partners that satisfied checklists often looked for the rest of their life. Yet, here she was. I laughed at the ridiculousness of the journal entry and marveled at its seemingly magnetic power. She appeared spiritual and was definitely sexy. But who knew if she could stand the hardships of cycling in Africa. Who knew if I could? Love wasn't a list. Love was faith. Sophie wasn't a journal-entry job description. She was Sophie. Over the coming days, we lingered and spooned, listened and loved. *She can do it. Faith.*

The time with Sophie made me ponder not just our relationship, but my relationship with everyone on the Peace Pedalers journey. She was the embodiment of karmic attraction. To receive, give. To be loved, love. I grabbed my journal again.

When I started this this journey I made, for the first time in my life, a decision to have something I created not only be about my desires and benefiting only me. I wanted the trip to mean something more—to make a positive difference in the world. Out of that intention grew the name Peace Pedalers. Then came the inspiration to ride tandem bikes. Next came the inspiration to start visiting orphanages.

Peace Pedalers has experienced progression and evolution. Of this I am proud. But there have also been stagnant cycles of destructive and reckless self-absorption. It's this tendency that pushed Garryck away, a tendency that led to me being alone right now. At times, too many times, Peace Pedalers has been insincere. On occasion I've made it look like a charity venture when it's mostly been about me having the time of my life.

I can't take back those moments. But I can choose to make a shift.

What if I were to take all the energy spent chasing personal desires and simply balance it with a passion to be of service to my global family? Time and time again, this human family has embraced me, caring for me as if I were their son or brother. As I move into Africa, is it possible to <u>both</u> LIVE BIG <u>and</u> GIVE BIG? If I get the balance right, what would be possible? How much richer would life actually be for everyone—not just me?

Yes, it's time to make a shift. I'm grateful for the many lessons this journey has taught me, even the painful ones. Making stupid mistakes hurts. But ultimately they are just that—mistakes. I can choose to use the pain to shape the future.

Live Big. Give Big.

Simple. Catchy. Powerful. I like it.

21

SANTA CRUZ, CALIFORNIA. USA

--▶

"LEAVE YOUR DAMN surfboard down there! Use both hands to get back up!" yelled a surfer from on top of the cliff.

"Take it easy, man! Go slow!" yelled another guy from above.

Woozy, stumbling, I dropped my surfboard and tried to focus on putting my shaky, bloody hands on the rocks to help me climb up from the crashing surf below. My head throbbed, though less so with every pulse. Fading, fading. I saw the drops of blood stream from my forehead and splatter the sandstone like a Jackson Pollock painting. Red, all red. Fading more.

"That's it, grab this towel," said an onlooker, shaken, like he'd seen a spirit.

"How bad is it?" I mustered.

"Pretty bad. The worst I've seen."

"Someone call a helicopter!" yelled a teenager.

A silver-haired man stepped forward from the gathering crowd. He had dark, weather-wrinkled skin and an air of authority. He grabbed the towel from my hands and dabbed my forehead.

"It's not that bad," he said. "You need to wrap it up and slow the bleeding. I'll take you to the ER now."

"But my board!"

"Somebody will get the board. You have bigger concerns right now."

Zac was his name. And other than that, he didn't much as he drove me to Dominican Hospital in Santa Cruz. I started to pull down the sun visor to open the mirror and have a look.

"I don't think you need to look at that just now," he said.

"I need to see how bad it is."

"Suit yourself, pal."

I pulled the towel down just enough to see that my entire forehead has been ripped open by the sharp reef all the way down to the bone, stretching across the length of my head. Panicked and dizzy, I borrowed Zac's phone and called my mom down in San Diego.

"Mom, you have to come up here. I ripped my face open in a surfing accident"

"Where are you going?"

"Dominican ER Room in Santa Cruz."

"I'll be on the next plane. It'll be okay, Jamie."

One of the Bay Area's top plastic surgeons just happened to be on call and in the area. She arrived by my side just as the heavy drugs kicked in, assuring me that she would do everything possible to fix me. Her hands felt cool, soothing. Trustworthy. The exact reassurance I needed until Mamacita arrived a few hours later.

I left the hospital in a drugged-out daze with 47 stitches holding my forehead together. I spent the next several days in bed wondering what the hell had just happened.

Not just with the accident. With life. With Peace Pedalers. It's been more than a year since Australia. What happened to the "Live Big, Give Big" declaration?

Love? Maybe. The decision for Sophie to move to California was a good call, the right call. There was too much of a connection not to see if it could work long term. Looked like it would, didn't it? Those late night planning sessions, maps and guidebooks strewn across the floor. The promises in bed. Proposing to her in San Diego.

Still, that wasn't the complete answer. I rolled over and stared at myself on the big closet mirror and knew.

Fear. With Garryck gone, you're terrified to ride Africa by yourself. So you took the first woman who said "for sure" and declared her perfectly suited for the expedition without either of you knowing if she was.

She didn't want to ride. She wanted to be in love. With you. When you finally figured that out you chose the bike over love. Then you broke her heart.

And now it's dashed, against the reef at the surf spot. You deserve every one of these 47 stitches for all the pain you put Garryck and Sophie through.

I rose from bed to take a new look at the wound up close. The scar snaked its way across my forehead, puffy and caked in blood. Nasty. *But look, there. At the edges.* The skin had already started to fuse and heal.

22

CAPE TOWN, SOUTH AFRICA

THE ONLY VOICE I heard was my brother Gino's. "They will rob you and leave you for dead just to steal your fancy video camera," he said after I informed him I would be filming my journey through Africa. "Watch your back and stay safe! I want my brother back at the end of this crazy trip of yours."

Petrified yet inspired, I surveyed the impoverished township, a sea of tin roofs and beehive wires as far as I could see, with Table Mountain looming in the distant background. Close, so close. And a world away. They said Khayelitsha was the largest and fastest growing township in all South Africa. Hundreds of thousands of uncounted, ignored "blacks" and "coloreds" and "mulattos." I still couldn't understand the definitions, probably because I didn't want to understand the definitions. The old tests alone seemed so bizarre and capricious. Like the "pencil exams": If the pencil stuck in a man's hair, did that make him black or colored or mulatto or all the above? I'd go with (e), who cares?

Since the fall of apartheid, the African Nation Congress had promised big improvements to townships throughout South Africa. Other than the occasional new school or road, I didn't see much change. People carried on, laboring, improvising, doing anything they could to upgrade from a lean-to to a structure with brick walls and electricity and maybe, just maybe, a window to Khayelitsha and beyond.

Gino was right. There were plenty of people who would have gladly jacked my expensive video equipment and sold it to settle a debt or pay for a meal. "Uncaring thieves," I swore, before I spent time in the townships and wondered if I'd do the same. Funny how little things like borders and laws mean when you wake every morning with the herculean task of feeding a family, and the overwhelming odds that you will not. Same ol', same ol'.

I wanted to shake the same ol', same ol'. That's why I started Peace Pedalers in the first place, and that's why Africa sat at the top of my must-visit list. I knew dozens of long-term travelers who, after having set foot in Africa, vowed they'd never visit another continent. It offered the highest of highs...and lowest of lows.

Today was Valentine's Day, a hot and steamy Valentine's Day, though not the hot and steamy I would have preferred. South Africa had been the planned starting point for the grand tour with Sophie. I wondered how she would have handled it here. Peaceniks and lovers usually either dive deeper into peace and love or hightail it back to their yoga classes and incensed apartments. I think she would have fit in the former category, though I couldn't be sure. Not yet, at least. Africa will change everyone who stays for enough time. You just can't be sure what type of change.

Township. Shantytown. Project. The division starts with the name, doesn't it? And gets worse from there. What's wrong with, say, community? My destination that morning was Luhlaza High School. *Maybe the students will come up with better solutions for integration in the future. They can't do worse than the past.* I had no idea what to expect when we drove up to the school in the minivan. More corrugated steel and cardboard patches? No. The institution was a government-lottery winner. It had brick walls, tidy yellow paint, and well-manicured grass. Somebody cared about this school. And just then I heard the screams coming from the classrooms. Kids burst through the doors and launched into folks songs to welcome us. All the fears and doubts I had melted away, and I was left with eagerness. *C'mon. Let's go.*

We decided a raffle would be the fairest way to choose the winners of new bikes, though the approach didn't feel entirely right. *What about all the non-winners? Would they feel worse? What if we just posted a list of winners? No, that would make the whole thing seem rigged. The raffle might not be perfect, but at least it's fair and in the open.*

The excitement from our arrival carried on into the multipurpose room, the kids bouncing around, holding their raffle tickets aloft. My sponsor partners from the Bicycle Empowerment Network (BEN) and I took our places behind a table, and a teacher began to read off the numbers. *Yes, Give Big.*

The boisterous room quieted in anticipation of hearing the numbers. Seven-six-seven-one-four! Several kids slapped their tickets in their palms or clenched their fists. So close! But as soon as that last number was called, a child would burst through the crowd, a cannon ball fired towards the previously unobtainable...a new bicycle.

And they'd dance, they'd always dance. One by one, 33 times in all, the winners did their own unique South African victory dance—cartwheeling, moonwalking, shaking, jiggling, and often crying as they made their way to the front of the room for their new set of handlebars. *This is BIG. And you have several more sessions like this to go.* I thought back to some of the more selfish episodes of phase one. They seemed more distant now. I wanted to do giveaways like this every day.

After the numbers had all been called, we took the class out into a large courtyard. This is where the fun really began. A few winners knew how to ride a bike. They darted off for test rides, friends chasing behind them, wanting to have a turn. I stayed with the ones who'd never ridden. The good folks from Bicycle Empowerment Network were ready. They had multiple volunteers available to teach the children how to pedal and steer their new bicycle through a simple obstacle course. I paired up with a young boy, holding the back of his bike seat for shorter and shorter periods until he took flight on his own.

Vanessa did the same. She was one of many special characters I had met during my hiatus in the Bay Area. Vanessa was a petite, spunky, intelligent woman who was born in South Africa and raised, during the violent years of apartheid rule, in Johannesburg. Her parents, fearing for the family's safety, fled the violence to settle in Canada. When I told her that I planned to tackle Africa during the next phase of Peace Pedalers, she begged me to go along. She wanted to show me what she remembered, while rediscovering her roots.

She sold bracelets at grassroots fundraising parties to help buy the hundred bicycles for the kids, and now was seeing the fruits of her labor.

I was happy to start the adventure off with a partner, especially now that I was lugging around several extra bags of video equipment. I wanted to document moments just like this one. I wanted to bottle up the high we were all experiencing.

So I grabbed the camera, gave Vanessa a makeshift microphone, and we started interviewing the students one by one, asking them to put into their own words what the new bicycles meant to them. The stories made the bikes come alive. One girl walked three hours each day to get to school. For her, the bike meant more time with family and studying. Another girl used part of her family's limited resources to take public transportation to school. Now she could ride to her classes and free those funds for other purposes.

The winners shared their bikes with friends, and made me feel better about the kids who didn't hold winning tickets. Africa shared, I was learning.

Not wanting anyone to feel bad, I pulled out my tandem and gave rides to anyone who wanted one, including kids who had won their own bicycles. The tandem rides raised the energy level to even greater heights. Especially mine. I was enjoying the entire event as much if not more than the students. I felt alive and enriched.

This was Live Big, Give Big in action. Vanessa and I had mapped out a three-month journey through South Africa, Lesotho, and Swaziland. We planned to explore, dance, ride, surf, eat, and celebrate connections with new friends. All the while I planned to enlist something I called my Giving Radar.

This Giving Radar was simply an intention to be of service on a day-by-day, minute-by-minute basis as we traveled. When I was laid up after my surfing accident, I had ample time to think and reflect. I realized that giving extended far beyond actual gifts. It was more of an attitude and intention to be of service to others. Doped up on pain killers, I visualized a green radar antenna above my head as I rode around Africa. It was this Giving Radar that had inspired the bicycle donation program.

It also guided me to begin filming the African expedition with a 3-chip camera, microphone, and tripod. My vision was to shoot raw footage of a kind never seen before, often of heartfelt discussions with Africans, video that would not only lower baseless fears and inspire more people to travel to Africa, but create meaningful, supportive friendships along the way.

"You need to trust Africa, and stay alert for your messengers, Jamie," said my mom before I left California. "You are on an important mission, and God always sends angels to people on missions."

I vacillated between believing her and trusting the nightly news.

"I will, Mom. Thanks."

A few of the happy faces of bicycle owners

New bike owners waiting happily for their lessons

 Enjoy a mini-movie on this lovely Valentines gift for the students of Luhlaza High School. www.bb42b.com/valentines

23

BUTHA BUTHE, LESOTHO

SHADE!

I had only two goals at that moment. The first: do everything possible to avoiding further exposure to the skin-searing African sun. There's sun, then there's Africa sun. Within days of setting out in Africa, I understood the difference. In most places, the sun can be fought with glasses and sunscreen and water. Take a break and carry on. In Africa, the sun is an army with endless troops. You can win minor battles, but never the war. It not only braised skin; it fried brains. After an hour peddling in the direct sunlight, my mind tended to see landscapes as if they were a Dalí painting. I worried incessantly about accidents.

My other task, equally daunting, was to find an additional pair of strong legs to help me cycle up into the highlands of Lesotho. After several weeks of riding, Vanessa decided to skip the hard climbing in the coming days and saddle up for a pony trek instead. I'd miss her, but hoped to find an athletic guy to take her place on the bike.

After yet another afternoon of crippling heat, Vanessa and I called it quits for the day and checked into a rondavel for the night. These circular homes are constructed with a mixture of mud and cow dung for the walls and thatch for the roof. At first, we were thrilled to be staying in the house where a mother gave birth to seven children. Rondavels look great in photos. But, as we soon discovered, they're a breeding ground for other species as well, biblical hordes of insects that seemed straight from horror movies, bugs with cantilever legs and death-grip pincers and all kinds of buzzing noises. *Pffffsssst. Zzzzzshhhh.*

I sauntered down to the well to escape the insect onslaught and dip a towel in the water in a never-ending quest to cool down. A young man was washing his clothes and linens by hand beside me, using a bar of soap then thrashing each item against a rock. Occasionally he looked up. We made eye contact, smiled at each other, and we went about our business. Mine clearly was not nearly as labor intensive as his. We shared a few more awkward smiles before I finally mustered the courage to strike up a conversation.

"My name is Maruti," he said, before explaining he was the youngest of seven children, all boys. He had seen us pedal in on the tandem, which gave me an opening.

"Have you ever cycled up the Moteng pass?" I asked.

"No, I only hiked up a trail near there. But many guests have gone, and they say it is very beautiful."

"Well, I'm losing my partner soon and planning to ride to Mokhotlong on a three-day trip. Maybe you can take her place?"

He stopped swatting a cotton shirt against the stone.

"Are you serious? I would be so excited! I-I-I-I would be more than excited!"

I reached over to shake Maruti's wet hand and welcome him aboard. He dove in for a hug, literally shaking in anticipation.

We rose early, eager to tackle multiple summits and some of the steepest grades on the African continent. Maruti came to the door wearing khaki slacks, a long-sleeve shirt, and a huge down jacket. Not exactly optimal. Several times he refused my offer to style him in a full kit of professional cycling clothes. He stressed that he didn't wish to show an inch of skin, and there was nothing I could do to change his mind. His bag was neatly packed, and included several loaves of delicious steamed bread for snacks. He had done all his chores three days in advance, he informed me.

Our bellies full of bread and tea, we were off. Maruti was all grins. I looked at his sinewy frame and thought he could hold his own on the bike. Unfortunately, his power didn't match his enthusiasm. He spun the pedals the best he could, but it was clear he wasn't much of a cyclist. For the first half-hour, I carried the load of the bike. We had three days of increasingly tough climbs. A whiff of doubt passed through me, only to be shooed away by my resolve. Maruti would have to make it. There was no Plan B.

Slowly, my fears began to dissipate once Maruti finally found his rhythm. I coached him to relax and take deep breaths. I also taught him how to use the PowerGrip clip pedals to apply power on both the down and up strokes. "Don't fight the bike, be with the bike. Make love to the bike!"

After a multipart sales pitch, he agreed to take off his massive down jacket and pull on a yellow Assos jersey designed to maintain an ideal body temperature. The look, the rhythm, the attitude—we were a tandem cycling machine, chomping up vertical feet by the second, ready to tackle the big climbs in the distance.

The Butha-Buthe and Mokhotlong regions of Lesotho were fertile and wet. Homes sported bright green gardens with clusters of spinach, tomato plants, potato rows, and ripe fruit trees. Many had "keyhole gardens," three-quarter circular structures with stone walls and a tall compost basket in the middle that feeds crops grown on top. From above, the gardens looked like keyholes. Ingenious.

Maruti talked about the way the villages bought and sold goods. Looking out over the village, I could see colored flags raised above various huts. Each color flag represented a different product for sale, he said. Red flags symbolized meat, yellow meant milk, and "the blue is for homemade beer."

There was no electricity, no phones, and no roads in these villages. Many were accessible by mountain bike or horseback only. But the modest life of the Basotho people clearly gave them a sense of peace and contentment. Family and farming were the focus, bringing a relaxing energy in every village. After a couple hours, I felt comfortable enough with Maruti to broach the subject of HIV. Lesotho had some of the highest rates on the planet, with nearly one out of four people living with the virus. "It's like the mountains," he said. "We can't escape it."

After about 1,000 vertical feet of climbing, I could feel the rear wheel starting to act up. The chain sagged and slapped the wheel when we coasted, never a good sign. I stopped for a closer look while Maruti relieved himself. Because of the steep climbs, I had decided to take an extra light load into Lesotho, leaving the bulk of my gear in South Africa, more than 500 kilometers away. I did a quick mental inventory of the tools I had, and prayed they'd suffice. If the hub needed to be opened up, we'd be in trouble. Maruti looked over my shoulder as I inspected the wheel. Soon a handful of local men gathered. Like a gathering of surgeons around an operating table, they diagnosed the problem and offered competing suggestions for a fix. One man approached with a large bag of carpentry tools. Another gripped the back wheel, while a third spun the front tire over and over, "for good luck." Despite all their efforts, reality sunk in.

"Maruti, I'm afraid our ride is over," I said.

"Oh, no. Jamie, no," he said, shocked.

"I need a specific tool to fix the wheel, and the only place that might have it is way back in South Africa. It's at least a one-day trip there, then fixing it, then a one-day trip back. And I know you need to go back to work."

"Really?" he said, glancing over to the bike. "Are you *sure* we can't fix it?"

Are you sure the ride is over? 100%, no doubt, read-my-lips sure that you can't get it fixed in just one day and return in time to go over the summit with him the following day?

"No, I'm not sure," I said. "But I have an idea."

I had no idea how I was going to get the bike fixed in a day. Lesotho isn't exactly the bike repair capital of the world. Even finding the right supplies and tools would be next to impossible. But that face, Maruti's look of disappointment. I couldn't live with myself if we didn't try. *Help.*

A few minutes later, a Land Rover approached from above. I didn't bother to flag it down, instead leaping into the middle of the road, directly in front of the car, waving my hands as if someone's life was at risk. He stopped.

"We've had a major breakdown, and we need to get back to Mamohase guesthouse immediately," I said.

"Hop in, I'm heading just past there and can drop you off," said the driver.

Sean turned out to be an owner of the Afri-Ski Resort we were planning to pass on the ride. He offered not only to take us to Mamohase, but invited us to stay and eat for free at his hotel when we got back on the road the next day. *One of Mamacita's road angels.*

Back at Mamohase, everyone was understandably shocked to see us. I shared the bad news with a small group.

"Let's go," said an Israeli tourist, shaking his car keys.

"Now?"

"If we move now, I might be able to get you to the border at Ficksburg before the shops close."

"Dude, you are the man!" I yelled in my best California accent. I slapped him on the back, and piled my gear into his car.

Shaul and I got along like brothers immediately, so much so that we forgot to watch the road and made a series of wrong turns that caused further delays getting to South Africa. We arrived at the border just under an hour before all the stores would close. The owner of an auto repair shop offered to escort us with his motorcycle to the only store in town that sold bikes. "But I'll warn you: they don't have a mechanic, so don't get your hopes up, okay?" He slapped down his tinted visor and bolted off on his motorcycle, and we followed. Suddenly, heavy rain fell in blinding sheets and the worn windshield wipers fought a losing battle to keep the glass clear. We could barely see our escort. Shaul turned up the Israeli dance music and rubbed his short beard.

When we arrived at the small shop, Marie, a middle-aged woman of Chinese descent, confirmed the bad news. She didn't have a mechanic on staff. But she did know a man in town who fixed bikes. Or so she thought. She called. I looked at the clock. We had about a half-hour.

At 5:00 p.m. on the nose, Nathan, a tall man with a floppy white tennis hat and shiny blue windbreaker, knocked on the door. He listened to what happened, stroked the handlebar, and asked to look at Marie's tools. Miraculously, she had the exact tools we needed. She just didn't want to let us use them. She was leaving for the day. "Come back tomorrow," she said. I pled, begged, and flashed my best puppy dog eyes. "A few Peace Pedalers stickers?" Finally she caved, trusting Nathan with the tools. We were ready for late-night hub surgery.

But just as Marie walked out the door, Nathan threw us a curve. He needed both grease and paraffin. Shaul tossed me his car keys, and I began my citywide hunt, Israeli house music blasting. After several dead ends, I stumbled into a closed auto parts store with a few workers lingering inside. I banged on the window. "Pleeeeeeeease." Within seconds I was dashing out with a tub of grease, a jar of paraffin, and cheers from the workers inside. Price: free.

The rain redoubled its rampage, and an exceptional darkness overtook the town. The operation would take place under the light of my headlamp. Nathan quickly discovered a few small pieces of broken metal deep in the hub. He removed other pieces, and cleaned everything with paraffin. He laid out screws, bearings, clips, and bushings on a clean white washcloth, as if preparing for a root canal. I'd spent decades tinkering with bikes, yet had no idea how he would get it all back together again.

Nathan tilted back his hat and reassembled the hub as if he'd done it a thousand times. He spun the wheel with pride, demonstrating the smooth motion ready for rolling the steep hills of Lesotho. Mission accomplished. I ran back through the pouring rain to the market and got us three ice-cold Castle Milk Stout beers. We toasted, and I jumped into the street for a celebratory dance in the rain.

The next day Maruti pulled on the yellow racing shirt and re-mounted the good-as-new tandem. We stopped for a moment at the breakdown point to savor the victory. Now it was time to kick it into gear and begin the haul up the cruelly steep Moteng pass. *How could any government get away with paving a 20-degree grade? That's a prescription for disaster. And we're going to attempt it on a steel tandem, loaded with gear, with a guest rider who has almost zero cycling experience.*

We made progress...painful progress at a painfully slow pace. Two or three miles per hour, tops. We climbed, and climbed, up the mountain and through the clouds. Literally. The constant mist kept us cool while shrouding the daunting inclines ahead. Our conversation slowed as well, first to one-word observations, then to silence.

After five hours of nearly nonstop grinding, we stopped for lunch. *Ahhhh.* The restaurant owners led us to a crackling fire, and handed us hot cups of tea. *Ahh, ahh.* One of them assured us the Afri-Ski lodge was "Just up the hill. You can reach it in about an hour." No problem. We had already clocked more than a half-day of damp, steep, extremely taxing climbing. What's another hour? Sean's promised hospitality would pull us through.

The clouds grew opaque, and the light faded fast. One hour became two hours and onto the third. Still there was no sign of the hotel or a reprieve from the sheer grades. I felt my body slip into a danger zone, just prior to collapse. And I had been cycling for years. I could only imagine what Maruti was thinking. *That's one tough S.O.B.* Just then, a massive storm smacked us head-on, forcing us to charge into a punishing headwind with freezing rain that felt like shrapnel. Even if I could lift my head, I could no longer see beyond a few feet. The blackness swallowed everything.

Ill-advisedly, I had left my warmer layers back in South Africa to save weight. I could feel the bike shake with Maruti's shivers. *Idiot. To shave off a few pounds off your load, you jeopardize the health and safety of your guests.* I grinded my teeth, and a negative anger filled my body. I was mad at the "one hour" estimation and mad at myself for believing it. Slipping, slipping.

Just then, I bonked. I could feel it coming, and could do nothing to avoid it. I'd pushed my body to the limit, then a little bit more. Bonks are caused by low blood sugar—hypoglycemia—and result in extreme fatigue, dizziness, or hallucinations. I experienced all three, each one fighting the other for supremacy. *Sleep! No, fall! No, is that a lion!* Something deep inside warned me not to alarm Maruti. I dug deeper and fought to keep the bike upright and moving forward. Maruti continued to shiver violently. His down jacket was drenched, providing zero warmth. I was sure his fingers, like mine, were frozen. "Maruti, I think..."

A truck approached from behind and flashed its high beams. The motion startled me, shaking me out of my delirium for a moment. Just then I saw the dimly lit wooden sign: Afri-Ski. *Afri-Ski!* We would have been passed by if the truck hadn't flashed us.

When we opened the sliding glass door to the restaurant, every head turned to take inventory of our sorry condition. Dripping wet, shivering cold, beady-eyed, and delirious, we ignored the stares and went into action. I grabbed the Ortlieb pannier of dry clothes, took Maruti's arm, and made a beeline to the bathroom. He was dizzy and disoriented. We leaned on each other to say upright. We stripped off our clothes, splashed warm water on our bodies from the sink, and mercifully slipped into dry clothes. Underwear never felt so good. I could see Maruti springing back to life as well.

I felt bad for the other guests because we jockeyed our way to the fire and didn't give it up for the rest of the evening. They gave us kudos for surviving, and the staff refilled our heated beverages to calm our nerves and warm us up.

Sean was more than good to his word, as the resort treated us to juicy steaks the size of baseball mitts. I looked to Maruti as he tore through his sirloin. *We did it. We did it, amigo!* I confessed I almost crashed in the final minutes of the ride. "I have never done something as challenging as this," he beamed. And it hit me. I'd put my life in his hands, and he'd put his life in mine. Alone, we would not have made it. I raised my fist in triumph. Not once had he complained. I would try to follow his example whenever challenged ahead. *He's a good man.* As we waited for dessert, an attractive Basotho woman walked up to the table and handed Maruti a folded piece of paper. He unfolded it to see her phone number.

After the climb-from-hell, every other mile seemed tranquil and fun. Maruti pointed out special rock formations and mountain peaks in the background. Even the climbs felt enjoyable. No problem, we said to each other. *You hear a lot more "no problem"'s in the developing world.* Maruti exchanged pleasantries with the cattle herders, decked out in tall gumboots to protect them from the snakes, animal skins to keep them warm, and assemblages of sticks and bones to use as decoration or to toss at a stray cow. They got a rush seeing our tandem pass by, and often ran full speed from their cattle posts to greet us.

We were invited to eat our lunch with a herder family about 30 kilometers from Tlokoeng. They'd constructed their hillside house out of stone, mud, cow dung, and thatch. Like many other village homes in Africa, this one also served as an impromptu sundry store, where the family sold warm bottles of beer, candles, and bags of neon-orange, home-made corn chips that resembled Cheetos. There was no electricity, no running water, and no furniture. I was offered a seat on a lumpy, fetid blanket that covered a pile of rocks and cow dung. This area of the house served as the family bed, couch, and storage for empty beer crates. It was still an improvement over the bicycle seat, which, after the recent marathon, left my backside with sores that felt like inserted razors each time I shifted.

We were their first customers that day. And their only customers that day. Maruti translated, but very few words were spoken. We simply starred at each other, smiling and taking turns pointing out unique aspects of the other person's way of living. A son was curious how I clipped my cup onto my backpack. I was fascinated how they molded cow dung into a stove to heat my noodles.

Maruti and I were also quiet, knowing the end of our ride was near. We'd spend just a few short hours descending in to Tlokoeng. After three unforgettable days together, he had to make his way back to his village.

"Here's where the payoff comes for all those climbs, Maruti," I said, handing back my noodle bowl.

He knew exactly what I was talking about as we climbed back on the bike and dropped into the picturesque Seati River Valley below. The herder family came out to see us off, as did the sun, a penetrating, illuminating sun. And as we descended, the temperature rose, the colors grew more vivid, and the vegetation more fertile. *Whhheeeeeeeeee!* The road smoothed out, and we increased our speed without pedaling more than a handful of times. *Ahhhhhheeee!* We whisked past rondavels, corn fields, and kids playing in the fields.

As we neared the bus station in town dozens of locals ran behind the bike, joking with Maruti in Sesotho. A couple drunken men wanted rides, Maruti explained. "Tell them no drunks allowed," I joked.

Truth is I didn't want anyone on my bike that afternoon. Maruthi would be difficult to replace. These friendships were becoming tougher and tougher to leave. I gingerly swung my leg over the seat and propped up the tandem. "Goodbye, my friend. Thank you." We embraced for a final hug, a long and stinky hug, as his bus approached. He held his head out of the bus and waved.

And, just like that, I was alone. Again.

 Enjoy a mini-movie on this magical adventure in Lesotho at www.bb42b.com/lesotho

One of many colorful Basotho homes on our route

Working with the locals for any kind of solution

Nathan and Shaul hard at work with the hub operation

Yes, a 19% grade. Maruti taking a much needed break

Maruti's eyes now grateful and proud

The friendly and colorful cattle herders of Lesotho

24

MALKERNS VALLEY, SWAZILAND

--►

NORMALLY I WOULD just pedal off with the first taker, but there was something drawing me to talk to the shy woman hiding behind the others, peering with innocent curiosity at the tandem. I had come across the trio a few kilometers from my destination in the Malkerns Valley in Swaziland. The midday sun had me shirtless and dripping from every pore. *Sweaty, shirtless gringo pulls up and asks you to hop on. You do it? Um, I'll walk.*

Their laughter made me turn around. Laughter always made me turn around. This threesome obviously had no problem squeezing joy from their surrounds. Mid-twenties, I guessed. On their way home. One woman had a pink-and-black-checkered plastic bag on her head. Another sported a well-worn yellow sun hat. The shy one had a black t-shirt and Adidas flip-flops. Ms. Yellow Hat jumped on the bike, and started laughing hysterically. I laughed along before turning to Ms. Flip-Flops.

"Hi. Hello. Yes, you!"

"Who? Me?" she asked.

"Yes, you. What's your name?"

"Martha," she said in a demure voice.

"Hi, Martha. I'm Jamie. Would you care to join me for a ride?"

"Oh, no. I don't know how to ride."

"That's fine, you don't need to know how to ride."

"No, thank you. I have never ridden a bike."

"That's okay, too. Today will be your first ride."

"No, thank you. My friend will go with you," she said, gesturing to Ms. Yellow Hat.

They laughed some more.

"I want to ride with you, Martha."

"I don't know how to ride a bike."

"You just sit on this seat, and I ride the bike. You ride with me."

"I don't know..."

"Great! You're going to love it, Martha!"

"I ride with you?"

"You have nothing to worry about, Martha. You ride with me and just pedal. Look around, enjoy the scenery, wave to your friends."

"Really? I can ride with you there?" she said, pointing at the seat and slowly approaching the bike.

By now, I catered my sales pitch to meet the situation. Sometimes I took the "C'mon, it's fun" approach. Other moments I'd go with the "I'll save you the loooooong walk home" spiel. There was, "Let's make your boyfriend jealous," "I can help you get sober," and "You need to escape this heat." But the best pitch was no pitch at all. "I'd like to invite you to ride with me," always accompanied by looking into their eyes to let them know my intentions were pure.

I could never be sure if the person would enjoy the ride. Eager participants often begged off after a mile or two. Reluctant ones sometimes pedaled all day or more. The important thing was that they tried. I knew firsthand the significance of having someone open your eyes.

My high school biology classroom always had the same smell, a sour, salty-brine odor, a mix of teenage sweat, floor cleaner, and the formaldehyde solutions used to store dead creatures in glass jars. I wasn't so interested in biology, but I loved cutting stuff open. The teacher, Mr. Luperini, had to hold me back from grabbing a scalpel every time I set foot in class. He was one of the few teachers to whom I listened, probably because of the excited way he talked about humdrum tasks, waving his hands in every direction.

"Okay, everyone. Listen up. Listen closely," said Mr. Luperini one morning, his eyes wide. "I've got some very, very exciting news."

With that, he began to pass around colored flyers. *Probably some science fair.*

"I'm organizing a summer trip to Europe, and I think all of you should go."

Whoa. Wha?

"I'll be leading a group through Germany, Austria, Switzerland, France, and Italy. It's going to be fantastic!"

That was it. "Fantastic" sealed the deal. The way he said it in a rolling lilt, accent on the *tas*. Spoken like an Italian tenor. But I wanted more than the trip. I wanted his passion. Whatever he took to fuel it, I wanted a healthy dose. I didn't have a passport, and hadn't left the U.S. a single time during my eighteen years. It didn't matter. I stayed after class with my buddy Marc Quilici.

"So tell me, how great is the trip? Really?" I asked.

"Come on, Jamie! You are Italian. This trip is made for you and Marc. Half the trip is in Italy, for God's sake. Great food, amazing scenery—you don't want to miss it. Trust me."

I hurried home that day clutching my glossy brochure, waiting for the right moment to present the idea of a graduation present. Hell, my brother Gino got a car when he graduated from high school. The way I looked at it, I'd be *saving* my dad money.

Though deformed by polio as a child, my dad refused pain medications, opting instead for bourbon and water in the evening. This presented a problem for me. On a good day, when his business was profitable, his buzz was a jovial one. But if his beloved 49ers lost a game or a distributor swindled him, he could churn into a staggering, belligerent mess. Luckily, sales were up that week and he appeared coherent.

Late evening, I hovered, wanting to catch him between his second and third drink. Anything later and I'd be pressing my luck. I'd practiced my speech all afternoon. "My heritage." "Your family." "All the hard work." I approached him as he watched Fox News. Uh, oh. If the stories were overly pessimistic, the anchors could spin him into gripe mode. Europe would be a no-go if he pivoted into gripe mode. I needed to take decisive action. I came in to the living room, sat down, and turned off the TV with the remote, a high risk move. *Step one.*

"Hey, whatcha doing?" he said. "Ya know, you could learn something."

"Maybe later, Pops. I want to talk to you about something now," I said, placing the brochure in front of him.

Step two. Use props to show authenticity.

"What's this?" he asked while glancing at the flyer. "Europe, huh. What do you want with Europe?"

"Gino got a car for graduation. I'd like to ask for a trip to Europe for a graduation present. Save you some money."

Step three. Demonstrate financial savings.

"Well, Gino got good grades and went off to a good college. You don't even know where you are going yet."

"Well, I've got good grades too. In fact, I'll even get a 4.0 this semester just for you. How about that? Plus, you only have to send me to Europe if I get into a good school as well. Deal?"

Step four. Always look to close the deal.

"Why don't you just get a 4.0 every semester?"

"I could. I just don't want to work that hard."

Uh, oh. That's not a step. That's a step backwards.

"Well, that's your problem. You need to learn to work hard all the time."

Need to pivot back to sales pitch.

"How can you pass up a deal like this? I'm promising a 4.0 this semester...in your honor...and to get into a top-notch college. If I fail at either, no Europe trip. You can't lose."

He picked up the flyer.

"Ahhh. We'll see. We'll see. At least with a new car you own something. A trip you just burn money for a few weeks while taking pictures of buildings."

"Thanks, Dad. I'll make ya proud. I promise."

Step five. Declare victory.

"I didn't say yes, did I?"

"Sure ya did. 'We'll see' means 'yes,' and you know it."

"We'll see. We'll see," he said, turning his news channel back on.

What I didn't tell him was that I already had a bet with my principal, Mr. Teshara, that I'd earn a 4.0. Now I had two motivations to get perfect grades. I studied more than I ever had, and easily secured that 4.0. Mr. Teshara was so impressed he wrote a glowing letter of recommendation, which I used to be accepted by USC and a handful of other top-notch schools.

"We'll see" turned into "*bon voyage*," and I was off to Europe with a group of fortunate, albeit privileged, classmates. We sipped pilsners in Germany, climbed the Alps in Austria, and slurped spaghetti at back-alley cafés in Italy. I was hooked. Every experience was made to dream of more. I knew from that trip onwards, travel would be a huge part of my life. And I started the lifelong journey because a travel enthusiast had asked me to join him on the road.

Martha took a little more convincing, and I wasn't offering a European jaunt. I was hoping she would see the same passion in my eyes that I saw in Mr. Luperini's.

I believed in my offer. I knew she would have an amazing experience. "Fantastic!"

And I also knew that it was now or never. People have an uncanny knack for postponing opportunity for excitement. Who knows? Maybe she would never ride a bike in her life, never feel that wind in her face as she pedaled faster, faster, *free*. "C'mon, Martha."

She kept getting on the bike…then jumping off. "Just a couple pedals." Again on, then off. "You'll love it." Finally, I could sense her settling her weight on the seat, determined, rounding up any fears rumbling inside, then storing them away for another day. She got on…and stayed on. I counted down, *three—two—one*, and she let out the unrestricted, whole-body, child's scream of delight. *Heeeeeeeee!*

When I looked in my rearview mirror, I knew she was enjoying every stroke of our mini adventure together. "You're a natural," I said. And she was, with surprisingly strong legs. *Likely due to the fact that women do the vast majority of the work around here.* I took her across town to a backpackers' lodge.

"It's my first time to even see this bicycle," she exclaimed, getting off. "And now I've just ridden it! And I'm feeling so excited and so happy!"

  Enjoy a short video about Martha's first ride at
www.bb42b.com/marta

The first eager taker in the floppy yellow hat was easy picking. But I insisted on giving Martha her first ride.

25

OUTSIDE JOHANNESBURG, SOUTH AFRICA

SITTING ON THE last bus to Johannesburg, I finally had a couple hours to gather my thoughts about the months in Africa. First and foremost, it's nothing like the original vision I wrote down in my notebook. It's light years away from the stories they show on soundbite-obsessed television news shows or the dumbed-down generalizations of Hollywood. My fear of Africa, driven almost entirely by mass media, made me hesitate for nearly two years before coming here. Two years!

I kicked myself and wondered what other parts of the world I'd foolishly placed into the danger box. Sure, Africa had its fair share of negativity. Every place does. But for every unkind gesture I'd experienced, several hundred compassionate ones drowned it out. I made a vow to turn off the news and surrender to the flow of travel.

What if the rest of the world could experience what I'm experiencing in Africa? Even a taste of the truth about how hospitable, fun, and exciting it is to travel here? More travelers, more friendships. And out of those friendships there would be a natural, organic stream of support to help reduce suffering and increase connectivity. Idealistic? Sure. It's too important for people not to try.

Something inside me was brewing. I felt energized, and ready to take an important step, to do something bigger than I'd been doing. I just didn't know what that step would look like.

When I arrived in Johannesburg later that day, I checked my bank account. With enough money I could afford some more bicycle giveaways, or stage something even bigger, like free plane tickets, computers, or other meaningful ways to connect people. But when I looked at the bottom line of my account, I was nearly broke. *What the...?*

After a quick search I discovered my little sponsorship deal with

Aceva Technologies had somehow stalled. I had been earning $1,200 a month in passive income on commissions I had generated in the past. Now, nothing. An email from the Aceva CEO informed me the company had been acquired by a large multinational business. All commission arrangements had ended as soon as the deal was completed.

I then saw a second email, this one from my real estate investment company. I had been investing the Aceva income, along with the majority of my riding funds, with them, and the payouts had been great, generating a steady stream of $1,000 a month while maintaining my principal. The email said nothing about my money, only that the founders of the company were being charged with fraud. The company's assets would be frozen pending a long and costly bankruptcy proceeding.

With only a couple thousand dollars cash to my name, I grabbed a pen and a napkin and starting writing out options.

1. Sell extra and gear to buy time
2. Add more value from sponsors.
3. Find new sponsors.
4. Quit trip and get a real job.

I kept hearing Gino's voice in my head. *"If you ever decide to stop riding, you'll still be considered a success, not a failure."* He was right. *Wasn't he?* If the trip ended, at least I'd covered a decent percentage of the world and made a few connections that hopefully blossomed into others.

Gino was right, but...but....my dad. I made a promise to him I would finish whatever I started. Equally important, I made a promise to myself. No, quitting was not an option.

That night I got on my knees and called everyone together. For major times in need, I prayed to any religious figure I could conjure—Jesus, Mohammed, Allah, Buddha, all the saints and apostles from Catholic Sunday school. *Why leave anyone out?*, I reasoned. I then called upon my dad, grandparents, and relatives on the other side to add a good word or two. I might not have much of a bank account, but at least I'd be rich in spirits. I'd find a way.

A few days later I received an email from a friend who had seen some of my video footage from Lesotho and Swaziland. He suggested I check out Les Stroud, the famous TV producer and host of the hit show

Survivorman on the Discovery Channel. Within seconds of seeing his show, an inspiration came to me. If I could get this famous TV host to become my mentor and executive producer, I could realize my vision to capture and share the *real* Africa. And by having his name and reputation on board, I would be able to attract new sponsors and ask for increased contributions from my current sponsors. It could work. It had to work.

After hundreds of phone calls, countless PowerPoint presentations, and daily petitioning to the saints and apostles, it happened. Les Stroud came on as my producer, and Panasonic signed on as my first major sponsor. With those two on board, the rest of my sponsors upped their levels of support. I averted financial ruin, at least for the short term.

I was now a pedal-powered production with two HD cameras, a helmet camera, professional tripods, hard drives, batteries, chargers, cables, lights, Sanken microphones, and geeky field recorders. I had so much gear I needed to extend my bike with a single-wheeled BOB trailer to carry it all. My tandem was now a tandem train. With everything loaded, including my clothes and spare parts, the entire bike now weighed a thigh-busting 250 pounds. Uphill rides felt like pedaling with an NFL lineman on my shoulders. I justified it all by knowing the footage would be better. Plus, I'd be even more reliant on convincing others to ride, especially ones of the strong leg variety.

Mozambique would be scene one for the new caravan. Quickly I learned the equipment would take far longer to set up and take down than I'd imagined. It also posed greater risks and a bigger target for theft. On one of my first days in the country, the trailer flew off the axle while I pedaled, sending my Panasonic camera and tripod hurling toward the pavement. A bystander grabbed it just before it hit the ground. "*Obrigado,*" I said to him as he handed me the equipment.

As I fixed the axle and loaded the bike anew, I noted the man had a bicycle, a fairly nice one by local standards. As I pedaled away, he pedaled alongside. I pulled the iPod headphones from my ears. Wanting a better connection with locals, I had begun to listen to language tapes, in this case, Portuguese. I'm a firm believer in that if you want to better understand a foreign culture, you need to spend some time learning the language. The first door to connection is respect. Plus, the lessons helped distract me from the grueling heat. I put the iPod in my pocket and decided it was time to put my skills to use.

"*Qual o seu nome?*" I asked.

"Bernardo" he said was his name.

"Jamie. *Você gosta de andar de bicicleta?*"

"*Eu gosto muito!*"

We hacked through my broken Portuguese, and I discovered Bernardo was seventeen years old and rode 30 kilometers each way to school. *Experienced rider, hmm.* I was soon drafting off him at about 25 kph, then we switched, and I took the lead. *Wow. Been a while since I've done this. Not since, well, Garryck. Garryck.* Before we arrived at his home, I sprung.

"*Você quer vir comigo até Inharrime?*" I asked, inviting him to ride to the next town.

He rambled in rapid-fire Portuguese, the only word of which I caught, digested, and understood was "*claro.*" He was in.

We rolled into his homestead at noon. In the center of the grounds stood a massive shade tree, with six thatch and mud huts circling the trunk. Bernardo's mother, sisters, friends, and relatives busily tackled typical rural chores, sorting and grinding maize, cooking a broth, preparing fish, and minding the kids, who had free rein.

Within minutes, members of Bernardo's clan offered me delicious mangos, papayas, cold coconut milk, and yummy rooibos tea that sent me to a nearby ground mat for a nice afternoon nap. I had only slept a few hours by the side of the road the night before, sharing the tent with a couple of strangers. I could hear the mothers shushing the kids so I could nap in peace.

When I woke, I was offered more tea, fresh bread, and baskets of fruit. This extended family did not have much by Western standards— no electricity, running water, or gas, not to mention a car. But they had food, health, family, and an unforgettable peace that only comes when you live unplugged, connected to nature, and surrounded by loved ones. I felt light and at home, reluctant to leave for the afternoon ride.

I set Bernardo up with some Assos cycling clothes for our final 40 kilometers to Inharrime. Once his strong legs warmed up, we cruised at Tour de France speed across flat smooth roads. At that pace, it was impossible to hear each other, so we opted for some music on my iPod, with headphone splitters. We were soon grooving to local Mozambican artist Stewart Sukuma, and having the time of our lives as the late afternoon sun set through the palm trees and dense forests. It was all about the ride—breathing heavy, pushing our bodies, working as a team with the gears, reading each other's cadence desires, and connecting with the power of the tandem.

We made it to Inharrime in an hour and a half, then planted our gassed legs and backsides under a massive tree. *With this guy on the bike, I could cover all of Africa in a couple months!* Both Bernardo and I wanted to keep pedaling onwards to Tofo Beach, but he had school and work commitments. As an afterthought, we exchanged numbers before he left.

A few days later, I was having lunch at a local bakery with Cordoso, another guest rider, when I received an SMS message from Bernardo.

"*Onde está você?*" he asked.

"Inhambane," I said.

"*Eu também. Podemos montar?*"

"*Inscreva-me para Praia do Tofo!*"

Within minutes, Bernardo joined us at the bakery. He was glowing.

"Hey, when you guys get to Tofo, come grab a free meal and some drinks at my restaurant," said a dreadlocked man sitting at a nearby table. "I'm Dino. Just ask around when you arrive."

"Really? That's nice of you. Thanks." I said.

"I overheard you explaining your project during lunch. That's nice of you to invite the locals to join you on your trip. I've never heard of that before. It's the least I can do. Let me know if you need anything when you are in Tofo."

I sent Cordoso on his way with bus fare and a full belly, my standing deal with any riders who saddled up. Cordoso was good, but he was no Bernardo. *Bernardo!* He made me appreciate anew the pedaling part of Peace Pedalers. We pushed off after lunch, just in time for the siesta-inducing afternoon sun. But the scenery was so stunning I forgot about the heat. We breezed past endless rows of palm trees and rich marshlands, thatch hut villages and scores of curious locals on the roads.

"Incredible!" I shouted.

"*Eu também estou tendo um grande momento!*" he said.

First stop in Tofo Beach: Dino's restaurant, where we powered down fresh prawns, grilled fish, a "the works" pizza, plus cold Cokes and beers. We then took a victory swim in the Indian Ocean's gray-blue waters. I looked ashore and didn't see a soul. *We work a lifetime for these moments. And far too often we fail to grab them.*

Bernardo and I settled into a beachside campsite that evening, watching the sun set, set, set, and then it was gone. I loved sharing the warm post-ride glow with him as he relaxed in his hammock under a coconut tree. He fell asleep peacefully, and I continued to stare.

I tried to count the words we'd said to each other over the previous couple days. A hundred? A few more? It didn't seem to matter. Still, I looked at him as my Mozambican brother. Did we need the words? Does anyone? Clearly we communicated with our body language, smiles, high fives, laughs, screams, hoots and hollers of joy. Didn't that resonate more?

Sometimes language can be limiting, I concluded. We fall back on weather, sports, and pop culture, the shared lowest common denominators of the day. The lack of words often forces us to focus not on what is new, but what is good. And aren't the majority of communications unspoken? Allowing a motorist to merge, the morning wave to the elderly neighbor. This is what was happening with Bernardo. There was a warm, genuine connection between us. I could feel it.

I let Bernardo sleep while I walked down the beach, asking about long-term stay options for the Christmas break. The lodges were all full of South Africans on holiday, but the manager of one offered me an idyllic sliver of sand under a coconut tree. I could purchase a few cheap tapestries and create my own little beach shack. *Hmm. It's certainly warm enough here.* I looked nearby and saw a man, shivering. He said his name was Manekas.

"*Por que você está tremendo, Manekas?*" I asked him.

"*Eu estou sofrendo de malaria,*" he said. Another victim of malaria in Mozambique.

"*Como você se sente?*" I asked.

"*Dor de cabeça, calafrios, dor corpo,*" he said.

Malaria, all right. Intense headaches, chills, body aches. People fear lions and great white sharks and black mambas, but they leave humans alone. No, the biggest killer on the planet, by far, is the mosquito, claiming the lives of more than one million people each year in Africa alone. The ones who do not die suffer for weeks and months on end. If malaria doesn't kill them, it kills their ability to provide for their family. Manekas confided he could no longer work at a beachside shop, and the peak tourist season was approaching fast. "I'll be right back," I told him.

A few months prior, my brother Gino had called me.

"Mozambique, eh? Please promise me you'll be safe," he said.

"I don't want to get injured or killed any more than you do, trust me," I replied.

Gino was the most vocal member of the family members in sharing his fear and disbelief about my stubborn desire to travel solo through Africa. "That was bad enough," he said. "Now you're putting yourself in even more danger with all the cameras and expensive video equipment."

"They will kill you for the gear," he fretted. "Your equipment is worth more than a whole village's income combined."

"Violent crime is a much bigger problem in California than it is in Mozambique, brother. I can show you the stats if you want to see them."

"No stat is going to convince me I shouldn't be worried. I'm worried."

"I appreciate your concern, Gino. Trust me, I'm watching out for my health and safety."

"What about malaria? Mozambique is a hot spot."

"Ummm, I'll try not to get bit so much."

"You are going to get bit no matter how hard you try."

I got off the phone that day and realized I did not have a well thought-out plan concerning malaria. I had a few long-sleeve shirts, insect repellant, and a mosquito net. But what if I got bit and started feeling symptoms? What if I was far from a hospital, which would be most of the time on the route I had planned?

The call with Gino prompted several days of intense research on the subject. I was blown away by the extent of the damage. Of the million people a year who were dying, most were children. That equated in Africa to a child dying from malaria every minute. I read about the enormous social and economic costs to individuals and their families, including drug treatments, expenses for travel to clinics from remote areas, lost workdays and wages, and absence from school. By the end, most Africans couldn't even afford a proper burial for their loved ones.

I stared at the thousands of dollars' worth of video equipment in front of me. *Maybe I should sell it all and…*My "Give Big Radar" went off big time.

To treat malaria, most experts recommended a drug called Coartem made by the Swiss pharmaceutical company Novartis. Long-term travelers in Africa should carry an emergency dose, they said. The medication had an outstanding 85% cure rate. After taking it, intense symptoms of fever, chills, and aches generally eased within 24 hours.

I was fortunate. I could afford the drugs. So could most other fellow travelers. I planned to bring enough for me, and maybe a few extra emergency doses. But what if I could turn a few extra doses into thousands of extra doses, enough to give to village chiefs in remote villages during peak malaria season, the precise time I would be riding through the region of Sub-Saharan Africa?

I composed a one-page summary of a project I called "Spokes for Hope." In it I outlined a partnership between Novartis and Peace Pedalers. They would donate thousands of doses of Coartem, and I would deliver it to afflicted villagers in remote areas. After sending the letter, I called the company's headquarters in Switzerland.

"Jamie, we do not give Coartem to individuals. You have to be a health clinic or practitioner," said a program manager.

"Yeah, but in the remote villages they don't have time or money to get to the clinics. We need to bring the drugs to them."

"I'm afraid it's not possible. It's a nice idea but we won't be able to assist you"

Stiff. Typical corporate "no-man." But I'm sure there are a few folks over there who'd say "yes." I just need to find them. For the next several days I networked, emailed, researched the corporate website, read press releases, and tried different avenues. The idea was too good. I knew I would find a way. "No" was not an option.

After a few weeks of relentless pestering, I opened an email and smiled. Novartis had agreed to send thousands of treatments of Coartem directly to South Africa to avoid any legal risks. They would make Spokes for Hope a reality. I ran outside and started to dance, white-man-with-overbite style.

The next afternoon, I stopped by Manekas's shop. His fever was gone and his body aches had calmed down to almost nothing. He and his wife both gave me huge hugs, and loaded me up with a handful of free tapestries to use for my holiday home on the beach.

Gino! Your nagging paid off for once!

 Enjoy an adventure to Mozambique with this mini-movie at www.bb42b.com/moz

My new tandem train was a tank. Over 250 pounds

It was hot and hilly but Bernardo and I were in paradise

We took Dino up on his offer and ate like kings for free

Bernardo passed out in the hammock seconds after this photo

26

BIG BEND, SWAZILAND

--►

MAPUTO, MOZAMBIQUE, IS just a stone's throw away from Swaziland, which was one of my favorite countries on the trip to-date. It showered me with gifts the last time I visited. Now I wanted to give back. Armed with the shipments of Coartem, I decided to circle back to the malaria endemic regions of Big Bend and Siteki.

In Swaziland, I didn't have to seek riders. They tended to appear. *Wait and they will come*, I told myself as I sat under a tree one morning in Big Bend. Most of the men walking by were heading to work at the local sugar mill, the town's majority employer. I spotted an athletic young man approaching. He sported a blue workout shirt, red shorts, and tennis shoes.

"Hello, my friend," I said.

"Hello," he replied, staring at my bike and gear.

"I'm Jamie. I'm riding…this bike…to Siteki. Do you want to come with me?"

He looked at the bike, then at me, then at some other men under the tree. He said nothing.

"I will pay your bus fare back, and buy you lunch as well."

"The bus back to here?"

"Yes. I want to ride here," I said, pointing to Siteki on a map.

"Ah, Siteki. I know Siteki."

"So, do you want to come?"

We'd reached a critical juncture. There was often a time, right after the moment the potential rider understood my invitation and offer to pay for meals and bus fare back, when he or she could shift to the reasons to say "no" (work, school, "I'm too tired," "my wife will kill me") or the reasons to go. I knew my actions at those moments would either close the deal or kill it.

So I'd invented a deceptively simple, yet effective move: hand the potential rider a pair of riding gloves. If the rider put his hand out to accept them, he was mine. Go time. I did so now.

"Yes. We ride," he said. "Henry. I am Henry."

I could sense Henry's positive energy from the get-go. He was interested in the cameras. I showed him how they worked, and together we captured some nice shots of us riding. He was hooked. His English was limited, and my Portuguese didn't help in Swaziland. We stopped several times in the shade to cool down, take photos, and share stories.

"Do you work?" I asked him

"No, can't find work."

"Where do you live?"

"With my parents. Eight brothers and sisters."

"Do you have a wife or girlfriend?"

"No. You?"

"Nope. We are both bachelors."

"The Bachelor Bike!" he said, laughing.

Just as both our bachelor bellies were starting to rumble, we smelled a *braai* (a term used throughout southern Africa for barbeque), and made a turn into a colorfully decorated roadside store, where a jolly Swazi chap was cooking up some chicken on an oversized grill in the shade of a massive tree. Locally grown vegetables, maize meal, and a few mysterious pickled items sat on the nearby table. *HomeTown Buffet has nothing on this guy's setup.*

The chef's name was Raphy. He had a three-day beard and melon-sized beer belly protruding from his long-sleeve collared shirt that matched his khaki slacks. How these men could stand to be formally and fully dressed in the sweltering heat never ceased to amaze me. For about a dollar each, Raphy dished us up a half chicken, ample sides, and all the maize meal we could eat. We relaxed in the shade, and a Therm-a-Rest chair became my comfortable home while we digested Raphy's handiwork.

Drifting in and out of a food stupor while having a conversation with an older gentleman, I noticed a guy giving haircuts under a nearby tree. I asked him about the impromptu haberdashery. Turns out Vusani was the owner of the stand, as well as several other barber shops in Swaziland. I loved the African barbershops, the way they were decorated with cartoon-figure hairdos and plastered with images of Mike Tyson or Bob

Marley. They had names like Top 10 Hair Styles or One Love Cuts. I rubbed my hand across the chia stubble on my head, and decided it was time for my first African-style, open-air haircut.

The barber doused my dome with some kind of antiseptic tonic. "Keeps you from getting a disease if you get nicked." *Whoa, disease?* He then doused the blades and washed them for a long time. The HIV rate in Swaziland was about 30 percent at the time. *And I'm getting a haircut with clippers that more than likely have nicked others.* He scrubbed some more and I took a deep breath.

"Please don't cut me."

"I won't cut you. I promise."

I trusted him. And I walked away with a stellar head shave, not a single scratch of any kind. As if in a neighborhood barbershop in the U.S., we spent the afternoon sharing tales, laughing at each other's jokes, commenting on the haircuts. I toured a few kids and adults around the village on the tandem. During a ride, I discovered that several people had died in the past few years. Malaria remained a big problem in the village.

"Raphy, I would like to experience real Swazi culture here in your village."

"Yeah? What do you want to do?" he asked.

"First, I would like to meet the chief and make sure the village has plenty of malaria medication in case the kids or elderly get sick."

"I can take you to see the chief. What else?"

"And maybe we can ask him to arrange a place for me and Henry to stay as well?"

He paused, and I thought I'd overstepped.

"Of course we can find a place for you, my son," he said.

"So you are my Swazi father now?" I asked, patting him on the back.

"You are Mduduzi. My son," he said, putting his arm around me.

"What does *mduduzi* mean?"

"Comfort. It means comfort. You made me feel comfortable. That's why you are my son now."

Raphy hopped on the tandem, and we descended down a long dirt road as the scenes of rural Swazi living rolled by us—thatch huts, donkey-drawn carts, and shoeless kids chasing the bike. We arrived at a large housing compound. I handed Raphy a package of ten treatments of

Coartem, along with usage instructions. Raphy entered the compound and came out with a look of indifference.

"The chief is out of town."

"Oh, no. What do we do now?"

"He has four wives. I spoke with one of them."

"And what did she say?"

"She said to tell you thank you for the malaria medication, and you are welcome to stay in the village as long as you want."

"Great!"

"Come with me. We'll go to your house," said Raphy.

We walked the bike a few hundred feet and stopped in front of a modern, single-story cement house complete with electricity.

"Here. You live now in this house, Mduduzi," he said, opening the front door.

"This whole house is mine?"

"Only the best for my son. I will have the woman bring you hot water for a bath, then I'll be back in an hour. Get ready because we will go to dinner and drink homemade beer and find you a wife!"

By the time we offloaded the panniers, a couple of women had brought in two buckets of hot water and two other buckets with cold water. Henry and I were filthy and foul-smelling. Without talking, we stripped down and stepped into the buckets.

"You like the adventure so far, Henry?" I asked.

"Very much. Do they do this in America?"

"Um, well, no. Not that much."

I loaned clothes to Henry and gave him some of my essential oils to boot. He looked and smelled like a proper Bay Area bohemian. We were ready for the festivities.

Raphy came by just before sunset, and we walked slowly down a dirt road into the main part of the village. The elders greeted us first. They were sitting under the tree drinking homemade alcohol, a common sight. Raphy grabbed a cup, filled it up, and presented it to me. "Local beer. Made from this," he said, showing me a little red fruit and pointing to a tree. I gave it sip. Not bad. Not good either. It was overly sweet and the alcohol level was high. I sat down with the men, sipping the beer and relaxing under the tree.

In duos and threesomes, the women joined the festivities. I was introduced to each one, along with the children. And the babies. I always wanted to hold the babies. *Here, let me hold,* I'd motion. Many women were confused at first. A white man who wants to hold my infant? It wasn't a common sight. Especially since village babies don't wear diapers. Eventually, the women realized I was a free babysitter who would entertain their children with his shiny white dome. They all got a hoot out of my name, Mduduzi, and they kept telling me I would make a great dad. "You just need to get married!"

"My son," Raphy interrupted. "A mother wants you to meet her daughter, Thabsille. She is very beautiful, and she would make a great partner for you."

He pointed across the courtyard to a curvaceous woman with a zip-up sweatshirt and long skirt. She chatted with friends and ignored Raphy, though I knew she could hear his every word. *Wow. He's not kidding about this marriage thing.*

"Maybe, before we get married, we can take a bike ride, and, say, get to know each other?"

"I will ask," he said, patting me on the back, half drunk.

I was planning to leave the next day to continue looking for small villages in need of malaria medication. But if I could finally convince a female rider to join me, it would be worth staying. Female riders were a much tougher sell in Africa. I wanted to learn more about their views. A few minutes later, Raphy came back from the house with a smile.

"Jamie, tomorrow morning Thabsille will cook you breakfast. And after she will join you on the bike!"

"Hey, that's great."

"You must try this," he said, handing me a plastic plate with some tube-shaped meat.

"What the hell is it?"

"Barbequed intestines!"

I took several bites and concluded they were, without a doubt, the most disgusting things I had eaten on the continent, and even worse than the wok-fried bugs in China. The intestines had a consistency of shoe rubber and tasted like a soiled sneaker dipped in salt. I smiled and threw up a little in my mouth. *I hope her breakfast doesn't include leftovers.*

As the night wore on, other villagers got into the act. They started calling Thabsille's mom my "mother-in-law." Others forced us to sit together for photos. I placed my arm around her and felt the curve of her back. *Hmmmm.* She had rounded cheekbones and a slight droop on the sides of her eye, making her seem cuddly. The elders recognized something between us. *Maybe we could…nah.* Raphy, his beer buzz now a beer blotto, sidled up next to me.

"Listen, listen. I can see you…and Thabsille…together. And if you get married, then you can live here with your father!"

"Good night, Raphy," I said.

"Good night, my son," he said, reaching out for a hug.

The next morning Thabsille had breakfast ready before I woke. "You didn't need to do this, but thank you," I said, looking down at a large bowl of maize meal coated with slimy green sauce I had experimented with the night before. The flavor was palatable, a grassy root taste, but the mucus-like texture of the sauce made it tough to stomach. At least it wasn't intestine.

Thabsille looked far more appetizing. She was donning tight tights, an exercise shirt, and immaculate white tennis shoes. She smelled straight from a warm shower, with a hint of enticing natural oils. I knew she'd be in the saddle for at least a few hours, so I set her up with her own Assos cycling kit, head to toe. She looked just as sexy in those duds, accenting the outfit with a bright red bandana. She jumped on the bike without hesitation.

"That's the spirit!" I said.

"We are not permitted to ride bikes normally."

"All you have to do is keep your weight in the center and relax."

"Like this?"

"Perfect. Ready? 1—2—3!"

The entire village erupted in cheers. The newlyweds on their way to the honeymoon. All that was missing was the rice shower.

Thabsille and I hit the trails and rural dirt roads hard for the next three hours, building a nice little friendship. She opened up about the lack of opportunity, the chores that consumed every day, and how rarely African women got to do something as lighthearted as ride a bicycle through the country. Every time we stopped she would lean on me or brush against me. I enjoyed every ounce of contact, but knew it wouldn't lead to anything more.

"I love your village. Who does most of the work?"

"Women," she said without hesitation.

"What do the men do?"

"Sit under the tree and demand food from the women."

When we returned back to Thabsille's house, her mom had an enormous meal ready for us. The temperature had soared well past 100 degrees, and the shade, cool water, and food calmed our bodies. Thabsille and I took a long nap under a tree, allowing the heat to die out before the evening festivities. As we lay down on the mat, we inched a bit closer. I wanted to spoon her and explore her curves, but worried we'd be caught. So we played a little game of footsies as we drifted into a deep sleep.

Raphy woke us with a roar. He'd come back from a nearby town, armed with food, drinks, snacks, and treats for the kids. Thabsille's dad, Themba, arrived home from his week working in Big Bend at the sugar mill. He spent only two nights a week at home, and I could tell he was popular by the way villagers greeted him. After a quick introduction, Themba and I took a spin on the tandem—and he was ecstatic. "Your new son-in-law," bystanders cheered. That night we would share dinner, "a steak dinner," Themba declared.

As the sun went down, I settled in to another enjoyable evening with the village. *Is this the old-fashioned neighborhood feel my parents talked about? The days when parents reprimanded each other's kids, and neighbors gathered on stoops each evening to swap news and stories?* "It takes a village to raise a child," proclaimed Hillary Clinton. That child would be in good hands in this village.

Throughout the night, villagers continued to place Thabsille and me together whenever possible. Their over-the-top matchmaking had a welcome impact. It allowed us to laugh, and to critique the best attempts. We liked each other, but knew the evening would be our last. Henry and I would head out in the early morning, so I resisted the aggressive attempts to get me drunk as well as hitched. Around midnight, I turned in.

"Guys, I'm sorry, but I need to get up and out before the Swazi sun kicks in," I said.

"But what about Thabsille? What about me, your dad?" said Raphy, only half joking.

"You know I need to move on, Dad. All part of growing up, right? I'll be back one day, but I need to keep riding."

"I will miss you, Mduduzi," he said, lowering his voice and beginning to get teary eyed.

"I will miss you too, Raphy."

I gave Raphy, Thabsille, and everyone in the vicinity long hugs. I was getting teary eyed as well, more so after I closed the door and flopped into bed. I looked around the small house and envisioned what customizations I'd make if I did stay. *A killer patio with hammocks to watch the purple and red sunsets. Yeah, and a huge rock bathtub with candles all over. Big enough for two. I could also make a big organic garden and have chickens and other animals live on the land.*

Try as I might, I couldn't fall asleep. The "what if's" shook me awake. *Was it really such an insane idea? How about testing it out for a couple weeks?* The rains began, and the tin roof amplified every drop. I drifted off for what seemed to be about ten minutes, waking with a gurgling stomach filled with intestines, green slime, and homemade beer, ready to burst at any time. Along with the oncoming duodenal onslaught came a crush of emotions—connection and loss, gratitude and envy, excitement and regret. I let them all sink in.

 Enjoy an adventure to my return to Swaziland with this mini-movie at www.bb42b.com/return

Taking a break from the hot sun with my new friend Henry

My open-air barber shop

Thabsille and I out on our ride

Settling into village life

Before bed Raphy brought me one final meal of the green slime delight for Henry and I

27
BURMA VALLEY, ZIMBABWE

--▶

POP! POP!

The loud explosions in rapid succession woke me in a state of terror. They sounded very close and very real, almost certainly gunshots. Pistol shots. I recognized the staccato blasts from my days at USC.

Pop! Pop!

I jumped down on the floor and made my way under the bed in the pitch black. My heart rate soared. I tried not to move or make a sound. I prayed nobody would blast into my room.

I had arrived that afternoon on the farm of Hugh and Toffy, a vibrant, elderly white Zimbabwean couple, two of the last white farmers left in the infamous Burma Valley. The guidebooks said they made cheese for tourists. But Hugh and Toffy had stopped producing the cheese when tourism narrowed to a trickle thanks to the deranged policies and pronouncements of president/nutcase Robert Mugabe.

They invited me to spend the night, swapping the cheese for a curry dinner. We were joined by the only other white farmer in the area, Oliver, a man my age who was also fighting to keep his land from being snatched by the Zimbabwe government and redistributed to Mugabe supporters.

We had stayed up well past midnight as I listened to horrific stories of their friends being dragged away from of their land. Many of them were brutally beaten, some even killed, as Mugabe implemented his land redistribution regardless of law, humanity, or common sense. Many new landowners had no clue how to run a modern farm, maintain equipment, or manage an international business. Little by little, their farm equipment broke, the crops died, exports dried up, and the new farmers ended up using the highly fertile land to grow a few simple sustenance crops like maize and tomatoes. You could see the results everywhere. *This was once a leader of Africa, and now it's one of the poorest nations on the planet.*

The next morning Hugh nonchalantly told me the nighttime explosions were "just a few shots from a security guard." He'd fired off a round at a couple of men who hopped a fence and attempted to steal coffee beans. *Um, that would have been nice to tell me last night. Would have saved me a couple of hours barely breathing while under a bed.* The gunshots and the evening stories clung to me as I pedaled off solo into the deserted Burma Valley. How would their stories jibe with black farmers? Did they see events the same?

My ride on the long, hot road wove through old banana, tobacco, and coffee farms, once thriving, now withering. Global exports from these lands used to help fund the country's top-rated education system for decades, giving Zimbabwe the reputation as the "Shining Star of Africa." Now, more than 95% of the farms were abandoned or growing just enough food to feed a couple families. I'd heard many white farmers tick off the statistics and personal hardship stories. Most of them neglected to highlight the obvious, that the old successes occurred under white colonial rule.

The vibe in the small villages along the road was muted and depressing. Few people wanted to ride or even engage in conversation. Many of them were hungry or malnourished, and I felt guilty for even asking them to climb aboard the bike.

"Mugabe is killing us," said a young man. "He's killing his own people"

"We are suffering. Please tell the world we need help," another man told me.

"Let's take a quick ride and you can tell me more about it. We'll get it on film."

"No, thank you. No way."

"For what?" yelled another villager. "We are suffering! We don't need a bike ride. We need help! Bring us help!"

Like many travelers to Africa, I was planning on skipping Zimbabwe altogether. The country was beyond desperate, fellow travelers told me. Crisis mode. Not the best place to pedal solo with $30,000 worth of gear. So during the final days of my lazy holiday in Tofo Beach, I dusted off my maps and began making my plans to pedal east of Zimbabwe.

Then one day at a Tofo Beach holiday party I met Tony. He was a hip, scruffy, dreadlocked Zimbabwean who spoke perfect English. He was dating a white backpacker, and maintained friendships with people all over the world. I shared my project with him, and he became intrigued. One day he noticed me studying my maps at a restaurant and came over for a closer look.

"Hey, mate. So where are your travels taking you next?"

"I'm heading up to Malawi then over to Zambia," I said, showing him the map.

"What about Zimbabwe?"

"I keep hearing horror stories about the situation there."

"Like what?"

"Like wide-scale starvation, massive inflation, no fuel, black-market everything, ya know, chaos."

"It's not a horror story, mate. Sure, we are suffering, but you won't read any news about tourists being attacked. Nobody is harming tourists. They are welcoming them more than ever. We need tourists to survive."

"I hear you, but I am traveling with all this filming equipment, and just don't feel safe."

"Mate, you *have* to go. The country needs someone like you to go in undercover and capture the harsh realities there and share it with the world."

"What if I get caught?" I asked.

"You won't get caught. And if you do, just say you are a tourist filming your adventure."

I heard the voice of Mamacita in my head. "Look out for your guides," she had said. "It will be obvious what road to take next." I had long wanted to go to Zimbabwe. And I'd kicked myself for allowing mass media to define other countries, only to discover a different story when I arrived. Part of this trip was about facing down stereotypes and fears, about making the discovery for myself. *Just be smart. You'll be okay.* Perhaps I could help.

Due to hyperinflation and loony government banking rules, everyone exchanged money on the black market. To counter this, Mugabe and his cronies tried to force visitors to use credit cards and ATMs. Not only did this rip off tourists, it kept cash out of the hands of locals, cash they desperately needed to survive. As a result, banking was rarely conducted in the banks. Transactions took place in cafés and on street corners.

The night before my ride from Harare to Bulawayo, I went out looking for someone to change money. A large, muscular man with a black t-shirt and acid-washed jeans approached me. He rubbed his thumb and fingers together, the international sign for money. This happened frequently in Zimbabwe. I nodded. He approached.

"How much you need?" he said, looking around nervously.

"One hundred."

"Can I see it?"

"Not here. Let's find a restaurant."

Backpackers warned me against exchanging money out on the open streets. Too easy for thieves to snatch the bills out of your hand and run away, they said. I looked around for any suspicious characters as we walked across the street to a busy café.

"Okay, let me see the money," he said, as we sat down at a table.

I showed him the $100 bill, grasping it with both hands.

"Okay, I'll be back. Stay here."

I waited for about five minutes. He returned with a large wad of "Zim dollars" in his hand.

"Here's your money," he said, extending the wad. "Where's the hundred?"

"It's here," I said, pulling it from my pocket.

As if jolted by a shock, his eyes opened wide and his face twisted nervously. He pointed out the window.

"The police are here! Hurry, take your money. We should get out of here!"

Without thinking, I gave him the $100 bill, stashed the wad of Zim dollars in my pocket, and hustled out of the café to avoid the police. *Phew, that was close.*

"I don't see any police…" I started to say to the man, as we exited. But he was gone. As I walked down the street my heart sank. Everyone was just going about his or her business. I hesitated, then put my hand in my pocket and grabbed my wad of cash. The top note was a large bill, but all the others were one-dollar notes not worth even a cent each.

Immediately I began to regret my decision to come to Zimbabwe. *What am I thinking? I'm riding around aimlessly with gunshots going off at night and now being robbed in broad daylight. Is all this a sign to get the hell of here before something really bad happens?* Suddenly everyone was a crook, and on every corner lurked a crime.

Back at the hotel I pondered my next steps. I could easily catch a bus to Zambia and be done with the whole country. But the more I thought about leaving, the louder Tony's voice grew. "Zimbabwe needs you to document the realities. Show the world." Then the voices of despair I heard in the Burma Valley joined the chorus. As much as I wanted to flee, I had to keep riding.

The ride from Harare to Bulawayo started out ideal from a cycling perspective—smooth roads with a wide shoulder, no traffic, and pleasant temperatures without much wind. I was enjoying the solo cycling, but I was still not myself. The scam ate at me, and I'm sure I projected a bit of resentment. I observed how many able-bodied Zimbabwean men and woman I was passing up. Normally, I would stop near each one. Now I wanted to ride alone. I justified it to myself saying, "I just want to have some time to listen to music and enjoy my passion for riding." But, deep inside, I knew I was lying. I was scared. I was closed up in fear.

Must conquer fear. Must not paint entire country with one brush. I saw a man walking in my direction, and I slowed down to pick him up. Just when he nodded hello, I panicked and rode on. *Wimp.* I rode another kilometer or so until I received a phone call from a friend I had met at the border of Mozambique. He called to check in on me, and I gave him the update—the good, the bad, and the ugly. "Don't give up, Jamie! Zimbabwe needs you," he said, echoing Tony's words almost to the letter.

As soon as I hung up, I spotted the man I had passed before. *It has to be fate. I have to bust out of this funky fear and get my mojo back.* Before I could let anxiety overcome me, I stopped the bike in front of the man and smiled.

"Hello. I'm Jamie," I said, extending my hand.

"Bernard. Nice to meet you," he said before giving me a soft yet friendly handshake, mostly with the fingers, common among Africans.

Bernard was tall and stick-skinny. He wore a worn-out white t-shirt a size too large for his gaunt figure. After a few more words, he hopped on the bike with pleasure.

"So tell me your story, Bernard. Where are you walking today?"

"I am walking to my house. I walk to work every day."

"How long do you walk?"

"It takes me 90 minutes each way."

"Good job?"

"I work on a small farm. I used to be a truck driver for produce. But when all the farms closed I lost my job."

"Do you have family?"

"Yes, but I don't live with them anymore. They live in Kadoma. The only job I could find is out here," he said, his voice trailing off.

"Do you like your job?"

"No, it only pays $10 a month, and I have to pay rent here and for my family in Kadoma. We are struggling."

"You must miss your family?"

"Yes, very much. Even more because my daughter has been sick. I feel very bad I can't be there."

"How far is Kadoma from here?" I asked.

"Oh, a long way. Maybe 100 kilometers or more."

My Give Big radar flashed in my head.

"We can ride there together. You can be by your daughter's side tomorrow."

"This would make me very happy."

"You just have to pedal a little harder."

He patted me on the back and picked up his pace.

We wouldn't make it that day. The sun was going down and we had ways to go to get to the next town of Selous. I'd made a vow long ago never to ride at night. Too many bad roads, drunk drivers, and wild animals. When we arrived at the only hotel in town, the manager said we were in luck. They had two rooms left.

"Would you like one room or two?" the man asked.

"How much are the rooms?" I asked

"Two dollars each."

Two rooms gives us some privacy, and would prevent any theft. "I'll take two..." *But what message does that send to him as a friend and teammate? Is distrust the message I want to send?*

"Just one room," I said. "With two beds. Please."

The next morning we hit the road early for the long haul to his village, about an 80 kilometer ride. While we were loading the bike, I had an idea.

"Bernard, do you mind helping me do some filming today?" I asked.

"Sure. What is it for?"

"You're a good spokesman for your country. I'd love to record you and share your thoughts with others. Show them what's going on here."

He chuckled as if I was joking, then paused when he saw I was serious.

"I will help, yes," he said.

We spent the entire day not only riding and talking, but also stopping to film interesting scenes and conducting interviews with locals. We Westerners should know about the food shortages and the creative ways they can feed our families on found items like termites and groundnuts, they told us. How Tupac, Internet dating, and other Western tastes had reached the villages, but how the only thing needed for a party was an *mbira*, a thumb piano. Bernard was a natural show host, translating and deciphering the interviews and even conducting a basic Shona language lesson so the viewers could learn a few words.

He conducted the interviews willingly, but I could tell his mind often drifted to Kadoma. I called an end to the filming sessions, and we arrived in town just as the rain began. First stop: a small grocery store to fill his kitchen. As we made the final pedal strokes to his house, several kids from the village recognized him. By the time we reached his house, the escort party grew to a dozen children. They jumped and hooted, ignoring the rain.

When we rolled up to Bernard's house, his wife burst into tears and his daughter ran full speed to him for a big hug. He pointed to the bicycle and explained why this strange man with odd tan lines was standing in the house. Bernard's wife took the groceries and began cooking a celebratory meal. Following a couple of quick showers, Bernard took me out to play pool, drink beers, and meet his friends.

Bernard lived in a cramped, 12-by-12-foot room along with his wife and two children. He invited me to stay the night with his family, and I was honored. After a big meal and an evening of camaraderie with his family and friends, we all crashed on one queen-size mattress on the floor. *Love it! How many families in California would be willing to share their bed with a stranger?*

Bernard's aunt shook me awake. "Come, sir. Here you will sleep better," she told me. She then led me by the hand into another room, where I was pointed to a bed containing an elderly man who had passed out. Bernard's drunken uncle, I later discovered. I could smell the tobacco and beer emanating from every one of his pores. Then he started to hack—long, wet coughs, almost operatic in their cadence, that woke me every 20 minutes for the rest of the night. *I wonder how many families would share their drunken, chain-smoking uncle with a stranger?*

My heart stopped when I saw it, a police checkpoint ahead on the two-lane road. An officer pointed to me, and I knew there was no escape. I wasn't prepared.

The punishment for filming without a permit in Zimbabwe was severe, confiscation of all equipment, hefty fines, and possible jail time. I had heard stories, but I was halfway through my trip and had recorded more than 12 hours of footage without so much as seeing a police car the last couple weeks.

But my bike and I were an obvious filming machine, with two tripods in plain sight, a helmet camera on my head, and a Pelican waterproof camera case strapped to the back, loaded with multiple HD cameras, mics, lights, transceivers, and other equipment. I couldn't avoid the obvious, so I took a different approach.

"Hello, Friendly Police Officers! How are we today?"

"Where are you going?" said a serious policeman.

"I'm heading to Bulawayo. You want to join me?" I asked, pointing to the seat.

"What are you doing here?"

"Here? Here just happens to be on the route to Bulawayo. Do you want to try a quick ride on the bike?"

"What is all this camera equipment?"

"Oh, I'm riding through Africa, so I need tripods and cameras. Look, this is my favorite camera here. Want to see how it works?"

I pulled out my still camera, took a photo of the officers and showed it to them on the screen.

"Do not take any pictures of us. This is illegal."

"Oh, I didn't know that. But check out this picture. You guys look handsome!" I said, showing the camera to them. Digital cameras hadn't made their way to Zimbabwe yet. Curious, the other officers huddled around the small screen.

"So what do you say, let's hop on the bike and do a ride!" I said to a tall young officer who had inched his way near.

"Where will we go?" he asked.

"How about just up to those red cones and then we'll come back. 30 seconds. Tops."

He looked around.

"Okay, I want to try it. Take this," he said, giving his clipboard to his buddy and hopping on the bike.

I brought him back to the group, hoping the gesture would spare an arrest. A lead officer approached me.

"Sorry, I was just having a bit of..."

"May I have a ride, too?" he asked.

That ride lead to another, then a few more, and after a half-hour of touring policemen, they waved me on...though not before first posing for a photo.

A few miles down the road, I stopped for a bite to eat at a roadside café. A man with short dreadlocks and a green-and-red-colored tank top sat alone at a table. His eyes were bloodshot, but his laidback energy convinced me to sit down next to him.

"G'afternoon," I said. "Seems like a popular place. What's going on?"

He looked over his shoulders and cautiously moved his face close to mine.

"We are all gold miners."

Over the next half-hour, he confided he and the others were not only gold miners, they were illegal gold miners, waiting for spies to tell them when it would be safe to re-enter the shafts and scoop up as much gold as possible before the police came. His name was Chengu. "Welcome to our crazy world, mon."

Everything about the situation felt sketchy—the side glances and secret handshakes, even the dishes of *sadza* (maize meal) and sausages with their mystery flavor and slimy texture. Dog meat? Wild game? Who knew? Still, I didn't feel unsafe.

I went back out to my bike with a full belly of *sadza*, and had a tough decision to make. I needed some extra pedal power to get to the town of Kwekwe that afternoon, but would I be putting myself in danger if I asked one of these guys to join me? It was Friday, and I always liked to arrive in a city on the weekends to jump into the festivities.

Let's do it. These men were part of the real Zimbabwe, the one not featured in the guidebooks. I decided to set up the cameras to capture the entire recruitment process. A small crowd gathered.

"So does anyone want to come pedaling with me out to Kwekwe?" I asked.

The crowd stirred, clapping and pointing to each other as candidates. Then I spotted Chengu. When he smiled, his eyes closed to a crease, just like mine.

"Chengu! How about you, man?"

"I would like to accompany you. But I'm afraid I'm not as sharp as you," he said, pointing to my cycling clothes.

"Oh, I have something for you," I said, reaching into my bag. "Here, go put these on."

And I handed him a pair of professional riding shorts and a jersey. Chengu took the clothes and disappeared through the doors of a cement building. *Is he coming back?* I got the cameras ready, knowing his buddies would flip out. They did not disappoint. Chengu sported the blue jersey and black spandex like a runway model at Fashion Week, his friends catcalling from all sides.

The group seemed so supportive that I set up two cameras on two tripods to film our exit. This was shaping up to be one of the best exits of the entire trip. The miners high-fived me and continued to shout encouragements to Chengu. A middle-aged man in khakis tapped me on the shoulder.

"Excuse me," he said politely. "Can I have a word with you?"

He flashed a police badge, and the air inside me froze. *This is un-good.*

"Yes?" I said

"Please follow me," he said.

He led me to a quiet area inside one of the buildings.

"What's going on, officer?" I asked.

"What do you think you are doing?"

"Getting ready to ride to Kwekwe with my friend Chengu, is there something wrong?"

"What are you doing with the video cameras?"

"It's a hobby of mine. I love to shoot video."

"Don't lie to me. Those cameras are not hobby cameras. You know it."

Offer a bribe? Run?

"Here, this is the project I'm doing," I said, handing him a Peace Pedalers sticker from my wallet. "I am riding this bike around the world, picking up strangers and making friends in a gesture of peace. I wanted to capture some video clips for the project."

He paused.

"You could be in a lot of trouble right now if the wrong police officers saw you with all these cameras."

This is going to be an expensive shake-down.

"What do you suggest I do?" I asked.

"There are many police around here because of all the illegal mining. You need to leave this area right away and stop filming."

"Thank you, sir, I'll stop filming."

"Consider yourself warned. There will be no more warnings."

I went back outside, took both cameras down off the tripods, and told Chengu to get on the bike. Fast. He mounted without a word, and we pedaled off in silence. We rode for about 500 feet out of the village and beyond earshot.

"Oh my God! I don't believe that just happened!" I said.

"You are one lucky person, mon!"

"Yaaahooooooooo!"

"Woooooooooooooo!" screamed Chengu. "Off to Kwekwe!"

The close brushes with the police made me want to film more than ever. *If they're trying to silence the truth, the truth must be shared.* Chengu was a fascinating character, with a distinct point of view. I wanted to record his thoughts. He was my first Rastafarian guest rider. While I knew many people who claimed to be Rastafari just as an excuse to smoke copious amounts of marijuana, Chengu was a true believer. I wanted to learn more.

"For us Rastas, smoking herb is a spiritual act," he said. "Ganja cleans the body and mind and brings us closer to Jah."

"And what is Jah?"

"Jah is God. Jah sent us his son, Yeshua, Jesus; we accept and study most of the Bible. I often read it after I smoke."

"What's Babylon? I hear it in all the reggae songs."

"Babylon is the society we're living in now—materialism, persecution, sensual addictions. We reject Babylon and want to get back to our roots."

"What about food? Any special Rastafari diet?" I asked.

"I eat mostly I-tal."

"What?"

"You know, I-tal. Natural. No processed foods. And I don't eat red meat. Rots I gut, mon."

After an hour, we stopped under a tree for a break. I had two things going against me: I was in a rush to film Chengu before anyone saw us, and I was a bit spaced-out thanks to a sampling of his holy herb. Hurried and high are never a good combo. Sure enough, as I was setting up the equipment, I dropped my small HD camera on my only wide-angle lens, leaving a deep scratch and rendering the lens worthless. Then, while using my other camera, I somehow managed to break the wireless microphone. *Someone's trying to tell you something. Remember, no more warnings.*

"So what brought you to the gold mining business?" I asked him that night in Kwekwe.

"I had a great job in telecommunications for many years. I used to make good money. There is no work now, so this is the only way I can get food...for my family."

"What happens if you get caught?"

"I can't get caught. It's not an option."

The next day I finally heeded the police officer's full advice, putting the video equipment away and heading straight for Bulawayo. It was Saturday, and I was hoping to sample some nightlife. Shortly after arriving, I found some rocking live music, a great little hotel, and a couple local women who wanted to show me how to party, Zimbabwe style. The town was interesting and the hotel was so comfortable and cheap that I decided to stay for a few days.

After a night on the town, I returned to my room and noticed the door was open. I was sure I had locked it. My heart jumped. Someone had broken into my room. Walking in, I saw my bags split open and my clothes spread all over the room. *But what did they steal?* I took a deep breath, then I took inventory.

Laptop, hard drives? Check! *Phew!* Two HD cameras and microphones? Here. Still cameras, iPod? Right here. Passport, credit cards? *No way. I can believe they didn't take those.* As far as I could tell, the only thing missing was about $100 in spare cash.

I felt a wave of relief overtake my body, then just as quickly exit. It wasn't the money. It was the violation. I know I shouldn't have, but I took it personally. *I'm just trying to spread a little peace and understanding. And you break into my room?* I decided to call Tony, the cool Zimbabwean who convinced me to tour his country. He was at his home in Victoria Falls.

"Jamie! You decided to come to Zimbabwe after all, eh?"

"Yeah, it's been amazing, but I've had robberies, gunshots, and was nearly put in jail for filming."

"Hey, mate, be really careful. The police are harsh in Bulawayo. Rumor has it Mugabe killed thousands of his own people, and police don't want any evidence getting out of the country. These guys don't play around."

"Really? This is not good," I said, starting to get more worried.

"Listen, man, the road between Bulawayo and here is a no-go for cycling. Lots of robberies and bandits. Best bet is to get your butt on a bus. You can stay as long as you want here at the hostel. Just get up here, mate!"

I hung up and threw up my arms. I had had enough. My bike needed parts. My camera gear needed replacements. An extended stay at the Shoestrings Backpackers lodge was just what the doctor ordered. I heeded Tony's advice and caught the next bus to Victoria Falls.

Thump, thump, thump. I could hear the party music the minute I arrived at the hostel the next evening. I headed into the party feeling energized and proud of the friendships I'd made in Zimbabwe. Tony was right. They needed their story to be told. I bounced around the party on a high before meeting Eva, a sparkly British backpacker. She had voluptuous lips and perky breasts that protruded from her silk top. We began to swap tales from the road, and she was blown away by the concept of taking a tandem around the world. It was the equivalent of a royal flush in the backpacker world. We talked, then danced, then returned to my room. In the morning I spooned her, grateful for the friendly conversation and human touch.

As she slept, I decided to get some air. I felt like a king—free large, comfortable room; lovely woman nestled up waiting for me back in bed; a triumphant and jail-free tour of Zimbabwe and southern Africa. I walked around the grounds wanting to high-five everyone who passed. I ambled over to where I parked the tandem.

Where the hell is my bike?

I ran over to the pole and saw the lock, broken, on the ground. Before I had hit the party, I bolted my bike against a large steel pole using an alarm lock. This ingenious device was about one-third the weight of a big U-lock and had been serving me well through Africa. It was battery operated and emitted a bright red light every three seconds. If the lock was cut or tampered with, the lock would emit a loud siren. Or so they claimed. I had not tried to cut the lock, but just trusted it would work, mostly as a deterrent. *Who is going to be able take a tandem out of a crowded hostel with a siren going off?*

I looked left. Nothing. *No, no NOOOO!* My nightmare scenario was now a reality—a stolen bike in one of the most destitute countries in Africa.

I sprinted back to the front desk and found a security guard on duty near the bar. He was only half awake and claimed he knew nothing.

What's the point of a guard if you can't leave a bike with an alarm parked right out front?

I walked back to the scene of the crime and got on my knees and prayed. *Please, please please. I'm not done riding! Please!*

I got up, took a few deep breaths, and decided to take another look around. There were eight-foot walls in every direction, plus a big fence. *How the hell could anyone get the bike over that fence?*

I decided to take a walk around the perimeter of the hostel. *Breathe. Deep. Breathe. Deep.* I tried to channel the meditation lessons from India. *See the bike.* I rounded a wall and thought of Garryck. *We had faith in China. Have faith now.* Slowly I scanned the bushes and trees.

Then, a silver reflection. There, through the branches, a piece of shining metal. Next a spoke and a wheel. Then the best sight of the entire African adventure—my tandem. The bike was buried deep under a pile of branches in a hidden part of the complex. The thieves had stashed it there with plans to retrieve it later on. *Ha Ha! I got you!*

I dug through the branches, tossing them aside like wrapping paper on Christmas morning. There she was. Unlocked, seemingly unharmed. My trip wasn't over. *Maybe it's just begun.*

 Enjoy an adventure to Zimbabwe with this mini-movie at www.bb42b.com/zimbabwe

Hugh and Toffy were some of the last remaining white farmers in Zimbabwe

My Zimbabwean guide Tony and I planning my route through Zimbabwe

Bernard and I taking a break in the shade

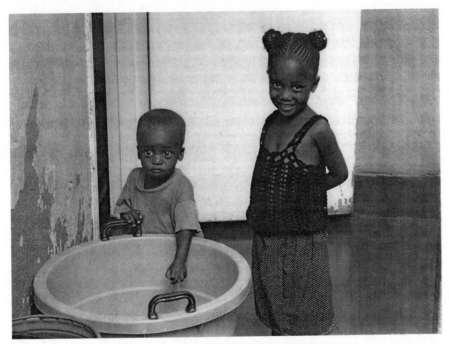

Bernard's two daughters were ecstatic to see him roll in

Jail, confiscation and fines evaded with big smiles

Chengu bathed, dressed and doused in my essential oils ready for a night on the town in KweKwe

28
CHOMA, ZAMBIA

- ▶

BIKES HAVE A way of amplifying moods. If you're feeling good, the exertion, the scenery, the fresh air will take you to an even greater height. But when you're pissed off at the world, the long hours on the bike can sometimes give riders ample time to stew. The roads suck, the towns suck, the people suck. *What am I doing here?*

What I'd learned is that a bicyclist's mood is contagious. It heavily influences surroundings and events, often for the worse. I was proving it soon after I crossed the border into Zambia.

I selected guest riders who demanded money or a piece of my equipment. Others were rude or refused to pedal. I picked up a rider in Choma only to discover he was a drunk, and an angry one at that. After a short ride, I tried to buy him lunch, part of my pre-stated deal with every rider. He didn't want food. He wanted Chibuku beer, and lots of it. When I cut him off, he became belligerent and stormed out. I paid for his beer and followed him outside. He was gone.

With my riding gloves! That bastard stole my gloves. I knew they were only worth a couple dollars. That's not why I was angry. For the first time in 26 countries and four years of Peace Pedaling, somebody broke the bond between riders. In a way it stung more than the bike thefts and near bike thefts. Those thieves were stealing an object. The drunk had stolen from me.

I pedaled off toward Lake Kariba sour and bitter, fighting against a pounding rain. I rode hard and fast, and argued with myself.

"Dude, you need to lighten up! It's just a pair of cycling gloves."

"There's never a reason to steal. I traveled for nearly two years in poor villages in Asia and they never stole from me."

"Where's the Give Big spirit? See the gloves as a gift."

"Quit talking about the gloves! It's not about the gloves!"

The angry Jamie won the round. I started the ride mad, and became more and more bitter with each pedal. *No more rides today, this week.* I noticed my front derailleur was acting up again, so I stopped to tighten it. I should have known better. Annoyed and tired, I tightened the bolt with every strand of strength I could muster.

Crack! I could hear the sound of metal snapping in my mind even before it occurred. I had broken my front derailleur and was now stuck with just one choice of gear on the front chain rings, making the ride in the hilly terrain next to impossible. I used some duct tape and a couple bungee cords to prevent the bike from getting any worse. And I knew I needed to do a little repair job on myself as well.

Several days and solo rides later, I went to lunch with a guest at a backpackers' lodge. Clair was a volunteer, one of many I'd met in Africa. I admired their devotion and priorities. Like the others, Clair was smart and industrious. She talked with certainty about the changes her group was making. I wasn't so sure. I'd seen a lot of money spent on Land Rovers and offices in towns, far from the people they professed to help.

Clair was a nurse and heading out soon to a clinic near the Malawi border. She had long dirty-blonde hair, no makeup, and smelled of vanilla. I tried and failed to hide my jaded attitude of late.

"Honestly, I'm thinking about skipping the country and taking a bus up to Malawi when my parts come. I'm done."

"I know it must feel terrible to have such a bad chain of events happen to you. But I assure you, there are many, many good people in Zambia."

"I know, I've met scores of them. It just feels terrible being here, by myself, with a huge bag of malaria medication, teddy bears, and camera equipment, trying to be of service and then to be treated this way."

"Well, maybe you need to find a way to tell the Zambian people how you feel. Write an article and give it to the local newspaper. Get the frustration off your chest. I'm sure the people would want to hear your feelings."

"Hmmmm. I never thought of that."

"You'll feel better," she said.

I thanked her for the suggestion and promised I would stop at her clinic if I decided to pass through Kamalaza. Through the night, I thought about her recommendation. She was right. I did need to get this anger off my chest. If I didn't it would only get worse. I felt like I was going to snap. Maybe I'd been on the road too long, but I wanted to let the people of Zambia know how horrible it felt to come into the country with pure intentions only to be treated with dishonesty.

A media mission, that's what I needed. I rode my bike to the largest television station in Zambia. They sent a producer out to talk to me. When he heard my story he booked me immediately on *Smooth Talk*, one of the country's top shows. He also gave me the contact information of several reporters for the nation's top newspapers and magazines.

For the next week I rode around town solo, still ignoring the friendly waves and invitations to stop. All I wanted to do was get to the next interview as quickly as possible. They printed and aired every gripe. Each time I saw a piece come out, I felt a little bit better. *At least they know what it feels like.*

The lifts were short-lived. As soon as I'd read or hear my words, I'd regret them. Perhaps the article Clair suggested would have been better to write...then tear up.

After an interview one afternoon, I passed up at least a dozen potential new Zambian friends. I felt a lump growing in my throat. It hurt to swallow. Each smiling face I passed, each giggling "Can I join you, mon?" drove a stake deeper into my heart and soul. I finally had to pull the bike over and collapse under a tree to cry and let it all out. This wasn't a whimper. No. It was a convulsing-shouting-exhausting cry. I pulled on my sunglasses in hopes they'd soften my sobs, but the tears just kept coming.

But then, all of a sudden, a new word popped into my head: *tolerance.*

I always said that Peace Pedalers was about tolerance and acceptance. Yet here I was, fumbling an opportunity to practice what I preached. I needed to accept the young nation and its growing pains. I needed to be tolerant of outlooks and histories that were different than mine. I had to believe in the people of Zambia. My lack of tolerance would only lead to more intolerance. I saw that now.

Overnight my situation changed. I gave more rides and worried less about being cheated or taken advantage of. I began to build amazing friendships with dozens of remarkable Zambians. Best of all, I was able to gather my confidence and reconnect with my passion to ride the northeastern region of Zambia up to the border of Malawi.

I wheeled into the small village of Kamalaza and quickly found the weathered, turquoise-colored medical clinic. As I approached, I heard the sound of babies crying and a woman speaking loudly in the local Ngoni language. I ducked my head in to see if Clair was around. Two babies seemed to be the center of attention, both wrapped in colorful *chitenges* and riding on the backs of their mothers. *Chitenges* usually made me smile, but these children were lifeless. I spotted Clair and walked over to give her a hug.

"Jamie! You made it! Wow, your timing could not be better," she said in a professional tone. "You told me you carry Coartem. Do you have any on you?"

"I do. Plenty."

"These babies here are burning up with malaria, and the clinic is out of all malaria medication. There may not be time to go searching in Chipata or Katete. Can you prepare a couple treatments?"

"Whatever you need."

My hands were shaking as I went to open my pannier and grab the Coartem. I'd distributed hundreds of packets to village chiefs, aid workers, and healthcare professionals, but had never prepared an individual treatment according to the dosing tables for infants.

As the screams intensified, I read and re-read the instructions. They involved breaking up the tablets and dissolving them in water so the infants could drink the solution. Clair and I then brought the cups to the mothers, who were able to get their babies to drink the concoction and keep it down.

I had one teddy bear left in my bag. I gave to a crying baby boy named Max. His face winced and contorted with storms of pain. Malaria is savage when it afflicts an adult, merciless when it strikes a child. Max's mother did not speak English. She put her hand on my shoulder after Max stopped crying. She didn't say anything. She didn't need to. Her eyes told me everything. Max would be fine.

My guest rider for that day was a nineteen-year-old man named Thomas Manza. I'm sure he had no idea what he was getting himself into when he accepted the invitation to ride earlier that afternoon. I had spotted Thomas sitting under a tree, working on a bicycle wheel with his buddies. He looked fit, with wiry muscles popping on the tops of his arms. I wanted to reach the clinic before sunset, but I was running late. Thomas's legs made it possible.

We spent the rest of the day at the clinic, trying to leave a few smiles. And when it was time for Thomas to leave, we both felt spent but grateful.

This was meant to be. When the bus was approaching he reached out and held both my hands and looked me in the eyes.

"Jamie, this was the best day of my life," he said.

"It was amazing for me too, Thomas. Without you we wouldn't have made it here in time."

I gave him a hug and smacked his shoulder as he boarded his bus home. *Remember, you were ready to quit. Max, the babies, the moms—they are happy you didn't.*

The next day I was blessed to be accompanied to Chipata by one of the clinic coordinators, a man named John. He was a highly educated, successful business owner who volunteered his time to help his community.

"Zambia, like any country, is sort of like an apple tree," he said. "There are ripe, delicious apples and there are young, bitter apples. You never know what you are going to pick. When you pluck the bitter one, you have to understand there are sweet ones nearby."

"You picked a few bitter ones in a row, Jamie. Next time it happens, don't grab an axe. Just go to the other side of the tree."

Thomas earlier that day getting ready to mount the bike

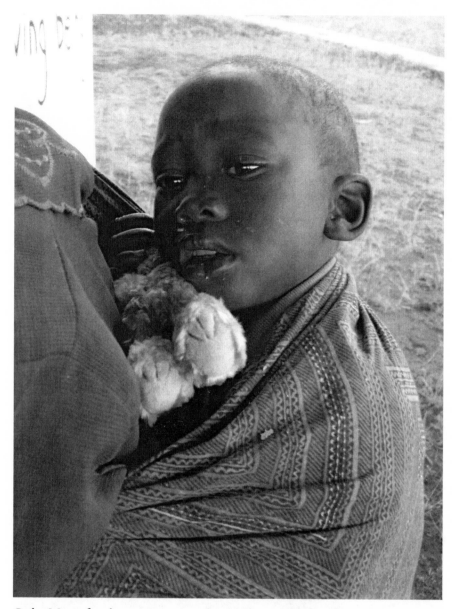

Baby Max after his treatment and teddy bear gift

Enjoy an adventure to Zambia with this mini-movie at
www.bb42b.com/Zambia

29
NKHOTAKOTA, MALAWI

TAP TAP TAP *tap tap*. I felt the rapid-fire pats on my shoulder.

"What's up, Gift?" I asked, glancing back at my guest rider.

"Jamie, you must turn around now! Shannon has fallen. She has crashed."

Without looking for any oncoming traffic, I hit the brakes and spun the bike around. A small group of Malawian woman hovered over the jumbled mess in the middle of the road. I put my bike against a railing and sprinted to see my beloved cousin struggling to get to her feet. She was covered in dirt, grime, and bloody scrapes. A thick clump of mud struck to her helmet. Not a good sign. I held her pink, freckled arm to make sure she didn't wobble over.

"Cuz! Are you okay?"

"I think so," she said, putting her rectangle-shaped glasses back on. "Minus, well, this blood here. And, uh, this blood here. And, all this here."

Just another reason why I loved having Shannon join me on the road—she always shined a light on the brighter side of situations, apparently even after bike crashes. I could tell she was in mild shock, shaking a bit, but in decent spirits. Her frizzy auburn hair seemed even more frizzed. The Malawians women gave her encouragement and righted her bike.

The last time Shannon came to visit me, back in Australia, she and her friend Heather clocked a week of riding without incident. She was an experienced rider, so I took her up on her offer to pull the camera trailer on her bike, freeing up the tandem for just shared rides. After only three kilometers, she got speed wobbles on a steep hill.

That was another thing I appreciated about Shannon. She was the epitome of thoughtfulness and empathy. I usually had to dig a bit and muster up a conscious effort to have a giving mentality. For Shannon, benevolence came naturally.

When I was planning Peace Pedalers with Garryck, I extended an invitation to family and friends to join us for a segment or two. Only a handful took me up on the offer. Shannon and my mother were the only ones who showed up multiple times. Her timing couldn't have been better, arriving in Africa as I was starting to feel a bit burnt out and lonely. I was craving more female energy and fantasized about having a girlfriend join me for the rest of Africa. Or more. I even put a profile up on an online dating site to see if I might get a few nibbles. Not exactly the easiest first date, I knew.

We got Shannon patched up and back riding through the hillside villages with their dirt brick homes and streams of kids who would run alongside us screaming *"Mzungu! Mzungu!!"* "White person! White person!" "I'm not white, I'm bronze," I'd yell back. Giant clouds kept the temperatures down and produced rainbows that seemed to stretch the entire width of the country.

As enlightening and enjoyable as the scenery was, the 24-year-old man three feet behind me, aptly named Gift, shared his thoughts on Malawi's emergence as a stable, inviting and scenic nation that had made the transition from colonial rule to independence better than many of its neighbors. He talked at length about corruption in Malawi, humanity, and "working together" as one giant global neighborhood. He dubbed himself a "Christian Rasta man."

Shannon and I had met Gift in front of our budget hotel one morning as he was trying to sell his handmade bracelets to tourists. He was a soft-spoken young man with stained eyes and a fluffy Afro. We liked how he repeatedly said, "For sure. Definitely."

It was getting late and we did not want to send Gift home in the dark, so Shannon and I invited him to stay for dinner. We then bought him a single room at a local guesthouse for about three bucks. As always, we had the local do the negotiating, cutting the total bill in half. The savings more than made up for having to rent more rooms.

In spite of Shannon's accident she was full of energy that night as we strolled the town in search of the best street food.

"I just love this!" she said, her body bandaged and bruised. "I can see why you choose to do this for a living."

We settled on some roasted corn, delicious sweet potatoes, and a few mystery meats dished up from roadside food stalls. Most vendors wanted to share samples, which was rare in my experience in Africa. We asked Gift before making each purchase. "For sure. Definitely." While we were eating, Gift shared an idea.

"Hey guys, I have many friends in the towns we are going to be heading through. I would love to stay with you for another day," he said. "I want to show you many things."

"For sure. Definitely," laughed Shannon.

"Yeah, Gift," I said. "We would love for you to keep riding."

"Great."

"I just want to be 100% clear that we don't need a tour guide. Same deal. We'll pay for your food and lodging as our special guest. Maybe buy some bracelets, since you're missing work. Sound good?" I asked, looking him in the eyes and awaiting confirmation he understood the offer.

"For sure...definitely. All I need is food and a place to sleep. And if you buy some bracelets, I would be most grateful. For sure."

I had learned it was better to be extra clear in these situations, to set expectations early in the process. If not, things sometimes got uncomfortable at the end of ride, with riders claiming they were working as my tour guide.

We were up at the crack of dawn, excited about our day-long ride along Lake Malawi. After fueling up on the local ground corn porridge *Nsima* and washing it down with delicious local coffee, we were soon pedaling in a gentle mist of cool rain, with multiple rainbows topping our vistas. The roads continued to be smooth, lightly undulating, and void of major traffic. Just right.

The villages nearest the lake were set in marshy conditions. I knew malaria was a significant problem here, and I was eager to have Shannon and Gift help me distribute medication to the less traveled locations. After a couple hours of cycling, we stopped in a pleasant village, where several leaders emerged from their huts to tell us about their community. Malaria had been extra destructive here of late, claiming the lives of several residents. The village was far from any medical clinics, and lacked regular transportation to reach them. We gave them a healthy supply of Coartem and wished them well. Shannon and Gift were hooked. They wanted to reach more villages and help save more lives.

"Hey, Gift," she said, pulling up alongside us on her bike. "Is there a way we can camp on the lakeshore with a local family?"

"Great idea, Cuz. Gift, do you think we'll be able to find a place to stay?"

"From his name of Emperor Haile Selassie I, we are going to find a place tonight," Gift bellowed with confidence.

Shannon and I were fascinated with Gift's unique comments and character traits. We fueled off them. Every moment was an adventure with Gift. He and I managed to talk to the chief of the next village and gain permission to stay overnight. Gift *was* a gift to our journey.

That evening we played a hotly contested game of soccer with local kids, followed by a cold plunge in the lake. The children stuck around to help us set up our tent, each taking a role. One boy cleared the ground, another clipped the poles together.

I had an extra sleeping bag and yoga mat for Gift, who chose to set up his camp inside the house near our bike and gear. He promised to keep watch and make sure nobody peeked into any of the Ortlieb panniers. I was grateful my trust had returned. *It's tiring to always be on guard.* Gift helped restore that faith.

We spent an unforgettable evening under stars that seemed to have grown exponentially in brightness and number, sitting by a campfire, eating barbequed meats and corn, chatting with fishermen, and learning the region's version of the Tonga language. *The necessary ingredients for a good time are always the same.* We hit the tent early hoping for a good night's sleep.

No dogs, I said to myself. Please no dogs. Dogs seemed to have a vendetta against gringos camping on their land. All clear, and we dozed off, only to be woken by a few drunken fishermen who had just come in from their midnight run. After an hour, I couldn't take it anymore and walked over to the revelers in my underwear. I don't know if it was the shock of seeing a half-naked, all-white man or the strength of the alcohol, but the men scurried to another location.

The next morning the chief invited us to his house for breakfast, then gave me a tour of one of the local charity projects.

"You see here, Jamie," he said, pointing to a crumbling cement building. "A church came here, and they built this orphanage saying they wanted to help us. But then they just left."

"And what happened?" I asked.

"Once they had their name on the building and they took all their photos, they were gone. But there were no screens on the windows, no plans to maintain the building. Just this."

"Is this common in Malawi?"

"Oh, yes. Everyone wants to say they are helping Malawi. But if you give us a building with no screens, and our children get malaria, well..."

I told the chief we had a long ride ahead and I did not have time to stay in the village. "But how about we continue the conversation on the bike?" After a little coaxing he agreed to come out for a morning ride. He looked half his 62 years, decked out in Assos cycling clothes, gloves, and helmet. I knew he could more than handle the pedaling. I gave him plenty of malaria medicine for the kids before we left.

Gift took a minibus 30 kilometers to the next town while the chief and I began our ride together. He shared his life story with me, but was eager to focus our conversation on the dilemma of his orphanage project. He had about 45 orphans of parents who had died of AIDS, malaria, hepatitis, meningitis, and other causes. During the peak farming seasons, he had enough food to feed the kids, but there were a few transition months where food was hard to find. He vowed to stay in touch so I could perhaps help with more sustainable strategies for the orphanage. I gave him my email address, but never heard from him again.

Finally we rolled into Chinteche, the end of the line for our Malawi adventures. Shannon had used up all her vacation time, and I was off to Zanzibar and Tanzania. Chinteche is well known for its "Lake of Stars" music festival. Many musicians lived nearby. So as a sendoff, we decided to make our own mini music festival and conduct some recording sessions with the locals. They were excited to show us their stuff. The jam/film/dance party lasted from 2 p.m. until well into the night.

The time had also come for us to say goodbye to Gift. We gathered for a farewell meal before we put him on a bus back home.

"Hey, Gift, may I buy some bracelets from you?" Shannon offered. "I'd like to bring some back as gifts. Gifts from Gift!"

"For sure. Definitely," he said, pulling out the bracelets from his bag. I handed him some money.

"This should be more than enough for the bus and a celebration meal back in Nkhota Kota," I said. "Promise you won't forget about us."

"Thank you," he said, counting the money.

"Thank you."

"I would like you to give me 60 dollars more for all my time and effort helping you to arrive here."

I saw Shannon's cheery disposition evaporate.

"Oh, Gift. Really?" she said. "We thought you were our friend. Not a tour guide."

"I am your friend," he said, continuing his businesslike tone.

"Gift, I was very clear from day one that we did not need a tour guide," I said. "You were invited as our guest."

"But I helped you in many ways. So I feel you should pay me for that."

"Gift, friends help each other," I said. "You helped us, and we helped you. I've paid for everything these past few days."

"This request makes me feel like the only reason you hung out with us was to ask for money in the end," said Shannon.

She got up to leave.

"Listen, we'll buy some bracelets as we promised," I said. "Then we will part ways."

"What can you offer?" he said. "Maybe $40?"

"We'll buy all your bracelets. Then that's the end of it, Gift."

We parted ways with a quick, insincere hug, my worst embrace in Africa. Shannon and I felt sad and violated, like a trust was broken. I told her this was the first time a ride had ever played out like this. *I told him!* I could tell Gift was disappointed as well, the way he shuffled onto the bus and didn't leave us with one of his trademark Gift-isms. "The Right and Honorable Gift shall now depart for foreign lands!" I'm sure he was counting on going home with more money in his pocket.

Several weeks later, I received an email from America. It was from one of my newsletter subscribers, a woman named Bishara.

Dear Jamie and Shannon,

I read your newsletter on your trip to Malawi. I felt your frustration and disappointment when you parted ways with Gift. What you experienced is a challenge for many of us. I was born in Nairobi and moved to England when I met my husband ten years ago. Every time I come to visit, my family asks me for money. They see me as rich because I live in England, not knowing how hard our life is and the stress we live with to get by.

What you should understand is that it is a cultural difference you are being faced with. It's part of our African culture and customs for rich friends and family to help those less fortunate. Whether it is between family members in the village or a friendship like you have with Gift—the expectation is to give to the poor if you are rich.

I encourage you to practice the compassion and tolerance you write about on your website and take this information to heart as you continue your journey. Gift did what came naturally to him—he asked his more fortunate family to share their wealth with him. He felt no guilt about it because, for him, that's the way it should be. It happens to me every time I go home to visit my family, and it's a fact that many Africans who live abroad have to deal with. We all also have to practice compassion and tolerance when it comes to cultural differences as obvious as these.
Safe journeys,
Bishara

I read the note several times, nodding my head in agreement more and more. From a half a world away, she'd been able to recast my encounters in a whole new light. Thank you, I replied. Thank you, thank you, *zikomo*. My future connections with locals would never be the same.

For sure. Definitely.

Enjoy a mini movie of the adventures in Malawi
at www.bb42b.com/malawi

Gift helped Shannon stay in good sprits after her wicked fall

We saw at least a rainbow a day in Malawi

Gift's big energy and bright spirit was a blessing on our trip

Our lakeside homestay Gift helped us arrange

My first village chief guest rider

One of the many musical acts that came to jam and dance with us

30

NAIROBI, KENYA

---▶

I FELT THE passion leave my body as soon as Shannon departed. I was getting used to these feelings every time a family member or quality rider took off. It didn't make them any easier, and I knew the only thing that could pick me up was another positive-energy person to take their place. This time, the letdown would be short. Mamacita had decided to join me in Kenya.

Just like Shannon, she had limited time. I wanted to show her some of the prettier parts of the country, so we decided to avoid Nairobi and head out to Nakuru Lake via bus. On the way, we used headphone splitters and watched *The Secret* on my iPod.

"So, Mamacita, let's put it to the test," I said after the movie ended. "What do you want to attract on our adventure to Kenya and Uganda? What kind of experiences and people do you desire?"

"Mmmmm, let's see." She thought about it for a while. "I'd like us to ride with an older Kenyan person, someone closer to my age. I'd like to tour with a female Kenyan rider and make a girlfriend or two. And I'd like to stay with a local family…one that has plenty of babies so I can hold them!"

"The baby-holding gene! You sure passed that one to me."

I looked out the window at the crush of cars, trucks, and buses hurtling down the roads. *She's 66, but she's never done this before.* A recent uptick in the Kenyan economy added more cars to the roads, more people to the country.

We arrived in Nakuru in the late afternoon and were instantly mobbed at the bus station. "Guide!" "Taxi!" "Meester, meester!" The facility seemed even shadier than most bus stations anywhere on the trip. Too many aggressive and shifty characters milled around us even after our chorus of

"No"s and "No, thank you"s. I went to work assembling the bikes, and the hustlers turned their attention to Mom. "*Usinishike!*" she finally said. Don't touch me. *Wow. Impressive.*

With our options limited, we recruited a glue-addicted guest rider to show us out of the station while his buddy ran besides my mom on her single bike. She was used to riding on my tandem during past trips. I wasn't sure how she'd do on a single bike with racks and panniers, but when I looked back I saw she was smiling ear-to-ear. "Yeee haaawww," she screamed.

We were excited to make our way through the high-altitude tea country towards Kericho. I found a guest rider, and Mom pedaled out in front. *So far so good.* I hoped I would be this passionate about life when I was her age.

"Remember, Mom, we ride on the left side of the street in Kenya," I said.

"I know, Honey! You told me already."

"Just being doubly safe."

"This is great!" she said, breezing ahead.

I knew she didn't see it.

"Mom!!! Bus! Bus! Bus!"

Beep! Beep! Beep! Beeeeeeeeeeep!

Nooooooo! At the intersection, she looked left instead of right, then pedaled on at full speed, happy and oblivious to the speeding bus. The driver saw her at the last possible second, swerved so hard the tires seemed to moan, and missed killing my mom by six inches. This was the closest near-fatal accident I'd seen in all my years riding—and it involved my 66-year-old mother.

"Mom, stop and pull over. Please."

"Oh my. Oh my. I'm sorry. I did not see that bus coming."

"You need to look right first and be extra careful, Mom. That was way too close!"

"Okay, I will. Don't worry."

But she wasn't—and I did. I saw her swerve back and forth on a dirt track beside a busy road. We'd reached a gentle incline, and she started to fall back. I could tell she was winded and ready to cry. *You've overestimated her abilities.* "You're doing just fine. We'll take it slow and stop whenever you want."

Finally we hit the turnoff to Kericho and were assured the roads would be far less crowded. The traffic eased, but the inclines increased.

What I failed to realize was that we were at 6,000 feet. The altitude, her age and condition, combined with the effects of her heart medication, made it difficult for her to handle any sort of uphill riding; she became winded in seconds. I grabbed as much gear as possible from her bike and strapped it on the tandem. That helped a bit, but still she struggled.

We were averaging about five kph, and the beautiful sights around Lake Nakuru below were impossible for her to enjoy. When we reached the crossroads to Elburgon, we made a decision to put Mom on a bus to our evening destination, which allowed me to ride the remaining 30 kilometers solo. I pedaled onwards with a mix of relief and fear. *She'll be okay.*

I decided to catch a catnap at a local park and try to calm down. When I woke, a curious man was inspecting the tandem. After exchanging a few bits of broken English, I invited him to come with me to Elburgon, offering the typical meals and a bus trip back. He accepted without hesitation, and I handed him cycling duds and helmet. The tight-fitting clothing always provided ample fodder for laughing villagers.

Just outside town, I noticed a minivan with a bike strapped to the roof. Joseph and I pedaled hard to catch up. Mom! When the van made one of its multiple stops, we slapped the window and waved. There she was, still in her bicycle helmet, holding a baby on her lap, surrounded by fifteen locals. She'd mastered the art of authentic Kenyan transport in a *matatu* bus.

Our ride started out bucolic and blissful, with rolling hills and baobab trees lining the streets. Joseph had hammered the pedals hard from the get-go, so we were making good time. "But hills ahead, Jamie." Age 24, he hailed from a family of ten brothers and sisters.

"So what is your dream?" I asked. "What do you want to do with your life?"

"I want to be an electrical engineer."

"Ah, good for you. So are you in school?"

"No. I finished only two years of high school and I had to stop to help my father. He lost his job and was unable to pay my school fees."

"How much are your school fees?"

"About 30,000 shillings a year."

Hmmm. That's about $350.

"So if you had 60,000 shillings you could graduate from high school?"

"Yes."

"Do you want to graduate from high school?"

"Yes, very much."

In Africa, and in most of the developing world, the distance between opportunity and discouragement was razor thin. I'd seen $10 change a life. Pocket money can improve the fortunes of a family forever. I thought back to the promise I made with my father to go on my high school trip to Europe.

"If I pay your school fees will you promise to get perfect grades?" I said.

"Yes, yes," he said.

"Okay, we'll talk about it at the hotel with my mom. We'll sponsor you to finish high school."

"That would be…very great."

The hills he promised did indeed arrive, as steep as I'd ridden since Lesotho, with grades reaching up to 16%. By the time we made it to the top of the last hill we were both cramping. The dozens of school kids who cheered and chased us had no idea of the pain we were in. I struggled to engage with them.

The hills he promised did indeed arrive, as steep as I'd ridden since Lesotho, with grades reaching up to 16%. By the time we made it to the top of the last hill we were both cramping. The dozens of school kids who cheered and chased us had no idea of the pain we were in but their giggles and cheers eased the pain and kept us moving.

As we rolled into the Hotel Eel in Elburgon, Mamacita was waiting outside with a few members of the staff, eager to greet us. It was nice having her around for many reasons—the cheerleading and encouragement, the deeper conversations, and a shoulder upon which to cry or lean. This trip felt different. I was more stressed than I'd ever been. I think it was mostly because of the conditions, with her on her own bike in such hectic and at dangerous conditions. I had my mom's life in my hands. I knew my brothers Gino and Nick would never forgive me if anything happend to her. I also took far too much responsiblity for her happiness and contentment on our journey together. This was some heavy excess baggage to lug around Kenya on top of her loaded panniers I decided to strap onto my trailer to lighter her load.

After our body temperatures and heart rates returned to normal we relaxed in the shade and finalized the Joseph's scholarship agreement. Mom and I would send $100 to Joseph's school headmaster for the first term and pay $100 per term, assuming his headmaster faxed us a copy of his perfect marks. *Was that asking too much?* Joseph was ecstatic, and both Mom and I felt optimistic about helping him continue his education. "Write us when you become president of a big engineering firm, Joseph," Mamacita said.

The town rested 7,000 feet above sea level, making it impossible for my mom to ride the next day. "Don't you worry," she said. "I'll take a bus and meet you in Kericho." There were no buses, but we found a large cargo truck and a driver willing to give her a ride. I hopped in for the first part of the journey to make sure everything was fine. "No problem," said the driver. He'd drop her off at the Kericho Tea Hotel and I would ride the 60 kilometers alone.

They let me off in a field with a half-dozen cows too busy chomping greenery to notice a stranger in their midst. I decided to get the cameras out and film the process of finding a rider in the middle of nowhere. As I'd experienced in most places in Africa, visitors couldn't go long without some local company. It was disconcerting at first, to have people gather. But quickly I came to depend on it, a friendly blend of curiosity and hospitality. If a stranger in California asked me what I was doing, I'd probably tell him to buzz off. Here I started conversations. Within minutes, despite being far from a town or village, I was surrounded by a small group of locals.

"Gentlemen!" I said, pointing to the bike. "This seat is available to any of you!"

I scanned the crowd to see if anyone changed his expression. An older man with graying hair and silver mustache raised his eyebrows. *Aha!*

"Hello, what is your name, sir?"

"My name is Richard."

"So Richard, you and I are heading to Kericho, yeah?" I asked.

"Okay, I will go," he said without pause.

He just needed to tell his 22-year-old son his plans.

"You will take good care of him, yes?" the son said, looking at his father all dressed up in cycling clothing.

"I will," I said. "Here, take down my number and I'll text you our progress."

"My father is 59 years old. And there are a lot of steep hills up ahead."

"He looks like he's in good shape. He'll do great. I promise."

Within the hour, I began to question that promise. "Steep" turned out

to be an understatement of epic proportions. And not only was the mountain precipitous, it was long, and it was full of trucks and buses spewing
rich, dark-black diesel smoke in our faces, enough to turn Richard's mustache dark. Luckily, a light rain appeared, preventing us from overheating
and helping to clean the air. I wanted to learn more about Richard's life,
but the severity of the climb kept our conversation to grunts and exhales.
Like most riders on the continent, he didn't complain. *Are Africans just
more polite? Or do they have a different threshold for gripes? The better question is "Why are we so quick to complain?" Only one bar of service! Arggh, this
traffic!* Richard fueled the pedals with everything he could muster that
morning. He was strong and fit from a lifetime of walking. The curtain of
gray parted, and the blue sky appeared front and center stage.

"You're a badass, Richard," I said after we reached the summit and
began to cruise down into a valley filled with green tea fields. "Sorry...it's
a compliment. What I mean is, are you still working?"

"No. I am a retired postal worker. With five children and nine
grandchildren."

"You must be proud."

"Yes."

We picked up speed.

"This ride was hard...but very nice," he said. "Like life."

"I agree. These rides are a lot like life. Challenging and rewarding.
You never know what you're going to experience. Even when you plan
every detail, there are always surprises."

"And now no more big hills. It will be *very* nice."

"This is the payoff time. Enjoy."

"You know *rafiki*, right?"

"Friend."

"Thank you, *rafiki*."

As we gathered speed, I heard a *clank* from behind. *Richard!* I turned
to see a video camera bounce, bounce, bounce, and then skid across the
asphalt. Dismounting the bike, we both said a little prayer. Not only did
the camera work fine, the wide-angle lens suffered nary a scratch. We
took our time the rest of the ride, stopping for Richard to point out the
different types of tea plants—black teas and green, orange pekoe and
white *matcha*, grown on small farms and harvested by hand.

We arrived at the Tea Hotel more than ready for a cup ourselves.

Mamacita sat in the lobby chatting with a few local women. *Of course.* We joined her and immediately she and Richard began to talk about the day's adventure as well as years past. She was good at that, finding the connections between strangers, then exploring the commonalities that bind. She told Richard she was proud of me.

After many shared experiences and cups of tea, Richard needed to catch his bus home. He hugged my mom, then paused before saying goodbye. Something wasn't right. "Are you okay, Richard?" I asked.

Suddenly his English escaped him. He looked to the ground then back up at us. I could see the tears gather at the bottom of his eyes. I put my arm around his shoulder and led him outside to a bench under a tree. I pulled out my video camera and asked him to share his feelings with the people of Africa. With the people around the world.

"I am so happy to meet my friend from America," he said in his native Kiswahili. "I didn't know we could meet. We simply met by coincidence. Thank you very much. It's God who created all of us. I am Black. And our difference is only in the skin. In the same way God created flowers of different colors, it is the way he created us. I will be telling everyone about my friend, and even to the whole of Africa. If we build these friendships even further, God will be happy and he will bring us all things. And there will be no wars or any conflicts, if we love one another."

The time with Richard convinced me to be a little more accepting of my mom. *Why is it that we grumble the loudest when they're doing things for us?* "I wanted pancakes, not French toast!" "You're supposed to pick me up at 3:00 p.m., not 3:30 p.m." Here she was, in Africa, supporting me and my passion, and I was getting bent out of shape because she craved attention from everyone. I kissed her goodnight and told her I loved her.

And after a day of rest, Mom was ready to tour again, especially now that we were at a lower altitude.

"I stopped taking my heart medication," she said after an hour of riding.

"What? Isn't that dangerous?"

"It was slowing my heart rate and zapping me of strength."

"I don't know, Mom..."

"How am I doing today?"

"Great."

"Voilà."

"Still, I..."

"You let me worry about my health. You focus on the ride."

As we made a descent, we noticed a group of young women in their school uniforms. Students, especially schoolgirls, were a tough group to recruit for rides. They had classes or homework or chores and couldn't spare a couple hours to ride. My mom was undeterred. Decked in her Spandex, she strode over to a teenager named Coreen.

"So, Coreen, we've had an 18-year-old boy and a 59-year-old man ride, but no Kenyan woman yet!" she said. "Please help me prove to my son that Kenyan women are just as capable as the men."

She looked at the bike, then at my mother's whiter-than-white legs.

"Okay, I'll go," she said.

On the downhill slope towards Kisumu, Coreen confided how she was studying to become a teacher of disabled children, while volunteering part time. She was a sweet yet shy young woman, soft spoken yet confident. And a natural cyclist. My mom gave her encouragement during lunch. They talked about God.

When Coreen headed home, Mom and I started to talk about lodging options for the night. I didn't want to push her too hard, especially knowing she was off her medication. The road's descent had leveled out, and a rain was settling in. I noticed a couple of local riders sharing a bike. He worked the pedals, while she sat on the seat sideways, a common riding style for women throughout Africa. *This should be the easiest sell of the trip.* Joseph and his wife, Beeni, were recently married and more than happy to join the festivities. Beeni transferred over to the tandem, and Joseph rode next to us on his rickety one-speed.

"Where are you going?" asked Beeni.

"We don't know," I said.

"What do you mean, you don't know? You must know."

"We're in search of a good place to pitch a tent," I said.

"Not the hotels?"

"Nope."

"You can stay at our house."

"Great! Hey, Mamacita! We've been invited to stay with Beeni and Joseph," I yelled.

"Oh, goodie! That's just what we wanted to do tonight."

Who says "goodie" anymore?

"Have you ever had a white person stay at your house?"

"No."

"I will try hard not to embarrass my race."

She hesitated, then laughed.

Beenie led us down a mysterious dirt road zigzagging through overgrown bushes. Within minutes the hard dirt turned to a mud so sticky it grabbed our wheels as if daring us to ride farther. We stopped every few minutes to kick away the sludge. When the mud became too deep to overcome, we hopped off and pushed. *I cursed myself with every step. You had to volunteer to carry every piece of Mamacita's gear, didn't you?* Whenever the pushing became too much to bear, it seemed like a local would emerge from the foliage to help us make our way; "the angels" Mom called them. They helped us through dozens of maize fields, over numerous rivers, some with rickety bridges and others without, and through languid villages in the Awasi region outside Kisumu.

Nearly an hour later, we arrived spent, dirty, and stinky. Joseph and Beeni's abode stood before us, a simple mud hut with a tin roof, no toilet, no shower, and no electricity. And perfect. That's because it had babies. They were all my mom needed that afternoon. As soon as she had a baby in her arms, she forgot about the day's labors. Joseph heated water on the fire, and we both got hot bucket showers in a stand-up shower stall. The experience felt like a luxurious mineral bath at the Four Seasons. Including the slippers.

We then settled into a beautiful evening doing, well, very little. We sat under clouded skies while conversing with their family and friends. Joseph and Beenie cooked an enormous meal of beans, potatoes, and cassava, all grown on their land. Dinner was served by a single candlelight, and the kids all ate on the floor while Mom and I were afforded a table, chairs, and even some silverware.

With no power in the village, silence reigned after dark. I could barely make out the pitters and patters of a light rain on their tin roof. Mom and I both felt at peace and at ease, as comfortable as if we were attending our own family potluck. We were grateful for the opportunity to experience a slice of real Kenyan living, to befriend people who were strangers just a few hours before.

In the morning, they had more cassava and tea ready. Beeni produced a loaf of bread she'd hidden, a purchase from the market the day before. Over breakfast we double-teamed Joseph, beseeching him and Beeni to join us for some more riding. They both had a big to-do list, and thanked us for the offer. But I could tell they enjoyed the riding, so we invited them again. "Okay," said Joseph. "We will ride with you to Kisumu." A neighbor agreed to watch their children for the day, and off we set.

The road to Kisumu was surprisingly busy and pothole ridden. I'd cycled in thirty countries to date, on surfaces that could be considered roads in only the most generous definition of the word. There was dangerous, then there was road-to-Kisumu dangerous. I regretted the decision to invite Joseph and Beeni immediately. The roads had no shoulder on which to ride, forcing us to go toe-to-toe with the buses or risk our luck on the adjacent dirt paths, which had steep drop-offs, more broken glass than a century's worth of Jewish weddings, and enough garbage to overflow a landfill. The ride was only 50 kilometers, but it felt like 500. *Please God, Allah, James Brown, Bill Gates, let us arrive alive.*

By the time we cruised in to Kisumu, my mom and I were nervous wrecks. The relaxation from the night before had disappeared after the first bus horn, not to mention the 994th. Add to this a record three crashes by a now bruised and bloodied Mamacita, and you can imagine how relieved we were to roll into the Imperial Hotel that afternoon. Joseph and Beenie didn't seem as fazed. We sent Beeni back early. She wanted to be with the kids. Joseph and I spent a few hours on a business plan for a community center in his village. We'd hashed it out while on the bike. He had hit a roadblock getting the project off the ground, and wanted some help in creating a proper budget and action plan. I flooded him with a business plan, sample proposals, and supporting information to kick-start the center.

I could tell the ride had taken its toll on mom. She hadn't uttered a word of complaint, but I knew she needed a little TLC. The only problem was money. I had precious little, certainly not enough to treat her to a nice hotel for a few days of recuperation. "Hang tight, Mom," I told her. "I'll be back in a bit." I then went to every upscale hotel in Kisumu to explain my situation and ask for a free stay for my mom. The best one in town said yes, and I cycled back to Mamacita to give her the good news. She checked in and slept for nineteen hours straight, then had a few soaks in the tub, a massage, a string of gourmet meals, and she was good as new.

At a candlelight dinner, I looked across the table at her. Whenever we got together on the road, magic unfolded before our eyes. If she willed something to happen, it happened. I couldn't put a finger on it, but I knew that we both shared a genuine intention to be of service to our fellow man each day. We also had a lot of love circulating, love for each other and love for everyone we met. I yearned to learn how to create that same magic when she wasn't around.

 Enjoy a mini movie of Mamacita and Jamie's adventures in Kenya at www.bb42b.com/kenya

Dead tired, cramping and delirious but still still giggling

Richard was proud and grateful. And one strong 59 year old!

Mom ready for action. I still strapped her panniers on my trailer.

Holding babies is Mamacita's favorite activity anywhere

We awoke feeling part of Joseph and Beenie's family

31

KAMPALA, UGANDA

I WANDERED THE congested, dusty streets of Kampala in a dazed and numb state. This was my first day alone in almost two months. Sharing the mission with friends and family was always a balance, usually following the same script. Excitement at the airport, curiosity during the first few days, a touch of crankiness at the end of the week, "Can we skip the village and stay at a hotel?" quirks growing to annoyances, quiet nights before they left, then a void. All the little things that bothered me—slow paces, big bags, snoring—would fly home on the plane with my visitor, and I would be left alone. I wanted to reach into the sky, pull the plane back to the airport, and tell them how much I appreciated their companionship, how much it meant to me that they would journey to some far-flung corner to share a few laughs and support my zany calling.

This time I felt extra lonely, partially because of the departures of Shannon and Mom, more so because of a deep urging I'd ignored and shuttled aside for months. Love. I wanted to love, and be loved. Not a road girlfriend or a quick fling. Love. Lasting love. This trip was about connection. I wanted the ultimate connection. The more I thought about it, the more I craved it. And the more I became depressed knowing I would likely never find it as long as I was on the road. With Europe and South America still to come, I played out endless Hail Mary scenarios. *Maybe I could write to a seasoned cyclist or go to a race in foreign country and convince the winner to drop her schedule and come on the road with me!* The road can lead to the occasional deep thought…and some damn ridiculous ones.

I decided to visit an Internet café for a taste of home. In my email inbox sat a message from an online dating service. The sender box read: Jeannie.

In Malawi, while waiting in a hostel lobby for Shannon to join me,

I chatted with the owners, a lovely couple who had met out traveling. They joined forces for a two-year, round-the-world journey, finally settling down to raise a family while running a backpackers' lodge near Lake Malawi. I marveled at how they worked side by side, finishing each other's sentences, seamlessly shifting between hostel logistics to traveler questions to family issues. They took time to hug and touch each other, even during the busiest times of the day. Ten years they'd been married. *I want some of that.*

Andy and Carrie were happy to oblige when I offered to buy them a beer so that I could pick their brains on the topic of love and travel. We sat at a table under a beautifully flowering tree one evening. Carrie was the first to speak. She was from Australia, wore loose-fitting, natural fabrics and sported a bushy, eclectic (aka uncombed) hairdo.

"I can only tell you that I wasn't willing to settle for anyone who did not prioritize travel," she said.

"So how did you finally find Andy?" I asked.

"I was out on a good ole Aussie walkabout for a few years and knew it was going to be a way of life for me. I had a lot of travel romances along my journey, but nobody who I felt was going to put travel first for the rest of their lives. Until I met Andy."

Andy came across as more polished, and perhaps a little more reserved. He was the businessman behind the hostel, while Carrie was the warm personality and free spirit who kept guests staying much longer than they planned. Clean shaven, he wore a quick-dry shirt and khaki pants, and spoke with a formal British accent.

"You see that camper van over there?" Andy said, pointing to a dusty van with bushes growing into the windows.

"Is that yours?" I asked.

"That was my adventure vehicle. It was small, simple, and allowed me to travel for more than four years while working odd jobs here and there to find gas money. Twenty-six countries, if you can believe it."

"If the van's a rockin', don't come a knockin'," I joked.

"Yes!" said Carrie. Andy blushed.

"Like Carrie, I had my fair share of travel romances. And, like Carrie, I was not willing to settle for someone who did not prioritize travel. She started traveling with me for a short stint… and just never left. We Carrie'd on, so to speak, for another 37 countries until we finally landed right here."

I wanted to clap. I wanted to cry. I wanted to grab a backpacker and start making love in the back of that camper van. I'd never been so envious in my life, more so each time they leaned into each other. They'd carved out a life where they work for eight months, then explore for the other four. "That's my dream."

The next morning, I composed an online dating profile. I called it "casting a big net and letting the right fish come." *Did you just compare your future love to a fish?* Yes, I knew it was crazy and improbable, with a whiff of desperation to boot. I didn't care. Andy and Carrie convinced me I had to at least put the "available" light on. I did it, then forgot about it. Until now.

Dear Jamie,
I don't want to toot my own horn or anything but I think I just about hit all of the attributes you are looking for in a life partner. And you seem to fit what I'm looking for as well. Just so happens that I'm very likely going to be quitting my job and doing some serious traveling in the very near future. So the big requirement of a gal who is willing and able to do some serious global adventuring may very well be met as well (and I'm sure that's not an easy one to find). So let's get to know each other and share the next chapters of our lives and see where it takes us.
Jeannie

Son of a… That's too good to be true. There has to be a catch. There's always a catch, right? I had put in my profile that I didn't want to consider a relationship unless they were ready and willing to join me on a tough cycling expedition in Europe and Latin America if sparks were flying. There I sat, staring at the computer screen in Uganda, wondering if maybe, just maybe, a butterfly might have fluttered her way. *Note: butterfly comparisons are better than fish comparisons.* Ignoring all advice and common sense that I should keep things brief at first, I sent Jeannie a long reply with far too many road updates, personal likes, relationship histories, and just about anything other than my grade school report cards.

I exited the Internet café perked up. *Remember, butterflies instead of fish.* I saw my bike and my mood sunk. Jeannie may be my virtual partner; the bike was my actual partner. I was alone. I hoped getting out of the smoggy capital to the scenic and hilly area of Kasese would help. From there I planned to ride south to Rwanda along the Congo border. But when I tried to settle into the tour I found myself uninspired, grouchy, and just downright sad. Had I felt that low during the 30-country trip to date? I didn't think so.

I should have learned my lesson. Never ride when you're feeling horrible. Bad feelings prompt bad experiences. But with no therapist couches within reach, I set the bike down in a field and started a conversation with a herd of stately black Ugandan cows. "What do you think my problem is? Loneliness? Lack of appreciation?" A group of children saw me talking to the creatures and came over to see if I was crazy. They inspected the tandem and quickly convinced me to give them rides.

I bid adieu to the kids and cows and hit the road for a couple kilometers before a motorcycle began following me. For some reason it didn't pass. Worse, the rider started honking his horn over and over. *Jerk! Just go around.* I signaled for him to move on. Finally, the driver gunned the engine, passed me, then pulled over so that I would stop. *What do you want from me?!* I could see two men on the cheap bike. *Is this some sort of L.A. road rage?* The passenger jumped off and walked toward me.

"Sir. Sir. I believe this is your camera?" he said.

"Oh my God!" I said, stunned. "Thank you...thank you so much."

"You left it back with the kids, and they told me I must take it to you. So here it is."

"I can't believe I...May I get a photo of you so I can remember this moment?"

"That might do it," I thought as I pedaled away. "That just might just do the trick in getting me out of this funk from hell." The red dirt roads were smooth, the verdant hills covered with thick palm groves. Some parts of the planet just seemed happier than others. This was one. I breezed along...until my chain stuck. I pried it out only to discover several broken teeth on the chain ring. I banged my head trying to fix it. I then had a tire blowout. Then another. And another. *Arggggh!* It was late, and I was far from any lodging, farther still from any semblance of patience.

"Hello, dear friend. Are you in need of assistance?" asked a man, as I repaired my tire for the umpteenth time.

"My bike needs some love, but it's getting dark. I need time and light."

"Please, sir. You can come to my house. There you can fix your bike."

"I don't know what to say. Thank you. Thank you very much."

"And you must eat. You need to eat."

I'd passed thatch roof huts all day, and expected the same as we walked to Pathius's home. Instead he led me to a modern, two-bedroom abode that looked straight from a blue-collar neighborhood in Los Angeles. It had electricity and a garage to fix my bike, the first garage I'd seen in weeks.

"You must take time to rest," said Pathius, a father of six, grandfather of eighteen, and an instant paternal figure to me. He cut up fruit while I went to work on my bike. When the sun went down, he held a spotlight as I finished the repairs. We ate pasta, and later in the evening he took me on a tour of his village. He had a leisurely gait and deep voice.

"Is this stay meeting your expectations?" he asked as we walked back to his house.

"Of course. You're a godsend. Why would you ask?"

"I've never had a white man stay at my house. Ugandans are afraid to host whites because they don't want to disappoint."

"Well this white man gives you and your house a five-star review," I said, patting him on the back.

I pushed off the next morning, upbeat from Pathius's hospitality. The day felt full of promise. I moved my legs extra fast in an attempt to outrun any bad moods. *They're back there.* Faster, harder. *They're gaining.* I shifted gears. *They're here.* I could feel the despair smother me like a pillow to the face. The numbness started in my chest before consuming my whole body. I had even picked up smoking cigarettes again in the past couple days. *Cigarettes? You kidding me? You don't think you need clean lungs out here?* The roads became rocky and steep. I pulled over to hack.

After what seemed like an eternity of coughing, cramps, and self-castigation, I finally reached a summit and settled in to a long and needed descent. *You ain't going to catch me now.* At the bottom of the large hill, I slowed to snap some photos of a bar-tailed trogon, with its red breast and tuxedo-like feathers. Just as I was coasting to a stop, I felt that my bike was unbalanced. I looked back and nearly retched. I was missing a large rear Ortlieb pannier.

My mind raced to remember what was in the bag. *Hard drives with all my content. Key repair parts. Spare cash. All to take a picture of a bird?* I was irate, at myself and at, well, life. I had no choice but to begin climbing back up the huge hill to try to find the pannier. *I'm going to crack. I feel it coming on. All the footage and interviews, gone.* Anyone who found the bag could pawn the contents for several hundred dollars, a fortune in Uganda. I started the deflating climb back up the hill, blurting expletives with each push. A motorcycle again stopped me in my tracks.

"Here is your bag, sir," said a man with a sonorous voice.

"What the...?! You are my angel! Thank you so much!" I said, running over to give him a hug.

"You must slow down, sir. So your bags do not fall off on the rough roads."

Slow down. Rough roads. Fall off. Slow down. Yes, I must slow down. His words hit me deeper than he could have ever imagined. I was burnt out. Bonked. No nap or conversation or act of kindness would revive me. I needed to get off the bike. *Slow down.*

With the help of a few van rides, I retreated to the Lake Bunyoni Overland Resort near Kabale, a place recommended by several backpackers. Stumbling in, I explained my burnout blues and depression to the owner of the lakeside resort. I didn't need to. He saw in my eyes that I desperately needed to recharge. Before I could continue, he handed me the keys to his best deluxe tent on the property. "For free."

My tent had an expansive deck overlooking the lake and a hammock ideal for sucking the life out of any afternoon. Here was my personal battery recharging station for the coming days. Within minutes, I was asleep.

This guy chased me down to give me back my camera

My host Pathius

32

KABALE-KISORO ROAD, UGANDA

"ARE YOU SURE you…want to…go to Muko today?" asked Innocent.

"Yeah, they have a campground up there, so I'm going to try," I answered.

"It will be raining very soon. I don't think it's safe."

"I don't mind rain."

"Are you positive you must go today?"

The clouds huddled together like a street gang getting ready to attack. By now I could predict the beginning drops to the second, whether they'd come in sideways or straight, if they'd pass in 15 minutes or linger all day. *Hey, if nothing else comes of this trip, I at least have a future as a meteorologist.*

Innocent tilted his head and made eye contact with me. I stared at the gap between his front teeth and decided his smile looked forced. Surrounding him were our cycling teammates for the day, our peloton, a group of playful, shoeless boys riding handmade wooden bicycles. Even they seemed to share the same concern. *When a child questions an idea you know it's a bad one.*

"We can ride in the rain, Innocent. I do it all the time."

He looked at the boys, then back at me.

"Okay, then I will accompany you as long as I can so you are safe."

"That's the spirit, Innocent!" I said, patting him on the back as he began to remount the tandem.

Before he could even strap on his helmet, a massive bolt of lightning stuck no more than a hundred yards from our bike, followed by thunder so loud it stole not only my hearing but also my breath. *Kaaaa-Boooooo*! Within seconds the rain came, blinding sheets of rain. Don't-mess-with-me rain.

"Jamie, it is not safe for you to ride! You must come with me, now!" he yelled over the downpour.

Normally gentle and deferential, he now sounded like a cop with a megaphone.

"Okay, tell me where to go."

"To my house. Down the hill, that way!"

We scampered down the slick road to his home, nearly crashing several times as the rain instantly turned the dirt lane into a mudslide. His father, mother, and brother were all there. Nobody asked any questions. They all went into action, clearing space in their back shed to get the tandem under cover. They served us hot tea and poured me a hot bath in a makeshift tub. I dripped water all over their house, and my gear took up about 80% of their floor space. They carried on, nonplussed. *Out here, you do what needs to be done.*

Warm, dry, calmed, I finally got to meet the entire family, as well as neighbors and friends, over a festive meal of beans, cassava, beef, and potatoes followed by endless cups of warm tea with honey that Innocent's father harvested. After dinner I cornered him.

"I know Innocent has school, but I would love to share a day with him and ride to Kisoro," I said.

"There are many, many hills between here and Kisoro," said Innocent's father.

Innocent heard us talking and shuffled over to join the conversation.

"You know I have never ridden a bike before today," he said.

"I know it's hilly, but it's only 40 kilometers. We can make it. We will stop often and rest."

"Do you think I can make it?" Innocent asked.

"You're a stud, Innocent!"

"I don't understand," said his father.

"He can make it," I said, turning to Innocent. "You can make it."

Innocent and his father began talking in the local Luganda dialect. I had no idea what they were saying, but it seemed Innocent had made up his mind and was going no matter what his father advised. He was small in stature, with muscular arms and sloped shoulders that gave him a look of relaxation. From the few hours we'd spent together, I knew he also had a quiet determination about him.

"I will go," he announced.

"Great! I will take good care of him," I told his parents. "I promise."

The next morning Innocent woke charged up and ready to go early.

We devoured the standard bread-and-tea breakfast, and Innocent's father presented me with an oversized jar of his rich honey, perfect with the organic peanut butter produced and sold in the area.

Virgin riders are a blessing and a curse. I loved introducing them to the wonders of two-wheeling. That first *wheeeee* fueled me for the rest of the day. But usually, when the *wheeee* wore off, I was stuck with a rider who was more deadweight that carry-your-weight. Ninety-nine times out of a hundred I'd spend the rest of the ride doing double duty. Innocent wasn't an outlier. After only an hour he was already cramping and complaining about his legs being exhausted.

I stayed optimistic and knew that we would get there. Eventually. Even if we showed up a couple hours late, barely able to walk. The slow climbs gave us the chance to get to know each other. He seemed mature well beyond his years.

"Here in my village there are many orphans who cannot afford school fees," he said. "There needs to be a school for them."

"You want to start a school for AIDS orphans?"

"Yes, I want to build my own school. So I can teach the children and help them grow up to become important citizens."

"So what's the plan?" I asked.

"I don't know how to do it. I'm not sure."

"I don't know how to build a school either. But I know you can find a way if it's really your dream."

"It is beyond my dream, Jamie. It is me. I think about it every day."

Without warning, I felt a greater push from his pedals. Innocent's legs were getting stronger, as if the discussion of the dream had released an anchor. As we moved closer to Kisoro, we shifted into a hill-tackling machine, working seamlessly together. We sailed through bamboo groves and rain forests and over two major alpine passes. We were the living embodiment of the Postal Service—neither rain, wind, freezing temps, or scorching heat could slow us. We fell a few times on the muddy roads, scratching a knee here, a palm there. None of it mattered.

We plowed ahead, faster, smoother, as coordinated as an Olympic rowing team. On the last climb, a brutal one, a slow-moving truck lingered behind us. I wondered if he knew Innocent or was just curious. When we hit the summit, the truck driver signaled us to stop.

"I have something for you," he said, popping his head out the window.

"Oh yeah? What?" I asked, curiously.

"We found this about 15 kilometers back."

He handed me my tripod.

"This is yours, yes?"

"Whoa! Yes, it's mine! Thanks so much! Can I give you some money?"

He waved me away.

I climbed up the truck cab, ripped the door open, and gave the driver a huge hug. It was all I could do to restrain myself and express how jacked up I was. The ride. Innocent. Now, for the third time in just a few weeks, I'd had a Ugandan man chase me down and hand me critical and expensive gear I'd lost. *I love Uganda!*

We arrived in Kisoro just as the sun turned in for the night. The managers at the Travelers Rest Hotel took one look at us and gave us a posh room for 20 dollars. I sent shivering Innocent into the shower first while I went to work cleaning the bike and all the gear so we could bring it into the room. It was the last thing I wanted to do, but it had to be done. *Like Innocent's family last night. Don't ask, just do.* When I entered the room, I saw that Innocent was still trembling, even after the shower and warm clothes.

"You need to stand here and jump up and down," I said.

When I got out of the shower he was still jumping and still cold. I was cold too.

"Come, let's jump together," he said.

So we both just jumped up and down in the hotel room, trying hard not to laugh—and failing miserably. There was something special about this young man.

The jumping didn't do the trick, but a hot dinner near a warm fire did. We spent the rest of the evening so close to the flames our shoes and clothes would occasionally smolder. A group of Dutch tourists sat near us, and we recounted tales of our crazy adventure together. Innocent was so content and proud that he glowed in delight as he fielded questions from the tourists. With little prompting he even shared his vision of his school and how I planned to help him.

"You two should start the school *together,*" one Dutch traveler told us. "Maybe this is your destiny."

Innocent's aunt lived in Kisoro, and he planned to stay the night with her. It was time for us to part ways. But before I let him go, I wanted to make sure he knew I was serious about helping him realize his dream.

"Innocent, my brother. It has been a grand pleasure," I said, reaching out for a hug.

"My pleasure," he said smiling.

"I'm honored you shared your dream with me today. Do you *really* want to start this school?"

"Yes," he said, turning serious. "I *really* want to. It is not an option not to start it."

"Do you *promise* to follow all the steps I plan to give you?"

"Yes, I promise," he said.

"Remember, the first step is to send me a one-page summary of your dream and a hand-drawn floor plan of the school."

I gave him a handful of bills.

"Here is enough money to pay for several hours at an Internet café. Get an email address and email me this first step," I said.

"Yes. Email address, floor plan. I will do it."

"I don't know what the next step is, but after I receive this I'll give you a next step, then the next, then the next. I want to help you wake up one day and see that your dream has come true."

He started to cry, and I followed suit. We gave each other an extended embrace, and he walked off into the darkness. I hoped our adventures together were far from over. I had just met a man who had a dream, a *real* dream he was passionate about achieving. His passion lit a fire in me as well, a fire to do my best to help him realize it.

I had had dozens of riders share their plans with me on the bike. Some asked for help, with others I volunteered it. With each one I offered the same deal. I gave them a little cash to open an email account and begin a dialogue with me.

I had yet to receive an email from any of them.

 Enjoy a mini movie of the adventures in Uganda at www.bb42b.com/uganda

These kids thought I was crazy riding into the storm

Innocent's entire family came out to see us off and wish us well on his maiden bike ride

33

ZANZIBAR ISLAND, TANZANIA

--►

"IS THIS GUY sleeping while standing up?" I mumbled to myself as I approached the security guard at my oceanfront hotel. His polyester shirt was untucked, his face unshaven, and he had creatively wedged himself between a wicker basket and the doorway in order to stay on his feet. *Gotta give him props. He probably has two or three jobs.* I hated to wake him.

"Excuse me, sorry. Did you move my bike?"

He straightened and opened his eyes as far as they could go. They were yellow and bloodshot and blasé.

"Bike? What bike?" he said.

"What do you mean, what bike? I left my bike locked up right here with the guard last night. He assured me it would be okay."

"It was not here when I started working," he said without expression.

No, noooo. There must be some mistake. I had the bike locked up with an alarm lock. Right here! In front of your face. It can't be gone.

I scurried around every corner of the hotel looking for it. *Nada.* I ran over to the hotel manager's office and burst in without knocking.

"Jonan, I left my bike locked up next to the guard last night and now it's gone," I declared.

"You left it outside? I told you to put it inside," he said, shaking his head and taking a deep breath.

"I figured with the guard there and the alarm lock it would be fine."

"You figured wrong, Jamie. There are thieves everywhere here in Stone Town."

"This can't be happening. Not again."

"Go have some breakfast. Let me talk to the staff. I'll meet you in the restaurant."

Jonan was a chubby, cheery man I had met while I touched down in Zanzibar a few months prior. He fell in love with the Peace Pedalers project and invited me to stay at his luxury lodge on the ocean when I came back through. He had been very clear since day one that the bike should be put inside every night, no exceptions. I kicked myself for not listening to him. I just figured with the alarm, the lock, the guard...I kicked myself some more.

I sat in the restaurant staring at my eggs, which had long gone stale. The ocean was calm and inviting. My stomach was anything but. When Johan walked up he looked like he had good news.

"The guards know nothing about it, Jamie. The other guard comes in tonight and I'll talk to him. But for now, you need to assume it's been stolen. You should start trying to find it elsewhere on the island."

"No...way. This is a bad dream."

"You need to move fast, before it leaves the island on a boat. They steal things here and sell them in Dar es Salaam. If it leaves this island you will never see it again."

I drained my coffee mug and scampered out of the restaurant. As soon as I reached the light, the voice hit me, so clear and loud that I turned around. It was my dad, scolding me for being so careless. "That's exactly what got me into trouble when I was your age. C'mon, son. You're smarter than that." I had been out partying hard the night before, being a showoff.

Before I could answer, Garryck's words replaced my dad's. "Dude, we could find a stolen bike in Xian, China; you can find the bike here on this small island. Get it done." I was not ready to stop riding, not even close. I nodded in agreement to both of them, then called Anna, my adorable, vivacious, five-foot-tall Italian friend who had volunteered to be my filming assistant. She was a huge believer in Peace Pedalers and was as crushed as I was to hear the news. "I'll be right there," she said.

I started to craft a flyer offering a 1,000,000-shilling reward for the return of the bike, nearly $600 U.S. I needed to get an island-wide buzz going right away and penetrate the island's well-known mafia. I knew that money was the surest way to get folks talking. Just as I was putting the finishing touches on the poster, Anna showed up with two beat-up bikes she had rented from a friend. We were armed and mobile.

First stop: the port. We needed to make sure the bike didn't leave the island on any of the daily ferries to Dar es Salaam. We handed out fliers to anyone who would take one and plastered walls and doors. I looked over at a group of fishermen and saw them pointing to the paper and talking. The buzz had begun. We agreed to hand out flyers until we ran out.

When we rolled in back to the hotel for some lunch, a young man idled outside. He was dark-skinned with a short Afro and wore a green and white t-shirt.

"You are Jamie?" he asked.

"Yes, that's me. What's your name?"

"I'm Wilfred. I have an idea to help you find your bike."

"Talk to me, Wilfred."

"There is a TV station here called TV Zed. I know some people there."

"Really? We should get them to run a story," I said, instantly flashing back to our media pleas in China.

"We can go there," he said.

"Let's do it," I said. "Anna, we'll meet up later. Wilfred will use your bike, okay?"

As Anna went off to print more flyers, I followed Wilfred as he weaved through the narrow alleys of Stone Town, the city's melting-pot history spilling over at every turn. Arab mosques, European cafes, Indian storefronts, much of it hidden behind hand-carved wooden doors and latticed verandas. Stone Town had long been an important global trading center for goods ranging from the necessary to the nefarious. The British closed the slave market in 1873, though people still whispered about modern-day human trafficking. Stone Town and Zanzibar had long operated in the shadows. I was finding that out firsthand.

The TV station agreed to put us on the 6 p.m. news that night. They also offered me advertising space at a deeply discounted rate. So not only was I going to be on the news, but I also had my 1,000,000-shilling reward flyer flashing on the screen in between programs all day. I paid the station roughly $40.

"We should go to the newspaper as well," he said.

"Thanks, Wilfred. You are my Zanzibar angel!"

At the newspaper offices, we received a similar level of support. They agreed to write a feature article that would appear the next day. Wilfred and I spent the rest of the afternoon putting more flyers up downtown.

"Now let's go to the police," I suggested.

Winfred looked at me like I'd proposed a trip to Santa's Village.

"We can try…but the police are not going to do much."

"What's the downside?"

He started to talk, then muted himself. "Okay, let's go."

At the police station we sat, then sat, then sat some more. We were ignored. Totally. The officer stared at his computer, refusing to acknowledge our presence. After several hours, we were able to corner another officer, who half-listened to my predicament. He suggested we see someone else, who suggested another, who was on leave and wouldn't be back for a month. *These jerks probably have the bike sitting out back.* After imploring them repeatedly to "do something," an officer handed me a piece of paper and had me write down the details. Winfred said nothing.

"I see what you mean, Winfred," I said as we walked out of the station.

"It is very corrupt here. If they find it, you will have to pay to get it back. And more than the reward you've offered."

For the next two days I wandered the tangled streets of Stone Town, tacking up more flyers and chatting with anyone who'd spare me two minutes. The town, which seemed open and welcoming before, now seemed sneaky and padlocked shut. Whenever I heard men talking behind the ornate wooden doors, I wanted to knock loud and grill them about my bike.

Rather, it was a knock on my hotel room door later that day.

"Excuse me, sir. There are some men here to see you," the male voice said.

"I'll be right down," I said.

I pulled on a shirt and flew down the stairs, praying I'd find a police officer…and my bike.

Instead it was Wilfred. He stood with a few African men in wrinkled business suits. He approached me to have a word before I reached them.

"The police are not going to help," he said. "These men are, well, they can help."

"But who are…"

"They know where your bike is," he said, cutting me off.

"Really? Great! Can we go there now?"

"They want to make sure they will get the reward."

I paused. *Are you in cahoots with these guys, Wilfred?*

"Bring me the bike; I'll get them the reward."

"They want you to come with them to identify the bike and meet the thief."

"What should I do?"

I wonder how much they're going to give you.

"Go get the money. They will come back later this afternoon"

I went to the ATM and pulled out more than $500 in Tanzanian shillings, all the while thinking about how many meals and rooms that would purchase. I hadn't pulled that kind of money out of the bank the entire trip.

Later in the day, I was taken to a small village in a steamy van with a few silent characters. They led me through a courtyard in a large concrete housing complex. Kids, chickens, and dogs seemed to be having a scurrying contest. We turned a corner and entered a small room...taken up almost entirely by my tandem. A man sat in the corner, head down and tied up with rope around his wrists.

"Is this your bike?" asked one of the men.

"Yes. This is it."

"Meet the thief."

I turned to the man. He didn't move or look up.

"He is a well-known drug addict," the man continued.

They brought the man over to me. His head remained down. As he moved closer, I could smell a vinegary body odor and could tell he hadn't showered for days. One man yelled something Swahili and whacked him in the back with a large bamboo cane. The thief immediately lifted his head. He had a creamy muck ringing his lips and a week-old, salt-and-pepper beard. I should have felt remorse. I did not. Nothing but anger surged through me.

"Would you like to beat him?" the man asked, handing me the cane.

Something clicked. I felt the anger spill out of my body like a bathtub after someone pulled the plug.

"Uh. No," I said.

"What? I can't hear you."

"No. I just wanted to look him in the eyes."

"Really. You can beat him if you want."

"I don't want to beat him," I said.

I continued to stare at him, though this time I was trying to find a speck of compassion in him. He was clearly a drug addict, and I had no idea what was going through his mind. I looked some more.

"I think I'm ready to take my bike now," I said.

"Nothing?"

"No, I forgive him. Can you tell him this in Swahili?"

"You forgive the man?" he asked curiously.

"I forgive him. Please tell him."

The man translated my request as they pulled him away from me. I thought I noticed a change in the thief's expression, though I couldn't be sure. My attention shifted to my tandem, my muse and savior. My, well, everything. *Don't go leaving me like that again.* It seemed okay, though I wouldn't know exactly until I took it out for a spin.

"Take the bike," said the man. "We'll meet you later about the reward."

They handed it to me, and I grabbed the handles like a man meeting his love after a long stint apart. For the second time on the trip, I'd recovered a bicycle stolen and sure to be lost forever. I tried to calculate the odds of recovering them both and gave up after reaching one in a million. A bigger force was at work. Fate, faith, my father. I didn't ask anymore. I just rode, rode fast and straight back to Stone Town, filled with a mixture of gratitude and fear. I saw another man waiting for me when I arrived at the hotel. He had a newspaper in his hand.

"I read about your project," he said. "It's a beautiful gesture to ride the bike the way you do."

"Thanks. I appreciate you guys finding my bike and allowing me to continue."

"Listen, you don't have to pay the full reward."

"Are you serious? Yes, um, yeah. That's a lot of money for me."

"Pay what you can."

"Would 400,000 be okay?"

"That would be fine," he said kindly.

I counted out the money and happily left it into the guy's hand. 400,000, 400 million—it didn't matter. I had my sweetheart back.

And a half-world away, I was beginning to know another. Though we'd never met in person, Jeannie and I were planning a first date. The email conversations were thoughtful and easy, with neither of us writing something that would doom the budding relationship. We met on Skype one afternoon.

"You know, I'm going to be in France next week," she teased. "That could be a romantic place for a first date. Can you bike on up?"

"Hmmm. I do have to take a flight over the Congo to West Africa.

Maybe I'll take a detour to Paris," I replied.

"Are you serious? I'd love to meet you in Paris if you can swing it."

"How about a bike tour in the south of France and do some camping?"

Camping tended to be a make-or-break issue. Women either loved it or ran away faster than I could say "room service." I decided not to waste time. *Please, please.*

"Camping on the beach? French wine, yummy cheese, chocolate, you. I'm in!"

I didn't know if I should be elated or terrified. What kind of a woman would say yes to a first date, blind date, camping date? In France?

"I'll see what I can do," I said. "If I can swing it, I'm there."

 Check out the Zanzibar Island mini-movie at
www.bb42b.com/zanzibar
Parts of this were reenacted to fill in the holes.

34
COTONOU, BENIN

I CHECKED MY email and was stunned to see the message. It was from Innocent. *You're the first!* He had secured a plot of land, tracked down free construction materials, started building his first structure, recruited a board of advisors, and hired his first instructors, who had already started teaching his very first students. *Wow*. He had more than lived up to his part of the deal. Way more. Now he was requesting the support I promised him. I needed to raise some money, and fast.

I decided to start by hitting up my cycling sponsors. I thought they would be inspired, and also benefit from Innocent's project. I had no problem asking them for money for a worthy cause, but worried they would dismiss a simple email. No, I needed something more tangible.

So I decided to plan a major event in San Francisco that fall, a combined fundraising party for Innocent's school and a screening party for some of the best footage I'd shot over the years. I sent out proposals that promised my sponsors a good turnout and a supportive crowd, an event for people to touch, sample, and bid on donated products. Did they have anything to offer? The requests were significant. I asked for tens of thousands of dollars' worth of gear. Still, I figured product donations were a likelier bet than cash.

For the next several weeks, I spent 15 to 18 hours a day sealing deals with sponsors, cranking out PowerPoint presentations, making follow-up phone calls, and editing video footage for an event set to take place in November in San Francisco. By the time I was ready to kick off the West African expedition from Niamey, Niger, I had successfully secured more than $30,000 in sponsorship contributions. I emailed Innocent the good news. "Keep on truckin', amigo. I'm doing the same."

Promise fulfilled, at least on paper, I rode in Niger with ease. The country garnered as many bad headlines as Zimbabwe, but the reception couldn't have been more different. With few tourists, Nigerians took time out of their days to walk me around vibrant outdoor markets, grand mosques, and music jam sessions that seemed to sprout as soon as the sun set. Backpackers and journalists stressed this was "one of the poorest countries in the world," and that was certainly true. But the people here appeared far less desperate and far more optimistic than their brothers in other disadvantaged African nations. Niger felt like old-school Africa, Africa before the colonial sins and Western influences. I felt my Africa burnout receding with each pedal.

A few days later, I was approaching my final destination of Ayorou and feeling confident that I would find a strong-legged guest rider, probably someone heading to the city's legendary markets. Finding riders in Niger had been easy, my highest success ratio to date. As I was making a voice recording for Jeannie, I saw a group of elaborately dressed Tuareg men up ahead. I stopped the bike about 100 meters before them, and decided to roll my cameras. They wore indigo robes with matching turbans wrapped around their heads. In Tuareg society, it's the men who are veiled. *About time!* They were waiting for a bus, idling with their goats and bags.

"*Je vais au marché,*" I told them in my horrible French accent. "*Je voudrais inviter une personne.*" I was heading to the market as well, and would like to give one of them a ride.

I turned to see the biggest man in the group approach the bike. He wore an olive green turban and pumped his fists in the air. Welcome, Sambo Gali!

Miracle upon miracle, Sambo was able to decipher my ragtag French, and I was able to learn he had two wives and two children. "Twice as fun...and twice as expensive!" He was a strong pedaler, but he knew numerous people on the road, forcing us to make several about-faces so he could say hello. "This man, he has four wives and the other man three," he said after we chatted with a group of his friends. "Two is the best...not too many, not too few." Married life must have been good for Sambo. Every time I looked at him he wore a broad smile and talked about the blessings in life. I could have used some of that positive energy on some of my darker days.

The highly enjoyable ride mirrored most of the others in my new favorite country of Niger. The final hour to Ayorou was one of the hottest I'd experienced in months, but Samba promised a cold river and, hopefully, a cold beer in town. We pedaled hard, passing dozens of shepherds, artists, farmers, potters, stick bundlers, musicians, and women carrying everything on their head from fruit baskets to chicken cages. Sambo seemed to know every third person, taking the time to wave and yell. In between he giggled like a lottery winner, a contagious giggle that had me laughing along.

The legendary Sunday Ayorou market was in full swing. Countless different tribes and ethnic groups, groups that would rarely if ever mix, gathered each week to buy, sell, see and be seen, exchange news, and even arrange love connections. Folks came from as far away as Mali, Burkina Faso, Chad, and Nigeria, bringing their finest camels, jewelry, and produce, not to mention their best outfits. Even the animals were dressed up. Part NYSE, part Love Parade, part Running of the Bulls, the market had a massive pull and rhythm of its own. Dive into the throngs, travel with them like rapids on a rushing river, going with the flow, and hope you reach shore safely.

Niger epitomized the spirit of Peace Pedalers. Its denizens were a rich and unique mix of ethnicities, religions, and cultures: Muslims and Christians; nomads and farmers; Tuareg, Hausa, and Fulani; to name but a few. But beyond all the surface "differences" was the common human curiosity and desire for connection. Sambo was just as curious to connect with me as I was with him. And something about the tandem bike—maybe its inherent vulnerability, sense of teamwork, connection of the pedals, trust between riders—created an opportunity to bond in a way that is not possible in any other manner of travel.

I was told the road to Gao in Mali was mostly sand, so the next day I found what appeared to be an old, yet strong, diesel Land Rover heading that direction. I booked a front seat and was ready to motor onward.

As instructed, I strapped the bike to the side of the Rover and fastened my gear on the roof. The Tuareg passengers slapped me on the back and welcomed me aboard. "*L'essence*," said the driver. We needed to stop for gas.

The men all joked and laughed as we barreled down the dusty streets in search of a petrol station. The driver pointed ahead and turned the car into the station at full speed. "Don't you want to stop?" I asked. "You're going to hit the..." And we crashed straight into a mud brick wall. There were no brakes! I tested the pedals as he gassed up. Nothing. I got out of the car and demanded my money back. The driver looked stunned and the others halted their conversation. "*C'est normal*," they repeated. The roads would be flat and devoid of cars, they said. I swallowed my better judgment, and we drove on.

I probably should have paid better attention to my inner voice. It took us 38 hours, 17 minutes, and 22 seconds to go a mere 150 miles. Every mile seemed to bring a new setback. We had two flat tires, a broken gear shaft, and a dead battery. We ran out of fuel and were finally abandoned by our driver 75 kilometers from Gao.

Each breakdown required us to sit and wait until the driver came up with a solution. My natural response would have always been to bitch. But after the first breakdown, I watched the Tuareg passengers relax in the shade, listen to music, laugh, and accept the inconvenience as a normal part of travel. I tried to do the same, convinced I didn't have the temperament to be as cool as the Tuareg men. But to my surprise I found myself liking it. Sure, I was baking hot, dirty, sticky, uncomfortable, and tired. Plus, I was going to be "behind schedule" again. But as soon as I gave in to the process, let go of my frustrations, and laughed with the locals, my mood brightened considerably. I noticed my back didn't hurt as much and my hunger subsided a bit as well. *We'll get there*, I told myself.

"Here is your package, sir," said the Malian customs official. "We just need you pay the $185 processing fee to release it to you."

"Like I told the official yesterday, I'm happy to pay any fees as long as you can provide me with a receipt," I said.

"Oh no, there is no receipt, sir. It's just an official fee."

"If it's an official fee then of course there would be a receipt for payment. If you cannot give me a receipt, I cannot pay the fee."

"I'm afraid we don't release packages with these kinds of contents without a processing fee. I'm sorry," he said, walking away with my package.

The standoff in Bamako had entered its fifth day. Five days of polite hellos, requests for money, requests for a receipt, denials of both, then walking away. The package from Mamacita was important, yes—needed parts for the bicycle, more gifts for kids, and some additional video equipment. Normally I didn't mind paying a few dollars at borders and post offices. Small bribes in the developing world came with the territory, as common as stray dogs and potholes. But $185? Mali was attempting to set the new standard for greed and corruption. I decided to try again, and again, and...

Caved. It wasn't the money that forced me to dig into my wallet. It was the boisterous and malodorous capital that changed my mind. *Curse you, Bamako! You can take your belching buses, muddy roads, fetish stalls with the rotting monkey heads, and police and pickpockets, both scheming for a way to get into your wallet. I'm headed to Dogon Country.*

On my way into the town of Mopti, a young man with puffy eyes and short dreadlocks approached me.

"Hey, mon, where are you going with this bike?" he asked, cheerily.

"Up to Dogon Country. Jamie," I said, reaching out for a handshake.

"Boobacon. Boobacon John Travolta!"

"Wow. That's the best name of the trip. Better still because you actually do look like John Travolta."

"You can call me Booba."

"Nice to meet you Booba. Where are you from?"

"Dogon Country, the best part of Mali!"

Fellow backpackers had stressed to me the importance of touring Dogon Country with a Dogon speaker. It's the best way to dive deep into the culture and connect with the people, they said. Perhaps Booba could do the trip with me. I loved his energy from word one. I explained to him in detail about Peace Pedalers and the malaria medication deliveries, and could tell before he replied he was a kindred soul.

"I am your man, brother!"

"You seem like a Peace Pedaler."

"Yes, mon! Love and kindness and generosity. This is me, Booba!" he said patting me on the back and helping me with my bike.

"So you want to join me?"

"Of course, mon!"

"Can you find a bike to use for the journey?" I asked. "That way we can host and film other riders while you translate."

"No problem. *Hakuna matata!*"

"Okay. So let's find you a bike and you can be my adventure partner in bringing a little love and connection to the Dogon people."

"Come, let's bring the love. Bring the love! Bring the love!" He began dancing around and swinging panniers over his head.

Booba was able to borrow a sturdy bike from a friend and assured me he was more than capable of towing the BOB trailer behind him to even our loads. He also found a safe place to store some unnecessary gear to lighten both our loads for the four-day off-road expedition to the mountainous Dogon Country, with its cliffside villages, sandstone grottos, talismans, sacred crocodiles, and spiritual rituals. Before leaving, we sat under an acacia tree, joking with locals who offered us local millet wine served in hand-carved calabash cups. "To Dogon Country!" we toasted.

"Look at this, mon," pulling up his pant leg to show me his calf. "What can I do?"

"Oh my God! What is that?" I asked.

His leg looked like an earth-toned cave with amber stalactites and ochre stalagmites, all dripping in foamy puss.

"We have to fix this before we ride off," I said.

I pulled out my overstocked first aid kit and gave him a long scrubbing and a clean dressing. A crowd began to huddle over me like medical students during a demonstration. I couldn't imagine how long the wound had gone untreated. A month? Two?

Just as I finished with Booba, I turned around to see a line of three other men forming. Each of them had nasty, infected wounds and asked to be treated by "Doctor J." I reached for more medical supplies. Two hours and several bowls of millet wine later they were all singing, dancing and showing off their white bandage dressings.

"When we come back from our trip, these men want to have a real party for us to say thank you for fixing their wounds," Booba remarked.

"Deal. Tell them my doctor's fee is for them to arrange some drummers. We'll see them in a few days."

Booba explained this to the men and they bid us *bon voyage* as we made our first pedal strokes toward the heart of Dogon Country. The dirt roads and climbing began just out of town, though nothing too difficult for the bandaged Booba and me. He handled the bike and trailer like he'd been on the road for the entire Peace Pedalers journey.

A few hours later, we stopped to take some photos of an attractive Dogon village with stone walls and mud huts with thatch roofs so thick and mop-topped they looked like Beatles haircuts. As was usually the case, our entrance into town was accompanied by running kids and curious onlookers. A young man with a shaved head sidled up next to me as I pulled out my camera. Booba explained the mission of Peace Pedalers in the local Dogon language. "I want to come with you," said the man. And just like that we had our first Dogon guest rider, Sekou Oulogme from the Sinkarma village. "You're good, Booba," I said. "Really good."

Sekou wore a torn white t-shirt that did little to cover his chiseled body. He never asked where we were going, or when he would return. He just wanted a little adventure. We handed out some malaria medication to the village elders and scooted on, Booba translating as Sekou spoke little-to-no French and no-to-no English.

Sekou was a 21-year-old farmer who worked on his family's property with his four brother and two sisters. At his urging, we made numerous stops to sample wild African black plums and desert dates, take photos of intricately carved caves and burial sites, drink millet wine, and meet Sekou's friends and family on the road, an extensive clan that seemed to include almost everyone. At one small village stop he introduced us to the chief.

"He says there are three people in the village suffering from malaria," translated Booba. "Can we spare any more medication?"

"Of course. Just explain the instructions carefully to him."

The chief was so excited, he insisted we accompany him into the village, where he filled our gourd bowls with endless quantities of warm millet beer stored in husks. After downing a couple servings, other locals came over to replenish our bowls. The beer was room temperature, tart on the tongue, and with a straw aroma. Hardly the cold pilsner I preferred after rides, but refreshing enough. After the fourth bowl, I understood that "no more" would not be an option. We stumbled out of the village, slightly intoxicated, with Sekou talking to the trees.

"Sekou says he has some friends in a village up ahead." said Booba.

"How far? It's getting dark, so we need to find a place to sleep."

"He said it's just around the next corner."

After a few more miles, I was beginning to wonder if the millet was dictating directions. My buzz had long worn off, and we all needed food and rest. But just then, Sekou guided us off the dirt road to a hidden village not marked on the map.

"Sekou! Well done," I said, before turning to Booba. "Can you invite him to spend the night and eat with us?"

I saw him nodding his head, yes, within seconds. *Love it.* Booba went to work arranging dinner while I set up my tent under the stars. Like most villages in Dogon Country, this one featured no electricity, no traffic, no paved road, just conversation and connection. Our hosts Yaire and Djomty brought over a live chicken and asked me if I thought it would suffice for dinner. "Absolutely," I said. *As long as I don't hear the little bugger die.* They prepared the chicken, along with pasta and local grains, over an open fire. And no meal would be complete in Dogon Country without some famous Dogon onions, for which gourmands pay top dollar. We ate and drifted and huddled around a fire and talked about the blessings of family. Now I had a ready answer if anyone asked me my favorite dining experience.

When the flames died out, I invited Booba and Sekou to share my big tent. They politely declined, opting for the hut. Djomty delivered a large, warm tub of water, and I went to bed sated, clean, and perfectly content under the endless Dogon stars.

Sekou and Booba rousted me in the morning. They were dying to show me the "Peace Huts" up in the village above our campsite. We hiked up a trail, followed by a dozen kids, into the tiny village of Kama-Badjo. All the while, Booba explained the concept behind the hut. They were purposely built very low so quarrelling villagers couldn't stand (and fight) during an argument. Instead they had to sit and talk it out. Villagers have been adopting this technique for more than 5,000 years, and Booba swore it still worked.

Just as we were loading up the bikes Yaire came over to say goodbye. I paid her for the stay. She had her two little boys, Koumba and Djiguiba, in tow.

"Booba, will you politely ask her if her kids are okay. They look sick."

After a beat of hesitancy and a quick discussion, Booba turned back to me.

"Yes, she says they both have malaria."

"Stay right here," I said.

We got a later start than planned, but I would have lingered all day.

That moment is why you are riding. That moment will never get old or less important. We had a 25-km ride from Kama-Badjo to Sanga, the last town before descending into the center of Dogon Country valley. Sekou wanted to continue with us, and we were more than happy to have him. He pointed continuously at cave dwellings, tucked away villages, and other unique features in the Flintstones-like topography.

In Sanga, we caught some much needed shade and filled up our water packs for the next stage of the journey. Sekou would return home from here, and Booba made sure to spread the word that the tandem was in need of its next rider. Within minutes, it a young man named Harouna Dollo volunteered.

We sent Sekou back with malaria medications and some cash to buy food for his family. He and Harouna exchanged helmets and a few words of encouragement. Harouna took a while to get used to the bike and the effort required. I could feel the pace slow down, but it hardly mattered. On the way to Banani we wove our way through rich valleys with red rock walls, by cliffs, rocky river crossings, and waterfalls that seemed to spring from desert sand. A mountain biker couldn't have asked for more.

Harouna spoke decent French, and since my "Afro-French" was improving, we were able to have basic conversations. He was nearing his twentieth birthday and worked as a pottery artist in addition to helping his mother and family. He valued the close relationship he had with his brothers and sisters, and laughed constantly. I'd never had a rider who laughed so much.

As we dove further into Dogon Country, I thought, *it's no wonder people have been living in this region for millennia.* Endless vistas pulled at any visitor lucky enough to be there. Here, don't miss the Cliff of Bandiagara, a World Heritage site, or the endless verdant mesas. *Eye candy*, I kept repeating. *Eternal eye candy.* Late morning, as I was taking it all in, I heard a loud *snap!* from the back of the bike.

Immediately the back tire grinded hard against the rack, stopping our tandem steed with a vengeance. "Un-good," I mumbled. At the same time, the weather was quickly changing from warm and sunny to cold, windy, and dotted with ominous black clouds. My enthusiasm dipped.

Booba had enough optimism for all of us and then some. It was infectious. He went into "solution mode," refusing to let my spirits wane. He arranged for the bikes to be stored at a friend's house for the duration of the storm. And he somehow managed to find a generator that allowed us to charge our equipment and batteries. Next, we went to work on the rack and found just the right trinkets in my spare parts bag to fix it. For the first time, I was glad I paid the $185 to the corrupt Mali customs agents.

Horouna had to get back to his village, so I gave him some Coartem, a bracelet, and money to find a lift home. A stranger approached as Horouna and I hugged each other goodbye. He was curious, too curious to just walk on by. You didn't see many white guys and locals riding tandems through here. Jacque Quirou couldn't resist the "worldwide invitation to ride." *Is it this country's can-do spirit? Or Booba's energy? My good looks? Or all of the above that is making Dogon Country the easiest place on the planet to pick up guest riders?*

The valley floor became soft and sandy as we rode onwards. Challenging, yes, but still traversable. We continued on paths near the Bandiagara Cliffs, trying to focus on the hillside dwellings instead of the condition of the road. The ecstasy was short lived. Soon we were buried in deep sand, my least favorite road surface. By far. No matter how easy it looks, deep sand keeps you off the bike, sucks all the energy out of you while pushing, and slows any progress to a crawl.

I asked Booba if the condition would be the same throughout the entire valley. "*Hakuna matata*, brother! No worries. It's only bad today. Tomorrow it will be better." I loved how residents of the developing world started sentences with "No problem," even when they didn't know the answer or how events would unfold. *Why not? If you don't know the outcome, why not side with the best case scenario and leave the worst case to others. Note to self.*

Booba was right…about the rest of the day being bad. We were only able to ride a quarter of the way. We pushed the rest. But each time we were forced off our bikes, local boys and young men came out of the bush to help. *These guys are better than a NASCAR pit crew.*

When we finally saw the village of Ireli in the distance, Booba, Jacque, and I, along with about ten pushers, broke out in cheers. The setting sun cast the area into an intoxicating sepia tone. I looked up to the red rocks where Telem tribes once lived inside small caves situated hundreds of feet above the ground. Booba explained it was still a mystery how they got into their caves, as researchers have found no evidence of stairs, ropes, or vines.

Our mystery was where we were going to sleep or eat that night. I had grown to love those moments. They were like Christmas Eve—you had no idea what you were going to receive, but past experience convinced you it would be good. This time it was the village Catholic priest who first approached us and invited us in for some tea. His name was Emmanuel Douyon.

We pushed the bikes into a corner of his house before walking up a flight of narrow stairs, where we were blessed with a priceless view of the entire valley on one side and the cliffs and Ireli village on the other. He filled a large pitcher with cold water and started some tea as we finally relaxed our exhausted bodies.

Emmanuel was more than happy to host us, and Jacque decided to stay the night as well. Road hospitality had rewarded us yet again. It pleased though no longer surprised me. But Booba was so was so delighted with how our adventure was unfolding that he jumped out of his chair, did a few pushups, and danced around the room. His giddiness overflowed to Jacque and me as we toasted with a glass of warm millet beer, catching both the sunset and the moonrise on our Dogon penthouse balcony.

Over a pasta dinner, consumed in the dark with our headlamps providing the only light, Jacque and I continued to hack away at conversations in broken French. He was a sweet man and gentle in the way he did everything from holding handlebars to gripping a fork. Though I'd only known him for an afternoon, he seemed genuine and bighearted. I asked him about his dreams and passions, and he always drifted back to "*ma famille.*" He had four children and a wife he adored. They were his life, his passion. In his 47 years, he had never traveled more than a few miles from his village. "It's my dream to one day take my family on a journey," he told me in French. The tandem trip reminded him of his dream. He planned to get working on it.

The next morning we woke to the sound of roosters and cows. I peeked out of the tent and devoured a giant, 360-degree view of the picture-perfect valley. There are only a handful of places on the planet where the scenery moved me to tears, landscapes so stunning they demanded every ounce of emotion in my body. This was one. I decided to do some yoga and focus on the serene beauty of Ireli, meditating for the next hour on the ancient granaries and burial caves, red and green mesas, and jolly baobab trees.

After a breakfast of homemade doughnuts, bread, jam, and fresh-brewed coffee, we were more than ready for a long day's journey to the end of the valley and back up to the top of the plateau. We knew it was going to be a tough day of pedaling, but we were all fueled by the surrounds and the villagers we would meet. I gave a hearty hug and a Peace Pedalers hat to our host, Emmanuel, and vowed to be back. That gift-giving session led to Jacque and I exchanging our favorite necklaces. *What can I give Booba?* I looked at his socks, threadbare and black. "Here you go, amigo," I said, handing him a pair of Peace Pedalers socks. "You are official now."

Booba was spot on again about the terrain changing after Ireli. The cumbersome sandy road turned to hard-packed red dirt that meandered through one picturesque Dogon village after another. Women in color-ful *kanga* wraps and mud-dyed *bògòlanfini* dresses, many with swaddled infants riding on their back, paused from their chores to extend sincere and elaborate greetings. *Booba's flirting. It must be the socks.* I couldn't get enough of the villages or the *terroir*.

The only hiccup turned out to be no hiccup at all. Our trail disap-peared into a lily-filled pond about neck deep thanks to recent rains. A group of Dogon women on the other side washed clothes in the water. They confirmed we were on the right path. So we simply clipped tight the seven Ortlieb dry bags and practically floated our way across the little pond to continue on the other side, refreshed and a bit less smelly.

About five kilometers later, we stopped for a break and met a friendly man name Michel who was intrigued by our expedition and interested if we had any room for him to join. Since Jacque couldn't spend too much time away from his wife and family, he handed his helmet to Michel and bid us a touching adieu.

We had at least another couple hours of riding before reaching the next town, and Michel jumped right in, even though he was a newbie or "Fred," a term used by experienced mountain bikers. New female riders are often called Wilma. *Fitting here in the land of Bedrock.* Unlike Jacque, Michel spoke almost no French and not a lick of English. From the first couple pedals I knew I'd be unable to give him verbal instructions. But Michel had strong legs, great balance, and massive trust, the best ingre-dients possible for new riders in these conditions.

Tight, technical, single-track trails comprised the ride, and Michel and I soon became a well-oiled machine with an ideal cadence. We hit every corner at maximum speed, flew over all the rooted sections, and drifted over wishy-washy sand spots as if floating. We were little kids hammering trails in the neighborhood, with no words needed. When we stopped for rests, with our heart rates rushing and our adrenaline pumping, we'd look at each other and scream in ecstasy whatever came to mind. "Baobab!" "Flintstones!" "Ôôô!" (good).

With the day's end and the town of Dourou approaching, Booba gave the single bike to Michel before running up a rocky trail to find a campsite for us for the night. This left Michel and me to muscle through the last bits of steep, sandy terrain alone. We began to slow, then fade, then stop altogether. But as soon as we lost our pushing power, we miraculously attracted what seemed to be every kid from nearby Dourou. Child after child jumped on the tandem or pushed one of the bikes up to the plateau, where the sand finally gave way to hard-pack dirt and, eventually, pavement.

When we finally arrived in Dourou there stood a large crowd, cheering and greeting us at the entrance. I felt like a rider at the end of the Tour de France. Booba soon joined the festivities and gave me some more good news.

"You must ride also with a Dogon woman, Jamie," he said. "They are very strong, and this woman they say is the strongest in the village."

I was tired and hungry, but was not going to turn down the opportunity to ride with the "strongest female rider in the village." It had always been difficult to convince any female rider to hop on a tandem and cycle away with a Western man, especially here in countries like Mali with large Islamic populations. Too many whispers, too many problems. "No, thank you."

A moving posse of women and girls led my guest rider to the bike like a prize fighter entering the ring. She was shy and timid at first, feeling all the eyes of her village on her. Booba translated as I asked her name and confirmed that she *really* wanted to come out for a bike ride. Her name was Fatima, and her determined smile and emphatic grip of the handlebars made it unnecessary to wait for Booba's translation.

I strapped on my helmet and pushed our steed through the still-growing crowd. "Farewell, fair villagers!" As soon as we hit the open road, Fatima hammered the pedals. Hard. This woman wanted to ride. *So let's have some fun.*

As soon as she mastered her balance and knew how to strap into the pedals, I veered the tandem off-road and we made our way over the rocks of the plateau, taking big dips and drops, Fatima yelling with every one. There are mountains of inequity in the world, more than we will ever conquer in my lifetime. The women of Africa face an especially daunting climb. But sometimes a little thing like a bike ride can inspire another step, then another, and who knows? We turned back to the village before the sun vanished. What seemed like the entire populace stood there to greet us and hear details of the ride.

"*Merci*, Booba. How do I begin to thank you for opening the door to this magical land?" I hugged him and patted him on the back. Goodbyes were tough. This one would be brutal. Days flew by with Booba, yet each moment seemed to stand still.

"If you have the unity to live together," he said. "And the peace and love, then you have the big energy and the strong luck for the life. Everybody will have the luck. To live together is important."

"You, Booba, are the reason I am on this trip," I said. "I want to meet the Boobas of the world, the people who make this planet special."

Another bus stop, another goodbye.

"Listen to me," he said. "My family. We have some extra land. I want to offer it to you so you can build a house in Dogon."

"Are you serious, Booba?" I asked, touched and stunned.

"I am very serious. You always will have a place in Dogon, my brother."

I hugged him again and worked my way through the logistics. *This is some of the best mountain biking territory anywhere. And the people couldn't be nicer. A small house here? Nothing fancy. Just come and be inspired and ride?*

I looked down at Booba's leg and noticed how well it was healing. Then I saw the Peace Pedalers socks, stretched out and blackened from the dirt. I took a deep breath and shut my eyes, as gratitude filled my body to the brim. I hoped the bus would never come.

 Here's a 22-minute taste of Niger, West Africa. I cut this for the fundraising party for Good Hope School. www.bb42b.com/niger

Although poor the joy and laughter was in every direction

Sambo Gali took about zero seconds to accept my invitation to ride

Sambo usually goes to the market in a bus like this. He preferred the bike.

And we're off! Booba with his borrowed bike and BOB trailer

Booba on his 4ᵗʰ cup of millet beer and properly ripped

The "Peace Huts"

The road to Sanga

Celebrating another epic day in Dogon with Jacque & Booba

Michel speaking the language of love—tandem mountain biking

 Here's a 22-minute taste of Mali, West Africa. I cut this for
the fundraising party for Good Hope School.
www.bb42b.com/mali

35
SAN FRANCISCO, CALIFORNIA. USA

-->

I LEANED MY head against the warm window of the airplane and felt the butterflies in my stomach. Were they doing the tango? No. More like a flamenco finale. After eleven months and thirteen countries of highly challenging—and equally rewarding—travel in Africa, I was minutes away from setting foot back home in the San Francisco Bay Area.

I hadn't seen Jeannie since France, and memories of cool champagne, warm couplings, and our initial connection mixed with uncomfortable fears and doubts about my recent decision to move in with a woman I barely knew. Yes, the European first date went well, better even than I could have imagined. We started the affair in Paris, then meandered our way south, playing footsy on trains, lingering in parks until dusk, toasting the roads ahead.

The bike rides weren't quite as smooth. During climbs I found myself doing the vast majority of the work. Jeanne admitted she was not doing a lot of cycling in the hills of San Francisco. Would she be able to handle a months-long ride? I had packed those doubts aside as we planted ourselves on oceanfront campsites, fed each other French chocolates, swam in the warm water, and made love in the tent.

She had long, sculpted legs and an all-consuming smile that made her eyes squint and twinkle when she grinned. She was about as laid back as they make 'em, with a ribald sense of humor that made me laugh. She snorted when she laughed, which made me laugh some more. *Any woman willing to have a first date in Paris and then escape to the south of France was okay in my book*, I had thought to myself. That more than made up for her lack of cycling prowess.

Jeannie's house in San Francisco was going to be my base camp for a planned two-month stay in the U.S. I had three objectives. The first was to get my footage edited and ready for the fundraising party on November 15th. The second was to raise as much money as possible for Innocent's school in Uganda and for the expedition into Europe the following year. Finally, I needed to help Jeannie get ready for her first big multi-year international cycling expedition.

And there she was, her tan face and that infectious smile. In a scene straight from a Meg Ryan romantic comedy, we ran to each other at full speed and embraced in a long, deep hug, followed by a passionate kiss interrupted with "I missed you so much" and "I've been dreaming about this moment for months." And it was true. I had been thinking about Jeannie since our last rendezvous. But something didn't feel right. The emotions seemed a bit forced, the words slightly strained. *Is this supposed to be more natural? Or are these types of situations always a bit awkward at first? What would Meg do?*

I dismissed the doubts and gave her another hug. The transitions back to the States were always tough those initial days. Now add a budding relationship to the mix, and the heavy question of commitment and long bike rides and, well, yikes.

As Jeannie carried on with her job and her life, I dove into long work sessions with a local production house to begin editing my endless footage from Africa. I secured an ideal venue for the party at a swank two-story bar, printed and distributed invitations, and worked the phones to ensure a large turnout.

Meanwhile, Jeannie's house was quickly turning into a storage unit with stacks of boxes containing donated gear from my sponsors. I counted more than $20,000 worth of equipment filling her spare room and overflowing into the hallway. I knew I had far more gear than I would be able to sell at the screening party, so I began an eBay hawking mission, auctioning off cycling apparel, panniers, laptop computers, video cameras, bicycle components, and flat-screen plasma TVs.

The party would be a success, I had no doubt. The partnership with Jeannie, on the other hand, well, I wasn't as confident. In her most recent email just days before arriving in the states, after months of talk about quitting her life here in San Francisco and hitting the road fulltime, she hinted that she might have an opportunity for a tenured teaching job too good to pass up. Just a possibility, she said. We'd talk about it when I was in town. At the time, I dismissed the notion. Who would choose a job over a massive cycling trip through Europe and Latin America?

She said we'd talk about it...but we didn't. We lingered in the honeymoon phase of the relationship, talking more about the adventures in France. Everything I was doing focused on the future. Neither of us seemed rooted in the "now."

One morning, over breakfast, I finally cornered her.

"I know, I know," she said. "I'm totally avoiding this discussion. It's just, well, I'm still not sure if I'm going to take this job or not. It's a really good opportunity, exactly what I've always wanted."

"Don't you think there will to be other opportunities after we get back?"

"Yes. No. I don't know, Jamie. It's very competitive in my profession, and a tenured opportunity exactly where I want it doesn't come around very often."

She's pulling out. Now what?

"I don't think I want to have a girlfriend in San Francisco while I'm traveling solo over the next several years. It's just not what I signed up for."

"Signed up for?"

"I was very clear from day one that my life is on the road and I'm looking for a partner to join me and share that adventure. You read this in my profile and know that's why I'm here with you now."

"I would really love to travel. I mean it. And you know that. France? The Mediterranean? I'm just confused now, and need more time to figure out what I'm going to do. Please be patient with me."

She leaned into me for a consoling hug, and I smelled tobacco smoke in her hair. *I thought you only smoked when you partied. What else didn't I know? And what else didn't she know about me?* I kept hearing my mom's advice she gave me after I broke up with my Australian girlfriend, Sophie. "Now you just get out there and ride your bike around the world. If a woman is meant to join you, then let her pedal up alongside you on her own bike." Was she right?

That night I couldn't sleep a wink. I tossed and turned trying to figure out a solution to the harsh reality in front to me--Jeannie was not going to join me afterall. And even though we had an amazing connection I continued to have zero intereset in a long distance relationship for the next several years. Now what? I was living in her house with all my gear scattered in every nook and cranny with more boxes on the way. If

I end it now where would I go? Was there a chance she might still come? Did she just need more time?

As I watched friends and strangers pour into the two-story bar of my long-anticipated fundraising event I thought about Innocent. I should have flown him over to join the festivities. His presence would have doubled contributions, which were already very high. In addition to all the donations from the sponsors, the bar agreed to donate a generous percentage of all drink sales. And this crowd knew how to drink. "A toast to the Good Hope School!"

The event showcased a glimpse of the school's future, but also afforded me an opportunity to take inventory on all the events that had transpired thus far. Watching the edited footage, I thought about all the friends I'd made abroad, all the lives touched through rides, malaria medications, or just a friendly wave. And they'd touched me. They turned my passion for travel, cycling and now philanthropy into my full-time career and the most enriching lifestyle imaginable.

After the credits rolled, the crowd rose and clapped heartily. I could feel the emotions darting toward me, a mix of support, attaboys, inspiration to follow my passion, a touch of enviousness, and a huge dose of *bon voyage*. We were able to auction off all of the gear, and far surpass our fundraising objectives for both Peace Pedalers and Good Hope School. It was time to party.

Jeannie had to leave, as she had to teach the next day. I wasn't leaving. I didn't ever want to leave the party and the warm camaraderie. I had family there, including Shannon, who would soon be wed. She thanked me again for the open invitation to ride.

I had friends, oodles of friends from all over the country and a few from abroad. This included Eva, the British backpacker I had befriended in Zimbabwe. We lifted a glass to the Good Hope School! Then another to recovering my tandem in Victoria Falls! To cyclists! The road! To woman who really know how to travel! To road romances!

Then, I kissed Eva. I regretted it immeditaly. But it was too late.

36

TOGO, WEST AFRICA

THE MIDDAY HEAT of Togo in West Africa can easily trigger heat stroke, even with seasoned extreme athletes. The problem this day was that I was no longer seasoned or athletic. I was a mess.

I clutched my handlebars while convulsions of violent chills cursed my ride as I relived, again, the drunken kiss with Eva back in San Francisco that started my emotional and physical tailspin. That kiss led to another and one more. Eva and I turned the playfulness into an affair. Affairs usually end in a flaming wreck, and this one was no exception— the discovery ("Were you holding hands with a woman last weekend?"), the lame defense ("I don't know what I was thinking. I figured since you were taking the job our relationship was heading nowhere"), the ultimatum ("Relationship? Get the hell out of my house!"), the wimpy apology ("I'm sorry"), the exclamation point ("Now!").

I hurriedly crammed my belongings into a rental car, trying and failing to justify or even make sense of it all. Guilt, shame and resentment lay heavy on my soul as I drove my way down to San Diego to prepare for my West African expedition. Sure, the relationship was going nowhere once she decided not to join the ride. But that was the very worst way for me to end it. And rather than take a closer look at how alcohol abuse was destroying relationships in my life I ran right back to heavy drinking and chewing tobacco use to numb the pain every day until I left California.

When I finally arrived back in Ghana to finish the final countries of the African expedition I doubled down on dumb. Upon arrival, I made sure to find a pack of cigarettes, and stayed as close to the party crowd as possible as I rode towards Benin through Togo. *The party's still going, right?*

I was paying for all those festivities now in Togo. As each hour passed, I was feeling weaker and weaker, while my body pinballed between sweats and chills. I looked back at my guest rider, Bridget, a professional dancer whom I had met the night before while filming a cultural performance. We made plans for a three-day adventure together. She smiled and patted me on the back. Her gentle touch felt like an ax to my torso. This wasn't good.

Knowing the difficulties of finding female African riders, I was thrilled she had accepted my invitation to join me on an extended trip. She had a strong body and a huge smile that filled her face with bright white teeth. She giggled sweetly when she heard my horrific attempts to speak French.

We stopped for lunch, but I had no appetite whatsoever. Another bad sign. The plan was to ride 70 kilometers that day to the town of Vogan. But by the time we rolled into Aneho, just past the halfway mark, I could barely move my body. The sporadic chills turned to constant shaking. We'd need to stop for the night.

The lodging options were slim, and I ended up checking us in to a dingy hotel near a beach littered with trash and sewage. It took every ounce of energy I had left to lug a half-dozen bags up to our second-story room. I took a cold shower and hopped into bed, hoping a long sleep under a fast-moving fan might snap me out of my misery. Bridget held my hand.

Several hours later my fever shot up anew, giving me body-shaking chills I tried to stop by curling up into a ball. Sweat poured from my body as if from a juicer, leaving the sheets stained and stinky. I stared at the fan and prayed for the fever to break. *Water, I need water.* Then the voices came, along with horror-film music and visions of drownings and slow-motion "endo" crashes that sent me tumbling into a ravine. Suddenly, Jeannie appeared. She wasn't angry or hurt. Worse, she stood before me as if I wasn't there. I was dead to her.

Stumbling in and out of consciousness, I relived the events in my mind well into the evening. My mishandling of the relationship with Jeannie triggered a string of self-destructive behaviors and past addictions like alcohol and tobacco. For weeks I had beaten myself up. I knew this couldn't continue, and that I needed to carve out some sort of peace. *Yes, peace.* I began to make plans for making amends, when a new thought floored me. *Maybe the worst is yet to come.*

Over the coming few weeks I was able to recover enough to get back on the bike and slowly make my across West Africa. I hosted guest riders, slept in villages, and cranked the pedals as always, but nothing felt the same as before. A burning sensation was growing across my chest whenever I rode, and my strength was a fraction of what it once was. My body wasn't healing, and I feared for my deteriorating mental health as well. I was depressed and lonely, and still kicking myself for my senseless actions in San Francisco. Guilt and shame were my heaviest load.

In Benin, violent coughing fits and a constant stream of yellow phlegm forced me back into bed. After a few days of rest, I tried to power through Gambia and Senegal, only to experience the same. "Pneumonia," said the doctor in Dakar, Senegal. He showed me the X-rays before giving me stern advice: "Get off the bike. At the very least, skip the ride across the desert."

The Sahara? No way I'm skipping the Sahara. I decided to ignore the warning and ride from Mauritania to Morocco during one of the worst times of the year—the Harmattan wind season. The Harmattan is a take-no-prisoners, wicked, seasonal desert wind that blows over West Africa from December to March. It delivers bone-chilling nights and searing, windy days that shoot stinging grit into the eyes, throats, and lungs of any fools who venture outside. I lasted three days before the coughing convulsions made it nearly impossible to breath. I had to swallow my pride and booked a seat in a fruit truck for a 2,000 km ride to Agadir, Morocco, where I hoped to find a place to heal before riding in Europe.

An hour before the planned meeting time, several blasts from an automatic weapon pierced the afternoon. *Bap, bap, bap, bap, bap.* At first I thought it might be an army drill. Then a cavalcade of military and police trucks came speeding past the hotel, full of armed men screaming at everyone to get out of the way. The hotel owner quickly ushered everyone inside.

Earlier that year, four French tourists had been killed by extremist Islamic groups, and the famous Dakar Rally had been canceled due to terrorist threats. The "Country of a Million Poets" was now more famous for its government coups and terrorism. I felt quasi-safe inside the hotel, only to have the sense of security shattered by more gunfire and far-too-close bombs. Each blast sent me to the floor, then to my knees in prayer. What had been a normal city was now a war zone, or so I gathered from the glimpses I stole outside. The explosions continued for more than an hour, then stopped. *Had the armed forces found their man?* Just then, as the sun faded, the fruit truck pulled into the carport, ready to take me to Morocco. *And straight towards the area of the rebel gunfire.*

As we loaded my bike and gear into empty fruit crates, the driver and his crew broke into an animated discussion about what to do with me. After several minutes of back and forth, a debate that broadened to include several concerned bystanders, the decision was made to hide me in the back cab and cover me with blankets in case of a roadblock. Each bump and stop caused my heart rate to skyrocket. I felt like a box of contraband being smuggled out of a country. Every pause could be deadly. *Go, go, go!* We arrived at the border around midnight.

We slept, in frenetic, 15-minute intervals, at a dilapidated roadside truck stop, only to rise before the sun to join a long, loooooong line of other trucks at the border. The recent terror attacks heightened security at every entry. I had no idea what was in store. Stay hidden under the blankets, emerge and show my passport, offer a bribe?

I had heard the Moroccan government was doing a major crackdown on all trafficking—people, drugs, and anything coming from the south. I convinced the driver to allow me to emerge from my hiding space, confident I could help expedite things. "I'm great at borders," I said.

Instead, we idled for the next seven hours, my presence not helping to expedite things one iota. I tried to regain any lost standing by helping to load the dozens of crates we were forced to unpack for inspection. *Um, this is not the easiest way to Morocco.*

After squeezing through the border, I was told to return to the back of the cab, only now I had to share the cramped space with a Moroccan man named Bachir. The driver, wanting to make a few more bucks, had also picked up a gypsy woman, Nadia, at the border and agreed to take her more than 1,000 kilometers to the Western Sahara city of Laayoune. "No more than three people," assured the man who had convinced me to buy the ticket. "Trust me. I've done it dozens of times. It's the best way to go. You can sleep all the way in the back and stretch out!" Instead, Bachir and I huddled next to each other, practically spooning, our sweaty legs touching for the entire ride as we picked up passenger after passenger.

Near midnight I felt the truck make a sharp right turn. *Great! We're stopping for the night. Get some food!* But the truck continued on for another 100 kilometers on a side road. *I thought this was a straight shot on the main highway.* When we stopped, I jumped out to see a large fruit truck that had flipped over and dozens of Moroccan men arguing how best to right it. The driver of the fruit truck was Rachid's brother. They hugged and chitchatted.

As I walked toward the overturned rig, Rachid grabbed me by the arm and told me, in French, to get back inside the cab. The rolled truck had a seriously injured passenger who had been whisked away in an ambulance, he explained. The authorities would be here soon. If they saw me, they might not allow me to continue on. Translation: "I am operating an illegal transportation service and don't want to get caught or be forced to pay bribes." Once again, I was hidden in the cab under a dusty blanket until the police came and went, leaving it to the bystanders to flip the truck back upright.

I was eventually allowed out of the truck; they needed as many able bodies as possible to right the rig. The first several attempts resulted in snapped ropes and a few people almost being crushed when the truck slammed back to the ground. It was now 3 a.m. Drivers rifled through their own cars and trucks for anything that could aid the effort—more rope, jacks, wooden crates. *No way. No way.* After a few more failed attempts, the crowd managed to flip the truck over and onto the road. In the process, a massive dust cloud blew into my face, sending me into a coughing fit so strong I vomited. *Can I please just get back to my foul blanket in my cramped quarter of the cab?*

After 51 hours—*51!*—I was dumped off, dust-clogged and diesel-smelling, in the sleepy, and sleeping, beach town of Taghazout, Morocco. It was nearly midnight. I knocked on locked doors looking for a place to sleep. Nothing. No answer. The beach seemed to be my only option. How could I sleep there without getting robbed? Under one of the fishing boats? To my surprise, a skinny, dark-skinned man with thick eyebrows and mustache named Mohammed appeared out of nowhere and invited me to stay at his house.

And I stayed. For several days. Mohammed and I became friends. He helped bring me back to life with his cooking. Using his well-worn tagine, he would simply cut up veggies, toss in some meat for flavoring, douse everything with ginger, turmeric, cumin, and paprika, then turn on the fire and allow this small pot do its magic.

During one of our savory dinners, Mohammed introduced me to his niece, a production manager from Casablanca. Nadia was a tall, tan, jolly Moroccan woman who offered to help me settle in town. She and Mohammed teamed up to help me negotiate an oceanfront apartment, cook me more delicious meals, stop by for visits, and shower me with friendship and tenderness.

Taghazout was a healing cocoon. I sensed, early on, that the longer I stayed the healthier I would become. But only if I fully committed myself to restoration. I resisted the overwhelming temptation to surf. I quit smoking. Again. I drank ten liters of water a day. I slept as much as possible and wrote dozens of pages in my journal. I had to heal before going up to Europe.

But the cough would not go away. It had grown so bad I suffered coughing attacks every time I shifted body positions. Whenever I sat up or sat down, rolled over in bed, or even lifted my arms, my torso would launch into a volley of violent, unstoppable hacks that would lock up my airway and stop me from breathing through my mouth. The rest of my body, including my mind, made steady progress toward recuperation. My lungs lagged far behind. Doctor visits and medicine did nothing. My cough was getting worse, and I made plans to fly home.

At a loss, I sent requests for prayers to my friends and family. I begged them to please send any shard of positive energy and healing powers from afar. A week later, I wrote something in my journal.

Yesterday was a breaking point for me. I was in tears several times, on the floor coughing my lungs out until I vomited and quivered from lack of breath. I was congested beyond belief—the worst I've felt in months. But in the heat of the suffering, I wrote out a prayer that went like this:

"I am done being ill. I have suffered enough. I call forth healing, cleansing, and purification. I call forth full forgiveness from my wrongdoings and maximum positive vibrations that no illness can survive. I pray in the name of Jesus, Mohammed, Allah, Buddha and all the Saints and Aposteles and every sprit in the universe to help me be healed in 48 hours"

I got on my knees, crying and begging, and prayed this prayer over and over. I took two Tylenol PM pills to knock me out, and off I went to bed. I was out until 10 this morning... and I woke feeling better than I have in a long time. For the first time in more than a month, I stood up and did not cough. I moved around some more—and did not cough. I cleared my chest and did <u>not</u> have a coughing attack. *It's been a few days now, and I still haven't had another attack.*

A realization jolted me out of bed one morning in April. *The most profound awakenings come after suffering.* I flashed back to going bankrupt and destroying relationships, then the inspiration to Live Big and go after my dream of connecting with the world. I relived Garryck's departure from our expedition and the subsequent decision to Give Big with bikes, malaria medication, Innocent's school and more.

This is no different. I've experienced ample suffering of late, suffering that has occurred...right over my heart. Right over my heart. I grabbed a pen and notebook.

It's time to <u>LOVE BIG.</u> Here's my plan:
1) Put LOVE first. Surrender to love. Simple as that.
2) Forgive myself and realize that <u>I AM ENOUGH</u>! I don't have to DO more. I can just BE me and accept who I am fully.
3) Cause no harm to others, or myself, ever.
4) Less DOING and more BEING. Don't overwork. Enjoy the ride.
5) Turn on the Love Big Radar.
6) Head to Europe!

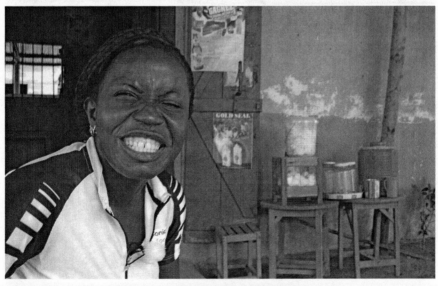

Bridget was all smiles and ready for a long expedition

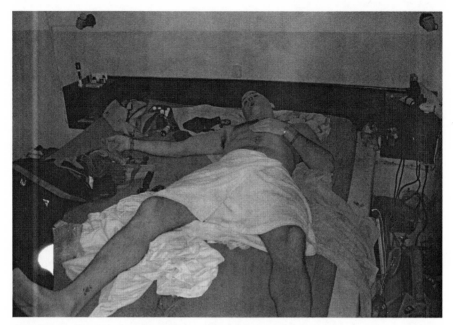

Laid out. Canceled ride with Bridget. Bummed.

My chest X-rays at the Dakar Hospital says Pneumonia

My transport across the Sahara—a Moroccan fruit truck

Mohammed working his tagine magic

 Check out a video of my final miles on the African continent.
www.bb42b.com/westafrica

37

AULLA, ITALY

---►

MY BACK AND hips ached as I rolled over at first light and peered outside. The rains, which treated my tent like a timbale all night, showed no signs of leaving Aulla, Italy. My chintzy air mattress had long lost its fight with dozens of protruding stones, giving me an unwelcome Rolfing session whenever I shifted. A mutt on his morning walk approached, sniffed my pile of sweaty gear, lifted his leg, and took a pee. Or maybe I should say left a pee. Its elderly owner caught sight of me, then clutched his wife by the arm. They quickened their pace away from the river, whispering to each other while shaking their heads in disgust.

No, no, no. Europe was supposed to be the postcard-perfect place to try on my new Live Big, Give Big, Love Big triple punch of goodness. In fact, I purposely planned my European expedition after the trip to Africa. I figured it would be a reward for all the hard work and tough rides in places like Mali and Zimbabwe. But there I was, waking up in friendly and bike-friendly Italy, having failed at both the "Peace" and the "Pedalers" part of my mission.

I had arrived in Aulla with plenty of daylight and a clear vision of finding my first Italian home stay, preferably with a large family who would give me an Italian nickname and insist I drink only the area's finest vintages. In preparation, I'd polished my Italian to a passable state and was ready to test it out. *Bianchini, my name is Bianchini. I won't even have to say my name. They'll know I'm of Italian descent just by looking at me.*

I parked my bike in front of the town's main restaurant and idled nearby, hoping to strike up a conversation within, say, ten minutes. Tops. That warm chat would lead to a giant pasta feast, homemade pasta of course, a long hot shower, a couple of new friends, a deep sleep under one of those all-consuming down comforters, and "Oh, have you met Paolo? He's a tour champion. He lives next door. He will insist on joining you up into the Tuscan Alps."

To my surprise, the curious stares and eager conversations of Africa were now replaced with suspicious glances and bowed heads. I could see locals cross the street just to avoid me and my giant bike. *The odds would be better indoors,* I concluded. And everything is better with a beer in hand. I saddled up at the bar in between a few locals who had just finished work. Soon the place filled up. For the next several hours I explained to dozens of locals the mission of Peace Pedalers, how I was a fellow *paisano,* how I was planning to ride through the Alps the next day towards the town of Lucca "where my grandparents were born."

"Very interesting story. There is a campground not far from here," suggested one cheery businessman.

"I'm sure there are rooms at the hotel," offered a grumpy truck driver.

"Have you tried the priest at the church?" said a distracted man.

Is it my Italian?

It was getting dark, and I had to find shelter. I decided to take the distracted man's advice and pedaled to the local church. A timid and frail priest opened the door just enough for him to see me and my massive bike. I explained my tour and my desire to stay with the holy men that night. *"Non possibile."*

He shut the door firmly and locked several deadbolts. *Shut down by a priest. A priest?*

As I pushed my bike up a steep hill, defeated, the rains began. The only shelter I could see was an old bridge. That would have to do. As I pulled out my wrinkled, mildewy tent, I felt like a mangy dog dispatched outside during a storm because the owners didn't want to muddy the carpets. *I miss you, Africa.*

In the morning the rains paused, and the majestic Italian Alps began to emerge out of the clouds. At least I had the scenery. My spirits lifted as I mounted my tandem steed and pedaled through crisp spring morning air. *It's just a different sales technique here. Tweak your pitch and you'll be fine.* I began looking anew for my first Italian guest rider.

"Italians love to cycle, especially in Tuscany," an Italian friend had assured me. "Your problem will be too many cyclists wanting to come aboard." I could see why. Italy is world-renowned not only for its excellent cycling equipment and racing history, but also for its charming back roads and biking culture. On any given morning in Tuscany, rain or shine, you are likely to get overrun by dozens of colorfully outfitted pelotons enjoying a ride with friends. I just needed to slip into one of those groups.

Climbing toward the Alps, the road weaved through rolling farms with trees beginning to burst with tufts of green. Spring had sprung. I waited for the first pack of cyclists to pass me by. Within minutes I was in luck. Bedecked in neon Lycra and cycling brand advertisements, the group slowed for a few moments to say hello…then just as quickly whizzed off. Another determined group did the same shortly thereafter. Throughout the morning, I asked dozens of riders if they wanted to join me as I made my way to Lucca. "*Lavoro*," they said. "*Posto.*" Work. While Italy worked, I rode solo.

The scenery and terrain helped distract me from the lack of companionship. Snowcapped mountains lined the horizon like a jagged baseboard, as spring flowers and rushing rivers rumbled to life along the country roads and stone farmhouses. *Surely I can find one person to play hooky.*

After a full day of climbing to 2,400 feet, I was right knackered, with just enough energy to seek a local family to host me. In an endearing village, I spotted a cheery Italian man trimming his bushes in the front yard as his two little girls played behind him. I rode my bike over and stopped in front of his house. His merry face turned stoic as he surveyed my tandem train. I hacked through my best Italian to explain that I was looking for an "authentic" Italian homestay experience that night: "cooking, playing with the kids, drinking wine, sharing photos and stories… just like I did in Africa!" I didn't even need to come inside the home, I explained. I'd pitch my tent on the front yard. His family would be my first hosts in Europe! An honor!

"Over there in the field, you can camp," he said without expression. He then turned and yelled something about chores to his little girls, who quickly ran into the house. Without as much a nod goodbye, he gathered up his gardening tools and followed his daughters inside. I could hear the series of locks being bolted shut. *What's up with the locks here? Why so many on the doors?*

I powered down a poor-boy dinner of bread, salami, and cheese, tossed on some deodorant, and rode to the only restaurant-bar in town, still hopeful to meet a host and a riding partner for the next day. After nearly two hours and numerous increasingly desperate attempts, I was once again directed to a grassy field. *Che cazzo?!?* What the hell?!?

The next day, like clockwork, the pelotons approached me, slowing to say "*buongiorno.*" I altered my approach with them. This wasn't just a simple ride. It was a "chance to prove to the world that Italians are as friendly as Malawians and Sierra Leoneans!" National pride did nothing to change their answers. "Ah, I wish." "Had I known I would have made preparations." "Not possible."

Frustrated, I stopped at a bike shop to see if any solo riders happened to be hanging around. A tall cyclist with dark, wavy hair observed me as I filled my tires with air. He wore a New York Yankees t-shirt, and I half expected a Bronx accent.

"My goodness! What is this bike all about?" he asked.

"I'm on a worldwide tour, inviting strangers to join me here on the rear seat to create cross-cultural friendships," I said.

"Reeeeeeeealy. How many Italian riders have joined you so far?"

I detected a hint of sarcasm.

"Um, none."

"Of course."

"Really? Why is that?"

"Oh, it's a long story."

"I have nothing but time."

He looked at me and saw I was serious.

"Okay. I can share it with you over lunch. Care to join me at my family's house?"

"Certo! Perfetto!"

"Antonio," he said. "Welcome to Italy."

Evviva per la famiglia di Antonio! I settled in to a long and leisurely lunch, topped by copious amounts of prosecco and homemade gelato. I wanted to kiss his father when he asked me if I wanted to stay in the family's hundred-year-old farmhouse on the banks of two rivers. Their village of Castelnuovo was one of those romantic hamlets you see on calendars in doctors' offices, complete with café-lined squares and a "Devil's Bridge" made of stone.

Anotonio looked much younger than his 34 years. He was a high-tech entrepreneur in addition to being an avid cyclist. We babbled for hours about million-dollar ideas and worst wipeouts. With impeccable

English, he expressed genuine interest in my project and we brainstormed about ways to be successful in Italy and Europe.

"Five years ago, we all left our doors open," he said. "We invited strangers into our homes. People were open. Not anymore."

"What's happened?"

"The media. All day, everywhere. Computer, television. Arggh. It has everyone living in fear. One bad story from another country, and, boom, it's like it happened in your backyard."

"Like what?"

"Unfortunately there have been some stories about Eastern Europeans coming over the borders robbing, raping, and even killing."

"So I might be a Russian thug, eh?"

"I'm afraid so, Jamie. If you just show up at their door asking to come stay with them, there is just no way most people will let you in. Would *you*?"

"Of course," I said, though I wasn't so sure. "What should I do?"

"You should announce your arrival. In advance. Give people time to go to your website, learn about your project, and decide if they want to participate."

"Work, work, work, they've told me so far."

"Exactly. I work for myself, so I can go with you to Lucca. But you are not in Africa anymore."

What is it about bad news that makes people want to seek it out and devour it like an all-you-can-eat buffet on a cruise ship? Is it some genetic urge to factor in any and all threats, or a morbid learned curiosity? Between radon and alar, the brakes of Audi 5000s and Y2K, salt and pop rocks washed down with Coke, aren't we all supposed to be dead by now? I didn't blame the media as much as our endless appetite for doom and gloom. They'd give us nothing but sunrise highlights and puppy births if we demanded it. We don't.

All cuddled up and safe and Bird Flu–free in a stately guest bed, I thought back to the recent days and felt the resentment creep up from my toes. The negative news fixation wasn't dimming, it was proliferating. Now on computers, cell phones, and bathroom stalls near you! I used to think it was a particularly American trend, but clearly the condition was widespread. If I didn't adjust something to counter the perceptions, I would end up camping solo, wedging into youth hostels, and staring at an empty seat on my bike.

Antonio was up early, decked out head-to-toe in high-end racing Spandex. His large cycling quadriceps popped from his shorts like fresh-baked loaves of bread. We planned to ride 60 kilometers to Lucca, where my grandparents were born and raised. Antonio estimated that he rode more than 12,000 kilometers per year, mostly fast road riding. *This could be the best ride of the trip.* He even arranged a support vehicle for my bags, a Mini Cooper driven by his girlfriend, Chiara.

We darted off from his house like seasoned pros, cutting into the crisp morning air that coated my arms in goose bumps. Within minutes, we were both properly warmed up and hammering the lush green rolling hills of Tuscany. *This guy is good. Bellisimo!*

"I think you're right, Antonio," I said. "When I was in Africa, I was focused on trying to help the communities. We delivered bikes and handed out free malaria medication. But Europe doesn't need this kind of support. I'm thinking…what it needs most…is a big dose of love and positivity."

"Oh yes, Europe needs more of that for sure," he said with a chuckle.

"So what if I invest my energy with local media to share the positive stories of friendship and connection from around the world? You think they'd publish stories like that?"

"Sure. And that effort can also let people know you are coming, and help you find more riders and homestays."

"I think I'm also going let all my friends and website followers know my exact riding schedule so they can spread the word as well."

"Perfect."

"I just worry about having the ride becoming too scheduled. I don't want to lose that serendipity. My best experiences have often been the least planned."

With Antonio aboard—and his advice still ringing in my head—the local populace seemed to change from uninterested to engaging and warm. Friendly Italians cyclists and motorists cheered us on as we weaved through picturesque Tuscan villages. I began to envision a new expedition style that would combine providence and planning. Would it be possible? I didn't want to bring peace to only the peaceniks. I wanted to touch the disbelievers and cynics.

Later in the day, after a leisurely picnic in Lucca, I said goodbye and thank you to Antonio and Chiara. They needed to get back to their jobs and families, and I needed to continue on, armed with their boost and advice. They left…and I got lost. I'd somehow managed to lose both my area map and Lonely Planet guidebook. I panicked at first, then assured myself I'd done just fine for years without guidebooks, and in places a hell of a lot tougher than this. Why do we insist on them in easy travel zones like Europe? I decided to ride around until some sort of "sign" appeared.

I had heard about a campsite overlooking the city of Florence. Seemed as good a place as any. I'd learned that people are more apt to help if you have a specific destination; they felt uneasy if you said you were just ambling around. I decided to ask directions from an older but spry cyclist with skin the color of a Thanksgiving turkey and white hair slicked back as if he had just hopped out of a pool. "Silvano," he said, introducing himself. After a couple minutes I learned he was 67 years young, had five bikes, and had toured around in more than twenty European countries. "*Bella, bella,*" he said, touching my bike.

Silvano spoke no English, but a little French and some Spanish in addition to his flowery Italian. We were able communicate with ease, using a mishmash of words in a handful of languages. He proudly led me to the campsite, and we set a date to meet at sunset to ride together in the city.

He promised a tour, but Silvano was incapable of just pointing out the towering Campanile of the Duomo or the medieval craftsmanship of the Ponte Vecchio bridge. Instead, we laughed and sang our way through the City of Lilies, high-fiving and flirting with jewelry-stand saleswomen and the sunglasses-at-night crowd on the piazzas. If Silvano was paying any attention to cars or traffic, I missed it. Miraculously, we came away unscathed. He loved every inch of this town, dousing me with this affection at every sidewalk café and historic building. *Bella, bella.*

He also loved the Peace Pedalers mission, agreeing that the positive stories of human connection on the tandem needed to be read by Italians. We set a time the next day to go to *La Nazione* to try to get a story published. He promised me he would smooth the way for a glowing piece, and I had no doubt he would.

That evening, overlooking the sparkling lights of Firenze, I grabbed my Toughbook.

I was told today that the word Florence comes from the Latin word for "flowers in bloom." I feel like a flower that's finally coming back to life after a turbulent winter. This Love Big addition to my journey has created several bountiful experiences so far. However, I have realized I am not in Africa any more. *Long gone are the days of just knocking on a stranger's door and asking to stay with him.*

After my first few weeks here in it has become clear that I have a choice to make: continue riding in my regular serendipitous fashion like in Asia and Africa, which would lead to many more days and night alone, or implement a new strategy to connect with people. So...like they say...when in Rome...

My new plan is:
- *Use Couchsurfing.org to find people who are trusting and embrace connecting with strangers from other lands*
- *Announce my route in advance on my website, and among friends and family*
- *Let the media know my story and try to let people know who I am before I roll through their country*
- *Turn the Live Big, Give Big, and Love Big radars on high*
- *And, of course, surrender to serendipity whenever possible.*

I just spent two hours sprinkling seeds of connections up ahead with emails and Couchsurfing invitations up in Northern Italy, Switzerland, Lichtenstein, Austria, and Slovenia. Off to bed while they hopefully take root...

Home on the rocks. Under a bridge. Night one on tour in Europe.

The picture perfect riding in the Italian Alps

Now we're riding! Antonio with his house in the background

My first friend in Florence, Silvano

38
SARAJEVO, BOSNIA AND HERZEGOVINA

--►

OVER THE NEXT several months, I put the plan into place like a cook following a new recipe of a favorite dish—a dash of planning here, a smidge of fortune there. The results led to some glorious feasts…some passable meals…and a few cases of heartburn.

The main ingredient in this new special sauce was the Couchsurfing website, which hosted online profiles of like-minded travelers and willing hosts. No fees, no quid pro quos. It was all organized in the name of connection, hospitality, and adventure, values I embraced and celebrated naturally. I felt like I'd hit a gold mine of kindred souls. And guest riders! I experienced the payoffs immediately.

In Sarajevo, I rode around town with Nevena, a Couchsurfing hostess. She took me to a popular TV station to record an interview on the *Good Vibrations* show. Then she showed me the aftermath of a different kind of vibration—apartment houses and office buildings senselessly shelled by Serbian troops from a nearby mountain that at one time had hosted the Winter Olympics, the self-proclaimed paragon of world peace and unity. With her matted black hair and architectural glasses, Nevena looked like she was straight out of a Seattle coffee shop. But she was from here, the war zone, and every block on the bike triggered new stories of snipers, grenades, and nights in the basement. Kids in other parts of the world collected stamps and Pokémon cards. As a child, she had a shrapnel collection "unrivaled in the neighborhood."

Nevana grew up in daily fear of murder, rape, sexual assault, torture, and beatings. I marveled at how she didn't let the war defeat her. She didn't try to rationalize human atrocity or make sense of the nonsense. She carried on, and focused on the positive parts of her life. Simplicity, she repeated. That was the overriding force in her life these days.

She and her friend Mirela, another Muslim-faith rider from Sarajevo, had vowed to rebuild after the war. Rebuild structures and relationships, jobs, and ways of life. Neither of them had dared venture to northern Bosnia, which was heavily populated by Serbs, the people who had terrorized their city. But in the name of peace and healing, they agreed to join me northbound. We cycled together into the Serbian section of Bosnia and Herzegovina. Mirela shared how fireworks still made her duck. But she also shared how growing up in the war shaped her positive outlook on life. We shared a victory meal with some Bosnian Serbs, talked about the future and the commonalities that bind us. We finished the ride feeling we'd added a penny to a wishing well of healing.

About an hour before my bus departed from Belgrade, we decided to take a "victory photo." Without me noticing, one of our new Bosnian Serb "friends" photo-bombed the shot complete with a thumb-index-middle finger hand signal representing the father, the son, and the Holy Ghost. During the war, soldiers flashed the same sign before beating, raping, or killing Muslim citizens. The war may be over, but some minds would never change.

Mirela would have none of it. She lit into the man, telling him to shove the three fingers up his nether region.

I cycled on to Prague, where the revelry and un-bombed beauty of the city inspired me to do something I hadn't considered in years—put away the video equipment. The filming, which I had so enjoyed in Africa, was now becoming a chore. The interviews felt forced, and my requests were sometimes unwanted or ignored. I struggled with this, wanting to keep a video journal and provide my sponsors with the promised scenes from the road. I also feared missing out on genuine friendships and authentic, stress-free moments while my head was stuck behind the camera. I decided on a compromise. I'd film only the most inspiring moments and keep the equipment packed away the rest of the time.

Relieved, I called up my Czech soul sister Irena, whom I had met on an earlier trip to Prague. Perfect timing, she said. She'd just finished a large tech project for Exxon and now had two weeks to play around on vacation. A bike trip to Germany sounded sublime.

Irena had never camped, so I was determined to get her hooked on outdoor living. We found a hidden back road that led to an ideal, not to mention free, campsite on the banks of a river. We set up a tent, skinny-dipped in the cool water, had some dinner and champagne, and lounged in the hammock. She had sleepy eyes and tea-blonde hair that tickled my cheeks. I grabbed her hand and led her back to the tent.

We were having so much fun, Irena decided to play through for a couple days and join me in Berlin. We stayed with friends, and Irena got along with everyone. During the days, we'd meander on the bike through the pastoral Tiergarten, to the flea markets in Mauerpark, ending at the bars that line the banks of the Spree. Berlin is the anti-Germany—more artistic, less methodical, more right brain, less left. We traced the boundaries of the old Berlin Wall, seeing sections frozen in time. The occasional Trabant car zipped by, reminding us of the divides not too long ago.

Berlin media outlets were interested in my mission, and Irena and I made the rounds to TV stations and newspaper offices. On the way to an interview, I heard a shout that made me slam on the brakes. "Jaaaaaaime!" What? *Was the voice in my headphones?* When I stopped I could barely believe my eyes. The bellow belonged to Mathieu, my host and surfing buddy in Benin! "What the hell are you doing here?" we both asked. He was in Berlin for a spell, studying German. Fate, we concluded. We took each other's local German phone numbers and talked about some adventures together.

After the TV interview, I ferried Irena to the Berlin Central Train Station, where we shared a weepy coffee session, wondering if it would be our last rendezvous. This was the part of my life I had grown to loathe yet accept as the price of a road romance.

She boarded her train, and I lingered in the café, debating if my feelings were real or if I was just a trigger-happy crier. The truth, I decided, is that the emotions were honest, but also that I loved everything about love. I knew the romance would end…and so did my companions. Sure, we talked about future rides and get-togethers, and sometimes they happened and sometimes they didn't. For those moments I was in love. A different kind of love, yes. We both got on the bike knowing the drill. And we both had a hell of a lot of fun.

I called Mathieu and invited him to pedal for a day heading north to Denmark. He had a rigorous school schedule, but agreed to put his studies aside for 24 hours. On the bike, he explained that he was dating a German woman he'd met in Benin. She convinced him to learn her native tongue if he wanted to get serious about the relationship. Mathieu is from Brittany. He's a gentle soul with a healthy appetite for outdoor adventure. If I staged a bodybuilding contest with everyone who had ever sat on the back seat, Mathieu would take the crown.

We talked about love and relationships, and the balance between commitment and freedom. Was there an "ideal age" at which to get married? Our parents settled down in their teens and twenties, but now people were living longer. Didn't that make the "ideal age" a little older? Neither of us had found a lifetime partner, yet we both believed we would be married. Someday. First he wanted to explore places like French Polynesia. It was fulfilling to be around some male energy after the string of female riders the past few weeks. Our time together made me think about the importance of male-female balance in life, and how wrong events can go when the equilibrium is disrupted.

One advantage of my new approach to travel: days and weeks of savory anticipation. Researchers claim that some of the biggest benefits of travel occur in the days leading up to the trip, the time spent mulling maps and must-visit lists, tasting that Parisian éclair or Brazilian *feijoada* far in advance. I tried to live in the moment, to not let the email exchanges or shared photos distract me from the locations at hand. But at nights and during solo stretches on the bike, I found my mind drifting ahead to my hosts. Would he or she be a shoes-at-the-door type or a feet-on-the-sofa person? Carnivore or strict vegetarian? Cuddler or platonic friend?

Of all the partners I planned to visit in Europe, none was as eagerly anticipated as Carina in Sweden. The last time I saw her was in 1979 when she lived with our family, working as an au pair. I was seven back then, and our family was going through a lot of upheaval. Carina was there to lend a hand and provide a steadying presence for three anxious boys and a newly single mother.

Now 48, Carina found me, and Peace Pedalers, on the Internet while searching for news about our family. I received an email from her while in Africa. She not only accepted my invitation to ride, but started a training regimen for the trip. I gave her a call at her vacation home near the Kattegat Sea on Sweden's west coast. She said the weather throughout southern Sweden would soon soak the area and flood the roads. Still the caregiver, she insisted on driving two hours to Malmö to pick me up.

Carina arrived with her sister, Anne, and we gave each other a big strong hug. *I remember that hug, usually coming after my stepfather had brought us to tears with his abuse, my mom distant and drinking heavily at the time. You'd rub my back and say, "It's all right, Jamie. Everything will be okay." Those hugs helped carry me through some tough months.* She looked hale and fit, a decade younger than her age. Climbing into Anne's posh Volvo, she vowed she was "ready to ride," though we were both grateful not to be out pedaling that day.

After the storms cleared, we saddled up and wove our way from Gothenburg to Halden, Norway, sticking to the bucolic roads along the rugged Bohuslän coast. Rocky islands with brightly colored fishermen's houses popped up at every vista. We ate fish for dinner and berries for breakfast. Simple, serene, stunning, the area lulled us both into a leisurely trip down memory lane. Carina was interested to know what had happened to my brothers and me, especially my decision to chuck it all and hit the road for all these years. She was stuck in a dead-end corporate job, and dreamed about escape. After all these years she still cared for us. Deeply. She was worried we'd be scarred from our upbringing, and seemed relieved to hear everyone was doing well.

Though I'd largely shuttered the video equipment, I felt a strong urge to pull out the cameras and ask her about life.

"It's *today* that counts, and I wish I was more like that," she said. "We say 'I'll be happy when I'm rich,' but then we are not happy when we are well off. It's like a wheel, and once you are in it, it's hard to get off. You stop appreciating the moment when you get like this."

The cold gray skies matched my mood as I left Carina on a train from Halden to Oslo. She'd been a big comfort to me as a child. Her words and companionship were equally bolstering now that I was an adult. *You can go home again,* I thought, *and sometimes that home is in a foreign country.*

I took a deep breath and stored my bike in the luggage bins. A Norwegian guest rider would pick me up at the station, and we'd ride into the capital together. I called Carina again to say thank you.

"Excuse me, sir. Would you kindly get off the phone?" a man asked/ordered in an officious tone.

"I'm finishing up a phone call with a dear friend," I replied, annoyed. "I'll be off soon."

He stood by, waiting for me to burn up the last minutes on my prepaid mobile card. Ignoring him, I kicked up my feet on a disorganized pile of heavily soiled dry bags, panniers, and camera cases. The stench no doubt filled the entire section of the train, boosted even more by my musky mix of body odor, essential oils, and cheap sunscreen.

"Sir, I need you to get off the phone at this moment," said the man.

He flashed police officer badge.

"Carina, I have to go."

I hung up the phone and looked up at the officer.

"Okay, I'm off the phone. What can I do for you, sir?" I asked in a sarcastic tone.

"Are you carrying any drugs with you?"

"No. I don't think so."

"Well, the dog seems to think you have drugs in this bag here. Might we have a look?"

"Sure, go ahead. Um, well, there might be something left over from a tandem passenger I picked up down in Christiana, Denmark. Where marijuana is legal. He was smoking down there."

He opened up the side pocket of my pannier, and found a well-worn plastic bag that contained a single joint of marijuana about one-quarter smoked. *Damn Christiana.* Before heading to Europe, I promised myself I was not going to do any drugs. I kept my pledge until Christiania, an eclectic and artsy neighborhood in Copenhagen. Marijuana has been legal there for years. Locals bragged it was the best in Europe. I had met some residents who gave me the royal tour of the hippie community, which, of course, included a few joints of their finest cannabis. I accepted the gift out of habit, and carried the satchel with me in my panniers. Several guest riders had enjoyed it without a care through Denmark and Sweden.

"We are going to have to get off the train," he said, holding up the bag.

"Are you serious? It's half a joint, nothing more. You can take it if you want."

"I'm afraid it's not that simple."

He handed the bag over to another undercover officer and radioed ahead.

"Um. Sir, should I be afraid here?" I asked.

"Well, a little bit afraid, yes. We don't tolerate any drugs whatsoever here in Norway."

At the next stop, they ordered me off the train. A group of police officers came onboard to confiscate my bike, bags, and gear. I was not

allowed to touch anything until after inspection. They grabbed my arm
and led me to the back of the police car, which sped me to a nearby
police station. They strip-searched me, rifled through my belongings,
and placed me into a cell where I was to await my sentence from a judge.
I guess the ride with Magnus is out of the question. They allowed me to
make a call.

"Hey, Magnus, it's me, Jamie."

"Hey, Jamie! I am almost off work and very excited to ride with you!"

I shared the news.

"Oh Jamie, that is really not good. Norway is the *worst* place in
Europe to get caught with marijuana."

"Do you have any advice? Or any idea how much money I should
expect to pay in fines?"

"Just be as nice as you can, and ask them for the smallest penalty
possible. Probably, at least 5,000 kroner."

"What? That's more than $1,000!"

"They are very serious about it here."

"I don't know how long I'm going to be here, so let's meet up at the
house, hopefully later tonight. I'm really sorry, Magnus."

Not that I'd spent a lot of days in jails during my nearly four decades
on earth, but this seemed to be a nice one. It had a comfortable bed,
modern toilet, and sparkling floors. *Wonder where they get the money to
pay for all this?* Then I realized the night's stay could cost me $1,000.
Never mind.

Another officer asked if I had an explanation I wanted to share with
the judge. I panicked. Should I take an Atticus Finch approach or just
play dumb like in *Legally Blonde*? Are you supposed to admit guilt here in
Norway, or deny, deny, deny? Still debating the best approach, I handed
him several Peace Pedalers stickers and begged for the smallest fine possible. *Stickers?*

Several hours later, I was handed a bill for nearly $600. "That's the
lowest bail available," said one officer. "It's a common fine for people who
pee in public or disturb the peace. I've never seen a drug smuggler get such
a low bail. You are lucky." *Drug smuggler? For half a joint left in a bag? I'll
tell you who needs a smoke—Norway's lawmakers.* They escorted me to an
ATM machine, where I pulled out the wad of kroner. It was more than I'd
spent on lodging the entire trip. I called Magnus and gave him a heads-up

that I was finally released, but my spirits were at an all-time low.

"Let me buy you a pint," said Patrick in his thick Irish brogue.

"I'll never turn down a pint from a...what do you call people from Belfast?"

"People from Belfast."

"I'll never turn down a pint from a person from Belfast."

He laughed. Cheers.

"So what are you doin' with that crazy long bike anyways?" he asked.

"I'm traveling around the world, inviting strangers to become friends on a project I call Peace Pedalers."

"So what's your business here in town?" he asked, his tone becoming a shade more suspicious.

"It's on my route... and I wanted to better understand the reasons for the past violence and current peace."

"Aw, Christ. Another bloody do-gooder."

"I was just over on the other side of the Peace Wall, on the Shankill Road, chatting with folks over there. I wanted to get another perspective over here."

"Ah! I hate Protestants! I bloody hate 'em!" he yelled.

I was speechless. I looked at him closely, and he was shaking. Veins pulsated on the side of his head as he clenched his teeth and returned my unintended stare. *There's a lot of venom in there. Quite a bit of booze, too.* I tried to appear casual as I looked away, admiring the dark wood walls that surrounded our booth. *No.* Avoiding tough conversations wasn't my goal for the journey.

"But why, Patrick? Why do you hate a person because of the way they choose to celebrate their spirituality?"

"I just hate 'em. Always have and always will!"

A piece of his spittle hit my cheek. *Do I wipe it away or will that make him ever more mad?*

"Okay, okay. Got it. How about we forget about religion and take a bike ride?"

He exhaled through his nose, making a sound like a leaky tire.

"Ah, brilliant. I'd love to," he said, getting on. "Where do you want to go?"

"Through the Peace Wall, Shankill Road."

"You taking the piss? Not a bloody chance in the world am I going over there!"

"What's the big deal?"

"I'd be a dead man if I did"

"Why?"

"Because I killed a bunch of them, and they all know me too well. Not…a…chance. I'll ride downtown or anywhere on this side, but no way I'm going to the Shankill Road."

"C'mon."

"Get lost, ya crazy Yank!" he said, sitting back down in the booth with his buddies, who suddenly looked much more menacing.

My knowledge of Irish history was limited. Patrick proved that. I'd read up on "The Troubles," trying to get a better understanding of the roots of the conflict and just how and where it spilled over into the streets of Northern Ireland. Belfast had long been a hot spot, that much I knew. But authors and information sources from all sides of the conflict talked about the peace accords and the progress being made.

So, as I did down in the Balkans, I set out with a generic intention to sprinkle some seeds of love and healing, one bike rider at a time. Just a simple ride, I told anyone who would listen. How much harm is there in that? Then let's head to the pubs and celebrate life right proper, pints in hand.

Discouraged though not defeated after my chat with Patrick, I walked outside onto the Falls Road where my bike was parked in front of the bar. During the The Troubles, roughly the late 1960s until the "Good Friday" agreement of 1998, much of the violence happened on or near either Falls Road or Shankill Road. After the treaty was signed, Catholics and Protestants created a "Peace Wall" between the two infamous streets.

Earlier in the day I was drawn to a pub on Shankill Road, where the RUC (Royal Ulster Constabulary), a British loyalist police force, used to gather regularly, making it a prime target for IRA gunfire and bomb attacks. A pint of ale sounded refreshing that warm afternoon, but I had a greater thirst for conversation. As always, the tandem bike made it easy to strike up conversations. I met a few locals who shared their take on The Troubles. They then pointed me to Mark, the bar owner, a man who had seen it all from his perch. I asked if he could simply educate me on the whole subject. We took a seat outside. He looked like a Member of Parliament after an all-night session, with a slightly wrinkled dark blue business suit, gray hair thinning at the top, and crow's feet that stretched nearly to his ears. He let me run a voice recorder, but didn't want me to film him.

"I am a peaceful man, and don't have any issues with anyone until they come in and try to impose their will on me. When somebody does this, it can take a peaceful person and make them violent."

"Are you happy with the current peace agreement?"

"For the most part, yes. The city is thriving again, and we needed that."

"And what do you think is going to be key to keeping the peace in the future?"

"The children. I send my kids to a public school where both Protestant and Catholics study and mingle together like kids should. Their generation is the best hope for continued peace in Ireland."

The children. *The children.* Both sides talked about the children as the key to peace. The whole world talked about children as the key to the future. At times it sounded obvious. Of course kids will decide the future. The rest of us will be long gone. But they weren't just talking about children taking over control. They were in agreement that kids entered the world without the biases and prejudices that we adults tended to grab onto and never let go. The most ardent Unionists or Nationalists, the ones who will go to their grave believing in their cause, still told me their sons and daughters were born with clean slates. Peace was there from day one. It's the most natural path. It's the divisions and hatreds that take time and effort to build.

After listening to Mark, I was even more determined to find a rider for the next day. I struck out numerous times, including with Mark himself, but I figured I'd just keep hanging around. While I waited, I gave a handful of children rides up and down the road. The boys all had shaved heads and clothes that fit like they'd been handed down from an older brother.

Pulling back up to the pub, I nearly ran into a handsome bald (is that redundant?) man. Joe was his name. He had heard me talking to Mark, and asked if I was still interested in finding riders. I didn't ask about his politics or religion, only that we gather during his lunch break the following day. We met outside City Hall. He rolled up his jeans so as not to catch them in the chain. He was old enough to be my father, yet more athletic and three shades paler than Dad had ever been.

"Hey, Joe! How are you? How you feeling?"

"I'm okay. Pretty nervous, I must be honest. But I'm excited. I really want to do this."

"You'll be fine. I've given rides on four continents so far, and haven't lost a rider yet."

"I just don't want to be recognized over there, ya know?"

"Here," I said, handing him my sunglasses. "Put these on."

"Do ya mind?"

"Not at all"

"I think I'm also going to button up my shirt so nobody sees my shamrock either."

Joe led me through his own neighborhood first, sharing a bit about his life. He had been passionate about the IRA movement. Everything changed once he had a son. He didn't want his child fueled with the hatred that at times had consumed him. So he quit the IRA, and felt guilty for any destruction he'd supported. The blocks around his house were crammed with dilapidated red brick buildings, like worn Legos lined up in row. Walls once coated in political slogans were now filled with band names and graffiti art.

"So when was the last time you crossed over to Shankill Road?" I asked him as we approached the Peace Wall gates.

"Um, let's see. It was, no…1969."

I don't know which of us was more surprised.

"They still close these gates at night, ya know," he said, making sure I understood the situation was still quite fragile.

"Here they are."

I expected him to ramble, or at least say something. Instead I heard nothing. After what seemed like several minutes he cleared his throat.

"Oh, oh, oh. This is strange."

His voice sounded nonplussed.

"So what's the emotion as you cross over?"

"There's still a wee bit of butterflies in me stomach. Not quite fear, but uneasiness."

There are some distinct moments in the Peace Pedalers history that I know I will never forget. This was one. Turning back to him, I saw his face, a leaky dam trying and failing to keep emotions in check. Fear, frustration, sadness, pride and nostalgia all seemed to be dripping out. Joe fought them off. He replied to my questions with one-word answers. Fine. Yup. Cool.

"I have been doing a lot of work on myself lately," he said after we crossed back over. "This was a great opportunity to stretch and grow."

"I feel the same."

Nevena in front of the tattered buildings like she grew up in

Mathieu and I rocking northern Germany towards Denmark

Rolling the pristine bike path along the coast

Kids didn't care one iota if you were Catholic or Protestant

Joe and I making our way to cross the Peace Wall gates

39

PARIS, FRANCE

--►

LIVE BIG, GIVE BIG, LOVE BIG. It was in Ireland where I finally found my groove and a way to balance these three simple intentions I set off to experiment with in Europe. From Belfast I meandered my way to Sligo, Ireland on the west coast where Mother Nature delivered perfect fall surfing and the locals greeted me with a free surfboard and a rich homestay. I rode across the country towards Dublin with a Sligo man named Sean who just happened to be a musician with a song about peace we were able to perform and even record on our last evening together. I was in the flow. And this was where I wanted to stay.

Heading into Wales and down to England I bunny hopped blissful moments with the locals all the way to the ferry station to Holland. An endless stream of European riders continued as I made my way on the empty Dutch cycling paths into Belgium. In Belgium I reunited with my dear friend Phillip, my very first long distance rider from way back in China. Phillip took a week off work to explore the Belgian back roads together where were hosted by beer-brewing monks and saved by a Flemish stranger who drove our battered team to Luxembourg after my rear wheel died on us out in the pouring rain.

But, just like so many times in my life and on my tour, Mamacita would save the day. My tandem was out of commission unless I found a new wheel. So she carved out time to come join me and hand delivered a new wheel. Problem solved. Mamacita had clocked many days on the bike in Japan, India, Thailand, Australia, Kenya, and Uganda; now it was time for a taste of France. I hadn't seen her in more than ten months. I knew she'd give me a boost.

Unlike previous visits, she was coming to France without a bike and without any intention to ride. She'd been slowed recently as a result of a nasty biking accident, a blowout of her knee, and the natural brakes of old age. She received cortisone injections for her knee, packed pain-killers, and managed to arrive with a new rear wheel for the tandem. I hugged her without stopping—for just everything.

As a bonus, I had lined up a special guest for our adventure: Carina, my former au pair. She was excited to reconnect with Mom after nearly three decades. And I was happy to have her back on the bike. She'd assured me she'd kept up her cycling since Sweden.

We had planned to stay in Paris for five days to take in the sights. But by the time I arrived, I had received an email from Mathieu, my French *ami* who had spotted me on the streets of Berlin. He said the surf and the weather were ideal near his hometown in Brittany. "You all have been to Paris many times. Come to the coast!" It was an offer too good to refuse. We tossed back some *pot-au-feu* with a few bottles of Burgundy Pinot Noir, and headed west.

It would be the third time I'd pair with Mathieu since meeting him in Benin the previous year. Back then he had received word that a globe-trotting cyclist and surf nut was in town. He offered to host me for several days at his pad near the beach in Benin. We built a solid friendship as I surfed and learned French for a few weeks. At first glance, Mathieu looked straight from the Kennedy compound in Hyannis Port. He wore polo shirts and chic sunglasses. But Mathieu was an old-school adventurer at heart, probably on this planet a century too late. He would have fit right in with the Peary or Shackleton crowds.

In Benin, he had talked up the waves near his home in France. "Come anytime," he said. "I'll show you them myself." The sales pitch continued in Germany, then on our two-day cycling adventure north. I never used to believe in fate while traveling. But after countless "chance" encounters and "accidental" angels, I had changed my tune. Of course I'd run in to Mathieu in Berlin, and in other parts of Germany, and of course we'd end up on the Brittany coast with long, sloping waves and warm afternoons as the exclamation points.

Mathieu lived in the tiny town of Plozévet, about two kilometers from the Atlantic. On our first night together, while he chatted with my mom and Carina, gathering all my worst bedwetting and temper tantrum stories from childhood, we could all hear the pounding swell coming in. The offshore winds had picked up, and there was nary a cloud in the starry sky. We talked about childhood misdeeds, but our minds were focused on one thing...surfing.

The next day we began a daily ritual of blissful activities following a strict order: wake up late. No alarm. Devour a mouthwatering breakfast of fresh bread, croissants, fruit, and oats. Hit the world-class surf for two or three hours. Linger over a huge lunch in the sunshine. Nap. Head back out for another pleasurable surf session until the sun went down. Start the evening with local apple cider and wine. "May I refill you?" Eat meals we somehow managed to prepare between the four of us. Soak in a relaxing bath. Bed. Rinse, repeat.

This is the perfect trip for me and Mom, I thought. I can surf with Mathieu, and she can reminisce with Carina. They chatted from the minute they arrived in Paris, stopping only to eat and sleep. I realized how important Carina was to my mom at a time when she needed a boost. I saw it in the way she reached for Carina's forearm when Carina talked about her life in Sweden, or how she devoured Carina's stories like they were free popcorn from movie theaters.

Sadly, Carina had to return back to Sweden after a week. Mathieu had business to attend to as well. That left Mom and me to once again embrace—or kill—each other on the road. After several long talks, she decided she wanted to ride. She'd ridden on every other continent, she averred. Why should France be any different?

I'd seen her cry from pain and frustration in Australia, nearly get killed by a truck in Kenya, and conquer 80-kilometer days in 100-degree heat in Uganda. If Peace Pedalers ever awarded an MVP, my mom would be the odds-on favorite in Las Vegas. This was different. Yes, France is a country that feels like it was sculpted by a greater force specifically for the purpose of pedaling on two wheels. Hmm, said the Creator. Let me give you smooth roads between quaint villages that just happen to have five-star bistros. Care for a break at a world-class winery? Done. Expert bike mechanics and repair shops in every town? Deal. Oh, and you want just the right amount of sunshine and clouds? *Voilà!*

Cycling in France was too good to pass up, we both concluded. We'd hit the road, though I worried incessantly she'd suffer another crash or emotional breakdown. I loved her very much. I never wanted her to suffer; never wanted to see her scared or uncomfortable in any way. If it wasn't for her, I wouldn't be out here in the first place.

We started slow, just a Sunday ride across town. No particular destination, no schedule we needed to meet. Free and easy we pedaled, past the sea-breeze grasses and slate roof homes. She was doing it. She was still strong. I felt the push from the back of the bike and gave her a thumbs-up. She was now 67. After an especially quick stretch of riding alongside the Maine River, I peered in my rearview mirror and saw her proud and content face.

Mamacita was always happier on the bike. I never wanted that to end. Giving up bike riding was the equivalent of taking away a driver's license from an elderly driver—often it triggers a decline. Maybe it was losing my father, and the guilt I carried for never pushing him to exercise. I wanted to make sure this parent stayed fit. I wanted my mom, needed my mom. After a few days of touring through the French countryside, I suggested she get off the tandem and jump onto the single bike, currently being ridden by a friend named Sophie.

No, no, no. She declined, then hesitated, making excuses and justifications. The knee, her conditioning, blah, blah. I decided not take no for an answer. This was either going to be a massive blowout and months of not speaking or, well, who knows. *I need you, Mom. There are so many rides to come.*

"Okay, okay," she said, finally giving in. A few minutes later she was spinning behind the tandem, sporting a confident smile. I thought I saw her mouth "Thank you." Her smile, and the fact she was riding solo again, said it all.

I knew I would sink when she departed. I knew I'd mope around France (or Japan, India, Australia, Kenya, etc.) when she left me to go back to the U.S. I even had a name for it, "post-Mamacita-visit depression syndrome," a common affliction during the Peace Pedalers expedition. I felt closer to her this time than at any other stage of the journey. She was there for me. I got that. But her actions this trip—more laid back and accepting than she'd ever been—freed me. Look, we're all trying to please our parents on some level. In Europe, I felt that I had. It took me four continents, but, hey, I'm slow.

I hugged her goodbye, and released my mind to South America.

The daily dose of perfect surf and weather in Plozévet, France

Home cooked meals with family in friends in France after a surf. Nice.

Mamacita is always happier on her bike.

40
FLORIANÓPOLIS, BRAZIL

--►

IF I AM going to wear the skin-tight miniskirt, my lipstick should match, I told myself as I stared into a full-length mirror. *Nice gams.* I don't think I'd been in better shape in all my life. Six years of hardcore riding will do that to you. I tested a few shades before picking one that mirrored my hot pink skirt and top. *Perfect. Now just a little more accessorizing, and I'll be ready for Carnival.* I tossed on a fake flower lei, a sparkly golden wig, and oversized pink sunglasses, the kind Elton John would wear on tour. *Florianópolis, here I come.*

I'd been fantasizing about this moment for a long time. The envisioned scene tended to pop up during heat strokes in Africa or bike breakdowns in Europe. *Hang in there, man. Carnival is coming up. Brazil, baby.* Fellow backpackers and cyclers place Brazilian Carnival at the top of their to-visit lists. I know it was right up there on mine. I was more than ready for some thumping samba, anything-goes parties, and gorgeous Brazilian women in every direction. Ask a man or woman in Brazil how many people they've slept with, and they'll usually preface their answer with, "Well, not counting Carnival…"

Ice-cold Brahma beers flowed like liquid gold, handed to me from smiling strangers toting coolers in "borrowed" shopping carts. Mendes and Gilberto blared from bars and cheap car stereo systems. I looked up to see several groups of men gyrating on the balconies, all dressed in drag. "Nice boobs!" I yelled, before realizing they were plastic. He waved, then lifted his skirt to show me his hairy package. *Ah, Carnival.*

I had arrived in Florianópolis a few weeks prior, just in time for my 37th birthday. A small crew of local Couchsurfing hosts treated me to dinner and a birthday fiesta. We swapped travel stories and talked about my plan to stay in Florianópolis for the next three months. I wanted to master my Portuguese and experience Brazilian life as a local. The thought of a Brazilian girlfriend did cross my mind a time or two. It's the best way to learn a language, right?

However, once I blew out the candles, reality settled in. My hosts rattled off details of a few recent robberies and warned about an uptick in crime, "especially against gringos." I left the party with a crippling sense of fear. Shopkeepers and bored teenagers morphed into potential robbers ready to jump me at any moment. Maybe this town and I wouldn't be such a great fit after all. I felt uneasy and alone. I lingered in bed the next day, recalling the numerous warnings I'd ignored in the last few months.

"I had a knife put to my throat for my iPod," one traveler told me.

"You made it sixty countries without being assaulted? Let's see if you can make it through Latin America," said a Brazilian.

"They will kill you for that case of cameras, and leave you in a bush. Watch your butt!" said my brother Gino.

I finally came out of my paralyzed state on day three in Florianopolis. I took a deep breath, and rode over from my host Marina's house in Rio Tavares to a small local surf shop. A short, chubby surfer named Victor patiently allowed me to hack through my broken Portuguese. He responded in perfect English that he might have a solution. Victor was one of the many Brazilians who had logged several years in San Diego, California, before returning home to a more laidback lifestyle. He just happened to know of an open apartment above a board-shaping business nearby. Within a few hours, I went from a fearful hermit hiding out in a Couchsurfing host's room to holding the keys to my own apartment just steps from the ocean. My rent was a whopping $200 a month. *Now* it was time to get ready for Carnival—local style.

I could feel Florianópolis's pulse start to quicken in the days leading up to Carnival. Impromptu parties and jam sessions popped up on street corners. The smell of roasting meat at sidewalk *churrascos* assaulted my nostrils like an assassin, bam! *Where's that coming from?* The samba schools finalized their parade routines, and new lovers kissed and groped on the sandy shores. Dressed in my pink miniskirt and gilded wig, I stood on the banks of it all and watched the river of revelry stream by. *Ready, set, jump!* And I was in, all in, drinking, shaking, and hugging until the sun split and returned again. "What's your number?" "Do you surf?" "Ever ride a bike?" The entire week was a blur.

I was spent from all the drinks, lack of sleep, and lust-fueled bursts of serotonin, dopamine, and testosterone. I wanted to doze for a week, but the grand parade was about to take place at the Florianópolis Sambadrome. The dancers from the samba schools rushed to pin their elaborate costumes and headdresses in place, a frenzy of glistening women and men dressed as lions, aliens, and historical figures.

Carnival came and went. I tallied the damage from a hammock near my apartment. My liver was still intact, my wallet in my pocket. After the music died down, I snuggled into Rio Tavares's sleepy way of life. There was no bar, no singles scene, just families and kids who begged me for a ride on my restless tandem. The laid-back atmosphere gave me ample time to do something I'd yet to do on the trip—reflect on the entire journey. There were no distractions to keep me from having to take a hard, sometimes painful, sometimes satisfying, look at who I really was, the values that guided my decisions, and the character traits that dominated my personality.

I relaxed one day on the comfortable shores of Praia Mole as dozens of beautiful people socialized, drank, and admired each other's bodies. Men readjusted their johnsons more than a Little Leaguer with a new cup. Women took quick dips, then chose to air dry their curvy figures rather than use a towel. I half expected a pornography director to yell "Action!"— then have the bathers slip out of their suits and jump on each other.

I sat back and observed the action. I went from hot and bothered to just bothered. I noticed a string of lip enhancements, Botox foreheads, and liposuction dents on derrieres. The beach suddenly seemed like a plastic surgery convention, with patients sporting this year's model. More cosmetic surgeries are performed annually in Brazil than in any other country on earth. Save the United States.

It's not that I had any strong moral conviction against plastic surgery. It's your own body, do with it what you like. Heck, I had a hair piece. I get it. But it's the focus, the fixation on physical appearance that got me down that day. What happens to that bikini body after a woman has a few kids? It changes. And it's *supposed* to change. We're supposed to wrinkle, gray, and sag. Beautiful. I wrote in my journal.

April
Florianópolis, Brazil
Pretty soon I'll be back on the bike, homeward bound. Although it's still

a long way off before I officially land, I find myself already thinking about the realities of re-entering society. I've asked hundreds of people, "What makes you happy?" I'd say more than 90% said the same thing: "family."

Soon enough I'll want to start my own family. And I'm excited about that. But, before I do, I want to know who I <u>really</u> am. How can I partner with a woman if I don't know who I am and what I am looking for? What kind of father will I be? Brazil could not have been a better place to get face-to-face with some tough truths about myself.

Along with being some of the friendliest people in the world, Brazilians are also the some of the most infatuated with outward appearance. Hey, we all are to some degree. And I'm at the guiltiest end of the spectrum. Countless times I have subconsciously categorized men and women based on looks. I never noticed how much until now.

For the last few months I've been hanging out with a woman I adore. Her name's Natalia, and she digs me as well. She's sweet, thoughtful, fun, easygoing, creative, authentic, caring. We have great chemistry together. She turns me on. I was ready to have an exclusive relationship here in Brazil. She was up for it too—ready to have picnics, help me with my Brazilian Portuguese, travel, make love. But my ego wanted someone taller, thinner, and more like the photos of those classic Brazilian beach beauties. So I opted to call her my "Little Brazilian Sister," and avoided a relationship with her.

Why? Really, Jamie, why? So I can spark a few "duuuuude!" comments on my photos on my Facebook page? How many other great people have I blocked out of my life before I ever gave them a chance? On the flip side, how many women have seen my bald head and said, "No, thanks."

Before I set off on this journey, I set an intention to use the expedition to help me become a better man. I see Florianópolis as an opportunity. It's insane to continue to live like this. I don't want a trophy wife. I want a soul mate.

I thought I was coming here to Brazil to party, chase women, and check off Carnival from my good-times bucket list. Yet here I am in a quiet, family-centered town, seemingly the only single guy in town. It's like going to AA in Burgundy or Napa.

And I'm excited about it.

I looked down at my bag and saw the jumbo pack of 36 condoms. Unopened. *Ordem e Progresso.*

Ready for Carnival!

The Florianópolis Sambadrome.

41

PUNTA DEL DIABLO, URUGUAY

--►

I called my brother Nick from Punta del Diablo, Uruguay, excited to reconnect. The calls with family were like chugging a big ole nutritious fruit smoothie—they'd fuel me for the entire day. It had been several months since we'd chatted. He'd called to give me the welcome news that his wife was pregnant with their first child. "I'll have the kid seat on the bike primed and ready for him!" I'd responded.

"Hey, man, *buenos días!*" I said. There was a long silence, then I heard him sniffle and cry. His wife, Kari, had had a miscarriage. We cried together, and I apologized for not being there to comfort him and his wife in person. I got off the phone and curled up in a ball on the floor, surrounded by a rat's nest of cables, battery chargers, and hard drives. I took a deep breath, and tasted the stench of the gear and clothing, a noxious mix of sweat, grease, and mildew. *Am I getting too old for this crap?*

Even though I was on the final stretch home, I couldn't bear the thought of another year plus without regular contact with my family. The thought of getting back on the bike solo was the last thing I wanted. The sunshine I'd been enjoying had been replaced by cold wind and rain, and I was getting no takers to venture off with me into the storm.

Then there was the fear. I knew if I rode in my current state I'd end up attracting negative experiences, and attracting the wrong incidents in South America can be deadly. The more I focused on the fear and negativity, the more fear and negativity I produced. I told myself not to spiral down, but had no idea how to arrest the fall. *Am I done with this? Would I be able to live with myself if I just packed up and went home?*

"Focus on the positive," "focus on the positive," I repeated in mantra fashion. I had just wrapped up three unforgettable months in Brazil. My mind and body felt renewed. But just a few days after crossing the border into Uruguay, the little changes began to trip me up. The Brazilian Portuguese I'd mastered gave way to an impossible-to-understand dialect of Spanish. I had been told the dialect was strong in Uruguay, but trusted my fluent Spanish would suffice. Wrong. Potential guest riders looked at me as if I were babbling in Inuktitut or Urdu.

I missed both my families—my clan in California and the one I'd shaped in Brazil, including my "Brazilian dad," Oliver. Before pedaling down off the plateau towards the border of Uruguay, I had stopped for a few days for a rural farm stay with Oliver and his family. We spent countless hours cooking, eating, and chatting in his kitchen with his wife, Janlice, and a soulful Argentine farmhand, Lucas. Oliver explained that he was once a strapping adventurer himself, out exploring the faraway lands, fit and strong. But, like my own father, he had failed to take care of his health, and it was catching up to him.

He was falling into depression with a broken foot that did not want to heal, and smelled like alcohol and stagnation. *I know this drill.* Oliver was in his mid-sixties, with greasy gray hair and a scruffy bead. Looking at him, I saw my own father the months before he died. Oliver had several adult children, and they were all concerned about his health. I told Lucas and Janlice I was determined to get him out on the bike.

"*Amanhã você estiver vindo na bicicleta comigo,*" I said. He was coming riding with me the next day whether he liked it or not.

"*Não. Eu estou ferido,*" he said. He was injured.

But Lucas, Janlice, and I kept it up until Oliver understood "no" was not an option. And the next morning he reluctantly mounted the tandem. The complaints came fast and repeatedly. My foot, my back, my lungs. I ignored them all and told him he was doing great. Just like the old adventuring days, eh? The complaints dried up, and I could feel his effort increasing. *Yes, the road. The big, beautiful road of adventure and possibility. We're doing it, Oliver. You, me…and my father too. We're all young and healthy.*

After a couple kilometers, he tapped me on the shoulder. We pulled over to a café and Lucas pulled up in the family car. "*Obrigado,*" said Oliver, looking me in the eyes and letting the words linger. "*Obrigado.*"

We sat at the café and I fueled up for my ride down to the ocean. I wanted to capture his spirit, so I pulled out a video camera that hadn't had much action of late. I couldn't understand his every word; they were fast and muffled in sobs. But I knew exactly what he was saying.

I had said hundreds of goodbyes to guest riders and hosts over the years. I had gotten better at the farewell part, but this one rocked me harder than any other. I thought about my dad and all the shuttered dreams, about my brother and his wife and their crippling loss, about Oliver and Lucas and how I may never see them again. Snap, gone.

The emotional roiling stayed with me all the way to the Uruguayan border. I had several fun riders and homestays, and on the surface everything was fine. But at any random moment, I downshifted from joy to wretchedness. Fear, loss, confusion, desire, ambition, doubt, plans, dreams—my mind felt like roulette wheel of emotion.

Now here in Uruguay I made the executive decision to charge off into a powerful headwind and peppering cold rain. *Perhaps some rigorous exercise and a good dumping will wash away the blues,* I convinced myself. I hammered the pedals for six hours straight and only managed to cover 40 kilometers. Some riders actually enjoy the headwinds. They say it's like sailing into a storm, a challenge that requires endurance and strong technical skills. I am an awful headwind rider, and a cranky one as well. This time I cranked up my iPod and fantasized about a warm shower, a fat steak, and glass of *vino tinto*.

Cantankerous and spent when I arrived at the hotel, I scoured the place for a rider to help power the bike to La Paloma the next day. The forecasts pointed to clearing skies. A twenty-something man nodded hello, giving me my opening.

"*Qué interesante,*" Martín said with a smile.

"I leave tomorrow morning at eight. I'll pay for your bus ticket back and take you to lunch in La Paloma. Sound good?"

"Really? I think I'd enjoy that. What do I need to bring?"

"A change of clothes. I have cycling garb for you."

"Ok! I will come! See you tomorrow at eight. Meet here?"

"Here in the restaurant at eight."

"Thank you, thank you so much! I'm excited!" he said, shaking my hand with gusto.

My spirits shot up immediately, thanks to the steak, wine, clearing rain, and now a serendipitous guest rider. *He looked fit,* I told myself.

We'd make it to La Paloma in no time. Maybe he'd know a friend or two in town. We would carve out some fun.

I looked outside the next morning. The wind and rains showed no sign of relinquishing their stranglehold of the skies. No problem. I had rain gear for Martín. Martín. *Where's Martín? I didn't tell him nine, did I? No, I never say nine.* He's probably in the lobby, I told myself. I searched the lobby, then the grounds, then the restaurant again to no avail. So I waited and paced. Nine o'clock, still no Martín. *Locals joke about Latin American time, but this is ridiculous.* At ten, I gave up, guessing the rains or a hangover changed his mind. I would ride alone.

My grouchiness grew with each pedal and raindrop. *If you say you are going to do something, do it. Or at least come and cancel out of respect.* I kept my head down and tried to channel my inner Garryck. *He'd love this…and I hate it.*

The next day, I met an affable woman who agreed to join me on a day trip to Sierras de Rocha, mountains just 50 kilometers from the shore. Isabel had an overbite grin and a seeming sense of adventure. Before we started pedaling, I asked if I could tape a little of our conversation.

"I just really don't want to do it, Jamie."

"C'mon, share your story with the world."

"But I don't have a story I feel like sharing."

"Please?"

"Huhhhh," she said, letting out a big sigh. "What questions are you going to ask me?"

"Just two—'What brings you happiness?' and 'What's your message to the world?'"

"Those are lame questions. I don't want to answer them."

"Ummm."

"I'll make up something if you really want me to."

"No. No, I don't want that."

"C'mon, let's go."

I'd never had a guest rider decline to share a few thoughts on camera, and her refusal surprised and silenced me. As we made our way down a wide walking path a few days later, I thought about a fresh approach with Isabel. I don't know precisely what happened that afternoon, but one second we were weaving around a few pedestrians, and in a flash we crashed into them. Down went the bike and trailer, hurling my cameras up, up, then, *smack*, right into the cement. I picked up one and saw it was cracked beyond repair. Isabel said nothing. I packed the cameras away, and we pedaled off in silence.

This camera accident was not the first. A few days before, I had been filming a shot with another rider and a freak wind gust blew another video camera into the ocean. A few days before that, I mysteriously lost an expensive still camera. Three pieces of expensive equipment, destroyed. What was I supposed to be learning from this? My spirits were at an all-time low, and I struggled to understand why. I needed an energy change, a location change, a mindset change. Fortunately I had a key restorative ahead in Argentina.

"It sounds to me like you're forcing things, honey," said Mamacita as we cycled back to our hostel after a morning at Iguazu Falls in Northern Argentina.

"I feel much more serious…and stressed lately. Now that I'm heading home, I'm nervous about reentry. What's my résumé going to say? Focused on peace? I don't think that's going to pad the bank account."

"I beg to differ. If you keep putting your heart into this project, and make a big difference in the lives of others, you will eventually be presented with ways to make money. But you have to have your heart in the right place first."

She started to rub my back. Those magic hands tended to heal more than just sore muscles.

"Your rainbow will be back soon. Just be patient," she said.

A loud squawking interrupted my train of thought. Then screeching from another bird. *A pair of macaws or toucans*, I surmised. *Either fighting or making love.*

"Okay, forget résumés," said Mom. "Better subject."

"Shoot."

"How's your love life?"

"Don't ask."

"Does that online stuff really work?"

"We'll see. I just posted a profile on Match.com. My plan is to get something going before I land back in California."

"Ha, plans. You don't plan love, you just love."

"It's just, well, I think I'm looking for a partner with a unique set of characteristics. Someone athletic, adventurous, sexy…"

"Whoa, whoa. You need to stop forcing and start flowing."

"Mom, nothing's going to flow out here in the sticks."

"Let me ask you a question. Do you think this journey is the result of force or flow?"

"Both," I said. "It was a lot of work, but the best times have been created by flow."

"Exactly. You should do the same with your heart."

For the rest of the afternoon we talked about force and flow. She had forced the relationship with my dad because she wanted kids. She had forced the relationship with Jim to fill a void in her life. "Don't make the same mistakes," she said. "Just be patient."

On our last evening together, Mom tried to brighten my spirits by taking me to a touristy tango show at our hostel. Dancers with fedoras and heavy eye makeup performed a few numbers, then invited members of the audience to join them for a try. Of course, my mom volunteered. She was terrible, giving us both a good laugh. I ordered another bottle of wine, and she meandered over to one of the hostel workers, a hefty, slow-talking man named Luis. She approached the table beaming.

"Luis is going ride with you tomorrow towards Paraguay," she announced.

"Are you sure that wasn't the wine talking? He looks pretty drunk."

"No he's excited. And I think he's in better shape than he looks."

She left later that night and my mood plummeted. I was already an emotional wreck even with her around. I bought a pack of cigarettes, my first in years. I lit up and fought with myself to believe her encouraging words. Hopefully Luis would add a little positive energy to the mix. I was horribly lonely, scared, and lost.

Luis did not show up the next morning at eight. He blew me off at nine as well. Ten o'clock and still no Luis. *What the...?* At 10:30 I received a text: "It's too cold out. I don't think I'm going to join you." *No apology? Is this entire continent flaky?*

I did my best to shake it off, continuing on my journey with sunny skies with a nice tailwind. I didn't have a definite destination, only knew that I needed to make it out of the Iguazu National Park if I wanted to find some guest riders. As I moved deeper into the jungle and the sun began to set, the road turned into an ice-hard mudpack. I took two high-speed falls, snapped a chain, cut myself several times, and damaged my front rack. Then darkness finally set in. *Poorly planned, poorly executed.*

I thought, *(a) I am alone in this jungle; (b) it's pitch black; and (c) jaguars live in this jungle and operate only in the dark.* I tried to keep the faith as I rode the slick roads, guided only by my small headlamp. The light from a small house felt like seeing the Statue of Liberty after an Atlantic crossing. The structure was inhabited by a park ranger, who looked at my bloodshot eyes, bloody knees, and mud-caked bike, and let me set up a tent for the night.

The next day I made my way out of the park, rejoicing when I finally hit pavement. I felt the urge to stop the bike to and kiss the asphalt. Several times I did stop to extend an invitation to potential guest riders idling at bus stops. They all glanced up to the steep hills before answering. *"No, gracias."*

I stopped for lunch at a small country store, resting my bike against a wall. The weight shifted, forcing the handlebars to turn quickly. The new valve cover an Uruguayan mechanic had installed on my front shock smacked the frame so hard it literally exploded from the valve, rocking the area with a blast that sounded like a firecracker. After flinching from the fire, the crowd approached slowly. Upon further investigation, the valve was shot, the front shock had no more air, and the camera case on my front rack had locked up my brakes. I hopped on the next bus heading to El Dorado, and considered leaving Argentina all together.

Catching a second wind on the bus, I went into problem-solving mode as soon as I arrived in El Dorado. Step one: I called Garryck for his MacGyver-esque suggestions, which usually involved duct tape and zip ties. *What did we do before duct tape and zip ties?* It was comforting to hear his voice, though it made me wish we were out here together. I then found a way to make the bike operable by adjusting the brake handles up into a horribly uncomfortable position. It wasn't pretty, but it would do until I received replacement parts.

Step two: reignite my mojo. I hit the town hoping to meet a few friendly locals whom I could recruit for a ride south. I ended up connecting with a group of high school kids at the local pizza joint. We had a round of beers, then another. I bought the group a giant pizza, and we laughed, shared photos, and exchanged numbers.

After the second beer, I went to the bathroom. When I returned I noticed my new camera was missing. So was a kid named Diego. Not to worry. I had just entered his number in my phone as he had told me he might want to come ride the next day. I called Diego. No answer. I looked at his buddies at the table and started to boil.

"Guys, where is my camera? It was right here."

"I did not take your camera," said Manuel. "I don't know where it is."

"Me either," said another guy, standing up and showing his pockets.

"I just bought you guys dinner, and you steal from me? Really?"

"I did not steal from you. I will try to call Diego. Maybe he took it by accident," said Raul.

I knew it was no use. Diego was not answering his phone, and my brand new camera was history. I had bought it a few days before to replace the other one that went missing in Porte Alegre back in Brazil.

I went back to my cheap hotel room in a cloud of rage, frustration, and bitterness. My head throbbed from the cheap pizza-parlor beer. *Tasted like it was cut with cat urine.* I sat up on my flimsy bed and typed:

June, 18. El Dorado, Argentina

Bottom line is that I'm just not into this ride anymore. Ever since I left Brazil and realized that I have this huge final leg in front of me, I've just wanted it to be over. I could have ended this ride after Europe on a good note. But now I feel this constant sense of "having to ride" and "having to film" when before it was about "enjoying the ride" and "sharing the ride." I'm done. I'm considering heading down to Buenos Aires and flying home.

Ahhhhhhhh!!!! I hate writing this. Right now I'm still pretty buzzed from partying with these high school kids, pissed off at Diego, and am in no condition to make a major life decision. I'll write more in the morning.

I shut the Toughbook and got down on my knees.

Please, God! Tell me what I have to do to get my mojo back and start enjoying this gift of Peace Pedalers again. Or, please give me a clear sign if I'm meant to stop riding and go home. Please, I need a bit of guidance right now. Tell me what to do and I'll do it.

I crawled into bed and tried to go to sleep, running through all the ramifications of quitting. What would I say to my friends and family? Would I ever be able to live with myself? What about the promise to Dad?

I don't know what time it was when the noise in my head finally settled, but I went to sleep expecting clarity in the morning.

Oliver, Janlice and Lucas became my family in Brazil

Mamacita and I at Iguazu falls

Mud like ice, getting dark, alone. Scary.

No suspension and the Andes next on the agenda? Bummed.

42

EL DORADO, ARGENTINA

I WOKE UP the next day feeling groggy and emotionally drained from the previous evening's shenanigans. I knew I needed to make a decision—continue the expedition to Paraguay or bus down to Buenos Aires to catch a flight home. I grabbed my Toughbook computer, the evil pack of cigarettes, and a map of Argentina. At a local café, I ordered a cup of coffee. I started to hand the waitress a two-peso bill when I noticed the handwriting on it: *Si el amor es su mayor debilidad, sos la persona más fuerte del mundo.* "If love is your biggest weakness you are the strongest person in the world."

June 19. El Dorado, Argentina

I just reread what I wrote last night. Do I really want to quit right now? I was pretty angry last night, and maybe I deserved getting my camera stolen. What kind of idiot leaves a fancy camera on the table with a bunch of strangers and walks away?

Is it possible that all of these challenges since landing in Latin America are really just lessons? And could it be that all of these setbacks are actually just a fertile environment for growth and transformation?

"Si el amor es su mayor debilidad, sos la persona más fuerte del mundo." Where is the love? Seriously, what happened to the love that I used to carry in my heart? Live Big, Give Big, Love Big?? Stress Big is more like it.

I didn't set off to South America with any meaningful intention except to party and learn Portuguese. Since then I've been living in a state of panic and worry about the fact I'm on my final continent in the Peace Pedalers' journey. That fear has been making me live in my head and not in my heart. I've been forcing, forcing, and forcing more—forcing riders to join, to be interviewed, get good photos and video clips. I have lost touch with my Live Big, Give Big, Love Big philosophy and intention. This is the reason why I'm so miserable— whenever I am too focused on myself it always bites me in the butt.

    So I've decided to turn up the love higher than I ever have and carry on my mission through South America. I also need to remember that I am traveling through different cultures and I must try harder to practice the tolerance and compassion that I preach. For starters:

    •   *I forgive you, Diego, for stealing my camera. I forgive all the people who have not kept their commitments to me. I forgive myself for slipping off track. I commit to finishing this journey and will do it with love in my heart.*

    •   *I'm on my way to San Ignacio to connect with the Guaraní tribe as planned and feeling good. Let's do this!*

I chowed down some *medialunas* and calmly returned to my room, packed up my bike, and headed south. I was as eager as ever to hit the reset button and have a fresh start down in San Ignacio. I wanted to explore the indigenous Guaraní culture and Jesuit ruins, as well as find a rider to join me to the border to Paraguay. Up until then, I had been unable to convince a single Argentinian to join me. That had to end.

As I exited the bus, I made my way into the forest to look for local Guaraní tribes. I had no clue how I would find them, but was told they were in a general direction. *Por allí, por allí.* "Over there." The vines and trees had the feel of a giant movie curtain ready to part, and I decided to film a clip of me riding under the lush canopy. Just as I got the cameras rolling, I heard a car beeping from behind. I was too busy filming to stop, but the driver continued to lay on the horn. Finally I paused.

"That's quite a bike," said the man. "Looks like you've come a long distance. Do you need a place to stay tonight? I run a hostel."

"I am actually trying to find a way to camp and stay with a Guaraní tribe. But thanks anyway," I said, beginning to get back on my bike.

"Wait, wait. I have a good friend who knows the tribes very well. Maybe he can facilitate a stay for you. They can be wary of strangers."

"I've heard they can be afraid of white men. I'm Jamie, by the way."

"Diego. *Mucho gusto.*"

"Ha! I just had a Diego steal my camera in El Dorado yesterday."

"*Lo siento.* I assure you, I only want to help you and not steal from you."

"I can tell. You are Diego Bueno. The other guy was Diego Malo," I said with a chuckle.

"Let me pull over and call my friend."

Before I knew it, I was following Diego Bueno to his friend Juan's house. Diego then hopped on the bike as Juan guided us by car through the forest to a Guaraní tribe. Signs and road markers were as tough to spot as the elusive jaguar. Even lifetime locals relied on asking directions, wishing to connect with countrymen as much as finding the proper route. I had no idea what to expect as we pulled up to a simple village at the base of a mountain. I vowed to let local customs guide my actions. *Flow, Mom, flow.* Juan went off to speak with the chief.

"I told the chief you wished to live alongside their tribe. You have his permission."

"Thanks, Juan. I appreciate your support."

"No problema."

"And Diego, I'd like to invite you to ride with me from here to Posadas. Sound good?"

"For sure, Jamie. I will accompany you. Just come by the hostel when you get back into town."

Diego and Juan drove off, and I was alone with a dozen Guaraní natives who were wondering what the heck I was doing with this enormous contraption and filming equipment in the middle of their little village. I felt honored they allowed me to stay here in the heart of the Misiones Province, an area shaped by indigenous tribes, Jesuit missionaries, smugglers, Eastern European businessmen, and power companies that have dammed up area rivers, forcing the Guaraní to move their settlements.

Ramos was one of the few people in the village who spoke Spanish; the rest all communicated in their ancient Guaraní tongue. He was outgoing, and excited to show me the surrounds. He and his daughter, Santa, helped me pitch my tent next to their green bamboo hut in the jungle. Then it was off to enjoy a relaxing bowl of mate with Ignacio, the head chief, as the sun faded through the trees.

Ignacio and Ramos described how, for the Guaraní, drinking maté is a spiritual ritual. They explained that Jesus told their people not to eat the fruit of the yerba maté, but to drink it as a tea on a daily basis. When the Europeans came in to exploit their resources and enslave their people, they also stole the maté tradition, and the practice spread throughout Latin America.

Their stories were spellbinding, tales about gods who did everything backwards and Kurupi, a short, hairy, forest monster with a penis so long it can wrap around his waist several times. I wanted to learn more. *And to catch sight of Kurupi and his enormous member!* So for the coming days I recruited locals to join me for joy rides. Ignacio promised to come, but got cold feet just before departure. A twelve-year-old boy named Renato happily hopped on as his replacement. Like the other boys in the settlement, he had a crew cut, with tufts of auburn-tinted hair on top. We spoke only a handful of words, but worked together to explore the entire community. *Yes. This is what Peace Pedalers is all about. Sharing, connection, peace.*

On a high from sharing a few days in a rich and remote culture, I bid my adieus and cycled back to the hostel. Diego greeted me warmly, then gave me the bad news.

"I really wish I could ride with you to Posadas, but I'm afraid I will have to cancel."

"Damn. But, no worries. I know you're a busy man."

"Listen. There is a Spanish woman staying with us. I like her. She is adventurous, traveling by herself. I think she may be interested in joining you."

"Um, okay. Can she ride?"

"She was planning to take a bus south the Santa Ana ruins today. That's in your direction. Let me see if she's around."

Diego ducked inside as I readied the bike. A woman carrying a light daypack approached. *An experienced traveler,* I thought. She wore no makeup or flashy jewelry. She had donned loose-fitting parachute pants, and smelled like natural oils. *A touch of hippie there, too. Nice.* She surveyed the bike slowly, carefully, then introduced herself. Cristina.

"Ah, man. This is incredible. What a journey you are on!" she said, patting me on the shoulder casually.

"So, Diego said you were heading south to the Santa Ana ruins today. You up for a ride instead?"

Cristina barely reached my chin, but I'd learned that height was no indicator of pedal power. Some of my best riders came in small packages.

"Absolutely. This seems much more interesting!"

I handed her an Assos riding jersey, and she left to change. When she returned, I had the camera and tripod ready for a "*bon voyage*" photo of us with Diego Bueno. Three…two…She slipped her arm around me and I reached around her waist at the same time. My hand cupped the small of her back with an ease and a knowledge as if I'd done it a million times before. She settled in to my embrace, and I sensed the trip was going to be a fun one. *Bueno, Diego. Bueno.*

As we loaded the bike, I thought back to a conversation from my college years. Phil and I had met on a chairlift. We chitchatted as we made our way up to the top of the slope, the conversation shifting from ski gear to plans after college. He was a successful businessman who seemed to have created a rich and balanced life. I was curious to learn more about him, so I asked if we could ski together.

For the rest of the day, he opened up about his experiences, sharing how he had the same ambitions when he was my age—travel, sports, and also making good money to enjoy his passions. He took a year off college to live in Spain, which allowed him to graduate bilingual and helped him land his dream job with and import-export firm. After our last run, he took me to his mountain house for dinner. His luxurious all-wheel drive had heated seats.

"So you think *I* should do a year in Spain?"

"If you go, make sure to take it seriously. Don't hang out with other Americans."

I looked around at his Klipsch stereo system and original oil paintings. "I'm gonna do it."

"You won't regret it. Just remember, ditch the Americans. It's the easy way out."

From that day on, I knew I was going to Spain. As anticipated, my dad freaked out when I told him I wanted to take a year away from college. I knew it would be a much harder sell than my two-week trip to Europe after high school graduation.

"Just wait until after you graduate and get a job," he said. "Save some money and go then. That's how normal people do stuff like that."

"Dad, graduating bilingual in California will help me find me a better job and open more doors of opportunity."

"Just graduate first," he said as if the conversation was over.

"With mom's flying benefits I can get to Spain for 50 bucks. I can get a job, find an apartment, and be on my own learning Spanish."

"Just..."

"I'm going no matter what."

He turned to stare. I half expected a backhand for my bratty outburst.

"I mean, I might not do things like normal people. But I only have this one life, and I think this is the best way to spend it."

"You promise you'll come back and finish your last year and graduate?"

I was on the plane to Madrid next fall.

Once there I took Phil's advice, shunning the gringos and living with the local Madrileños. I put up posters seeking *intercambios*, language exchange partners, and made friends with many of them. The immersion strategy also helped me woo a comely Spanish *novia* (girlfriend), Isabel, who just happened to have a house in the mountains and an insatiable appetite for skiing. Second semester, I decided to take Phil's advice a step farther. I started a consulting business with a Chilean man and moved into a flat with two Spaniards. I cooked, ate, worked, dated, partied, traveled, and bonded deeply with my new Spanish crew.

When I returned home, I cornered my father and thanked him for the best gift he ever gave me. "This is going to pay off," I told him. "*Veras.* You'll see."

Cristina and I tore through our conversation as quickly as we rode. Her Castilian Spanish was clear and easy to understand, a straight shot back to my college year abroad. We stopped at the crossroads to the Santa Ana ruins and decided to share a soda and snack. I didn't want her to leave.

"So, it's Friday night and I think there's going to be some music and dancing in Posadas. So you have any plans?" I asked.

"No, I'd love to keep riding and join you. I've seen enough ruins. Where are you headed after Posadas?"

"Across the border to Paraguay. I've got a homestay lined up with a nice family."

"That sounds amazing. I've never been to Paraguay."

"Well, I'm sure we could work something out with my host. Maybe we can go to Posadas tonight, then cross the border to Paraguay together?"

Cristina's spontaneity and relaxed nature fired me up. It had been a long time since I had a proper adventure partner in South America. I got on the phone and called my Couchsurfing host, Jazmin, in Paraguay. Cristina crossed her fingers, hoping it would be okay for her to accompany me. "Of course," said Jazmin. "We're having a Father's Day party that afternoon. She can join the party." Cristina's face lit up like a little kid allowed to ignore bedtime.

"Oh, no," she said, pausing her enthusiasm. "I don't have my passport with me."

"That's not a problem. It's just part of the adventure."

"That's true. I can take a bus back to the hostel, get the passport, and meet you on the road."

"Exactly. When you see me, just tell the driver to stop."

We exchanged a comfortable, warm hug, interrupted only by a jolt of sexual energy piercing my body. *Wow.* I watched her bounce joyfully across the street and board the bus, and hoped she felt the same.

If there were any problems with the ride that afternoon, I sure as hell didn't notice them. Instead, I closed my eyes and glided up and down the rolling hills. The tailwind added a few miles-per-hour to my pace, and the sun warmed my back.

At around sunset, a gleaming Cristina Morales popped her head out the window and yelled "hello" as the fast moving bus bolted past me. The bus did a drunken weave, finally stopping a few hundred meters ahead. Out bounded Cristina with her small daypack, arms open for another hug. We had limited light remaining, so we hammered the pedals hard to reach town before nightfall. I asked her to give it all she had, as I was on empty. We made it to the city center, exhausted and adrenaline-fueled after a few close calls with fast moving cars and buses.

We treated ourselves to ice cream, found new maps at the tourist office, and landed a room at a stately historic hotel for about $10. It was time to celebrate. I hustled out to buy us a bottle of champagne, and we sipped bubbly in the room while getting ready to hit the town. There was an electrifying energy in the room that evening, a connection between us that created an added a sense of mystery to our adventure together. Everything about her turned me on—her smell, an intoxicating mix of oils and musky sweat, the way she purred my name, the fact she no prob-lem getting naked right in front of me, allowing me to catch a glimpse of her shapely butt as she entered the shower. She wasn't trying to be sexy or seductive. Everything was part of her laid-back, hippie nature.

The warm temperatures cooled down, prompting the entire city of Posadas to take a stroll, or so it seemed. We ran in a fountain with some kids, sought restaurant recommendations from locals, shared a steak din-ner, and looked around for a taste of the nightlife. "Do you mind if we skip the clubs?" I asked. "I was thinking the same," she said. Instead, we held hands and strolled along the riverfront Avenida Costanera, nod-ding to the dog walkers and hot dog vendors, and staring at the lights of

Paraguay across the water.

Back at the room neither of us needed to say a word. I'd already tasted that kiss a thousand times in my mind. Long and sweet, easy as an afternoon nap on a hammock, with a dash of spice and hint of more to come. I don't remember thinking or planning my next move. We just swayed and melted, kissing again and again.

Deep into the night, we both rolled over and stared at the ceiling. "*Wow*," she whispered. "*Wow* is right," I said.

I couldn't let her leave. No way. And at breakfast she said the same. "I only have a few pieces of clothing, but I can manage," she affirmed. My kinda gal. Now we just needed a bike. After I detailed the goal and experiences of Peace Pedalers, Cristina insisted she wanted to help me in my quest to meet guest riders and learn more about their cultures. We found a Paraguayan touring machine in good condition, along with a helmet and gloves that fit her. The bike shop owner charged $65 for the whole ensemble. She'd be a full-fledged, Peace Pedaling partner all the way to Asunción.

For two days, generously paved, nearly empty roads with broad shoulders allowed us to ride side-by-side while gazing at the pink, orange, and green stucco farmhouses that dotted the landscape like a display case of macaroons. Flowers gleamed in purple, neon pink, and sunshine yellow. Everything seemed brighter and new. Tailwinds pushed us the entire ride to San Juan. Our luck continued as we learned our arrival into town coincided with the Festival of San Juan, an annual celebration that takes a staid Catholic remembrance of Saint John, adds fire-walking, cross-dressing, and other Guaraní rituals, then washes it all down with copious amounts of food and drink.

The only thing missing was a guest rider. We had struck out at least a dozen times on our two-day ride, and I was starting to lose hope. As we approached the city, we saw a group of young men huddled at the local gas station. I had become a bit discouraged with all the rejections, so I just passed them by. But Cristina would have nothing of my pouting. She forced me to turn the bike around and give it one more shot. *Good luck*, I thought. These guys were already celebrating the festival with beers and guffaws. Then Cristina smiled, a long, genuine smile, and told them they needed to ride with us. With almost no prodding, a young man named Christian accepted her invitation even though he was still on duty at the station.

The three of us meandered into a town ready to boil over with revelry. Kids ran around with sparklers. Paraguayan polkas blared from all directions. Crowds wandered over to a Main Street Carnival, complete with a rickety Ferris wheel, whirring cotton candy machines, and even a bullfighting ring. Christian guided us into a tent with vendors serving up food and drinks. His buddy Ronald was working at the tent, and when we explained the project, his eyes lit up. Ronald was free the next day and said he would love to come riding with us. He also invited us to stay with him that night at his house, just a few hundred meters from where we stood. I doubted we'd get much sleep...and didn't care one iota.

The multi-day festivities began with Noche de San Juan. For centuries, locals have practiced a tradition of lighting the streets of San Juan with candles so Saint John can find his way when he comes to visit. "And you must help," urged Ronald's lovely mother, Severiana, as she handed us candles she'd made from orange peels and pig fat.

Cristina and I hit the fairgrounds for some good old-fashioned fun, Paraguayan style. We danced to live polka, tried our luck at roulette, held hands on the Ferris wheel, survived a dangerously steep blowup slide, laughed with locals, and allowed ourselves to just be kids again. We were both good at that. And for the next few days we proved it.

Moving on to the nearby town of San Bernardino on Ypacaraí Lake, we called our Couchsurfing host, only to discover he was busy and our room was no longer available. *All this celebration with the masses has me itching for some private merriment with Cristina. But I just got CB'd—Couchsurfing Blocked.* I scoured the alternatives, but only saw the lakeside Hotel del Lago, a posh resort dating back to 1888, with white turrets and gothic windows, a budget crippler for sure. After another meditative sunset, I had an idea.

We cycled back to the hotel, and I asked to speak with the manager. To my shock, they dialed his number and handed the phone to me. His name was Osvaldo, and he spoke impeccable English.

"Ah! You are on the long bike? Ha! I saw you earlier with my friend."

"That's great!" I said. "I wish I would have known; I would have given you a ride."

"I told my friend that if you came by our hotel I would give you a free place to stay. And here you are! Welcome. Put the front desk back on the phone and I'll have them arrange a room."

We woke in a suite with an expansive patio overlooking the lake, and decided to envelop each other anew.

At breakfast, we thanked Osvaldo again for his generosity. He was eager for us to stay a second night to experience another unique indigenous festival. Centuries prior, men in the area used to camouflage their bodies with banana leaves and hide in the dark, ready to capture the woman of their choice if she happened to amble by. Women thwarted the plan by traveling in pairs and by carrying lit torches, which they would use unsparingly to burn any unwanted potential captor. The modern-day festival featured colorful and rhythmic reenactments of these attacks, all choreographed and set to music.

My personal dance with Cristina felt every bit as festive and effortless. Like the village celebrations, our connection was part fairytale, part fortune, a mélange of cultures and commonalities. I wanted it to continue.

I loved her can-do spirit, but also how she could leave me and go do her own thing. She was social and independent, fluttering off for extended periods of time and having long conversations with new friends she seemed to meet without effort. She had but a few items of clothing, but never complained. When one shirt was dirty we would wash it and let it dry on the bike the next day. *That's my kinda travel partner.*

I wanted Cristina to continue on with me to the Gran Chaco region, but knew she had to get back to work in Brazil. I moped around the morning of her departure, scanning my mind for places she might want to join me in the weeks and months to come.

"You think I'm going to miss riding in the Chaco for a silly job?" she asked.

"But your work…"

"Sorry, Jamie. You're stuck with me."

As I hugged her, I realized the date was July 1st, my dad's birthday. I think he would have liked her. I looked up and thanked him again for the trip to learn Spanish in Madrid.

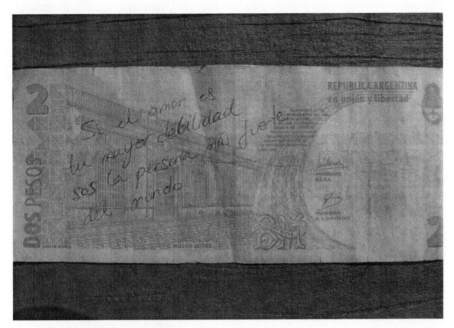

I saw this 2 Peso note as a sign.

My home with a native Guaraní tribe

My farewell crew before leaving the village

Wrapping up a perfect day in the saddle with Cristina

Christian left his job at the gas station to take us into town

Sereriana placing candles out for Noche de San Juan

43

CHACO DESERT, PARAGUAY

--►

FOR SOME ODD reason, I thought about those cheesy corporate motivational posters—the ones with headlines that scream ACHIEVEMENT or VISION, accompanied by photos of the pyramids or a tortoise and a hare. One from a dentist's office popped into my head. SYNERGY, it read, with a picture of gears underneath, "The bonus that is achieved when things work together harmoniously," and it was attributed to Mark Twain. Hard to believe that Twain was the father of corporate speak (*did Dickens invent the memo, Frank Lloyd Wright the cubicle?*), but the words and imagery perfectly described my partnership with Cristina as we made our way into the Chaco desert.

With each mile, we realized how similar we were in many ways—our passion for raw, intercultural adventure, our desire to connect deeply with others, and our trust in the overall goodness of humanity. One of the most powerful beliefs we shared was the conviction that much of the Western world was living in an unconscious state of far too much fear and prejudice. We wanted to help change that any way we could.

Cristina did her Peace Pedalers part by learning how to use the video camera, capture broadcast quality sound, and take stunning photos that documented the beauty of our intercultural adventures. She'd bike ahead at full speed to capture a scene, or rise early to film an indigenous village at first light. Like me, she felt that if we could deliver some positive, inspirational images and stories, we could hopefully warm a few hearts.

With that intention, we continued to attract a wide range of stimulating characters who shared their hearts, cultures, religions, stories, and talents. Together we recorded musicians jamming in Encarnación and Asunción, and a German-speaking Mennonite family that shattered the perception that Mennonites are unapproachable. They welcomed us in for a gracious homestay.

It looked like our luck might have run out one day when the massive thorns of the Chaco region shrubs caused a whopping four different holes in our tires and delayed us more than two hours. We were trying to reach Toledo, but we knew we wouldn't make it before dark. Just then a car drove up from small dirt road. We flagged it down. According to the driver, we'd reach a very small town about six kilometers away. So we pedaled into the moonlit night on a mysterious dirt road that seemed to stretch to the horizon. It was as barren, dark, and eerie of a road as I'd ever experienced. We were both starting to get a bit scared and frustrated. *Let's see how she does in challenging situations.* I was about to suggest turning back to the paved road when a dog's bark punctured the silence. Soon there were more yelps, filling the air like a cranked car stereo.

"Dogs are a good sign," I said. "That usually means people."

"Let's just hope they are friendly people."

"They will be. Trust me."

"I do trust you."

After a few minutes we saw a light, then a house, then smoke coming from an outdoor grill, then a family enjoying a Sunday *asada* barbeque, on their porch.

"*Buenas noches,*" said Cristina.

"*Bienvenido,*" replied a woman, motioning us to come sit down with them on the porch.

"I'm sorry to disturb your party," I said in Spanish. "But we are doing an adventure here in the Chaco and had some bike problems. We, um, well, we don't know where we are going to stay tonight."

"Now you know," said a man. "You are staying here with us. Have a drink."

He handed me a cold beer, and Cristina looked at me with a sense of wonderment.

"Are you hungry?" the woman asked, grabbing a plate.

"Yes, very hungry," I said.

She gave us plates and led us to a large spread of barbequed meat, grilled veggies, and side dishes of cheese rice, corn cakes, and cassava.

Cristina dove into the family camaraderie, dishing up food for others and holding babies. I shared a cigarette with Grandma and talked about the differences between the Dry Chaco and Wet Chaco regions, some deforestation we'd seen, and if Chaco really had the best empanadas in Paraguay. *"¡Claro!"*

It was yet another magical evening spent gabbing, laughing, and sharing a meal with new friends who immediately trusted and accepted us into their clan. I nodded to Cristina as if to say, "Forget the headlines and scares. This is what the world is all about." The family told us to keep our tent in our bag, instead handing us the keys to our own little house. Sated and infused with hospitality from people who would be classified as "below the poverty level" in America, we snuggled our warm bodies together and made a perfect night even more so.

The rest of our adventures through the Chaco Desert continued in the same magical, bordering unbelievable, fashion. Our synergy and combined passion to connect and serve led us to enriching homestays, deep friendships, jaw-dropping stories and tear-jerking good-byes with the locals. Neither of us wanted it to end. But eventually the smooth pavement would give way to rough roads and dirt as the road made it's way to Bolivia. We both knew the end was near.

Cristina and I donated her trusty Columbus bicycle to the last community who hosted us and we came together for one last day of riding on the tandem to Mariscal Estigarribia, our last stop in Paraguay. As we approached the town the emotions began to surface. We enjoyed our victory ice cream at the end of our ride and sat face to face, hand in hand, gazing into each other's teary eyes.

"So, Jamie, what do you think about us?" she began.

"Oh my God. We're…unstoppable."

"I mean, what do you think about the possibility of us coming together?"

"Our connection is amazing, Cristina. These have been the best two weeks of my tour by far."

"I'd love to find a way to explore our connection further."

"Yeah, me too. I wish you had a stronger bike to keep rolling with me. I guess we need to just surrender and trust. If it's meant to be we'll adventure together again."

"Yeah. I know. I just don't want it to end."

"Me either, *Guapa*"

Cristina's and I waited for her bus to arrive, holding hands as a steady stream of tears fell from our eyes. When she finally boarded the bus our tears shifted to violent sobs and hysteric emotions I had never experienced on the entire tour. I looked through the window deep into her red, puffy eyes as tears streamed and her mouth quivered. The bus revved its engine and beeped its horn. I had a strong, genuine desire to jump on board and grab her off the bus. As it began rolling away the urge grew stronger, I saw myself chasing the bus down. I couldn't let her go. She ran to the back of the put her head out the window crying profusely. We were both feeling the same thing. *Stop the bus! Let the adventures continue!*

But the reality of the expedition held me back from chasing the bus down in the end. She needed a better bike and proper gear to ride into Bolivia or the Chilean Andes. We would have to surrender our connection to our trusty Travel Angels that took such impeccable care of us.

I cried for two days after she left. She cried for a week straight.

I rode with Mauro to the Ipati, Bolivia, bus station at the end of our three days of riding together. After exchanging thank-you's for the hospitality and shared experiences, I moved in to give him a hug like I did with all my guest riders.

"Are you okay?" I asked him.

"I don't like to hug," he said.

"I'm sorry, amigo."

"It's okay. I have to work on it."

"Wanna try again?"

"Ummm. Okay, one more time," he said, hesitantly.

I gave him a bear hug and held him close for a few beats. He squirmed at first, then he settled in. We both smelled of multiple days' worth of red dirt and adrenaline-fueled sweat. I touched his black hair and looked down at his face. He had only half of a brow over his left eye, the result of an accident.

"That was better," he said, starting to get emotional.

"Much better" I said. "Much better, brother."

Mauro was the first Bolivian rider I hosted after leaving Cristina in Paraguay. He was gregarious yet low-key, and his companionship helped ease the sadness of losing her as a riding partner. Mauro was an orphan who had never met his parents, raised by the Catholic Church, and was working at a guesthouse six days a week in Camiri, an old colonial town spouting new riches thanks to oil discoveries. Mauro had never ventured far beyond Camiri. It's not that he didn't want to; the opportunity had never arisen. He was curious to explore, and we both embraced the mountainous countryside like eager tourists, roughly following the trail Che Guevara took with his band of guerilla fighters as they sought to make Bolivia the hub of a socialist revolution.

After Mauro departed I inhaled the fresh, oxygen-deprived air and took in my surroundings. I stood at the starting line of a long, challenging journey into the highlands of Bolivia. Ipati sat at about 4,500 feet, and I planned to tackle some of the world's highest roads, up to more than 13,000 feet. Unsurprisingly, I had no takers to my invitations to climb. *I wonder how Cristina would do.* I cranked up the iPod, took off my shirt, slathered on sunscreen, and off I went, fired up for the challenge. *I know how Garryck would do.*

The steep, rocky climbs gave way to rough, wild descents that made the climbing more than worth it. However, I was still riding without a front suspension, ever since my fork blew up in Argentina. My forearms and shoulders reeled from every bump and crack. *Of all the areas to ride without a suspension...This feels like I'm strapped to a jackhammer on full speed.*

After 30 kilometers, I stopped for lunch, mostly to give my arms a rest. I slapped them repeatedly to stop the continued twitching, making for a few wisecracks from passing motorists. I then decided to check a small crack I had noticed in my titanium bike frame a few days prior. In Camiri, I had put a yellow paint mark at the end of the crack to track if it was getting worse or not. It stayed the same size on the paved roads. Now it had fissured and spread like a windshield after being hit with a rock.

Nooooo! Garryck and I had daydreamed about riding into the Bolivian Altiplano for years, and now, just a couple dozen kilometers into the ride, it was over. I had two choices: carry on and risk the frame breaking, or climb even higher to a road that was paved. I idled in the shade, did some meditation and praying, and waited for my answer.

Be prudent, I told myself. I didn't want to risk a major accident or repair job that would require sending the bike back to the U.S. I began to take the bike apart, but, man, was I bitter. It felt like a dream being snatched away. Just then, I noticed the wind shifting. As I turned the wrenches to disassemble my bike, the wind was stiff and in my face. I had learned to trust and surrender to the wind. This time it signaled I'd be aided on the higher road. I just needed to get to smoother pavement and stay off the dirt roads.

After four hours of waiting at a barren crossroads, I finally got a lift from an empty truck that zipped me over a pass to the next town of Muyupampa. *"Gracias, amigo."* The second I got off, I saw two friendly-looking Bolivians with giant wads of coca leaves in their mouths. I thought I could have some fun with them, so I rode over to their bench at full speed, then screeched to a stop just inches from their feet. *"¡Que tal!?!"*

"What the hell are you guys doing here standing around on such a nice day?" I asked.

"We are both water engineers. We are doing a project here," said a man, who introduced himself as Baimair.

"I was talking with a bunch of people about the water problem here. Is it true that thirty percent of the country lives without clean water?"

"More than that, I think."

"We should do something," I said, my brain spinning with ideas.

"Definitely," said the other man, Bruno. "I have also always wanted to start something as well."

"Where do you live, Bruno?"

"Sucre."

"Hey, I'm heading to Sucre in the next week or so. Just need to do some bike repairs. Maybe you can join me for the ride."

"Yeah, maybe."

We swapped phone numbers and talked about getting together later that night. I rode away feeling blessed and guided. Sure, my frame just cracked and I was less than happy about that. But meeting Bruno and Baimair sparked an idea. I found a hotel room for four dollars a night, showered off a few layers of grime, and met up with the boys for some food, a beer, and my first wad of coca. The omnipresent green leaves, which have been chewed or consumed as tea by indigenous South Americans for centuries, are banned in the United States for fear they will be processed into cocaine. Chewed or drunk in their natural state, the leaves are only a mild stimulant and a cure for altitude sickness. They helped my breathing in the mountain regions, and I started to carry a wad with me whenever I attempted the higher elevations.

Bruno and I met several times over the coming days.

"I'm serious about starting a small charity organization," I said. "I came up with the name Operation Agua and registered the domain www.operationagua.org."

"So what do you need from me?"

"You are a water engineer, and you know the communities that are in most need of clean water, the ones the government is ignoring, right?"

"Yes, I know many. One community, called Ayango, is suffering a lot. Many people are getting sick from the water there."

"So I'd like to form a partnership. You and Baimair are the engineers on the ground here. I will look for funding to buy supplies and materials."

"There are many more than Ayango."

"To start, let's just have a pilot project. We'll focus on one community and see how it goes."

"Okay, Baimair and I work near Ayango, so we can begin surveying and making a plan."

"And the most important thing is to engage the community. They will have to do all the labor—digging trenches, pouring cement, and preparing for the materials. You need to get them to sign an agreement that they will provide the labor."

"Yes, this is a good plan."

"So it's a deal? We are partners?" I asked, putting my hand out.

Over the next several months, we put our partnership into action, including surveying the land, rallying the community for labor, finding a clean water source, digging several kilometers of trenches, and connecting the village to the water source with thousands of feet of tubing.

Cristina was great at capturing the essence of the Peace Pedalers spirit with the cameras

From strangers in the night to part of the family

Mauro with his pet cat and rat at his modest home in Camiri

Creating the website for our new project "Operation Agua"

44
SUCRE, BOLIVIA

--►

AS I IDLED in the plaza waiting to meet Bruno, I chuckled to myself thinking of the scene more than a decade prior.

"Gino, come downstairs. It's important," I whispered, trying not to wake up my brother's wife while I shook him awake.

"This better be important," he grunted, slowly getting out of bed.

Gino and Aimee had moved back home to live with my dad, Dick, while Gino worked his way through law school. They wanted to save enough money for a house of their own. Half asleep, he followed me downstairs. Outside the bathroom, I handed him the electric hair clippers.

"Cut me," I said.

"What?"

"I'm cutting off the rug."

"Now? Are you sure?"

"I'm sure."

"Are you drunk?"

"It's time, bro. I want to just be me. No more hiding behind the rug. It's who I am. People can take it or leave it."

It was 1 a.m., and he fired up the clippers.

I began losing my hair in high school. I didn't think much of it until I became a pledge at Sigma Chi, where I was reminded daily that a thinning hairline made me look like a geeky professor. "Dude, that head's the ultimate beaver dam. You're going to be the only brother in the history of Sigma Chi to graduate a virgin." I wore a red baseball hat for the next two-and-half years. I put it on the minute I woke up and hung it by my light when I went to sleep. I never liked baseball hats.

During Christmas break of my junior year, I went to Hair Club for

Men, where they styled me with a fancy, high maintenance toupee. The "before and after" shots sold me. Sure, the rug made me look more my age. But the more I looked at it, the more I regretted the decision.

"Ah ha! Here it is!" said Gino, holding the toupee high above his head in victory.

"Let me see."

"Wait!"

He threw a shoulder check to keep me away from the mirror. Then he changed the bit on the clippers and got back to work. I peered up to see his tongue protruded from the side of his mouth, a lifelong trait he'd displayed whenever doing something that required concentration.

"Okay, I'm done. You can look at yourself."

"Jamie. Jaime!" called Bruno, snapping me out of my flashback.

"Hey, man. Sorry I was just…I have a question for you. Before I get back on the road to Potosi, I wanted to ask your advice on how to better connect with Quechua locals."

"Quechua are very weary of white people. There is a long history of abuse."

"I know, on my ride from Muyupampa to Sucre, not one person joined me on the bike."

"Do you speak Quechua?"

"Uh, no. Just Spanish."

"We need to teach you basic Quechua. Outside of Sucre, many people won't speak Spanish. So this will show respect to their language and culture."

"Anything else?"

"You should bring a gift of coco leaves and know how to offer it to them. This is an ancient tradition."

"Got it."

"I think it would also be fun to use that sound system on your bike and play some Bolivian music that they will enjoy. That will be a nice way to arrive in the community."

We spent the next few hours in the plaza reviewing handy Quechua phrases. Afterwards, Bruno took me to a place to buy an oversized bag of coco leaves, then taught me proper chewing techniques and how to invite others to join. Finally, we rode over to a record store, where we bought some popular Bolivian music to play on the bike's sound system. Mission accomplished.

On the road, I reached for the iPod and cranked up the music. The first song reminded me of Cristina. The second one reminded me of Cristina. They all reminded me of Cristina. Heck, everything reminded me of Cristina—setting up the cameras to capture a stunning piece of scenery, high-fiving children, even the flat tires and *"no problema"* attitude. Incubus's *I Miss You* hit me especially hard and tears streamed down my face as I powered up a steep hills with a wad of coca in my mouth.

The long day of pedaling gave me time to consider how I might get Cristina back on the bike after all. She had no bike, no panniers, no clothing. Nada. That was the first challenge. Then the fact that she was all the way in Brazil and would need to somehow get out to me, if she even wanted to come out to ride again in the first place. Finally, there were the fears and doubts that surfaced about what expectations she would have of me or me of her if we came back together for a longer tour together. In Paraguay we took each day as it came. If she joined me again it would take our connection to the next level. Would we be officially dating? Even though I had some fears I could see us coming together and envisioned more amazing times touring the rest of South America together.

At sunset, I spotted a small village coming up in the distance. *This will be my home for the night. And this is where I will recruit some indigenous riders to come play.* I could feel my cold worsening. I needed to find a warm place to stay.

I stopped the bike about 200 meters from the entrance to the village to prepare myself. I popped in a fresh wad of coca leaves, turned on some Bolivian music, and brushed up my Quechua phrases. I even put a few Quechua cheat sheet phrases on my handlebar map in case I forgot. Showtime.

The village was so small it failed to make any of my detailed maps. It looked inviting enough, though, with kids playing soccer while the elders examined brown papers at a small community center. They were busy with the Bolivian government's recent census project. Seemingly the entire town gathered near the one building and I received ample smiles and a few claps as I spun up the steep rocky hill.

"Napaykullayki!" Hello. *"Imaynam kasanki?"* How are you? I parked the bike and began to invite numerous locals to enjoy some coca with me. *So far, so good.* The conversation turned from my broken Quechua to their broken Spanish, as a handful of locals grabbed a wad of leaves and chewed with me. After several minutes of friendly conversation, I shared

my intention to stay in the village that night, learn more about the culture, and find a rider the next day to pedal at least to the beginning of the major 5,000-foot climb at Retiro Baja.

Word spread fast, and I was assured I would have a place to stay that night. And over the next three hours I had five different people tell me they wanted to ride the next day. Assuming most would flake out at the last minute, I told them all to be ready at 9 a.m. sharp. If several showed up, I planned to give short rides to everyone, partially to reward them, but also to select the one with the strongest legs.

A red-cheeked, stocky indigenous woman who promised to host me disappeared, but a new character, Modesto, stuck around. We hit it off right away. Modesto is *mixto*, mixed. His mom is pure blood Quechua, and his father had Latin and European roots. He had eyes that looked Asian, and brows that bent at the corners.

"You want to stay with a local family? You are welcome with my family," he said.

"Thanks, Modesto."

"Follow me. I will introduce you to my wife and children. They work at the market."

We walked across the street to a room with a few stacked dry goods and soda bottles; his wife Tica, his daughter Kusi and his son Apu greeted me warmly. Modesto took me to his humble house nearby, and he went to work clearing a chunk of floor space for me and my gear. I set up my mattress and sleeping bag, and we meandered back to the village for some food and chitchat with the locals. We spent the rest of the evening with his friends, chewing coca and sharing stories.

The next morning, he and his mom brought me breakfast in bed—a bowl of fried corn, a piece of freshly made bread, and a cup of herb tea. I felt warm, welcomed, and yummy inside. Looking out the window, I saw Modesto's mom cooking up corn and doing chores outside. I gave her a polite smile, which she returned.

I walked out of my room smiling, with the camera rolling in one arm and my cup of tea in the other, explaining how great I felt to wake up in this lovely village. As I made my way down to the fire, I could see her friendly expression change. She waved me away and screamed something in Quechua. A short, round friend who cooked alongside her joined in the clash, saying something in Spanish about blood and theft. Modesto came out and his mom began to rant on in Quechua to him.

"What did she say, Modesto?" I asked.

"*Piensa que estás aquí para robar su corazón.* She thinks you are here to steal her heart."

"Literally?"

"Yes, they think you want to kill them and take their hearts."

I froze, speechless, my adrenaline surging. Modesto's mom continued her hysterics. She shrieked at me, then shouted the same words to Modesto. Over and over. Finally, he turned to me. "She wants you to leave the house."

Still scrambling to understand what had happened, I abandoned my meal and hurriedly assembled my belongings outside the house. Modesto came over, his head hanging down.

"My mother told me she wants you to give her money for staying with us."

"Do I get an early departure discount?"

"I don't understand."

I waved off the comment and gave him 20 bolivianos, about three dollars at the time. He paused, holding the money in his hand.

"I would like to try your bike."

"Great. Give that money to your mom, and let's go for a ride together. I want to talk more about this."

I finished packing up, setting aside clothing and gear for Modesto. He took longer than I expected.

"Actually, I have a full day of work to do today," he said. "I cannot join you on the bike."

"I don't understand, Modesto. What's going on here?"

"It's just the *abuelas*, the grandmothers and old people. They are the ones with the biggest fears. They have seen a lot of abuse by whites— murder, slavery, rape. I have no fear of whites, but they do."

"Please tell your mom that I was not here to steal her heart. I came to create a friendship and inspire others to come out and create friendships too."

"I will tell her," he said.

I pedaled over to the community center, hoping to pick up another local for the ride to Potosi. I could feel my cold worsen, and knew I could use another set of legs for the long haul. I also wanted a friendlier soul to better explain Quechua beliefs and why Modesto's mother would react like she did. Was it the camera? My bald head? I didn't want the incident to color my views of the community.

I sat at the center, cranking Bolivian music through my speakers, a big ball of coca in my mouth, from 8:30 a.m. to 11:00 a.m. Nobody came by.

I put my head in my hands and broke down crying. I missed Cristina more than ever. This would certainly not have happened if we were together.

The stunning road from Sucre to Potosi

Chewing coca and chilling with Modesto's son Apu and wife Tica

Breakfast in bed with a real Quechua family

45
POTOSI, BOLIVIA

POTOSI'S FORTUNES ARE as dramatic and undulating as its geography. Located on a dusty, windy plain more than 13,400 feet above sea level, the city was once South America's richest. Miners carved shiploads of silver from the nearby Cerro Rico, "rich mountain." With the ore came elaborate churches and mansions, and tens of thousands of immigrants and fortune seekers. But once the world's appetite for silver was sated, the businessmen departed, leaving the once proud city with crumbling colonial buildings and slave-like conditions for the miners who had no choice but to stay.

One of the highest cities in the world, Potosi was also proving to be an inhospitable place to recover from a horrific head cold. Even after several days of bed rest, my body screamed for more oxygen, humidity, and warmth. I finally mustered enough strength to walk the earth-toned town, brightened mostly by colorful serapes and skirts. At an Internet café, I Skype-chatted with my upcoming host in Chile, Roberto.

Please, I begged. Could I come to Iquique a few days early? I was sick and freezing. He took a long while to respond ("I'm sick" isn't the best line to open doors), but said, "¡Claro, que sí!" Yes, of course. Come any time. I thanked him profusely, then added as a P.S., "Will you check to see if there is a welder in town who can repair my bike?" *No problema.*

Just knowing I had a welcome room waiting at a beach resort town made me feel warmer already. I decided to check the surf report for Iquique while I was at it. It was good, very good, with seven-foot waves and 80-degree temperatures. *I gotta get out of here today.* As I grabbed the top of my computer to fold it shut, an Instant Message popped up.

Cristina: Jamie, are you there?

Jamie: Guapa!!! Oh my God. So happy to see you online.

Cristina: I can't stop thinking about you. And I can't stop crying!!

Jamie: I've also been thinking of you a lot. And crying a lot, too. I miss you.

Cristina: I'm in Brazil, but my heart is still with you in Paraguay.

Jamie: I have been dreaming of riding with you again.

Cristina: I would love to! When?

Jamie: How about biking with me from Chile to Colombia?

Cristina: Sí, sí, sí.

Jamie: Amazing. We would have so much fun together.

Cristina: I don't have a bike or all that stuff I need like bags and clothing.

Jamie: I know. That's the challenge. You need a good bike, clothes, panniers, sleeping bag, and mat.

Cristina: How much would all that it cost?

Jamie: I don't know, maybe $1,500 or more, I'd say.

Cristina: Oh. I don't have that amount of money.

Jamie: Hmm. Let me work on it. I have an idea.

Cristina: Even for a bike?

Jamie: Maybe I can track one down in Chile. It's worth a try.

Cristina: If you can find one, you know I will be there right away by your side.

Jamie: If I can find a bike and all the gear, then it's meant to be, like we talked about in Paraguay.

Cristina: And if you can't find the bike then it's not meant to be?

Jamie: I'm only focusing on MEANT TO BE!

Cristina: I miss you.

The 18-hour bus journey to Iquique, Chile, transported me from fedora-wearing miners and farmers to sunscreen-wearing surfers and tourists drawn to area beaches, gambling, and duty-free shopping. It felt like parachuting from Hoth to Casino Royale. Roberto, with his hipster haircut and surfer t-shirt, greeted me with open arms.

"Any luck finding a titanium welder?" I asked the next day.

"I have been searching all over Chile for you. All the way down to Santiago even. I'm sorry, but nobody welds that metal here."

"That's not good. I may have to send it up to the U.S. to get it fixed."

"Why is it so hard to fix it?"

"It's a unique metal. Very few people know how to work with it."

"Well, the good news is that Francesca is coming over this afternoon. The woman I mentioned who did the bike trip from Chile to Colombia. She wants to meet you and go for a ride."

So now I had two challenges—get my bike frame fixed and find a bike for Cristina. I had no idea how I was going to do either. *If it's meant to be...* Later that day, Francesca rolled over, and we immediately swapped tales of our cycling adventures. She rode alongside while Roberto and I manned the tandem for a jaunt on a smooth cycling path that followed the moon-shaped shore, past crammed pedestrian walkways and paragliders angling for every patch of sky.

"So, Jamie, I see from your website you are heading from Chile to Colombia," she said.

"I'm excited. But I'm trying to find another bike for my friend Cristina, the woman I rode with in Argentina and Paraguay."

"What kind of bike are you looking to buy?"

"Actually, I don't have the budget to buy one. We're hoping to find a Chilean bike company to sponsor her."

"Well, my boyfriend and I were sponsored by Oxford when we did our trip. They are the biggest bike manufacturer in Chile."

"Really? Do you have any contacts there?"

"Sure. I know the owner of the company. His name is Raul, and he's a really nice guy. He may be willing to help you out."

As soon as we finished our ride, I dialed Raul's cell phone.

"Hello, Raul. My name is Jamie. I'm an American cyclist and friend of Francesca. She gave me your number."

"Great. What can I do for you, Jamie?"

"I'm doing a global cycling trip, and Chile is the seventieth country of tandem cycling. I ride the tandem solo and invite strangers to join the journey and create friendships."

"I love it! How can I help?"

"I have a partner I need to assist with the project. We need a bike for her to ride from Chile to Colombia."

"What kind of bike?"

I paused. *Go for it.*

"I'm thinking a 29er mountain bike, front suspension, XT components, disc brakes, touring racks, and light components."

"Where do you need it delivered?" he said.

"Santiago would be great! In, say, about a month?"

"I'll have it ready for you at our headquarters in a month."

"Really? Thanks. I mean, do you need a PowerPoint or sponsorship proposal?"

"No. It's not necessary. It is our pleasure to support your project."

Back at Roberto's place, I went to work trying to find the rest of the gear necessary for Cristina to join the ride. I sent a slew of emails to the sponsors requesting their products—cycling clothing from Assos; panniers and waterproof bags from Ortlieb; technical clothing, a sleeping bag, and a lightweight tent from Sierra Designs. Within 24 hours, they all responded the same way as Raul and Oxford: "Where do you want it delivered?"

Dad, you must really like Cristina. That's some impressive work. It just might be "meant to be."

Cristina was all set to ride from Chile to Colombia. That is, if I could find a way to get my cracked bicycle frame repaired.

I called Cristina with the good news...only to have second thoughts the minute I hung up the phone. *Was this really a good idea? What is your true motivation?* I wanted a partner, someone strong, independent, and affectionate, someone who shared my passion for Peace Pedaling. Cristina and I worked well together, both on and off the bike. I wanted another taste of our adventures together. I wanted to explore our connection further and so did she.

But mixed with the excitement of seeing her again was a pit of fear and doubt in my stomach. I could not quite put my finger on it. I had tried and failed in love so many times and the thought of trying another relationship was scaring the crap of me. One part of me was eager to explore the connection with Cristina deeper while the other side of me was screaming no way. I figured it was just the normal jitters and carried onwards preparing for our big adventure together. Based on the ease of her bike and gear coming I knew it my heart we were destined to travel again together.

After failing to find a welder in Chile, I shipped the bike up to America for repairs. And instead of using FedEx to return it, I had a far better messenger...Mamacita. She flew in from California, happily toting my mended bicycle frame along with Cristina's panniers, clothing, and equipment.

"I'm your personal FedEx delivery system," she grinned, giving me a big hug.

"FedEx never looked better than right now, Mom."

"I'm excited about meeting Cristina. I told you if you were patient a woman would ride up beside. Forget all that Internet dating nonsense."

"I'm excited for you to meet her as well. But I have to be honest and say I'm still feeling scared and doubtful"

"That's normal. Remember, it's just a bike ride. It's not a wedding."

"I just don't want to hurt her feelings if it doesn't work out."

"Look, something inside you inspired you to invite her. Honor the inspiration. Honor the forces that brought you together."

We continued the conversation as we waited for the boxes at baggage claim, then talked some more in the days that followed. Force versus flow, force versus flow. *How many moms would fly around the world to deliver bicycle parts for their son?*, I asked myself over dinner. She made the whole trip happen, then gave it a boost every time it looked like it would end prematurely. "Thank you," I said. "For everything."

When I saw Cristina at the Santiago airport a few days later, all the warm memories I had from Paraguay drowned out most of the doubts. She was a good woman, decent to the core. I knew she was taking a bold step coming to join me. I hugged her and stroked her hair.

Mamacita embraced Cristina as well, mixing embarrassing stories from my childhood with thoughts about the universe bringing us together for a reason, her own unique sales job. Cristina nodded politely and held my hand. After a day of getting acquainted, Mom left for California. "Leave you two in peace." *I hope.*

Oxford and our sponsors took great care of us. Cristina's bike was just what I ordered, and we were both enthusiastic to get back out on the road. Soaking in a hotel hot tub, I thought it would be a good time to share an idea I had about how our partnership might work over the next several months as we made our way up to Colombia.

"Cristina, can we have a talk about a few things?"

No, don't do it. Don't go there.

"Of course."

"What do you think about an open relationship?"

Too late. Jack ass.

"What do you mean?"

I could see her face tense up.

"I was just thinking how it would be nice to be partners, but still have the freedom sometimes to go our own way for a bit."

"You mean you want to sleep with other women and are asking me if I'm okay with it?"

"Uh, well. I just don't know if I really want a girlfriend, Cristina. How about us just being riding partners."

In the history of man, has this line of thinking ever worked?

"¡Mierda! If I knew you wanted this kind of arrangement, I wouldn't have come. You told me you wanted to 'explore our connection.' You said this in the email. If you are sleeping with other women, we can't explore any connection, can we?"

"I'm sorry I brought it up. That was stupid."

She shifted to the other side of the hot tub.

"And are you open to me sleeping with other guys?"

"Umm. No. That wouldn't feel so nice."

In the history of Jamie, has there ever been a dumber line of thinking?

She started to cry.

"I'm sorry, Guapa," I said, moving next to her. "I'm just...well, I'm scared. I've never had a woman join me for four months. I *do* want to explore our connection. Now that I know how you feel, I'm really sorry I brought it up."

I regretted bringing up this silly idea. It was a bad start to our partnership. A few friends had told me stories about their "open relationships." They sounded fun at first, but, on closer inspection, the arrangement never seemed to last long. All started with one partner more enthusiastic than the other and ended quickly in anxiety, depression, jealous rages, and, surprise, new STDs. When she posed the same question right back at me, I felt nauseous thinking of another man stroking her cute little butt. I felt like a complete jerk, but, man, this fearful freedom-freak voice inside just would not shut up. It continued to mess with my thinking, and I had no clue how to muffle it.

Fresh from the beaches of Brazil, Cristina got a rude awakening trying to pedal her own bike up and over summits that reached more than 13,000 feet. I could hear her cursing at the ruts in the dirt road that made her tip over every quarter mile or so. I should have pushed her a little harder to train in Brazil, but I had to hand it to her. Each day she got stronger, and learned how to maneuver that steed in the tough terrain. The breathtaking Altiplano scenery helped power both of us, offering an ever-changing panoply of active volcanoes, treeless mountain tors, and, at night, a bed of stars so bright and plentiful you could read under them.

Like the ups and downs of our riding, so went the tone of our relationship. Sure, we had an exciting guest rider and a rich homestay with a Quechan family in Peru. We made our way to Machu Picchu with a hitchhiking Brazilian hippie. We embraced at the top of Wayna Picchu. We were charmed by our charismatic guest rider Christian, who showed us the back roads of Cuzco. It was "almost perfect." Some days the emphasis was on the "almost," others it was on the "perfect." The more we rode, the more we realized the door to my heart was only half open, while Cristina's was fully ajar and vulnerable. The impasse led to many silent nights and more tears than I'd like to admit.

"ALMOST perfect" continued down from the mountains to the surf at Punta Hermosa, where we were hosted by the generous Mifflin family right on the beach. From there it was off to Lima and more enjoyable homestays and forged connections with locals. These were the experiences both Cristina and I craved more than anything. Far beyond the cycling, those moments helped stoke the memories we both cherished of our two weeks in Paraguay.

But we were not in Paraguay anymore. We were in only the second of four countries we planned to cross. Sadly, the emotional ups and downs were weighing heavily on both of us. I had was scared to let Cristina in my heart. Cristina is a thoughtful and intuitive woman, and her sensitivity and perception were able to detect my second-guessing at every turn, making what should have been sweet moments into bitter experiences. I looked at her, as she continued to get stronger on the bike, and felt a swell of love and respect. But she deserved a better travel experience than this. She deserved a better partner.

"Cristina, I know you feel the tension that is building between us," I said one evening.

"Of course. It's very obvious."

"I think I need some time alone. I need to really think about whether or not we can carry on together like this."

"Really? Can't we just talk about it?"

"No, I need to clear my head. I'm going to head up to Máncora and do some surfing and be alone for a few days. Maybe some salt water will clear this funk I'm feeling. Why don't you head to Trujillo and we'll meet up later."

"If this is really what you need to do, I will do it," she said, putting her head on my chest.

"I don't know what's going on inside me now, Cris. It feels like there is a battle going on between my head and my heart, and I need to sort it out. Alone."

"Okay, so you will email me when you are ready to talk?"

"Yes. I don't think I will need much time. Just a few days."

"Take all the time you need. Call me when you're ready."

She gave me a kiss.

Alone, drunk several big bottles of Cusqueña beer, I looked for the most lively nightlife in Máncora, a fishing village turned seaside party headquarters for the Peruvian leisure set. Live music pulsated throughout town, and I decided I needed to dance, beginning my groove on a dusty road next to an outdoor bar with ample revelers shaking their drug-fueled *culos*.

I boogied right over to the dance floor and began shakin' my thang with the local ladies and having a blast by all appearances. But within a few minutes the effects of the booze shifted, making me feel as if I were watching myself from grandstands twenty feet above the party. I started to shake my head, no, no, like a frustrated parent wondering when his child would snap out of it.

No matter how much I danced or drank, there was no escaping the truth—I didn't miss the party times. I missed Cristina. I wanted to flee the dance floor and teleport her to the beach, where we'd stretch out a sarong and cuddle up under the stars. So I started to walk away, far away. I walked until I couldn't hear the music anymore. To the beach, feeling more sober with each step. On and on into the night. As the sun rose, I grew clear and grounded. No longer did I wish to fight the deep love I had for Cristina.

I collapsed on the sand. I rubbed my bald head and started to chuckle. Scenes from the trip blasted my mind like a movie trailer—the unused box of condoms in Brazil; the embrace of Carrie and Andy, the happily married travel couple who ran the hostel in Malawi; the Indian guru at the ashram who said, "Shining the light of awareness is the first step to transformation." I knew, at that moment, in that morning light, the old party had ended.

The cold, dusty city of Potosi

The stunning and challenging Altiplano of Chile

Magical Machu Picchu

46
MÁNCORA, PERU

AND ANOTHER HAD begun. It was no accident Cristina came into my life the day after I re-committed to start living from my heart again. Or that we found her a free bike so easily. She was supposed to be there. Mamacita was right. The right woman had ridden up beside me.

Staring out at the ocean, I knew from where the screaming voices came—fear and resistance. I was afraid of love and commitment. Once I shined a light on that part of me, I came to peace with it. I asked her for forgiveness and thanked her for being so tolerant of my complicated and painful process. I asked her to please start making her way up to Máncora so we could enjoy the beach together and begin our life anew.

Sure, the riding got easier after shifting from the mountains to the Pacific shore. But what really made it glide now was jettisoning all the emotional past. Cristina didn't want to talk about the past, *thank God*, and neither did I. We spent our days eating fresh ceviche from roadside stands and pitching our tent on beaches without footprints. After a week, we decided we wanted to stay with a local family, an energy boost we shared and craved.

Coming around a turn at the end of a long day of sun-drenched touring, I spotted a long, secluded, sandy beach with waves breaking gently on shore. On the far end sat a simple bamboo shack. In the U.S., the beach would have been fenced off and owned by an eccentric tech billionaire with hobbies like lunar mobiling. We pulled up at the fence and motioned *hello* to a woman.

"Cristina, you want to take the lead here?" I asked.

"What do you mean?"

"You be the one to ask her if we can set up a tent next to theirs."

"Okay, no problem."

A short, dark-skinned woman with tight curls came over. Up until then, I had been the one who usually asked about homestays. After seven years of doing so, I felt like I'd earned a PhD in the subject. Cristina confidently launched into her pitch, asking about land for the tent and if we could cook dinner with them tonight. The woman immediately swung open the gate, and we became a part of the unpretentious lives of Maria, Rosa, and Juan.

After pitching our tent in a spot of sand with a million-dollar view, we saw a fruit and vegetable truck pull over to the side of the road. We offered to buy the ingredients for the evening's meal, and Rosa came out to choose the items—fragrant guavas, *lucumas*, and green-scaled *chirimoyas*, perfectly ripe avocados, *yucas*, and potatoes of all hues. Total bill: $3. Juan had reeled in a tuna earlier in the day, which he'd add to the feast. We'd cook everything on a small grill outdoors, where the family prepared all its meals. I had never been as envious of a housing setup as I was at that moment. The multilevel marketers could have their Utah mansions in the mountains. I'd take Juan, Maria, and Rosa's one-room, slat-wall beach shack any day of the week. Cristina and I went for a swim in the warm waters, holding each other.

In the morning, Juan, our 65-year-old host, accepted the invitation to ride with us about twenty kilometers to the next town. He prepped for the journey by putting on tennis shoes to go with his business slacks and short-sleeve dress shirt, making him look like a retired engineer, minus the pens and protractors in the front pocket. Juan combed his piano-black hair back into a pompadour, covering some thinning at the crown, then put on a white baseball cap. He was good to go. During the ride, he shared that he got the most pleasure in life by being of service to others, volunteering at his church, working hard, and providing for his family. He was a humble man of few words. We were the first foreign visitors to ever stay on his land, and he stuck out his hand to express gratitude for our experience together. "*Yo tambien*," I said. Ditto. I looked at Cristina, and we shot each other knowing smiles.

Cristina was addicted, the same addiction that had plagued me the last seven years on the road and, frankly, for my entire life. We wanted to not only explore, but embrace. Everywhere. We saw the world as a neighborhood block, *our* block. We wanted to know everyone on it.

I never understood how neighbors in the United States could live next to each other for years and get by on nothing more than, "g'morning" and "looks like rain." I cringed thinking about all the things that prevented meaningful human contact—gated communities, smart phones, take-out deliveries, headphones, cubicles, teleconferencing, ready-cooked meals, personal shoppers, virtual tours, point-and-click, drive-ins, drive-thrus; hell, just drive right on by life. In the developed world, it's easy to go an entire day without having any real contact with another human being, let alone a heartfelt conversation or a warm hug.

It's like we were given an amazing gift by our Creator—the ability to connect in ways that no other animal can come close to matching—and now we're doing everything in our power to give that gift away. Why befriend the person sitting next to me on the train when I can pretend to make friends on Facebook?

Peace Pedalers was my own effort to take all of that dehumanization and turn it into my own unique "re-humanization." One of the most common refrains I'd heard in all developing world countries was the sentiment "We're all human." At first the phrase sounded simple and obvious to me. But the more I heard it, the more I understood the deeper meaning, that we spend so much time focusing on the differences—Christian or Muslim, red state or blue, Pepsi or Coke, iPhone or Samsung—we forget about the commonalities. We focus on the one-percent and forget about the ninety-nine. Yes, we are all human. We're all here on this planet for a quick spin, then we turn to dust. So why stay inside? Go meet your neighbors.

I could see that Cristina's addiction to human connection would be lifetime affliction, and I couldn't have been happier. We spent the following several weeks weaving our way from the Pacific Ocean to mountainous regions inland, zigzagging north to Ecuador. The ride continued to reward.

With Cristina now as engaged as I had ever been, we picked up guest riders who took us to hidden waterfalls and secluded beaches; stayed in more shacks and urban apartments; transported sandwich vendors, homemakers, banana farmers, students, slackers, believers, alcoholics, daydreamers, first-timers and, probably, last-timers.

And kids. Always kids. Oodles of kids. Pedro Pablo swore he'd be president someday. Christian took me to the market and pointed out the tastiest foods to buy. Rai showed us how to build a proper sandcastle.

One, two, three, even four at a time—we gave rides to children at every stop, even if it delayed us for hours. Cristina never tired of playing with a child. I couldn't live with the thought some kid would be heartbroken if he didn't get to test out the tandem. So we ferried them all, hopefully spawning a new generation of cyclists.

For Cristina's birthday, we hunkered down in Mompiche with a handful of new Ecuadorian friends, twenty-somethings who brought surfboards, guitars, and ample good cheer. The fishing village had long been a favorite haunt for backpackers and surfers who loved the town's low-key vibe, grilled seafood dinners, and exhilarating waves. We capped each day with a beachside campfire. This was the life we both wanted—travel, nature, culture, adventure, meeting new friends, long conversations about life. We played footsies and daydreamed.

Before Cristina and I took off to Quito, the group drove us to their favorite waterfall in the jungle nearby. A recent hard rain had turned the natural spigot on high, filling the swimming hole below. We all stripped down and dove in.

"Ahhhh. This water is perfect," I said. "In California, the waterfalls are gorgeous but colder than a well digger's butt."

"Ah, I like that phrase. I'm going to use it," said Jorge.

"The whole area is stunning."

"Take photos now, because it will all be gone soon," said Eduardo.

"What do you mean?"

"The people, they like the environment, but they don't have the time or energy to fight for it. And the politicians are too corrupt to save it. So the big corporations come in and do whatever they want to the land."

The more we swam and talked, the more I realized how passionate Jorge and Eduardo were about doing something to preserve their natural paradise. Cristina and I wanted to help their cause. I had an idea, and shared it with them while we dried off on the rocks. "Ecuatopia," I said. "A grassroots environmental group to educate, inform, and run projects that keep Ecuador the natural Utopia that it is."

They loved the concept and the name, especially since the word "Utopia" is the same in both English and Spanish. In fact, they'd been thinking about starting up a group before they even met us. Now they had a partner to help them get started. Ecuatopia. It had a ring to it.

Within a few weeks, we had a website up and running and helped them plan their first event.

Home sweet home

Juan's ocean view ride

Pedro Pablo on his way home from school shared his dreams

47

CALI, COLOMBIA

--▶

IN CALI, COLOMBIA, I took my first steps. Forward with the left foot, rock back on the right. Step back left, hold, step back right, rock forward left, step forward right, and again. *Okay, I can do this.* Forward left, rock back..."That's it," said my salsa instructor. Cristina gave me a thumbs-up, and practiced her part on the side of the mirrored room.

Being in Cali without a few salsa steps is like going to London without an umbrella. You're going to need them every day. More important, the dance was important to Cristina. And I owed her one. Or two. Or two hundred. Forward left, rock back. *Got it.*

Sensing my confidence, the instructor inserted Cristina into the mix and added a couple twists and shakes. I felt out of step from the beginning. My palms started to sweat, and I rubbed them repeatedly on my thighs. *Damn. Latin rhythm is tougher than I thought.* At several points, I nearly quit, but ended up gutting it out. Cristina took over with the instructor and quickly showed me how it was done, moving effortlessly, knowing precisely when to turn, twist, and wiggle. Her shimmies and thrusts made me see her in a whole new light. Frankly, it made me want to turn off the lights and jump her bones. I vowed to work on my salsa as we adventured around Colombia.

"Crime ridden," "pickpocket haven," "drug infested"—the guidebooks and family members didn't give Cali the best build-up. If you're solely in the hands of a guidebook, those things might be true. But if you're in the hands of a local, problems are avoided. Just like in the U.S.

Roberto, our young, affable Couchsurfing host in Cali, had prepared a tasty smorgasbord of local treats for us. He had lined up a concert with a world-class marimba band, securing us front row seats to experience the

African-influenced rhythms. A fellow adventure-addict, he led me on a grueling yet beautiful mountain bike ride from Cali to the jungle terrain almost 3,000 vertical feet atop the city. He even managed to help us secure free entrance and filming rights to the opening night of one of the world's best salsa shows, *Delirio*. And we salsa'd. Night after late night we danced, Cristina helping me with my steps. I was learning.

One morning, Roberto and I planned to tackle some more mountain biking. I was up early and excited to ride. But I saw no sign of Roberto, and I assumed the lazybones was still in bed. So I went up to his room and peeked into his door only to see his body under the covers. "¡Roberto, vamonos! ¡Levantarse ya!" I whispered. Nothing. "Wake up!" I raised my voice. Nothing. The mound didn't move. Itching to hammer some trails, I reached out and grabbed his foot and started shaking him over and over. Finally movement. An arm removed the bed sheet, and I was face to face with Roberto's mother, Olga. *Yikes! "¡Lo siento! So sorry!"* I was in the wrong room! Roberto's was on the other side of the house, and he was up and getting ready. *Doh!* Luckily, Olga was a good sport and we all got a huge chuckle out of it in the end.

The road finally called. We set aside our salsa shoes and strapped on our cycling shoes for a 500 kilometer ride to Medellín. Roberto would join me up the road as my guest rider. First stop: a lunch break in Palmira, just 25 kilometers away. A Peace Pedalers volunteer named Micaela, a woman I had yet to meet in person, emailed me saying she planned to go to Africa and wanted to support Innocent's Good Hope School in Uganda. When she heard we would be pedaling through Palmira, she gave us the name of her step-grandmother, Maria Zoila. "You have to meet her! She'll show you the best spots for lunch." I was eager to meet her, but what should have been an hour-and-a-half trip was now coming on three hours.

"Guapa, what's up with you today?" I asked. "You are doing, like, twelve kilometers per hour and normally you do around twenty."

"I don't know! I'm doing the best I can. I just have no energy."

"Do you want me to take your bags?"

"No, I'll be fine. I'm just tired."

By the time we arrived in Palmira, we were battling a stiff headwind as well as a threatening rain. Maria Zoila's smiling son, John Jairo, and his sister, Patricia, met us on the outskirts of town and escorted us by motorcycle the final few kilometers to their house. Maria Zoila stood at the door, all 4-foot-6-inches of her, clad in a loose fitting pink knit skirt and jacket. She threw open her arms and made us feel welcome instantly.

"You cannot go back out now that you are here," she said. "The rains are coming, and it won't be safe. No, you must stay the night with us."

"If you say so," I said. "I've never turned down a homestay on this trip, and I don't want you to be the first."

We enjoyed a leisurely lunch and relaxed with the family until deciding to hit the town for some dinner and dancing with John Jairo, Patricia, and her husband. Cristina relished the chance to show off her sharpened salsa skills, while I fumbled with my beginner steps. But just as I was getting the hang of it, Cristina complained she didn't feel well, so we called it an early night. On the way home I cornered John Jairo.

"Hey, you mentioned you like cycling. Why don't you join us tomorrow to Tulúa."

"I would love to," he said.

"Excellent. With two of us, we can carry Cristina's bags. She's not feeling so hot."

"Too much salsa."

"Too much salsa."

The next morning, even with all her bags strapped to the tandem, Cristina still struggled.

"This is so frustrating! I thought I'd get better at this, but it's getting harder."

John Jairo became a Peace Pedalers all-star by extending his time on the bike day after day, and we were more than jazzed to have him. Cristina's fatigue continued to frustrate her, so we decided to put her on the tandem and load up John on Cristina's bike. We gave it everything we had in the morning hours, sensing the afternoon heat would be unbearable for all of us. Once in town we found a pool-bar combo and planted ourselves with one foot in each. It was just what the doctor ordered—cool water, friendly locals, and tons of shade.

Cartago was John Jairo's last stop, alas. He had a job interview the next day back in Palmira, something he had landed while on the road, his first nibble after being unemployed for many months. We were cheering for him and peppering him with practice interview questions and advice. "When they ask if you have any negative qualities, say, 'Yes. I'm a workaholic.'" He was a natural Peace Pedaler, strong on the bike and even more giving off it, quick to lend a hand with the filming or point out a part of the scenery. As a thank you for his above-and-beyond showing, we sent him home with a custom made t-shirt, Peace Pedalers socks, and some new pedals for his bike. We knew we were unlikely to find such a willing and able guest rider anytime soon. But we'd try.

Cristina continued to lag, so we decided to stay in Cartago to let her rest up. I found a cheap hotel, and we caught up on our sleep and spoon sessions.

"Jamie, wake up. I need to talk to you."

"Hmm. Huh," I said, rolling over.

"I'm two days late on my menstruation."

"What? I mean, you can't be pregnant. We practiced safe sex. So come on back to bed and let's practice safe sex some more."

"Jamie, seriously. I'm *never* late on my menstruation. Never."

"C'mon, it'll probably come tomorrow. You're on a bike tour. Your body is not operating in normal conditions."

"You think we should get a pregnancy test just to be sure?"

"You're not pregnant. You can't be, Guapa."

"Something's wrong."

"If you want to be 100-percent sure, let's go get one."

An hour later Cristina came out of the bathroom with a perplexed look on her face.

"Look. You see the line?" she said, handing me the white and pink test kit.

"I don't see a line. That pink thing? That's not a line."

"It's a line."

"It's these cheap pregnancy tests. They're probably wrong."

"Maybe you're right."

"But, hey, let's try another brand just to be sure, okay?"

We went out again, grabbed some fine Colombian coffee and then walked over to a different pharmacy. *She's not pregnant. You practiced safe sex.*

"Oh no," she said from the bathroom. "I peed on my hand."

"Well, what does it say?" I asked through the door.

"Um. This."

She emerged and held out a stick with a faint purple line.

"So same as the other test? If it's got a line you're pregnant?" I asked

"Yep."

"Great! You're not pregnant. It's not a real line."

"But there is a line."

"That's not a line. I can barely see it. And it's fading."

We decided to head back to the pharmacy for a third test, a different brand. This time I watched her pee.

"See, it's the same," she said.

"Lemme see."

"There's a line."

"That is not a *line* line, Cristina. It's just a mark, a smudge. That's it. It's a smudge."

"But it's a smudge that was not there when it was new."

"I still don't trust this."

"We can get a blood test. That's 100% accurate."

A hotel clerk suggested we go to the local Red Cross. We held hands, feeling both giddy and nervous. I told her about Kurupi, the Guaraní god of fertility who walked the forest with his wraparound member. Still, underneath everything was a feeling of calm. She said she felt peaceful too. Whatever happened would be fine. *If it's meant to be...*They told us the test results would be ready in three hours. *Three hours?!?*

We walked around nearby shops and held hands some more. I was *almost* certain she wasn't pregnant so I wasn't on edge. *But, what if?* She admitted to a few "what if" thoughts as well. We distracted ourselves by doing something neither of us liked to do—go shopping. We tried to be casual and relaxed as she helped pick out a new shirt for me. As we continued to stroll the streets, I gazed over at Cristina. Part of me fantasized about how amazing it would be to have a baby with her. The time...moved...veeeerrrrry...slooooooooowly. I didn't just watch time, I stared it down, daring it to click, click, go! Finally, we walked back to the office and were directed to a window.

"Your name?" asked the receptionist.

"Morales. Cristina."

The woman left for a moment and came back with a folder. She looked down at the paper inside, then up at us. Smiling.

"*Felicidades*," she said, handing us the paper.

We both gaped at it. "*Positivo*," screamed the single word in the middle of the page. Cristina was pregnant. *"Positivo."* I felt dizzy. *What happened to that calmness?* I needed to sit down. We walked over to a bench.

How? I practiced the same safe sex measures with Cristina that I did with every woman on the trip. Did I break a condom? Did one slip off? Was it that night in Quito after our salsa dancing? I turned to Cristina and could see she was struggling to process her emotions as well. She seemed to be cycling through them—surprise, fear, excitement. Then the waterfall of tears began to fall from her sweet green eyes.

"Let's go for a walk, baby," I said softly, reaching my hand out.

"Yes, good idea."

After a long stroll, some deep conversations, and a good night's sleep, we decided she should take the bus to Medellín. She was in no condition to continue the tough rides. I had our good friend Roberto on the way to join me as my guest rider, so we decided to keep the plans and meet at the hotel in three days. The time apart would allow us think, meditate, and pray. She promised not to make any decisions until she saw me again.

That night, while Cristina was sleeping, I got down on my knees and prayed for clear signs to know what we should do next. I rose and sat on the bed next to her, just watching her breathe for several minutes. She looked like a seraph, a seraph with a child growing insider her. Our child.

Taking my first steps. Salsa dancing is hard!

 This is how to Salsa dance! Cristina became my Salsa guru. Check out her moves at www.bb42b.com/salsa

Roberto taking me out on the epic trails above Cali

John Jairo stayed with us for several days as an honorary Peace Pedaler

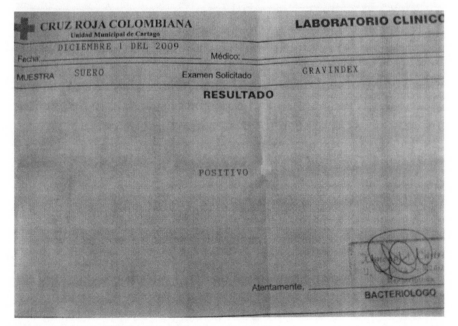

The photo that changed our lives

48
MEDELLÍN, COLOMBIA

--▶

I LAY IN a padded lounge chair by the pool in Medellín waiting to see Cristina again for the first time in three long days. On the ride up, I tore through the million different scenarios. Would she keep the baby? Abort it? Stay with me? Dump me? Spain? California? When she turned around the corner and walked towards me, I looked at her and tried to guess everything. *She's smiling, that's good. But is it a polite smile, a friendly smile, or a loving smile?* I couldn't tell. We embraced for a long, deep hug.

"It's good to be back in your arms," I said.

"How was your ride?" she asked.

I gave her the play-by-play as she settled into a chair next to mine, describing our days cycling through high coffee lands and being invited on a ranch to pick and drink coffee with the growers. She sat there, absorbing every word, imagining she was riding alongside Roberto and I. Cristina was the best listener I'd ever met by far, and I loved sharing with her. But we both knew the travelogue was avoidance.

"Enough about me. How are you feeling?"

"I'm feel pretty bad in the morning. Sometimes I vomit or get really close to it. But I feel fine in daytime," she said, rubbing her belly.

A belly rub means keep the baby.

"Do you still want to keep our plans and ride on Providencia Island?"

"Of course. I've been looking forward to that for months."

We paused.

"Have you had any thoughts about our little gift growing inside of you?" I asked.

"I want to have some time with you alone so we can talk about it. I think Providencia will be a good time for that."

She stopped rubbing her belly.

"I don't want to make any fast decisions on that either," I said. "Why don't we give ourselves a few weeks? Come up with a game plan by the end of the trip to Providencia."

Providence. I always thought the word meant divine fate. That's only partially correct. A more comprehensive definition includes God's care or guidance. And Lord knows we could use a world full of divine TLC. I felt a calming presence as soon as we stepped off the three-hour ferry and onto the sandy shores. Locals welcomed us with waves and thick Creole English, and we cycled past bowed palms and clapboard houses on the tiny Caribbean island.

Providencia is only five miles long, perfect for a couple of cyclists with a chronic case of wanderlust. *Tour the island in an hour, ride with a few locals, capture some epic footage, then plop yourself on a hammock, relax, and talk*, I told myself. I looked forward to those talks, whatever their providence. We started up a hill to begin our adventure. The gradient grew steeper, so I shifted up into the granny gear.

CRACK!

I hate that sound more than gunfire. With gunfire, as long you're not hit, there's no harm. On the bike, a sudden evil crack means a world of hurt ahead.

"What. The hell. Was that?" I said, trying to remain calm.

Cristina got off the tandem and put her hand on the brake lever to keep the bike from rolling back down the steep hill. I bent down and examined the drive train.

"Our ride is over," I said in an angry, annoyed voice.

"What happened?"

"The derailleur shattered. It's in two pieces."

"We can buy another one, no?"

"Guapa, there are no bike shops on this island. We would have to go back to San Andres. Even then..."

"What are we going to do?"

Providencia.

"I think we're meant to not ride or film on this trip," I said, calming a bit. "Let's push the bike off the road over there."

We knocked on the door of a small B&B nearby, and explained our situation to the proprietress. "*No hay problema*," said Mayo, leading us to a spare room we could store the bike and filming gear in for as long as we wished. We grabbed only our camping supplies, flip-flops, sunscreen, and a few other bare essentials. For the first time together in six countries, we were finally traditional, bike-less backpackers. No riding, no filming, just us. Mayo suggested we head to Manzanillo Bay to camp. And when we arrived I wanted to kiss her. There were no hotels, no guesthouses, no B&B's, only a powdery, private shore and a lone structure, a roots-'n'-reggae restaurant/bar made from bamboo.

We set up a tent under the coconut trees and spent the next five days staring at the water, marveling at the stars, skinny dipping, resting in the hammock, reading, doing yoga, meditating, and, most importantly, talking. The pregnancy was a huge surprise to us both, and we made a commitment to move slowly.

At mealtimes, we lingered at the restaurant and chatted with Roland, the bar owner. The fifty-year-old sported fine dreads, a furrowed brow, and a Rasta-colored belt and necklace. He boasted of fathering four different children with four different restaurant patrons. His infant daughter, Estrella de Mar, and her mother were currently on the island visiting Roland from Holland. I shared our story with him one evening.

"You have been given the best gift God can give, mon!"

"We just want to make the right decision. We don't have plans to be a couple, so it's a bit awkward."

"You don't have to be a couple to be a good father. You just have to love your child and be willing to help any way you can."

"Do you ever regret having all these children and having them raised in another country?"

"No mon! Neeevah, mon! I love my children and they love me. Each one was a gift. Your baby is a gift. The only decision you have to make is how to be a good father."

Cristina and I sunk into the hammock in front of Roland's reggae bar one late afternoon. I could hear his low rumble laugh, mixed with the babblings of a toddler in the background.

"So if we did keep the baby, how do you see us raising our child?" I asked.

"I know you don't envision us coming together as couple, so I would be a single mother living in Spain. It would be difficult, but my family would help."

"And what would you expect from me?"

"I would expect you to be a good father."

"And how could I be a good father if I'm living in the United States and you're in Spain?"

"Financially, of course. But most important, I would want you to come visit as much as you can. And to chat regularly on Skype so you can watch the baby grow up."

"It's just not at all what I envisioned for my first child. But every time I think of the option of abortion I want to vomit."

She paused.

"I have already had an abortion...and it was terrible. But, I'm...I don't want to be a single mother without an active father."

"But if I'm in the States how can I be an active father?"

"I just told you. The distance is not what I'm worried about. It's more of a decision to be a part of this child's life."

"I just wonder if I'll end up suffering every day of my life, missing my child. Skype parenting? That's no way to live."

"It would be difficult...for us both."

"Do you think we could have happy lives like that?"

"I don't know."

"I guess that's why we're here on this island, why the derailleur blew up into two pieces."

"I'm enjoying the process," she said, pulling herself closer.

"Me too," I said, coming in closer for a kiss.

On our last day on Providencia, Cristina and I decided to hike to the peak of the island. Up the steep, lush, rugged terrain, we trekked in silence. Unsaid was the fact our decision would soon crest as well. The steady rhythm of the ascent prompted me to enter a relaxed, deeply meditative state. I sought to tap into my very highest self, to overcome ego, and to connect to the love in my heart.

I remembered the two-peso note back in Argentina. *Si el amor es su mayor debilidad, sos la persona más fuerte del mundo.* The very next day, I had met Diego Bueno, who led me to Cristina. There seemed to be some higher force pushing us together and keeping us together, presenting sign after sign since that fateful day—from finding her own bike in Paraguay to the magical second bike in Chile, free nights in four-star hotels to the steady stream of openhearted family homestays, to the derailleur breaking to meeting Roland to, well, now.

The hill grew steeper and more sylvan as we approached the top. The climbing got tougher, but the pace and rhythm sent me deeper into a dreamlike state until I couldn't feel my legs. I was watching the entire event from above now. Quicker, calmer, quicker, calmer. I'd experienced the same on the bike, though rarely. Sometimes a tough climb at the end of a long day's ride miraculously turned placid and easy. *But only when my mind was right*, I realized now.

Above the action and out of body, I heard my father. He was a soft-spoken man, but when he felt passionately about something, he made sure his three sons listened. While we were in high school, he'd plop boxes of condoms on our desks, in the bathrooms, or in our cars.

"Dad, I have enough condoms," I said after he handed me yet another box.

"Just make sure you *use* them."

"What's the deal, Dad? Why are you like the condom king?"

"Listen closely. When I was younger I got a girl pregnant. I knew we shouldn't abort the baby, but we did anyways. There has not been a day in my life that I haven't regretted that decision. I've been living with guilt and sadness my whole life."

"I...I had. I never knew."

"Use condoms!"

And I saw the children, all the children on the trip, the ones who waved and ran alongside, the ones we hoisted up on the bike, the newborns we held at night. She had a charmed touch with all of them. *She's going to be a great mom.*

My rear derailleur mysteriously blows up? Hummm.

Roland with one of his love children Estrella de Mar

Not a bad place to figure out our future

Proud parents and officially "parenting partners"

49

PANAMA CITY, PANAMA

- ▶

"SO, HONEY, ARE you ready?" asked Mom, putting her arm around me and pulling me closer.

I didn't know how to answer. *Was I ready to be a father? A partner? Was I ready to come back to the United States after eight years on the road? Was I ready for all of this to be over?* Mamacita and I took a break from the morning cycling and stared at the massive cargo and cruise ships lining up to enter the Panama Canal like a giant assembly line.

"I am, I guess. But I'm pretty scared. There's so much uncertainty in my life right now."

"Like what?"

"Like what's going to happen between Cristina and me? Or what am I going to do for a living to support her and the baby?"

"So what is your biggest fear?"

"That I'll fail. That I'll make the wrong decisions and screw up again. That I won't be a good father. Just a boatload of fear, Mom."

"What's the WPO?

Hmmm. The Worst Possible Outcome? That the baby wouldn't come to term or would be born with a lifetime of challenges. That Cristina would decide she wanted nothing to do with me, and that I'd never see her or our child for a long time if ever? That all of the connecting and documenting and embracing I'd done over the past eight years would amount to nothing, a colossal waste of time. I couldn't go there. I didn't want to utter any word of it. *No fear, no more fear.* Instead I muttered something about it being a difficult transition back to the U.S., and an uncertain road with Cristina.

"So, even the WPO is not that bad, is it?" she said, putting both her hands on my shoulder and turning to me. "Sweetie, you made it this far.

You are almost home. You don't think God is going to let you fall on your face now, do you?"

"He might. I might."

"Falls are lessons."

"Yeah, I suppose. But they hurt. And I don't want to be hurt right now."

"Just take the next step. Show up, suit up for service, and leave the results up to a greater force."

This would be our last time together on the Peace Pedalers journey, and we spent our days reminiscing about countries past. She came under the guise of wanting to help me transport some of my belongings and gear back to the U.S. But we both knew the real purpose was to toast the ride and talk about the roads ahead. We lingered in Panama City for a few days, and capped our time at a posh jazz bar. In typical Mamacita fashion, she'd bragged to the bar owner about my project, and he insisted I come by the next day to film one of Panama's top musicians.

As I sat across the table from her, sipping complimentary mojitos, it dawned on me that while she loved to grab the spotlight, she usually shined it on me. I reached across the table to grab her hand.

"I think I would have quit long ago if it wasn't for you," I said.

She put her knuckle over her lips, trying then failing to muffle a cry.

"Remember when I had my open heart surgery? You were in China."

"How could I forget?"

"The last thing I thought about before the anesthesiologist placed that gas mask over my face was, 'Jamie better not give away my seat on the tandem!' It got me through, honey. From the surgery…and through other challenges in the years that followed. I *lived* for these trips. I live for these moments with you."

I wrapped my arms around her and emptied every tear in my reservoir on her shoulder. The divorce, the weekends with Dad, those long bike rides as a child, the failures and triumphs, China, Australia, France, Uganda, and everywhere she rode with me—it all came out now. And here I was, poised to pay it forward to a child—a boy, we'd learned! I thought about all the sacrifices she had made for me and cried some more.

"Hey," she said. "We both need to stop crying or we'll flood the Canal."

We laughed.

"Now go get out there, finish your mission, and bring me my grandson."

"Deal."

I could feel the pace quicken as I made my way up through Central America to California. The thought of the baby made time on the bike whir past. I could meditate for hours on the places I wanted to show him—mountain biking trails in New Zealand, favorite ski slopes in the Alps—the best way to hold him, or the age he'd learn to ride a bike. *Ten minutes after he learns to walk!* I rose earlier, spent less time idling, and was aided by a constant flow of interesting guest riders. I spent nearly every night being hosted by indigenous and mestizo families.

In Damas, Costa Rica, I picked up an impoverished fifteen-year-old rider named Mauricio, with bushy hair and jeans that sagged like a New York City teenager's. He was looking for work and having no success. Over lunch, he told me his father died when he was young boy. He and his four brothers and sisters were raised by their mother, who was forced to beg just to keep the family alive. His life story shook me to the core, and I offered to pay for his schooling so he could get a better job.

We rode together for several days, but had little luck finding homestays. Locals seemed to enjoy interacting with me, but remained suspicious of Mauricio. One day I reached into my Ortlieb handlebar bag and was shocked to find that my camera was missing. As I dug deeper, I realized my iPod was gone too. I stared at Mauricio, nearly certain he stole them. *No big deal*, I told myself. I had just recently offloaded all the photos from the camera, and the iPod was seven years old and just about to die.

But, no matter how hard I tried, I couldn't shake the feeling of being violated. For only the second time in eight years and 75 countries, a guest rider had stolen something from me. When I asked him if he had seen the equipment, he just shook his head and said nothing. I began to question everything he'd told me on the ride. In the tent that night, we slept in silence.

We took a bus to San Jose the next morning. The whole while I performed mental machinations, trying to convince myself Mauricio was just a down-on-his-luck local and innocent of any theft. I wanted to believe in him, to end our time together on a positive note. When our bus arrived in town, I grabbed my bags and turned to say goodbye. Mauricio was nowhere to be seen.

"Thank you," said Dave, one of my final guest riders in Costa Rica. "That's my message to the world."

Over the years I had been asking guest riders to share their messages on the cameras. Many were similar. This message boggled me.

"What do you mean by that?

"Thank you. Thank you for exactly what is in front of me now because it's necessary for me to get where I'm going."

I had met Dave when we were both in our early twenties. We sold Cutco cutlery while in college and eventually both ran sales offices on our summer break. Since then, he'd pursued a successful career in real estate, gotten married, and relocated to Costa Rica along with tens of thousands of fellow Americans in search of an inexpensive and easygoing lifestyle by the shore. Dave ran Rip Jack, a thriving hotel and restaurant just steps from the surf in Playa Grande on Tamarindo Bay. His arms were freckled from a decade of surfing, and he had tattooed the words "Thank You" on his shoulders.

And he was right. I didn't say "thank you" enough. Both for the obvious moments and the hidden instances. How many "unfortunate" incidents seemed to morph into blessed ones after a week, a day, an hour? More than I could count. I looked to the skies and yelled, "¡Gracias!" as loud as my lungs would allow. For punctured tires and pouring rains, guest riders who barely pedaled, and the ones who flaked on me. They were all steps toward richer encounters, greater adventures, and, hopefully, personal maturation.

Thank you, Mauricio. You've made me less attached to my things. Literally and figuratively.

Thank you, Dave. And Double D. Mathieu, Innocent, Mr. Luperini, Shannon, Carina, Booba, Mr. Yamafuji, Assos and Novartis, Gino, Nick, Dad, and Mamacitaaaaahhh.

Thank you, Nuskin, yak heads, Fiji time, barking dogs, chest infections, saddle sores, unopened condoms, and the ones that obviously failed.

Thank you, Garryck.

And thank you…Cristina.

I Skyped with her often, giggling from afar as I watched her belly stretch and grow with each call. From poolside at Rip Jack's, I filled her in on the trip's final details. She soaked them up and asked for more.

"So how is little Luca doing?" I asked her.

"You keep calling him that, but we haven't agreed to a name!"

"I know, I know. Sorry. It's just the only name that keeps popping whenever I think about him."

Lucca, "he who bears light," is the Italian hometown of my family. I figured that since he would be raised by a Spanish mother in Spain, he should also have some of his Italian roots represented. Cristina shushed me, saying not to call him Luca (a spelling she preferred) until we both agreed.

"What about Bruno?" she asked.

"Bruno? Where did you come up with that?"

"I don't know. It just came to me. I love it."

"Me, too.....It was the name of our dog."

My father wanted to name me Bruno. He fought with my mom about the name until she started to dilate. But she would not have a Gino and a Bruno. The family would sound like a pizza joint. As a consolation prize, dad got to name the German Shepherd Bruno. I laughed, knowing he was still at it, whispering "Bruno" into Cristina's ear while she slept.

The mighty Panama Canal in action

Mauricio with our suspicious home stay family

50
BARCELONA, SPAIN

--➤

DOES TIME MOVE any slower than the period between airplane touch-down and baggage claim? Passengers who have checked the flight map incessantly since takeoff now decide to turn off all power to make a decision. Should I grab my bag or put on one of the eighteen layers of clothing I brought on board? Respond to my text messages or tell my kids to put their books in their backpacks? *People please. We've done this before. I have a belly I need to hug!*

Never, ever, under any circumstance or altered state of mind, would I have imagined pending parenthood to unfold like this. No, I was going to marry an outdoor enthusiast and have a bunch of little mountain-biking babies. Or partner with a fellow USC alum and pop out a clan of California towheads. Heck, even an arranged marriage seemed more likely than my situation with Cristina. And what was my situation with Cristina? Neither of us knew. Instead we focused our energies on the baby and trusted that the other details would reveal themselves.

I was lucky to be deboarding the plane. To utilize Mamacita's American Airlines benefits, I needed to fly stand-by, a near impossibility during the popular summer months. As my luck would have it, Spain had just qualified for the World Cup final, and no Spaniard would dare travel on that day. Score!

Better still, Spain won their first ever World Cup, and I arrived to a full-blown party and a country in a pretty damn good mood. I was in one too, especially after the doors slid open and I saw Cristina and her beautiful belly. We enjoyed a long, warm hug, during which little Luca (!) gave a few kicks to welcome Daddy to Spain. Cristina's sister and brother accompanied her, and seemed just as excited about the baby.

Our first stop was Cristina's parents' house in the Barcelona suburb of Sabadell. She had given up her apartment and sold her belongings in order to travel to South America. For the last several months, she had lived in her childhood bedroom. Though not an ideal long-term living arrangement, she had a comfortable home, supportive parents, and her sister, Nieves, and brother, Jose, just a few minutes away. What she lacked in material comforts and independence she gained in proximity to family.

But Cristina and I, since the day we met, seemed to have a combined energy that attracted amazing places for a couple of vagabond travelers to temporarily call home. From Argentina to Paraguay to Chile to Colombia, there was always a free house or room or beach at hand. Now in the final month of her pregnancy, Cristina sought refuge from the summer swelter of Sabadell and an escape to a less hectic retreat with a little more space. Within a couple days we learned about a woman who needed someone to stay in her restored farmhouse in the charming mountain village of Sant Llorenç de Savall. She planned to be gone for a month, and required someone to water the plants and look after the dog. Our bags were repacked within minutes.

And for the coming weeks we lived a life of simple rustic comfort, spending hours side-by-side cooking dinners, strolling in the countryside, making love, swimming in the pool or nearby streams, and making wagers on when Luca would stir next. I was certain his acrobatic kicks, along with the Spanish World Cup victory, meant we had a future soccer star on our hands. We talked about our relationship, though one of us would usually change the subject back to Luca.

When Cristina dozed off for a nap or her night's sleep, I shifted focus to another pressing concern: the end of Peace Pedalers. How do you end an effort that had lasted through eighty-one countries in eight years? *You gotta go big*, I told myself the entire ride. I wanted to make a splash, not only to inspire others to travel and embrace this wonderful world of ours, but to prove to myself the years were well worth it.

But my riding funds were close to empty, and the sponsorships began to dry up thanks to the growing global financial crisis. I would not be able to afford to buy an HD projector and sound system to show my footage, or hire a fancy publicist to help me make a media splash. I began to pare back my plans and accept whatever final outcome of the last leg. I let go, and in doing so, felt relieved. *Hadn't the highlights of the trip been the simple moments?*

I decided I'd do the very best with my remaining resources and find a way to ride the final miles, even if it was just Cristina, Mamacita, and me. And Luca, of course! That little man was going to get on a bike. I shuttered my laptop and focused all my energies on being fully present for the arrival of my son and supporting Cristina these last few days before Luca's birth. I had made it this far with my road angels paving the way. They were not going to leave me hanging on the final miles. I dedicated the last leg of the ride to them.

Luca was ten days late by the time we made our way back to Sabadell. I'm certain it was because of the relaxed surrounds at Sant Llorenç Savall. I don't blame him. None of us wanted to leave. Luckily, yet another family friend offered up their elegant flat in town near the hospital. As soon as we unpacked our bags, Luca stirred, attempting to unpack himself. Cristina was admitted to the hospital to induce labor after discovering her water had broken, though slightly, a few days before. ¡Vámonos!

Luca (not Bruno) Morales Bianchini was born at 3:16 a.m. on August 16 via C-section. "He has a big head," explained the nurse. *Just like his dad. A big beautiful bald head.* Spanish law prohibits the father being in the operating room, so the first time I saw Luca was when the nurse handed me a swaddled mass of pink cheeks and blue eyes. He fit into my arms. Perfect. Beyond perfect.

I'd held hundreds of babies on the ride. None were as sweet as this one. Then I heard the sobs. Mine. Luca, meanwhile, just stared at me in a state of total peace and contentment. I know the experts say a baby's eyes don't focus until much later. I don't care. I know we were locked on each other. *Get ready, little man. I promise you the ride of your life.*

Several weeks later and several thousand miles away, I grasped the handlebars and stared at my other baby, the one who'd carried my gringo butt around the world for nearly a decade. She looked pretty good for an old gal. The grips were worn to the metal and the bell was mostly rust. The handmade Brazilian heart Natalia gave me dangled from a carabiner, and a plastic rosary from elderly Italian woman wrapped around the stem. The names of past riders, hand painted on the frame, were now faded and cracked, though still legible. Oliver, Janina, Luis…Cristina. Each name triggered images and emotions through my body.

I had been dreaming of the day Peace Pedalers returned to America, and now I was here, staying in Seattle with a USC fraternity brother I hadn't seen in fifteen years. Kris Moore had followed the ride from the beginning. He was just as excited to host me as I was to reconnect with him. While I was globetrotting, Kris was carving out a successful career at Microsoft. He had gotten married to his lovely wife, Stacie, bought a beautiful home on a golf course, and had an adorable baby girl, Sienna.

After the birth of Luca, I took a quick ride through Canada and re-entered the United States by ferry to Seattle. The plan was to pedal south through Washington, Oregon, and California, ending at the Peace Pedalers starting point, the Golden Gate Bridge. The logistics weren't difficult. It was the mental preparation that had me twisted. For months I had been trying to prepare myself for coming home. *What would I do? How could I support Luca and Cristina? Would I want to escape at the earliest opportunity?* Peace Pedalers wasn't just a trip. It was my entire identity. In a few weeks it would be gone. *Going on a multiyear trip is easy. It's the returning part that's daunting.*

Kris left for work, and I sat alone in his garage, giving the bike a tune-up before heading out. We had been on a similar path years prior. I then took a different road, and now the divide was worlds apart. My home was a stinky tent, his a large house in an affluent neighborhood. I traveled via a beat-up tandem. He owned several expensive cars. I had a baby boy and a foreign partner living half a planet away in her childhood bedroom. He had a wife he adored, a daughter who hugged him every day, and plenty of money to pay for medical bills, clothes, education, and anything else his family might need.

My head spun more than the gears to the tandem. *Was this whole thing a colossal waste of time? How would I ever catch up to my peers? Is the eight-year gap in my resume going to prevent me from ever getting a job? Will I end up failing like I did after college?*

I got the bike packed up in silence, planning to depart early the next day. Kris came home, and noticed me puttering around.

"How's it going, Jamie? All set?" he asked, putting his hand on my shoulder.

"Yep, all set I suppose."

"You okay? You seem a little down."

"Yeah, I had a rough one today while you were at work. I guess reality came crashing in harder than I expected."

"I can only imagine. Tell me what's up."

"Dude, I have nothing. I have a tent, bike, some clothes, and video cameras. You have it all—house, cars, wife, stability, job."

"Ah ha! I had a feeling you might go down this road. Bro, listen to me closely," he said, putting his hands on my shoulders and staring at me. "What you have is priceless. You have real experiences. You have seen the entire planet. You have connected with the world in ways that folks like me can only dream of from our stuffy corporate cubicles."

"It's...it's just such a difference," I said, motioning to the house and cars.

"Dude. All that crap is easy to make, and you know it. It's also just as easy to lose it. But nobody can ever take away your experiences. They are yours forever. Never forget that."

"Thanks, Kris. I needed that."

I gave him a hug, and nodded my head.

"So are you going to come out riding with me tomorrow or what?" I asked.

He smiled.

"I thought I might be able to get off work, but I can't do it. Sorry, man. Ya see, you have freedom and adventure. I'm locked in. Enjoy it while you can."

Truthfully, I was relieved to begin my 200-mile journey to Portland solo. I craved a day alone, time to think about Luca and my relationship with Cristina. I also itched to do some hardcore touring, a power ride without stopping to film or interview anyone. So I rolled out on my lonesome, iPod cranking, under mostly sunny skies. That night I camped near a lake in a county park awash in fall colors. I asked the birds if they had any answers to my questions about career, relationships, and fatherhood. I listened to their replies. Homes and strip malls gave way to hills and evergreens as I stretched into the heartland of the state. I was happy to be alone, but when I saw a man hitchhiking at the side of the road, I reverted to old form.

"Where ya headin'?" I asked, slowing down beside him.

"Ah, my car broke down again. I just need a ride back home."

"Ya want to pedal with me?"

He looked at the bike for a beat, then hopped on.

"It's about ten miles or so."

Gary was grease-stained and decked out in the Pacific Northwest male uniform of blue jeans, fleece layers, rounded baseball hat, and hardy mustache. He could have been heading to work as a mechanic or out to meet friends at an indie rock concert.

"So what's up with your car?" I asked.

"Ah, man. The car's just the beginning. Lost my job last week. Both my parents and my best friend died this year."

"Sounds like a rough year for ya."

"Roughest of my life."

"Well, feel free to take some anger or frustration out on those pedals. They can handle it."

"Don't mind if I do."

I felt a surge of power as Gary's intense energy increased the speed of the bike. "You're a machine," I said. Gary also let loose on his recent tough times, and I shared my own fears about coming back to America and my uncertainly with Cristina. We both needed a good listener, and the ten miles went by far too fast.

"This is my stop here, buddy," he said.

"Are you sure you don't want to keep riding for a bit longer, then just hitch back?"

"Aw, man, that's a nice gesture. But I have to get this car fixed and try to find a new job."

"Okay, Gary. Thanks for sharing a slice of your life with me. I'm rooting for you."

He was starting to walk away, but turned around to give me a strong bear hug.

"Thanks for making my day," he said.

Thanks for making my day. I couldn't begin to count the number of riders who made my day by sharing a story or adding a little pedal power. And maybe I had made their day in return. "This was the best day of my life" was a common departing line from my guest riders. How many of them would continue riding, exploring, embracing foreign cultures? If only one percent of all the riders I hosted passed the camaraderie on to others, well, the trip was an overwhelming success. I'd like to think they all did. *And I'd like to continue to do something that makes people's days—one future guest rider in particular.*

In Eugene, Oregon, I stopped by the Burley Trailer company and traded my BOB cargo trailer in for a top-of-the-line family trailer.

A family lunch in our mountain farmhouse. Mamacita came in for the birth

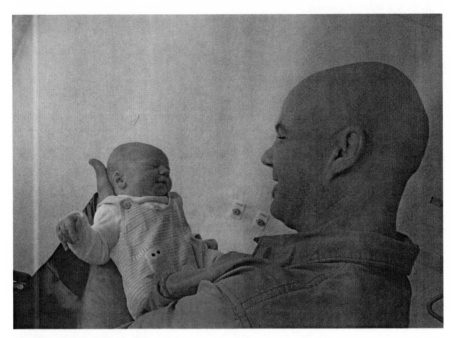

Welcome Luca!

Gary and I after our ride

51
SAN FRANCISCO, CALIFORNIA. USA

--►

I AM A CHRONIC quitter. Harley business, multilevel marketing, telecommunications jobs, relationships—you name it, I've quit it. I'd always chalked it up to a potent combination of ADD, envy, boredom, wanderlust, and ridiculously high standards. And here's the thing about a serial quitter: we're great at excuses. My boss stabbed me in the back; the economy went into the tank; she wanted to get serious too early.

That's one reason why I love cycling—you can't fool the bike. It lets you know about your effort immediately and without sugarcoating. Since childhood, the bike was the one thing I gave myself to completely. And now it had rewarded me in return. On the most audacious, harebrained, moving, and important quest I had ever undertaken, I did not quit. Oh, I wanted too. Many times. After every robbery, crash, major illness, or bout with depression, I wanted to give the bike away and fly home to California. Two huge forces dusted me off and kept me going.

My dad had never seen me complete anything following my graduation from college. I carried that shame with every pedal. At his funeral, I held his hand and promised to see this one through, and in every place I visited I looked to the skies and knew he was watching. *I did it, Dad. I did it.*

The other force was much more painful to admit. And it was one I was now ready to toss into the San Francisco Bay.

Over the course of the eight-year Peace Pedalers odyssey, I had learned many lessons from the planet, some insightful, some painful, some so plainly obvious I kicked myself for missing them all these years. The ride tore down stereotypes, set little bonfires of love and connection around the world, and shaped me into a man.

During those countless hours behind the handlebars, I conjured up many fantasies of how "crossing the finish line" might look. Of course I imagined my friends coming out to greet me and ride across the Golden Gate Bridge with me. But I also envisioned network television news teams, newspaper reporters, fans, website followers, and autograph-seeking admirers cheering me on. *Jay-ME, Jay-ME, Jay-ME!*

What propelled me on as much as anything during the tough times on and off the bike was the vision of a big, ego-puffing, PR firm–coordinated, finish-line party to celebrate me and my banner accomplishments. None of it felt right now. If I learned anything on the road, it was the importance of doing the right thing when no one was looking. My road heroes were the men and women who rose each morning under difficult circumstances, quietly and persistently went about their duties, and hugged their family at the end of the day.

Looking back, every time I let fear and ego got out of control, the ride—and my life—spun out of control. It robbed the purity of the Peace Pedalers mission. It damaged relationships. I didn't want it dictating events at the finish line.

No, a heartfelt, low-key ending would be far more apropos. After switching to a child-totting trailer in Eugene, I discarded any notions of a Big Bang re-entry with parties, media appearances, and public speaking events. Instead I craved meaningful reconnections with my close friends and family, the people who cheered and supported me throughout the journey.

The new plan was for me to cycle from Fort Bragg down to San Francisco and cross the Golden Gate Bridge on Sunday, October 24th. Dozens of family members, friends, and Peace Pedalers followers planned to ride with us over the bridge that day. *Including you, Dad.* Connection—that's what this trip was all about. Now it was time to reconnect with the people who mattered most in my life.

Then a funny thing happened. A TV news station and reporter from a large daily newspaper contacted me and said they wanted to cover the event. I could feel my ego starting to stir. I quieted it by telling the reporters they were more than welcome to join as long as it didn't take away from the private celebration. Truth is, I didn't know what to expect during those final miles home, especially after reading weather forecasts detailing a series of cold, wet storms.

Sunday morning, Cristina, Luca, and I woke to checkerboard skies, and I thought we just might pull this thing off after all. Then the text messages and phone calls started to pour in. "Freezing, horizontal rain pouring here in San Francisco. Not looking good." "My editor changed my assignment to storm watch." "Sorry, bro." "Rain check?" This was October. California never had freezing storms in October.

At least Garryck would be there. He wouldn't miss it. It had been more than eight years since we crossed the bridge together. Our friendship had grown stronger. When I saw his name pop up on my cellphone, I knew the ride was over. "Sorry, bro," he said. "I don't think you should take Luca out in this weather. And I work tomorrow. I'm sorry. I really wanted to ride with you."

The storms were set to clear Sunday evening, so we shifted the ride to the next day, hopeful some people would be able to play hooky from work. And what a glorious day it was. The rains scrubbed the skies and made all the roadside wildflowers burst open. I always loved riding after a storm. The invigorating air made me feel like I was mainlining oxygen. Sage bushes and eucalyptus trees and jasmine plants streamed fragrances when I passed by. Villagers were out and happy to continue on with their business.

Monday the 25th was no exception. Cristina and I loaded Luca into the trailer under azure skies and a handful of clouds shaped like pompoms. I sent dozens of text messages and emails to friends who made no promises but said they would try. Work, school, kids, they said. It was a Monday.

We made our way from Sausalito to where the Golden Gate Bridge hits ground on the Marin County side. I paused at the designated meeting place and looked around.

"It's okay, Jamie," said Cristina. "It doesn't mean they don't support you. It's Monday."

"Monday. Yeah, I know."

Still, my heart sank when I didn't see anyone I recognized. I thought back to the day eight years prior when Garryck and I launched the tandems on their maiden voyage. We had no idea how they'd fare, and indeed Garryck's broke down shortly out of town. But we'd patched them up, and broke them again, and fixed them some more, and more, and now I was standing in the exact same place where we began. And I began to smile.

I looked down into the Burley trailer, and did see someone I recognized. Luca's ever-curious eyes could now focus and take in everything in front of him. I bent down to kiss his forehead, and he stirred as if eager to cycle on. ¡Vamonos! *Of course*, I thought to myself. *Of course there would be no paparazzi or tickertape. Toss the ego off the bridge. Here's your welcoming party from now on.*

As I was leaning over to kiss him again, I caught a glimpse of a bald head with a bushy beard I'd seen before. "Hey, JJ!" I shouted. He rode over to us, a wide smile puncturing through his thick beard. Cristina and I had met JJ in South America the previous year. "You're the parade," I said.

And so we made our way on to the bridge and started the ride into San Francisco. Eight years, eighty-one countries, thousands of guest riders, nine hundred hours of video footage and seventeen thousand photographs, a thousand doses of malaria treatments, a hundred free bikes delivered to those in need, a flourishing school for AIDS orphans, a handful of charity projects, and countless new friends, a special partner…and one beautiful baby boy—yes, I'd say the trip was a success. "YESSSSSS," I screamed as we hit the peak of the bridge and started to coast down.

I didn't miss the crowds or bright lights one bit.

Proud Papa with Cristina and Luca at the finish line

52
SAN FRANCISCO, CALIFORNIA. USA

--▶

THE REST OF the welcome home tour rolled out in similar fashion. I had a screening planned in San Francisco later in October. Local media helped promote the event, and a popular bar agreed to show my footage on their wall-sized TV. Just my luck, the San Francisco Giants, a team that hadn't won a championship in five decades, managed to scratch their way into the World Series. Their first game took place in San Francisco at exactly the same time and date as our event. We ended up screening the video to a dozen friends after the game. The Giants ended up winning, 11-7.

Our next event was scheduled for October 31st in Santa Cruz, just 75 miles south of San Francisco. And once again a World Series game was set for the same date. The big attendance we expected dwindled to a few loyal fans, friends, and family. The Giants won the game 4-0 and eventually took the series from the Texas Rangers. Go Giants. *But can you please give me a little more heads-up before I complete another eight-year, trans-global journey?*

In San Diego, we planned a giant Peace Party bash complete with live bands, outdoor barbeque, and dancing, followed by a video presentation on a giant screen. In all my years in San Diego, I'd experienced only a handful of days with bad weather. Unfortunately, this was one of them. The temperatures dropped to near freezing level and the cold rains and strong headwinds chased the whole city indoors. Like the other three events, this one was attended by only my closest friends and family.

By the end of the tour, I just laughed and held Luca as much as possible. I called it my "humility tour," a final reminder of what the mission was all about—connection, inspiration, love, and truth. I wanted to know the truth about the world and its remarkable inhabitants, while also discovering truths about myself.

This included the mother of my son.

The more time I spent with Cristina, the more I realized I was crazy about her. As she and Luca spooned each other in bed, deep in slumber, I stared at them both in awe. How many women would drop everything for a multi-country bike trip with a flakey vagabond, supporting another's passion no matter how challenging or impractical it seemed? And then lug a two-month-old baby across the Atlantic solo to give Luca his first ride with his daddy? She was beautiful, just beautiful. And seeing her as a loving mother made her even more gorgeous.

"Guapa," I whispered soft enough so I wouldn't wake her. *Guapa.* I knew I couldn't live without either one of them.

The final miles of Peace Pedalers was in the pouring rain

EPILOGUE

▸

THE EMAIL CAME in as I was editing video footage. "Innocent!" I said aloud to the empty room.

We'd stayed in contact since riding together in Uganda four years prior, and each report from Africa brought better and better news. This email announced the graduation of a few dozen kids from the Good Hope School we founded. To honor my help over the years, the ceremony would take place on February 10th, my birthday, he said. Could I possibly come?

The trip could be a twofer, he continued. Innocent's first son would be baptized the day after the graduation ceremony. He and his wife, Mariam, had decided to name their child Jamie.

You play hardball, my man. How am I going to turn down an offer like that?!

I had not seen the school since its founding, but I knew I would be back someday. Innocent's personality and can-do spirit continued to inspire me long after the Peace Pedalers mission had concluded.

All those years ago, when I picked him up between Kabale and Kisoro while he was on his way back from school, I was hoping just to spend a few miles with him. Then just as I was going to say goodbye and pedal onwards to find a campsite, the skies unleashed deafening thunder and buckets of rain. Innocent and his family gave me shelter.

Innocent ditched his classes to come cycle with me the next day, despite the fact he'd never ridden a bike and the terrain in the region is grueling, with steeps hills, muddy roads, and unpredictable weather. Our 50-kilometer ride stretched the entire day, and during all the ups and downs, falls and near falls, Innocent shared his dream to start a school for those who couldn't afford an education, especially the area's numerous AIDS orphans.

He could see the school clearly in his mind, and the more he talked, the more I saw it as well. His heart was in it, so I decided to put mine in there too. I handed him a few dollars to open an email account and gave him his first assignment, to send me a one-page summary of his dream via email. I had given cash on faith to at least a dozen other riders who expressed business and community plans. None of them followed up. Until Innocent. That step led to another, then a few more, then some fundraising, and a bit more, and now he was hosting graduation ceremonies.

For the last four years, Innocent had worked day and night to turn his vision into the Good Hope School, now with more than 150 students and dozens of teachers, board members, and a supportive group of community leaders. Each year, he'd asked me to return to see the progress, but something always seemed to get in the way. I reread the email and smiled. "I would be honored if you were also to be Jamie's godfather." *You are one persistent, and damn good, salesman, amigo.*

Cristina and Luca weren't able to join me, so I invited my most frequent biking partner to come along. The touring duo was on the road again, marveling at everything that had transpired since the last time we cycled in Africa. "Thanks for coming, Mom." She was nearing seventy, but still game for adventures like this.

We could hear the party at the school before we could see it. At least a hundred students sang and screamed in anticipation of our arrival to the graduation events. I careened my head out the window as we wound our way up the hill in the van, desperate to see Innocent's dream, the Good Hope School. And there she was, two long, rectangular structures with dusty brick walls and no doors. *Just like you prophesized on the bike.* The words PEACE PEDALERS SCHOOL lined the base of one building.

The crowd noticed our van approaching, and redoubled their celebration. The girls wore simple green cotton overall dresses and the boys donned red sweaters with white piping and green slacks, making me think of Christmas. *It's all a gift—the kids, the school, Innocent, the ride, Cristina, Luca, life.* The drumbeats got louder. *Thump, thwacka, thump, thump. Thump, thwacka, thump, thump.* And I was lost in a pulsating trance of memory and the moment.

In the blur of it all, I caught glimpse of Innocent and Mariam. He'd filled out his wiry frame, and now sported a mustache. *You did it, my friend.* In her arms I saw Jamie, sweet Jamie, with his tiny Afro puffed up to its limits and his small body clad in red-and-white-striped dungarees, the color and pattern of a candy cane. They saw the van and quickened their pace toward us.

I leaned back in my seat and let it all sink in.

The Good Hope School's main structures

The students of Good Hope welcoming us with gusto

 Check out a short mini-movie about the impact Innocent's dream is making in his community. www.bb42b.com/goodhope

Baby Jamie and his godfather unite

The Good Hope School family

Thanks for taking this journey with me. If you would like to learn more about how to get involved with Good Hope School or wish to synergize on any current or potential project, please don't hesitate to reach out. This journey forever changed me as a man and I'm currently working on the next big Live Big, Give Big, Love Big project. If you are moved by any of this story and want to join a soulful, passionate group of people dedicated to love, connection and contribution please reach out.

Jamie can be reached at 831.465.4787 or jamiebianchini@gmail.com. We look forward to meeting you!

CPSIA information can be obtained
at www.ICGtesting.com
Printed in the USA
FSOW01n0210280715
9299FS